The NuyorAsian Anthology
Asian American Writings About New York City

1/9/2000

Querido Ben —

Maraming salamat for everything. I hope this year brings much happiness and prosperity to your family — Just a little millennium gift, hope you enjoy it

Bino.

Bino A. Realuyo, Editor

Rahna Reiko Rizzuto, Associate Editor

Kendal Henry, Art Editor

Library of Congress Number 98-072300

ISBN: 1-889876-07-0(paper)
        1-889876-08-9(cloth)

Cover Photograph: (c) Kendal Henry

Publication of this book was funded by
the National Endowment for the Arts.

This book has also been made possible by Jon Moon, Beatriz Tabios and the friends of The Asian American Writers' Workshop.

Cover Designed by Lisa Lum Chune
Book Designed by Jue Yee Kim
Art Directed by Kendal Henry

Published in the United States of America by The Asian American Writers' Workshop, 37 St. Mark's Place, New York, NY 10003-7801.
E-mail us at AAWW@panix.com. The Asian American Writers' Workshop is a not-for-profit literary organization devoted to the creation, development and dissemination of Asian American literature.

Distributed by Temple University Press, 1-800-447-1656

for Augusto Roa Realuyo and Dr. Amelia Roa Realuyo,

whose letters gave me New York City when I was young . . .

and who brought me to New York City when I was old enough to understand.

Acknowledgments

Salamat to the Asian American Writers' Workshop for the opportunity to edit *The NuyorAsian Anthology*. Former and current staff: Peter Ong, Barbara Tran (for having contacted me on this project), Derek Nguyen (especially for his great work on "Eavesdropping"), Jeannie Wong and my dear moonbeam, Andrea Louie, for her patience, dedication, understanding and always the great hair and smile.

Gracias to former staff at AAWW: Miwa Yokoyama, Ray Hsia and Erna Hernandez.

Salamat to the soldiers/interns, those who began the work: Mari Nagasawa (for her leadership), Dayna Poon, Joon Park, Jee-Eun Song, Michelle Yung, Kavita Kumar. *Gracias:* Jane Choi, Anne Maloney and Clifford Rivera.

Maraming salamat to my left and right hands at the Workshop: Cheng Hee and Miel Alegre!!! I will always cherish the discussions over the phone, the meetings in my apartment and all your great support. For the tedious phonecalling and letterwriting, a very special *salamat!*

To those whose email has sustained me during the work on this project: Eileen Tabios along with Rap and her wand, Jean Fong Kwok (from Amsterdam, for her deep reflections!), Raquel Deloatch, and Victor Tolentino (my brother companion—for always being there, wherever I am). To Rigoberto González, for being there, for always being there, *salamat.*

To Mexico, for the moments of reflection, *Muchísimas Gracias.*

Maraming salamat to Lisa Lum Chune and Jue Yee Kim for the wonderful design of this anthology, for being so patient with us, for agreeing to join our delirious group, and for everything they have accomplished under tremendous pressure. *Maraming salamat* to John McGhee for the extraordinary job on copyediting this massive book, for his valuable insights and suggestions.

Maraming salamat to Kendal Henry for directing the search and selection for artwork independently, for his kindness, generosity and artistic expertise. For always being there when I need him, a true friend, a true find.

Maraming-maraming salamat to Rahna Reiko Rizzuto for her insights, editorial skills, listening ear and, most, her friendship. She worked very closely with many writers in this anthology in editing their work for publication. *Salamat* for the great research for *NuyorAsian.* No one I know has the ability to finish reading novels overnight and still miraculously manage to discuss at length their inner workings. I couldn't have done this without you, Rahna. It is always an honor to work with you.

To Pusa, who kept me company during the solitary selection and reading process. *Salamat.* To my family, always, always, *maraming salamat.*

To all the writers and artists whose works appear in these pages: may you enjoy the book as much as I enjoyed putting it together. *Maraming salamat sa inyong lahat.*

Contents

ARTISTS

Not a Travel Essay, but an Attempt to Write an Introduction Fusing Landscape, Musings and Cyberescapisms—

Cuernavaca, Mexico June 11, 1998

They wonder what it must be like to live there, that vertical city up north. Ah, *increible!* they say, mouth open, wanting to know what I do during the day. I tell them how much my rent is.

I am thinking of New York City while I sit *en un zócalo, tomando una cerveza*, listening to Alejandro Fernandez, pondering the reasons I decided to take the offer to compile this anthology. It is the city of my immigration, where the cliché expression "beginning a new life" may mean exactly that; a childhood fantasy realized, an adult fantasy continuing. *Ahorita, no!* I tell the street vendor as he leans toward me. The boy wants to sew my name into a friendship bracelet. I look past him, at the horizontal landscape around me. Nothing grows vertically here, only emotions, dollars and hair.

The fascination has crossed borders, transcended fabrics. At a bar last night, a drag queen lip-synched Liza Minelli, "New York, New York," out of synch. Behind her, half-naked male dancers. How tired, I thought, but I paid attention to her makeup and glitter, and in a glance, noticed how the go-go boys in the cages wore nothing. I refused to clip a dollar; I wouldn't know where to put it. I was thinking then, as I am now, What can I possibly say to introduce this anthology? And I didn't know, still don't know what this book is about. I thought about the many ways such books have been presented: as a historical and literary mapping of Asian American life in New York City? A chronological arrangement by literary publication and merit? A collection in thematic divisions? Ah, so many ways. I choose not one of these.

Sitting here amid flies, fruit and afternoon gossip, I welcome the shadow of a tree. Unlike humid New York City, there is air here, in this city famous for its eternal spring, where mosquitoes outnumber the rumormongers in the plaza. The book is in between both seasons, or perhaps it is both. It is an anthology of heat and shadow. A melange of anger, and the lack of it. Of truth and disguise. It will be an out-of-synch drag queen. A New York one, glittering just the same.

Hey, Bino, I have this idea for a cover!
> What?
> Tchotchkas!

Choch what?

Tchotchkas! I want to photograph a group of tchotchkas for the cover. They would represent different aspects of New York: a yellow cab paperweight, little Asian dolls, an Empire State Building eraser, fans, little toys, Godzilla, Power Ranger key chains, buddhas, all kinds of tchotchkas!

But Kendal, that's like . . . Jewish?

I know.

Telephone message on June 4, 1998, a day after I repeatedly emailed Rahna Reiko Rizzuto for a final copy of her essay, How to Give Birth:

Hi, this is Rahna's friend, Kris. I'm calling to let you know she has given birth, and she is going to be Okay.

Flushing, April 2, 1998

The 7 train is the longest ride to nowhere, yet the worlds it passes through are fascinating. At night, you don't see much, but the trip reveals the strangest of smells. There is this concoction of food scents; and as the train slowly moves from one neighborhood to another, the smells separate and distinguish themselves. Close your eyes, can you tell who's cooking? I worked in Flushing for many years. The presence of immigrants in Queens is most evident in its semblance, noise and scent. I had my first bulgogi here. They have pizza with kimchi. Some of the stories were set here. Bharati Mukherjee's *Danny's Girls*. Marianne Villanueva's *Personal History*. And why not? Queens has the largest Asian American population in New York City. The Koreans have revitalized Flushing. The Filipinos find their newspapers and entertainment magazines at the kiosks. The South Asians sell them, but they don't know who Sharon Cuneta is, and she is perhaps the most recognizable face for the Filipinos in Woodside. Editing this anthology requires understanding such a landscape. The noise of the train: a never-ending pressure and excitement to a visitor, but to a resident, as subtle as a fake deaf-mute selling pens between Queens Boulevard and Jackson Heights, as unemotional as closing one's eyes when a beggar walks into a subway car.

Veterans Hospital, Manhattan, March 1998

My father was lying on his high bed in the Intensive Care Unit. A nurse came up to me. Her ID told me she was Korean. How a Korean could fit within an all-Filipino staff who spoke Tagalog all the time astounded me. Has she learned to eat *dinuguan*? She approached. She asked what I was writing about. My father, eyes closed, spoke: Ah, he's a poet, a writer, a poet! The nurse looked at me. Really? My daughter is a poet! Oh. Okay? I only realized then that whenever I visited my father, I wrote to kill time. I told her about *The NuyorAsian Anthology*. The Asian American Writers' Workshop. I gave her my card. You must ask your daughter to go there. In a week, I received a call from her daughter. Another week passed, and I received her poems. The last pages of this anthology present a group of very young writers. At sixteen, the nurse's daughter, Alison Park, is its youngest contributor.

From: ***@aol.com
Subj:　　TSISMIS
To:　　　***@columbia.edu

February 28, 1998

Hi Erna:

Thanks for sending me your story "Tsismis." I enjoyed it tremendously. I have very few comments then we're set. I would like you to remove the quotation marks because I believe that will give your writing a fresh look. Conversational narrative is difficult to deliver but you did it very well. I also don't feel comfortable with glossaries. As contemporary writers, we need not explain our literary compulsion to move language beyond the limits of the vernacular. I would hope that, eventually, Filipino words would merge with our vocabulary. That will not be accomplished unless we leave our writing alone, and do not explain parts that may not be comprehensible to others (subliminal: let them work with it).

If certain terms like "mga itim" get in the way. I suggest you find a way in the conversation to refer to blacks without having to explain the word. That is the challenge in literature. Find creative ways to do that.

Also, please remove the glossary from your manuscript. And PLEASE DON'T STOP TO

EXPLAIN.

Claro?

Anyway, please print this and review against your original. Once finished please send to me on a disk as a TEXT format, with hard copies (clearer ones, please, not photocopies):

Bino A. Realuyo
*** West 19th Street **
New York, NY 10011

Questions? Contact me . . .

Bino

It sounds cute, but what does "NuyorAsian" mean?
      I think the title is very imitative and derivative. Can't you come up with something else?
      I would bear a child for you if you changed the title.
      Oh, fabulous, fabulous, like the music of the streets.
      NuyorAsian . . . hmmm . . . is that like . . . Nuyorican? Oh—
      That makes me Iowasian then?
      I love NuyorAsian. It's like the cover. It means absolutely nothing.
      Keep it. It sounds dangerous.

Email to Derek, Nguyen, AAWW, January 1998

In a message dated 1/5/98 7:14:00 PM, you wrote:

<<i spoke with kimiko and left a message with jessica about the nuyorasian
fishbowl. kimiko was enthusiastic about the project and will give me a
couple of names of moderators she would feel comfortable with. once i
hear from jessica, i'll let you know. once the moderator is confirmed,
i'll give them your number so you can speak with them about the content
you would like to cover for the anthology. how does that sound?>>

I'm sorry I didn't tell you this . . . I actually planned to moderate this myself. I should have given you more detailed information before you called Kimiko . . . my fault.

It's not a moderator I want, it's a cochatter . . . I want Jessica and Kimiko to talk to each other about topics given to them beforehand. The job of the cochatter is to join in the conversation. As the editor of *NuyorAsian*, I feel compelled to do this cuz a stranger will not understand what I am looking for. What I plan to do in fact is to remove myself from the manuscript once it is transcribed. Ideally, I just want Jessica and Kimiko to have a conversation. I am just decor, a glamorous decor to say the least, the little colorful fly hovering over them. :-)

I think the original title was something like:

The NuyorAsian Lit. Cafe presents
"Eavesdropping: Jessica Hagedorn Chats with Kimiko Hahn About Motherhood, Literary Voyeurism and New York City Yellow Cabs" (joined by cochatter Bino A. Realuyo, editor, *The NuyorAsian Anthology*), etc.

Since this is experimental, a little mistake in terms of direction would be fatal to the anthology . . . fishbowls traditionally generate a lot of intellectualism, most of it unnecessary as far as I'm concerned, ranging from pure semantic garbage to pedantic meditations. I want to know if either one of them has been to a sex club and what they did there. (Then, of course, I inject the conversation with my own personal experiences, hmmmmm . . .) Did they meet their husbands at a sex club? Did they ever have sex in a yellow cab? Do they wear yellow?

Please call Kimiko again and find out who she has in mind, then tell her about the above and how the editor plans to join the conversation himself avec good Ethiopian coffee at their service. Sorry about this Derek, such communication breakdown, huh . . . and so early?

Anyway, keep me abreast.
Bino

Watermark: Vietamese American Poetry and Prose book party—*notes on the Asian American Writers' Workshop*

I wish Curtis Chin were here. I met him in 1991, that man from Michigan. I didn't like his hair. He had the word *Asian* all over his face, provoking activism every time he breathed, the

Asian sort. Someone told me he was a poet. A poet? How could anyone divulge a secret like that? He became my friend, a constant companion. I write too, I told him one evening. Weeks later, we were sharing work. In a few months, there were others sharing work. We would go to diners to talk, the six of us. From diners, we moved to borrowed tables at arts and community organizations. Our commonality was not writing, but activism. We were all young and angry. It was the early nineties. ACT-UP was in the streets. Anti-Asian violence was on the rise. *Miss Saigon* ignited anger. Lesbian and gay Asian Pacific Islanders started organizing. We had reasons to write. Our group soon changed, new faces, more serious writers, including Marie Lee, a young woman who was about to publish a book and Barbara Tran, a young MFA graduate from Columbia University. I told Curtis I wanted to call our group *Four Winds*. I had already made the flyers. Curtis named us *The Asian American Writers' Workshop* instead and had a friend draw a logo that looked like a patch on a superhero's chest. A's and W's that looked like fangs. The faces of the Workshop changed again. The office got bigger, whiter. Curtis moved to California. And the very few who remained are still here. Tonight, at this party for Barbara's anthology, I reflect on those moments. I look at this office. I look at the bookseller, the books the Workshop has produced. How far Barbara Tran has come! I remember when we first recruited her by giving her a piece of paper posing as a business card at a Li-Young Lee reading where she was an usher. She has gotten married. She has won awards. She is serving food.

Asian Cinevision Office, Chinatown, November 1997

I've heard so much about *Bridge*. It almost seemed like a myth. As soon as I started to flip through volumes and volumes of this magazine, I was immediately taken to the past. The seventies. The Basement Workshop. The birth of Asian American activism on the East Coast. Oh, there's a picture of Jessica Tarahata Hagedorn. Tarahata? They looked very very young then. Some of them are still writing now. Some don't even live in New York City anymore. Ah, there's the famous Frank Chin diatribe. His original letters were printed. Then, it was American-born Chinese vs. the immigrants. Now, it's Asian American women vs. the less-published men. No one was with me in the dimly lit room. The files were old, chairs rickety. I munched on Chinese pastry. I spilled coffee but didn't tell anyone. Some of the *Bridge* and The Basement Workshop writers appear in *The NuyorAsian Anthology*: Luis Cabalquinto, Fay Chiang, Henry Chang, Luis Francia, Jessica Hagedorn, Kimiko Hahn, Yukihide Hartman, Walter Lew and Richard Oyama. When I left Chinatown, I carried with me copies of *Bridge*. I wanted to include reprints of the actual pages in this anthology, but would soon be disappointed by the politics of design. But I am certain that the passion of those activists inhabits those who have persevered and continued to define American literature.

Peacock Cafe, West Village, August 5, 1997

The oldest waitress in the world works here. When she approaches, I often worry she won't make it to my table. But she always does. Then she tells me the same exact thing she just told the people at the other table: *Oh, what a beautiful summer day!* Beautiful? Today, I am taking refuge from the humidity in this air-conditioned coffee shop. American coffee, please. How does one begin an anthology? Whose work to choose? And why? Jose Garcia Villa is my most natural choice. A most influential poet. He invented a poetic form. He was published in major literary journals and is still highly regarded in the Philippines. All this was in the early twentieth century, when such a feat was nearly impossible. So I begin with his most famous poem. And I end his section with dedications from fellow poets. I sit here in this ancient coffee shop trying to imagine how the outside landscape looked during Jose Garcia Villa's prime. I stare at the oldest living waitress and wonder if she served him coffee as well. Oh, was it a beautiful summer day?

From the call for submissions, July 1997:

Since the first three Chinese students came to New York in 1847, the community of Asian Americans in the city has grown into a remarkable presence. As a whole, we are more diverse and urban, and our families have arrived more recently. We live in a vital, gritty microcosm of America, and are exposed daily to the best and worst this country has to offer.

In celebration of this historic milestone, the 150th anniversary, the Asian American Writers' Workshop is producing *The NuyorAsian Anthology* to capture the essence of what it is to be Asian American in New York City. The anthology, which will be published by the Asian American Writers' Workshop in 1999 and distributed by Temple University Press, will showcase who we are and what it means to be *NuyorAsian.* As such, we believe it will be a unique and indispensable addition to the growing body of Asian American literature available in schools, bookstores and libraries across the country.

We encourage submissions of poetry, fiction and literary essays from established and emerging writers that present their perspectives on life in New York City.

Bino A. Realuyo, Editor

Jose Garcia Villa

Biography

Jose Garcia Villa (1908-1997) was born in Manila, Philippines. A
legendary poet, editor and fiction writer, he was a seminal influence on
many poets in the Philippines. He lived in America for over fifty years
and was the recipient of numerous awards including a Guggenheim,
Rockefeller and Bollingen fellowships. An associate editor at New
Directions from 1949 to 1951, his published works in the United States
include a collection of fiction, *Footnote to Youth*, and poetry collections,
Have Come, Am Here and *Selected Poems and New.*

The Anchored Angel

And, lay, he, down, the, golden, father,
(Genesis', fist, all, gentle, now)
Between, the, Wall, of, China, and,
The, tiger, tree (his, centuries, his,
Aerials, of, light) . . .
Anchored, entire, angel!
He, in, his, estate, miracle, and, living, dew,
His, fuses, gold, his, cobalts, love,
And, in, his, eyepits,
O, under, the, liontelling, sun—
The, zeta, truth—the, swift, red, Christ.

The, red-thighed, distancer, swift, saint,
Who, made, the, flower, principle,
The, sun, the, hermit's, seizures,
And, all, the, saults, zigzags, and,
Sanskrit, of, love.
Verb-verb, noun-noun:
Light's, latticer, the, angel, in, the, spiderweb:
By, whose, espials, from, the, silk, sky,
From, his, spiritual, ropes,
With, fatherest, fingers, lets, down,
Manfathers, the, gold, declension, of, the, soul.

Crown, Christ's, kindle, Christ! or, any, he,
Who, builds, his, staircase, fire—
And, lays, his, bones, in, ascending,
Fever. Verb-verb, king's-spike—who, propels,
In, riddles! Six-turbined,
Deadlock, prince. And, noun,
Of, all, nouns: inventor, of, great, eyes: seesawing,
Genesis', unfissured, spy: His, own, Arabian,
His, love-flecked, eye!

The, ball, of, birth, the selfwit, bud,
So, birthrights, lanced, I, hurl, my bloodbeat, Light.

And, watch, again, Genesis', phosphor, as,
Blood, admires, a, man. Lightstruck,
Lightstruck, into, the, mastertask,
No, hideout, fox, he, wheels, his, grave, of,
Burning, and, threads, his,
Triggers, into, flower: laired,
In, the, light's, black, branches: the, food, of,
Light, and, light's, own, rocking, milk.
But, so, soon, a prince,
So, soon, a, homecoming, love,
Nativity, climbs, him, by, the, Word's, three, kings.

—Or, there, ahead, of, love, vault, back,
And, sew, the, sky, where, it, cracked!
And, reared, in, the, Christ, for, night,
Lie, down, sweet, by, the, betrayer, tree.
To-fro, angel! Hiving, verb!
First-lover-and-last-lover, grammatiq:
Where, rise, the, equitable, stars, the, roses, of, the, zodiac,
And, rear, the, eucalypt, towns, of, love:
—Anchored, Entire, Angel:
Through, whose, huge, discalced, arable, love,
Bloodblazes, oh, Christ's, gentle, egg: His, terrific, sperm.

From *Have Come, Am Here*

26

Silence is Thought converging
Unprecipitate, like
Dancer on tight wire balancing,
Transitive, budlike,

Till—her act finished—in
One lovely jump skips
She to the floor, bending
To make her bows, dips

Herself in bright applause—
Then silence is
No more. Now it is the rose
Called Speech.

34

Take a very straight line, Fermin, if you want to die.
The line at the middle of fire, that is.
So that it is perpendicular, central.

Die illuminist, Fermin, rising and particular.
Cohere at the electric center of death.
Ascend the incandescent rope and throw

Your tenderness to me below. If they call you buffoon,
Fermin, I have violins to drown them out—
But you have a Confrontation to make.

36

Be beautiful, noble, like the antique ant,
Who bore the storms as he bore the sun,
Wearing neither gown nor helmet,
Though he was archbishop and soldier:
Wore only his own flesh.

Salute characters with gracious dignity:
Though what these are is left to
Your own terms. Exact: the universe is
Not so small but these will be found
Somewhere. Exact: they will be found.

Speak with great moderation: but think
With great fierceness, burning passion:
Though what the ant thought
No annals reveal, nor his descendants
Break the seal.

Trace the tracelessness of the ant,
Every ant has reached this perfection.
As he comes, so he goes,
Flowing as water flows,
Essential but secret like a rose.

Nyabongo's Project

One of the strangest projects is
That of Dr. Akiki Nyabongo, an
East Indian prince residing in
Brooklyn. Ebito's historian, a handsome
Liquid-eyed man of forty-two, is a prince
By virtue of
Being a son of the late

Kyebambe, King of Toro, a state
In Uganda, and a doctor by
Virtue of a Ph.D. at Oxford. He
Was born in Kabarole, Toro's capital,
In the shadow of the Ruwenzori Moun-
tains, sometimes
Known as the Mountains

Of the Moon. Dr. Nyabongo is
Preparing a book about Ebito
Or Flower Language, a symbolic
Method of communication among his compatriots,
Involving the use of flowers, leaves,

Grass, seeds, twigs,
Clay, beads, animal hair and

Stones. He is engaged in setting
Down detailed scientific descriptions of plants which he
Will then key to their messages in Rutoro
And English. A typical one: "Akaisabi-
sabi, or Aspa-
ragus puberulus. A much-branched,

Climbing shrub. Branches long,
Flexuose, terete; branches long,
Spreading . . ." means "You are the
Puberulus that grows at the side of the road
And grasps the bark cloth of every
Passerby, and
I will grasp at your love."

(Collage. From an item in "Talk of the Town," *The New Yorker*, Jan. 26, 1952.)

The Bird

A little bird that is thirsty:
One takes it away from
The verge of death: its little heart
Beats increasingly

Against the warm, trembling hand,
Like the last wave of
A gigantic sea whose shore you are.
And you know suddenly,

With this little creature that
Is recovering, that

Life is recovering from death! And
You are holding it up,

    Generations of birds and all
    The woods over which
They fly and all the heavens to which
They will ascend.

(From a letter to Otto Modersohn, *Letters of Rainer Maria Rilke,* Volume 1, Norton.)

Dedication

● Carlos A. Angeles

From a New York Times editorial, 1956.

New York City is The Big Apple, or is it? It reminds me (to this day) of the Depression years and Jose Garcia Villa, the Filipino poet-expat who lived in Greenwich Village from the 1930s to his death in 1997, and whose letters to me always ended "life is just a bowl of cherries!" Whenever I pass an Automat during my sojourns in New York City, I think of Jose, dining on a soup of ketchup in a cup of hot water.

Carlos A. Angeles was born in 1921 in Tacloban City, Leyte, Philippines. He began writing poetry at age 12; crashed national publications while in high school; and continued writing poetry while a student at the University of the Philippines. He is the author of two books of poetry, *A Stun of Jewels* and *A Bruise of Ashes: Collected Poems 1940-1992*. He is a recipient of the Philippine Republic Cultural Heritage Award in Literature, a winner of the Carlos Palanca Memorial Awards in Poetry and holds an award in literature from the Balagtas Memorials.

● Luis Cabalquinto

Luis Cabalquinto retired early from his job at Pfizer International to devote more of his time to writing poetry and fiction. His literary work has appeared in numerous publications, including *The American Poetry Review, Prairie Schooner* and *International Quarterly*. Aside from English, he writes in two Philippine languages, Tagalog and Bicolano. He resides in New York City but spends part of each year in his birthplace, Magarao, in the Philippines, managing an orchid garden and a rice farm—as well as writing.

Portrait in Snow

(for Jose Garcia Villa)
by Carlos A. Angeles

When at last he stepped
onto two cold sheets that were
the twin seasons
misery-rain and hunger-snow
he forced a breath.

And on the surface
of the air about
he felt the heavens stirred
icy boomerangs
hitting him roundly
then squarely
then perpendicularly
and horizontally
yet
in such a manner that
they never met.

And where they did not meet
there was the tangent
and in the tangent
there was the Soul
and that
was bursting in his eyes.

II

With his thumb
he made a snowman
and with
the little bit caught
in his fingernails

he shaped a hat
and put it on
the snowman's feet.

Where it should not be.

III

But, at last, he tired
of building
and dug he more than a few
of the whiteness
which was about him.
Deftly
now, securely
he scooped and scraped
until he saw it was—
not all was whiteness now.

But that between the paleness
of his hands
and the cleanness of snow
he held grass.

And the grass was green
and had roots
and dangling earth
which was very brown
or very black.

IV

Look!
he said. Look now!
Yet no one stirred.

The surface of
the air perhaps?

But it had stirred before.

V

And the night it was
his back
was running water
his side
was chilling snow.

And where the two
may never meet there was
a space
and that space
was a vacuum
and that vacuum was called
Immortality.

VI

That was what he quested.

But in the summer
the people gathered around
the dusty road and claimed
no other miracle.

Icicles at a time like this?

So mouth gave way to mouth
and built a rope of rumor

whereon
Science was called to walk
upon like a circus
tightrope walker.
What was it?

It was glass
naught but shattered glass.

VII

And yet,
still as yet
Science trembled.

Hurrying fast away
the glass bits splintered
like snowflakes

melting
in his hands.

Night with Jose

(For Jose Garcia Villa, 1908-1997)
by Luis Cabalquinto

Pale angel, brown-anchored
        by shadowing old age,
In your cigaret-scented vintage
        studio Village flat

I hailed you with cheers
        to your precious heirloom
Of god-spun deathless songs
        that shame false art.

Always eating pink raisins,
        with your blue monks,
Bearing the gadfly emperor's
        resplendent new poems,

This night you fought with your
        old Lord and, with the
Upended comma of a young lover,
        brought forth another child.

While the hours stood
        drunk on their heads,
Death's messy tables turned
        and you boomed: "Hail, Decrepitude!"

Diamond-cut, eighty-proof,
        you knew you passed
From your gin-paced heart
        one unacknowledged craft.

When with the tossing lights
        were paired the missing hoards:
Somewhere in that comradeship I
        caught love's guarded art.

Louis Chu

Biography

Louis Chu was born not far from Canton, China, in 1915. His family moved to Newark, N.J., when he was nine years old. He attended school and college in New Jersey and was graduated with a major in English and a minor in sociology. He later did graduate work in sociology at New York University. During World War II, he served in the U.S. Army, finding himself in Kunming, southwestern China, in 1945. He returned home and then visited China again to take a wife just before the Communists took over. *Eat a Bowl of Tea* was adapted for the stage and made into a feature film, directed by Wayne Wang.

From *Eat a Bowl of Tea*

When July rolls around in Sunwei, there is no better way to escape the heat than to find one's self a spot under the banyan trees in the public square. In New York, where people are plentiful and trees are scarce, there is no banyan tree. And even if there were, Mei Oi could never get up early enough to reserve a spot under it for herself.

One particularly hot July afternoon, eight months after her arrival in New York, Mei Oi opened all the windows wide to let more air into the apartment. Even with the windows wide open, the air hardly stirred. Disappointed, she walked to the front door and opened it. Immediately a rush of wind pushed past her, flooding the apartment with a new coolness. Mei Oi was thrilled at this new discovery. She stood by the open door, inhaling deeply the fresh air. But as soon as she walked back to the apartment proper, even with the door open, the breeze vanished. Experimentally she returned she returned to the front part of the hall and immediately the breeze rushed at her.

Why not get a chair and sit down by the door and be cool? she asked herself. She walked quickly to the kitchen and brought out a straight-backed chair. Placing the chair squarely in the doorway she sat down to enjoy a cool afternoon. She lifted the bottom of her dress above her knees. It was cooler this way.

She had been using this resourceful cooling system for about a week, when one day, as she was sitting thus in the doorway, she noticed someone coming up the stairs. When the bobbing head came up higher, she saw it was Ah Song's. Even before he took another step up, her face had become crimson. The doorway was several feet away from the top of the stairs. As soon as his eye level came up to the landing, he could see a figure sitting by the open door. Any uncertainty about the person's identity soon evaporated as he approached the landing.

"Oh, hello," said Ah Song, with just a trace of surprise in his voice.

"Oh, it's Uncle Song," said Mei Oi, quickly pulling the hem of her dress down over her knees; but it was too late for Ah Song not to have seen her exposed legs.

"It's terribly hot today, isn't it?" Ah Song was in a dark cord suit.

"Yes, it is." She got up. "That's why I'm sitting here. There's no breeze inside." She stood awkwardly in the doorway.

"I . . . I was just going upstairs to see a friend . . ."

"Yes," Mei Oi nodded. She wished Ah Song would continue upstairs. When he just stood there and grinned at her, she felt embarrassed; and, after a moment of hesitation, invited him in.

"Ben Loy is at work," she said after they were seated in the living room.

"Oh, is that so? And you're home all alone?"

"Yes," replied Mei Oi uneasily. This was the first time she had been left alone with a man other than her husband. Ah Song was practically a stranger. Even when she was with her own father she would blush.

"What time does Ben Loy get home?" asked Ah Song.

"Some time after midnight." She wished he would go away instead of asking so many questions. He was not at all like that beggar man who used to come to her house in Sunwei and call out over the top of the half doors: *Good little girl, have a kind heart and give me something to eat.* She would always give him something. Even when the pot of rice was all gone, she would pester her mother to part with some taros or potatoes.

"Does your father-in-law ever come up to visit you?" Ah Song pursued. He pulled out his cigarette case and lit a cigarette. He puffed at it leisurely and contentedly. His left thumb and forefinger went up and touched his nose. He did this many times. Each time he did this the big diamond on his second finger sparkled in front of Mei Oi; so that she could not help but notice it.

"No, very seldom." Mei Oi shook her head. She was already getting alarmed at Uncle Song's obvious intention to stay. She had asked him to come in as a matter of courtesy and had not expected him to accept her invitation. If someone had seen him even near her apartment, she could be ruined by gossipy talk. And never again would she be able to lift her head to face either Ben Loy or her father-in-law.

"Uncle Song," she continued, her face frantic with fear, "you must forgive me; but, as you know, a woman alone having a male visitor . . . it's . . . well, it's the sort of thing that is not done. I'm sorry, it's all my fault. I asked you to come in. Now I must ask you to leave. Please come back when my husband is home."

"Don't be afraid. I won't stay long." Ah Song almost chuckled. "This is New York, not China. You can have male visitors if you want to."

"But . . . but what would people say?"

"Nothing. What *can* they say? We're not doing anything wrong." Ah Song's left hand went up, touched his nose, then came down and adjusted his tie. "What kind of life do you have here? Your husband goes to work and you stay home to stare at the four walls!"

"But I'm married to him," protested Mei Oi.

"Ben Loy will do whatever his father tells him to do. He's that way." Ah Song took great relish in revealing this to Mei Oi. He felt that the more derogatory things he could say about Ben Loy the better it would make *him* look in the eyes of Mei Oi. He knitted his brows and sought additional ammunition to throw at this young wife who, to him, was just a country girl who found herself in a big city. "Do you still think you're marred to Ben Loy? Your husband was a regular customer at the local whorehouses. Everybody knows that but you and Wang Wah Gay!"

"No, no, it's not true!" Mei Oi cried.

"My dear girl, you have been badly misinformed." Ah Song tried to suppress a chuckle . . . . He got up and started pacing the floor. "I'm sorry if I've hurt you by telling you the truth, but somebody has to tell you sooner or later."

Ah Song was very pleased with the turn of events. He had always enjoyed seeing a woman cry. Now, when sobs came to Mei Oi, he was particularly pleased. He believed that he held the power to sway the emotional outburst of this young girl to suit his fancy.

"Please don't cry," he said, wiping away the tears with his own handkerchief. His arm was now around her, comforting her. The delicateness and warmth of her flesh . . . the mere touch of her sent his heartbeat soaring. The large diamond on his finger blinked dazzlingly bright as he held the handkerchief in his hand.

"Please, I'm all right now." She gently lifted his arm and pulled away from him. "Will you please leave now?" She dabbed at her eyes with her own handkerchief.

"In just a moment." Ah Song followed her to another part of the living room. "After I've told you how much I love you!"

"What . . .what did you say?" Mei Oi was shocked.

"I've loved you ever since I first saw you at your wedding banquet at the Grand China Restaurant," continued Ah Song. "Day and night, no matter how hard I tried, I couldn't get you out of my mind!"

"How can you stand there and tell me these things?" Me Oi managed to blurt out between sobs. "Don't forget: I'm Ben Loy's wife." Good or bad, she told herself, still she was Ben Loy's wife. Today was the first time she had ever heard anything bad said of her husband.

"Yes, I know," said Ah Song. "But I also know that in this country divorce is a common thing. If a woman doesn't love her husband, she can get a divorce and marry another man." He shrugged his shoulders and turned his palms up.

"But I don't want to divorce my husband . . ."

"I love you. Marry me. I can give you a life that Ben Loy cannot hope to give you in a thousand years." Ah Song's imagination began to fabricate a fantastic family background. "Very few people know this, but my family in Canada owns a lot of land; in fact a great part of the State of Montreal . . . of course you've heard of Montreal. We own the biggest hotel in Toronto. My family owns the biggest theater in . . . in Vancouver . . ."

These names were vaguely familiar to Mei Oi, for she had heard of them before. She was immensely impressed; but she could not understand what Ah Song, with *his* family background, would be doing in New York. She was tempted to ask him when he resumed, "Some years ago, when my mother wanted me to marry a girl I didn't love, I left home, and I haven't been back since. From time to time my mother writes and pleads with me to go back. But I haven't wanted to go back. I liked this bachelor life. But since I've met you . . ."

He walked over to Mei Oi and placed her hands in his. "I no longer have a desire for this old life. I . . . I want to take you home with me as my bride." He patted her hands fondly. "My mother will love you, I know. You will never have to sweep a single room." He peered at her tearstained face briefly, then sat down beside her at the couch. "The last time I was home, my mother had eight servants."

"Please go now," said Mei Oi.

"My mother is the old-fashioned type. I know she would shower you with diamonds and jades and gold necklaces."

"Come and visit us when my husband is home," Me Oi sobbed and buried her head in her palms.

Ah Song put his arms around her. She tried to move away but he held her tight. "But I love you, don't you understand?" Instinctively he bent his head and kissed her on the cheek. She jumped up, walked a few paces away and whirled.

"Please leave me alone!" she implored.

"I just want to tell you I love you." Ah Song gestured with open arms.

"You've already told me that. Please leave now before somebody comes." She started walking toward the door, hoping he would follow her. But he only straightened his tie and peered at himself in the full-length mirror in the living room. It reflected a nonchalant, cold, and calculating individual. He would get what he wanted, he told himself.

"Can I borrow the use of your bathroom?" he asked flippantly, trying to delay his departure. Mei Oi did not answer him. She stood by the door, sulking.

"The toilet is outside," she finally said in a loud voice. She placed her hand on the door knob, anxious to see Ah Song leave the apartment.

"Brew me a cup of tea and I'll leave," called Ah Song from the living room. He was still admiring himself in the mirror.

Reluctantly Mei Oi returned, making her way to the kitchen in silence, a prisoner in her own home. She did not want to make a disturbance that would expose Ah Song's visit to her apartment. She wanted him to leave quietly, undetected, just as he had come. If she had known he was like this, she would never have let him take a single step over the threshold. She was hoping that, if she did what he wanted her to do, he would leave peacefully.

Inside the kitchen she let the water run into the white-enameled pot, then put the pot on the range for the tea. When she turned to sit by the kitchen table to wait for the water to boil, Ah Song appeared in the kitchen doorway. She stared blankly at him.

"You'll feel better after you've got to know me a little more," grinned Ah Song. He know she would not dare make an outcry; because if she did, she would place herself in a scandalous position. He knew, too, that he was free to stay as long as he liked because her husband would not be home until midnight. He would take his time with this naive country girl. He walked over and helped himself to a seat.

"After all," he resumed, "what does a woman want in a husband? Good looks, money, position. A life free from worry. My mother would never interfere with the life of *her* daughter-in-law—if she had one. And my father—he leaves the women-folks alone. He never bothers my mother."

Ah Song waited for Mei Oi to say something; but she was quiet, resting her chin on the palm of her hand, her elbow on the table top. Once in a while she glanced back at the pot. Once more Ah Song put his diamond-ringed hand to his nose. "We live in a big mansion . . . great big mansion, several blocks big. . ." He made a wide arc with his hand.

Unwillingly Me Oi followed his every word and gesture. She mentally compared her present existence to that of mistress of a mansion with servants and acres and acres of land.

"I wish you would leave," she said dejectedly. "My husband may come home early today. When he went to work, he complained of a headache." She stared at Ah Song hopefully.

"I'll leave in a few minutes after I have my cup of tea. That is, if that's no trouble to you."

Mei Oi got up, walked quickly to the shelves and returned with a container of tea. Just as she turned to face the pot, the trapped steam started to escape from the lid. She gingerly flipped open the lid, threw in a fingerful of Jasmine tea leaves, and quickly let the cover down. After a moment, she picked up the pot and started pouring its contents into Ah Song's cup. After she had replaced the pot on the range, Ah Song grabbed her gently by the wrist. "Mei Oi, I love you!" he almost pleaded.

The cry of *I love you* was a mixture of sweet and sour music to Mei Oi's ears. She was flattered and frightened.

"Please don't say any more," she said. Her hand pushed away the hand that had held her wrist, and Ah Song reluctantly let go.

"Believe me, little sister, ever since I first saw you, I have had you in my mind day and night." He shook his head. "It's torture to love someone who doesn't even know you exist."

Mei Oi nervously took a seat opposite Ah Song. "You have no right to talk to me like this," she protested, trying to conceal the quiver in her voice. "I'm a married woman."

"My mother has a right to acquire a daughter-in-law as much as anybody else," said Ah Song. "Fate has brought us together. We must not fight fate, but welcome it."

This sort of talk bewildered Mei Oi. Her attitude toward Ah Song was becoming less harsh. She saw in him a little boy wanting something—desperately begging, pleading. Like that beggar man in Sunwei.

"Uncle Song, I'm Ben Loy's wife," she began.

"Yes, I know that. I also know that I love you. Don't you understand?"

"No, I'm afraid not," she shook her head. "I'm a little confused." When she saw that Ah Song was staring at her, she quickly lowered her eyes.

Ah Song thought he saw an opening. Swiftly he was out of his chair and next to Mei Oi. He was on his knees, his hands holding hers.

"Please believe me," he whispered, "I love you so much, I'd do anything for you. My mother would feel honored to have you for a daughter-in-law." He put his head close to hers. "You are so beautiful, Mei Oi. I love you, I love you, I love you!"

Mei Oi said nothing. She could not think clearly. Ah Song's hands reached out to wrap her in his arms. He kissed her on the cheeks.

"Please don't," she tried to push him away; but he tightened his grip.

He kissed her full and long on the lips. Then again.

"Please don't." The protest was almost inaudible.

He pressed his lips over her face, whispering, "I love you, I love you!" Finally he lifted her from the chair and carried her into the bedroom.

"Uncle Song, please leave me alone . . ."

Ah Song's heart was throbbing madly. Drops of perspiration appeared on his forehead. He gently dropped her on the large double bed and lay down beside her.

"Please don't . . . please don't . . ."

The bed springs squeaked under their combined weight. The neatly-made bed was quickly disarrayed.

"I won't hurt you . . ."

"Please don't . . ."

"I love you. I won't hurt you."

In the kitchen the white-enameled pot stood mute and unused, the lone cup of tea on the table forgotten and untouched.

Later, when they both got up, Mei Oi started to sob, very softly.

One day several weeks later, Chong Loo, after making his customary rounds collecting rents, stopped by the Wah Que Barber Shop on Mott Street. This time he was in need of a haircut. At other times he would come to collect rent or just drop in to "fire" his *big gun*.

"You sonavabitch," greeted Ah Mow, the proprietor. "So hot you have to wear a jacket?"

Chong Loo dropped down on one of the waiting chairs, with his ever-present brief case beside him. He was almost out of breath. "I want a haircut. The last time I got a haircut here, you didn't do such a good job."

"Blame it on you hair," said Ah Sing, the second barber. "Your hair looks more like a brush than hair on someone's head. What is the latest news?"

"Wow you mother, how should I know?" Chong Loo lit a cigarette and the oscillating fan on the opposite wall blew his smoke away.

"That which does not concern me," he added nonchalantly, "does not worry me." He got up and walked toward the first barber's chair.

"Wow you, mother," said Ah Mow. "Take off you coat."

"Ha, ha. I let you be the judge," said Chong Loo, turning to remove his coat. When he returned to the chair he asked pointedly, "Ah Mow, why don't you get your *rice cooker* over here and . . ."

"That which does not concern me, does not worry me," Ah Mow began quoting him.

"Wow your mother."

"I'm just repeating what you said a moment ago."

"You sonovabitch, I'm telling you for your own good," replied Chong Loo. "If you have your old woman here, everything would be better for you. If you get sick . . ."

"What's the use of getting her over here?" said Ah Mow. "She's already many times ten."

"It's better than getting a young wife in this country," continued Chong Loo. "Hey, cut it a little shorter here." Chong Loo's hand went up and pointed to a spot of hair.

"You crazy man," said Ah Sing. "Which would you want? Sleep with an old woman or a young one?"

"That's just the trouble," said Chong Loo. "Everyone wants to sleep with a young one. No one wants to sleep with an old one. She's all yours, and you're safe. Heh, heh, that's what's good about it."

"Wow your mother. You go to hell."

"Look out. Don't cut my ear!"

"Wang Wah Gay's daughter-in-law." Ah Sing was making idle talk. "She's been here almost a year now. She has no big belly yet. I wonder why."

"Do you know what I've heard?" asked Chong Loo excitedly. "That son of his . . . he . . . when he was younger, he got mixed up with the wrong people."

"I thought his father sent him to . . ."

"Yes, Wang Wah Gay sent him to a small town to work so as to keep him from the evils of the big city. Ha, ha, he sent him to work in Stanton." Chong Loo smiled at himself in the wall mirror.

"Ben Loy's a good boy," said Ah Mow. "He don't gamble. His father was more worried about his son becoming a gambler than anything else."

"What he didn't know was that the son used to come into New York several times a week for women," laughed Ah Sing. "Didn't you tell us that, Uncle Loo?"

"The boy ruined his health," Chong Loo said sadly. "They say that thing can't come up any more."

"People talk too much," said Ah Mow. "Maybe there's no truth to it."

"He's had all sorts of diseases, from gonorrhea to syphilis," continued Chong Loo. "If that is not the case, why hadn't his wife been pregnant now? Why hasn't she been with child?"

"Wow you mother," said Ah Sing. "Maybe they don't want any baby. Many young couples don't want babies right away."

"We Chinese are different," said Chong Loo. "The old heads would see to it that the young ones produce. Anyway, I think Wah Gay's son is *no can do*. Heh, heh, just like me."

Ah Mow flipped off the white cloth apron from Chong Loo's neck and the rent collector stepped off the chair. He walked up to the mirror and examined himself, turning his head this way and that way. "Me? I look like a sixteen-year-old," he announced.

"Wow your mother," said Ah Sing. "You'll be sixteen in the next world."

Mei Oi's affair with Ah Song was the sort of thing that a country girl would never dream could happen to her. Once it happened it was not within the easy-going personality of Me Oi to halt it. Things might have been different if Ben Loy had gone back to Stanton to work; but to please his wife, he remained in New York. In his own words, he wanted his wife to feel more at home, close to Chinatown. He felt Mei Oi would be too unaccustomed to the living conditions in a small town like Stanton. Chin Yuen had recommended him for a job at the New Toishan at 53rd Street. He had decided to stay.

The seasons came and went. Ben Loy continued working at the New Toishan.

When Mei Oi got up one morning in April, she complained of feeling ill. She put her hand to her forehead and it felt warm, warmer than usual. "I think I have a little fever," she said.

Ben Loy put his palm to her forehead. "Yes, it feels warm."

"I feel a little dizzy too," added Mei Oi. What alarmed her most was that the day before she had eaten very little. There was a general lack of appetite. "I wish you wouldn't go to work today," she said.

Ben Loy immediately called the boss of the New Toishan Restaurant and told him he could not come in to work. Then he accompanied Mei Oi to the doctor's.

At the doctor's small crowded office, they took seats and began reading the scrolls hanging on the walls of the waiting room. Next they watched the old fish swim in the glass tank by the window. When they got tired of watching the fish, they looked up at the clock on the wall, whose sweeping second hand seemed not to move fast enough. Every fifteen minutes or so Dr. Long would open his inner office door and someone among those waiting would get up and walk in.

When Me Oi's turn came, the doctor greeted her with a perfunctory "hello."

"Name?" the doctor sat down at his desk.

"Wang. Wang Mei Oi."

"Have you been here before?"

"No, this is the first time," said Mei Oi.

The doctor led her into the examination room. "What seems to be the trouble?" he asked. "Open you mouth." The doctor stuck a thermometer into her mouth.

"Sit down," Dr. Long pointed to the stool. "Roll up your sleeves." He brought out the instrument for measuring blood pressure.

When that was done, the doctor announced, "I have to take a blood test."

"A blood test? What's the matter, doctor? What's wrong? How much blood are you going to take?" asked Mei Oi, timidly.

"Oh, not much," said the doctor. "About half a gallon. Ha, ha. Is that too much?"

The outer door could be heard opening and closing. Then footsteps. More people were coming in.

The doctor gave Mei Oi a little bottle to bring back the next day. "Don't forget," he reminded. "It's the morning sample that I want."

A week later Dr. Long called Mei Oi to inform her that she was pregnant.

The news jolted her like a bolt of lightening. She sighed and clasped her hands tightly. Of course, she never had been pregnant before and had no idea how it felt to be with child. She wished her mother were here to tell her what to do. She wanted to tell the whole world she was pregnant. She was going to have a baby after all! She found herself saying "I'm pregnant . . . I'm pregnant!" Everybody who gets married has a baby, sooner or later. Now her turn had come. She hurried to the mirror to stare at the soon-to-be-mother. She liked the way she looked. She dashed to the phone.

"Will you please call Ben Loy to the phone?" She waited.

"Hello, Loy *Gaw*?"

"What's the matter? Speak fast. I'm busy right now."

"The doctor just called. He said I'm going to have a baby!"

"Did you have to call me to tell me about it now? Is that all? I have six tables to wait on." He hung up.

Her husband's cool reception to the news did not dampen her own enthusiasm. Even her meetings with Ah Song did not hold any significant meaning for her in the light of her pregnancy.

Maxine Hong Kingston

Biography

Maxine Hong Kingston lives in California with her husband, actor Earll Kingston. Her first book, *The Woman Warrior*, won the National Book Critics' Circle Award in 1976. She is also the author of *China Men* and *Tripmaster Monkey*.

From *China Men*

Ed, Woodrow, Roosevelt, and Worldster held their bowls to their mouths and shoveled as fast as they could, chewing crackly pork and pressed duck in one bite, gulping while jabbing from the center dishes without choosiness. They raced as if food were scarce and one of them would be left the runt pig. Woodrow picked up the soup tureen and drank directly from it. "Uh. Uh," the others protested, but didn't stop gulping to say "You're cheating."

Worldster threw down his bowl and chopsticks, spit the bones "p-foo" out on the table, knocked back his shot of whiskey, jumped up—his orange crate hit the floor with a bang—and shouted, "I won. I won."

But Woodrow, the soup drinker, ran out the door. "Last one to leave the table loses," he said.

"You're still chewing and swallowing," Worldester yelled.

"Okay," said Ed. "Okay, I lose." His friends cheered him as he leaned back and sipped his whiskey. "That was a four-and-a-half-minute dinner," he said, looking at his new gold watch. "It's a record." They gave their record a cheer.

The last one to finish eating did the dishes. While the others returned to work in the front of the laundry, Ed set a kettle to boil, unfolded his newspaper, lit a Lucky Strike, the brand he had chosen, and poured another glass of whiskey and a cup of coffee. Reading while drinking and smoking was one of the great pure joys of existence. He read that a Gold Mountain Sojourner, upon returning to his village, had gotten bilked by relatives, most of whom he had never met before. They had flocked to him. They tricked him with an intricate scheme for investing in a bogus Hong Kong housing project for refugees. Another Sojourner put his life savings into a bank that the entire village had set up just to get his money. The Sojourners were quoted as saying they were coming back to America.

Ed scraped the dishes onto the tablecloth, which was layers of newspapers. Then he rolled up the top layer; the table was instantly clean and already covered for the next meal. He sudsed the dishes with laundry soap and put them in a drainer. From the whistling tea kettle, he poured boiling water on them; the water was so hot, the dishes dried before his eyes. It was a method he remembered the slaves in China using. Dishwashing just took common sense; women had made such a to-do about it. The Gold Mountain was indeed free: no manners, no traditions, no wives.

When he joined his partners doing the ironing, his favorite part of laundry work, they were planning "the weekend."

"I want to go tea dancing," said Worldster, "and take driving lessons." He had a thick moustache and tried to look like Clark Gable.

"Let's see the Statue of Liberty at night," said Woodrow, who vowed that he would make a million bucks by 1935.

"I want to go on a date," said Roosevelt, who was looking for a medical school that gave night classes. "A weekend date with a Rockette," he said in English.

"I know where *City Lights* is playing," said Ed. "Also *Little Miss Marker.* You know, someday, when the people from the future see the movies, they'll think people today walked and moved like Charlie Chaplin." Oh, it was wonderful; for a dime the ushers let you stay all day through the intermissions, and the shows ran again and again. "Every Saturday night is a party in this country." Customers were picking up the big bundles—cash for the weekend.

Ed placed shirt after shirt on the stack that was growing beside his ironing board. Friends were fairer than brothers; there was an equality. When Tu Fu left his village, friends cared for him; "we swore brotherhood for eternity," he wrote. How good life was. Ed was young, and he was in New York with three new true friends who sang at their work.

They were singing the Rainy Alley Poet, who lived in Paris and followed black hair in the rain: "'I will follow that gleam though stumbling in the haze, the twilight like a bubble of rose rising in the wine glass, and let my nostalgic eyes become ensnared in memory dark as her hair.'"

"Aiya," breathed Woodrow. "True love. True life. The free pursuit of happiness."

"Aiya. That's me," said Roosevelt, "'ensnared in memory dark as her hair,' except it should be blonde hair. 'Ensnared in memory yellow as her hair!'"

They sang Wang Tu Ching, a Sojourner, who had done all the wonderful things that a young man ought to do in Paris—having affairs, getting French girls pregnant. "'Oh, this endless journey home. I am Chinese, and must not expect happiness but tears and sacrifice. Farewell, Latin Quarter, chestnut trees, bookstalls along the Seine.'" "'Latin Quarter, chestnut trees,'" Ed repeated.

"'I'm madly in love with Europe,'" they sang, "'where I played my reed flute on an empty stomach.'" This was a song by Ai Ch'ing, a fellow Kwangtung man.

They sang an old poet, too, Yüan Mei, who had advocated educating women and written from a woman's point of view: "'For years I've been imagining a boat/Shooting over the waves as fast as any bird/But never taking the traveler away from friends/Always carrying the traveler back to his home.'"

"Oh, that's beautiful," said Roosevelt. He rested under the fan and smoked a cigarette with tears in his eyes. "That's how I feel." The men were thinking not about one another but of lifelong friends.

"And listen to this one," said Ed. "The first wife welcomes her man home: 'If it were not for Second Wife, you would not come home. She is your plum blossom.'"

"Oh, oh," moaned the lonesome men. "Welcomed home by two wives."

They worked very late at night, and after a while did not sing or talk. The two fans whirred, blowing the calendars, the monthly calendars swinging on the walls, and the pages of the daily calendars riffling. Ed's legs ached. At about eleven o'clock, he spoke the bitter verses of "The Laundry Song," by Wen I-to of Chicago:

> *A piece, two pieces, three pieces—*
> *Wash them clean,*
> *Four pieces, five pieces, six—*
> *Iron them smooth.*

No, they were not going to be welcomed home by wives; they would stay here working forever. He thumped his iron on the accents.

> *Years pass and I let drop but one homesick tear.*
> *A laundry lamp burns at midnight.*
> *The laundry business is low, you say,*
> *Washing out blood that stinks like brass—*
> *Only a Chinaman can debase himself so.*
> *But who else wants to do it? Do you want it?*
> *Ask for the Chinaman. Ask the Chinaman.*

The other men were so tired, they only grunted in agreement. At midnight they switched off the lights in the windows, turned the Open sign around to Closed, and pulled down the shades. They worked without interruptions from customers, then made the ironing tables into beds.

Under his desk lamp, Ed did the accounts on his abacus and wrote down the profits in ledgers. Woodrow, who had bought a Kodak with a part of his million, took a picture of him. "You can send this to your wife and tell her you study a lot," he said. When Ed finished the bookkeeping, the others were asleep. In the quiet of the night, he practiced his calligraphy by writing down modern poems for his friends to paste on the walls over their ironing tables. He wrote a letter to his wife, and went to bed.

On Saturday Ed and Woodrow went to Fifth Avenue to shop for clothes. With his work pants, Ed wore his best dress shirt, a silk tie, gray silk socks, good leather shoes with pointed toes, and a straw hat. At a very good store, he paid two hundred dollars cash for a blue and gray pinstripe suit, the most expensive suit he could find. In the three-way mirror, he looked like Fred Astaire. He wore the suit out of the store. Woodrow took a picture of him dancing down the New York Public Library steps next to one of the lions. "I don't see why you have to spend all this money on clothes," said Woodrow, whose entire wardrobe came from the unclaimed laundry. He was the one who had written the sign in English: WE WILL NOT BE RESPONSIBLE FOR CLOTHES UNCLAIMED AFTER 30 DAYS. He shot his cuffs and said, "You must admit I look pretty swanky in these secondhand outfits." The two of them strolled Fifth Avenue and caught sight of themselves in windows and hubcaps. They looked all the same Americans.

Suddenly a band of white demons came up from behind them. One picked off Ed's straw hat and kicked its lid through. Before Ed and Woodrow could decide what to do for the shame on China Men, they saw the whites stomp on other whites' hats. "It must be a custom," said Ed.

That afternoon, the partners trimmed one another's hair with their barber's shears and electric hair clippers. They copied Ed's professional haircut, parted in the middle and the two sides lifted just so in "pompadours." Then all four gentlemen went to a tearoom. Ed regretted having to check his gray felt hat at the door. It looked good with his new suit. Girls liked the way he cocked his head and looked at them sideways with his hat brim tilted at a smart angle. The hatcheck girl also sold them strips of tickets for ten cents apiece. The hostess escorted them to a table, where they ordered cookies, open-faced raw cucumber sandwiches, strawberry parfaits, and tea. They nibbled carefully at their sandwiches, chewed with their mouths shut, sipped tea, and dabbed their lips even though they had not slobbered or made crumbs. They looked around at the couples to decide which dancing girls they were going to ask. "Look at the legs on that one," said Roosevelt. "She must be a Rockette."

"The main difference between them and us Tang People," Woodrow observed, "is the shape of their nostrils, which are oval instead of small, neat, and round like ours."

They were saying those things in Chinese, so weren't being rude. They were sophisticated New York gentlemen, and knew more about American manners than white people. "When I was a waiter," said Worldster, "there were hick tourists who tipped us after every course. Every time we came to the table they tipped us." Since the music took so long stopping, he went over to a couple, tapped the white man on the shoulder, and cut in. "What's your name, sweetheart?" he said like in the movies.

The others waited until the orchestra stopped, then stood and walked out onto the dance floor. "Dance with me?" Ed asked, holding out his tickets. "Sure," the blonde dancing girl of his choice said, smiling, taking several tickets, which was a compliment; he would get to dance with her a lot. He smiled back and said, "Sure." The music did not start up right away. "You like come my table after you dance with me?" he invited. "Of course," she said. "You speak English very well," she said. "Thank you," he said. "You be very beautiful. Pretty. You be pretty. I like you." "How nice," she said. "Thank you. You're very handsome. You're good looking. Do you understand handsome?" "Sure. Of course. How nice. Thank you." A fox-trot started, and he put out his hand; she put her hand in it, and he led her, his feet in their new leather shoes, glissading across the waxed wood floor. He saw himself and her in the mirrors, and they looked liked the movies. He guided her a little closer with the intimate hand at her waist. He looked down at the gold eyebrows and curving eyelashes and her blue eyes. He pulled their two clasped hands closer so that her gold hair brushed his hand. Her hair was fine and soft, not like hair at all. He dared a dip, and her wonderful hair rippled near the floor and swung back against his other hand. When the music stopped, she said, "You're a very good dancer." "And handsome too?" he asked. She laughed with her beautiful lipsticked mouth.

The others had also brought their blondes over to the table under the potted palm, and they ate the sandwiches, drank tea, and smoked cigarettes. "Is he really a Chinese prince?" Worldster's girl asked. "What's 'prince'?" asked Ed. "A king's son," she said. "A king's son," said Worldster in Chinese. "Oh, yes," said Ed, "in China, we all be prince with so much money. To much money. But. Now we all the same Americans."

They danced until they had no more tickets. And they danced with as many different blondes as they pleased. And Ed was so handsome that some danced with him for free, vied with one another to dance with him. He became bold enough to ask the friendliest blonde, one who had been studying his eyes, his high cheekbones, and neat nose, who had made him unbutton his sleeve and hold his tan arm against her pink arm, "You like come home with me? Please?"

"No, honey," she said. "No."

Not one of the four of them told any blonde that they were married and were fathers. "See you next week," they said, learning new ways to say good-bye. "See ya." "So long."

On Sunday they rode the ferry boat to Coney Island. Woodrow asked a blonde to take pictures of the four friends with their arms on the railing and their black hair flying in the wind. At the beach, a bathing beauty photographed them in their bathing suits, nobody wearing a jockstrap, which might not yet have come into fashion. Ed had bought a beach robe, "which is different from a bedroom robe," he explained. He sent many pictures to his wife, including one of himself sitting on the sand with his arms around his knees and his sweat shirt tied around his neck; he was smiling and looking out to sea.

On another weekend, Worldster, who had taken flying lessons, rented an aeroplane and invited each of his friends up into the sky. (*Friends* in Chinese connotes play, good times, and youth.) "We're men of the Twentieth Century," he lectured as Ed marveled at the speed and height. "We're modern men, and have to learn to make use of the new machines." He explained how to move the plane right and left and up and down, then said, "You try it," and let go of the controls. Ed flew over rivers, trees, and houses, raced cars, and made the plane go back up when it fell into air pockets. They circled the airport and waggled their wings at Roosevelt and Woodrow down there.

Ed sent his wife pictures of himself in the cockpit; he wore a white scarf flying behind him, goggles, and a leather skullcap with flaps over the ears. He also sent several shots of the plane in the air, an insect against the white sky.

Woodrow bought a car, and Roosevelt a motorcycle. Each of the four friends stood by the car for his picture. They also took pictures of one another leaning into curves on the motorcycle. Ed did not pass the driver's test but drove anyway. "You can drive without a license here," he wrote to people in China. "It's a free country."

In the spring, Ed sent his wife a picture of the four partners with their arms around one another's shoulders, laughing next to a Keep Off the Grass sign. He was wearing another two-hundred-dollar suit, a navy blue one, and a shirt with French cuffs, which closed with gold cuff links. For a winter picture, he sat on a rock in Central Park in his new gray greatcoat and jaunty hat and leather gloves lined with rabbit fur.

In his quiet time at night, he mounted the photographs in a fine leather album. With his first spending money, he had bought a postcard of the Statue of Liberty, the album, picture mounts, white ink, and a pen with a steel nib. He pasted that postcard in his expensive album, then added the other pictures.

Ed's wife wrote often and sometimes sent lichee, which she had picked from the three trees that Ed's father had planted and the twenty trees that Ed's brother had planted. When would he return to plant lichee trees?

Then she wrote that their two children had died. What should she do? "I think you ought to come back right now," she said.

He did much worrying, and hit upon a plan. He would not end his American life but show her how to live one. "Here's what you have to do if I'm to bring you to America," he wrote, though there was a law against her. "I will bring you to America on one condition, and that is, you get a Western education. I'll send you money, which you must only spend on school, not on food or clothes or jewelry or relatives. Leave the village. Go to Hong Kong or Canton and enroll in a Western scientific school. A science school. Get a degree. Send it to me as evidence you are educated, and I'll send you a ship ticket. And don't go to a school for classical literature. Go to a scientific school run by white people. And when you get your degree, I'll send for you to come here to the United States." He would figure out later how to accomplish that.

When next she wrote, she had enrolled in medical school; she was writing him from there. As years passed and sometimes she became discouraged with how long her education was taking and how difficult the work, he wrote encouragement: "If you don't get that degree, I'll not send for you. We will never see each other again." He did not want an ignorant villager for his American wife.

So much time went by, he saved another two hundred dollars, which he spent on a gray suit and a Countess Mara tie.

THE NUVORASIAN ANTHOLOGY

At last she mailed him her diploma. He spent another few years saving passage money, and fifteen years after they had last seen one another, he sent for her. Applying for her, he risked having his citizenship again scrutinized. She would enter legally and gracefully, no question of asking a lady to ride the sea in a box or to swim to an unwatched shore.

At dinner one evening, he announced to his partners, "I've sent for my wife, who will be here in January." They were so surprised that they stopped their eating race.

"How did you save enough money?" Worldster asked.

"I guess you'll be moving to your own apartment," said Roosevelt.

"Why do you want to do that?" asked Woodrow.

After writing letters for fifteen years, Ed and his wife ended their correspondence. They were near each other, she on Ellis Island, where there was no mail, and he on Manhattan. When he saw her on the ferry, she was standing surrounded by bundles and bags, no child tugging her coat and no baby in her arms. He recognized her, though she was older. Her hair was slicked against her head with a bun in back, a proper married-lady hairdo. In spite of the law against her, she was landing, her papers in order. Her imigration verified the strength of his citizenship.

"Here you are," he said. "You've come."

"You look like a foreigner," she said. "I can barely recognize you."

"Was it a rough journey?" he asked.

"It was terrible," she exclaimed. "The Japanese were right behind me. When I tried to board the ship from Canton to Hong Kong, the man acted as if my papers were wrong and asked for a seventy-five-dollar bribe. So I ran to another gangplank and found out seventy-five dollars wasn't policy at all; this man wanted a hundred dollars. I had to run back to the first entrance. Then I paid another hundred to get off the ship. It was the last ship out of Canton before the Japanese took the harbor. And I was so seasick, I vomited the whole way across the Atlantic. And what a questioning I got on the Island. They asked me what year you had cut your queue, and a workman shook his head, hawked, and spat. It was a signal. So I said, 'I don't know.' On my way to be locked up again, I said to that workman, 'That was a delicious bun you gave me. Thank you. I hope you bring me another if you have more.' Get it? It was a code I made up, meaning, 'Thank you for giving me the right answer. Please give me more help.' Oh, I was so scared. If it weren't for him I might not be here."

"Don't worry anymore," said Ed. "That's over now. Don't worry anymore." Her big eyes had lines around them. "That's all over now," he said.

"I had to build roads," she said. "Since your father is too crazy to work, and you were away, I had to pay the labor tax for two men. Your father followed me and wept on the road when I left."

"Never mind now," he said. "That's all over now."

They rode the subway to the room he had rented in preparation for her coming. He taught her the name of the subway stop for the laundry. "Easu Bu-odd-way Su-ta-son," she repeated. "That's good," he said. "Remember that, and you can't get lost."

She unpacked jars of seeds. "But we aren't farmers any more," he said. "I'll plant in tin cans and put them out here on the fire escape," she said. "You'll see how many vegetables we can grow in cans."

She showed him a piece of cloth. "Do you recognize this?" she asked. "The Japanese were right behind me, and I had time to take just one keepsake—the trimming on the bed canopy." She had ripped it off and shoved it in her purse. She unfolded it. "This is the only thing we have left from China," she said. "The heirloom." A red phoenix and a red dragon played across the strip of linen; the Chinese words down one end and English words across the top said, "Good morning." She had cross-stitched it herself.

"You could write English even then," he teased her, "and getting ready to come here." "I didn't know what it said," she demurred, "I only copied it from a needlework book."

He took her shopping and bought her a black crepe dress with a bodice of white lace ruffles and buttons of rhinestone and silver. "You look very pretty," he told her. They bought a black coat with a fur collar and a little black-eyed animal head over shoulder, high heels, silk stockings, black kid gloves, and a picture hat with a wide, wide brim and silk fluttery ribbon. They strolled in ther finery along Fifth Avenue. "I washed all these windows," he told her. "When I first came here, I borrowed a squeegee and rags and a bucket, and walked up and down this street. I went inside each store and asked if they wanted the windows washed. The white foreigners aren't so hard to get along with; they nod to mean Yes and shake their heads to mean No, the same as anybody." New York glittered and shined with glass. He had liked pulling the water off the panes and leaving brief rainbows. While working, he had looked over the displays of all the wonderful clothes to own and wear. He had made the money to pool for starting the laundry. "In the spring," he promised her, "we'll buy you white cotton gloves."

"On the first day of autumn," he told her, "New Yorkers stomp on one another's straw hats. I wear my gray felt one as soon as summer's over. I save the straw for spring. I'm not extravagant. You ought to put your earrings in the safe deposit box at the bank. Pierced ears look a little primitive in this country." He also told her to buy makeup at a drugstore. "American people don't like oily faces. So you ought to use some powder. It's the custom. Also buy some rouge. These foreigners dislike yellow skin."

She also bought a long black rat of hair oil to roll her own hair over for an upswept hairdo. At a beauty parlor, she had her wavy hair cut and curled tigheter with a marcel. She washed, ironed, and wrapped her silk pants and dresses and never wore them again.

He took her to see the Statue of Liberty. They climbed the ladder, she in high heels, up the arm to the torch, then the stairs to the crown. "Now we're inside her chin. This part must be the nose." From the windows of the crown, he showed her his city.

They also went to the top of the Empire state Building, took the second elevator to the very top, the top of the world. Ed loved the way he could look up at the uncluttered sky. They put money in the telescopes and looked for the laundry and their apartment. "So I have been on the tallest building in the world," she said. "I have seen everything. Wonderful. Wonderful. Amazing. Amazing."

"Yes," he said. "Everything's possible on the Gold Mountain. I've danced with blondes." "No, really?" she said. "You didn't. You're making that up, aren't you? You danced with demonesses? I don't believe it."

Her favorite place to go was the free aquarium, "the fish house," where all manner of creatures swam. Walking between the lighted tanks, she asked, "When do you think we'll go back to China? Do you think we'll go back to China?" "Shh," he said. "Shh." The electric eels glowed in their dark tank, and the talking fish made noises. "There are bigger fish in China," she said.

They went to the movies and saw *Young Tom Edison* with Mickey Rooney. They both liked the scene where the mother took Eh-Da-Son into the barn, but only pretended to thrash him; she faked the slaps and crying and scolding to fool the strict father, the father "the severe parent," according to Confucius, and the mother "the kind parent." ("My bones, my flesh, father and mother," said Tu Fu.) After the movie, Ed explained to his wife that this cunning, resourceful, successful inventor, Edison, was who he had named himself after. "I see," she said. "Eh-Da-Son. Son as in *sage* or *immortal* or *saint*."

They also saw a movie where a big man bridged two mountain peaks with his prone body. He held on to one cliff of a chasm with his fingers and the other with his toes. Hundreds of little people walked across on him.

The four partners no longer had to race to get out of doing the dishes. Ed's wife shopped and cooked. She bought a tiered food carrier, filled each pot with a different accompaniment to rice, and carried it and a pot of soup hot through the subway to the laundry. The first day she did this, she got off at the wrong stop in the underground city. She went from white ghost to white ghost shouting over the trains, which sounded like the Japanese bombing, "Easu Bu-odd-way Su-ta-son?" And a conductor said, "Of course. East Broadway Station. Go that way."

"He understood me," she proudly told the men."I can speak English very well." She set the table with her homemade meal so they didn't get to buy restaurant take-out food any more. And they did not race but had manners. "Tell me how you started this laundry," she said. Woodrow described their Grand Opening. "Our friends sent stands of flowers tied in wide red ribbons, on which your husband wrote good words in gold ink. We exploded firecrackers out on the sidewalk, right out there on Mott street. And then the customers came." "Working for ourselves, we can close whenever we please and go do as we like," Ed said.

The partners did not tell her that they hardly ever celebrated holidays. They had learned that holidays do not appear with the seasons; the country does not turn festive just because a rubric day appears on the calendar. The cooking women, the shopping and slicing and kneading and chopping women brought the holidays. The men let holidays pass. If they did not go to the bother of keeping it, a holiday was another free day. It was that free a country. They could neglect attending the big public celebrations such as those at the benevolent associations and New Year's eve at Times Square, and no one minded. Neglecting the planting and harvest days made no difference in New York. No neighbors looked askance. And there were no godly repercussions. They had no graves to decorate for the memorial days of Clarity and Brightness. They did arrange cotton snow, reindeer, a stable scene, and a Santa Claus in the laundry window at Christmas. "We don't want them to break our window or not bring their laundry," Ed explained. His wife brought back the holidays. She made the holidays appear again.

Her arrival ended Ed's independent life. She stopped him from reading while eating. She'd learned at the school of Western medicine, she said, that doing those two actions at once divides the available blood between brain and stomach; one should concentrate. She kept telling Ed to cut down on his smoking. She polished his World's Fair copper souvenir ashtray clean. She cut new covers from brown wrapping paper and shirt cardboards for his books, and resewed the bindings. He inked the new covers with the titles, authors, and volume numbers.

When the partners took the couple to a restaurant, the men wiped their chopsticks and bowls with napkins. "That doesn't really clean them, you know," she said. "All you're doing is wiping the germs around. Germs are little animals invisible to the naked eye." "That must be a superstition from your village, a village superstition," said Worldster. "You ought to give up village superstitions in America." The next day she brought her microscope to the laundry and showed them the germs under their fingernails and on their tongues and in the water.

At one of their dinners, Worldster handed papers to Woodrow and Roosevelt, and the three of them started discussing business.

"What is this?" said Ed.

"Deeds for the business," said Worldster, "contracts for the partnership."

"Where's mine?" said Ed. "What contracts? Why contracts all of a sudden?"

"Where's his?" asked his wife.

"You weren't at the meeting," said Worldster.

"Since when did we have to have contracts?" Ed asked. "We had a spoken partnership. We shook hands. We gave one another our word."

"We wrote it down too," said Worldster. "I guess you have the status of an employee."

"I don't see why you didn't show up for the meeting," said Roosevelt.

"This is all perfectly legal," said Woodrow. "Look—registered with the demon courts."

It was in English. There wasn't anything Ed could do. They had ganged up on him and swindled him out of his share of the laundry. "You were always reading when we were working," somebody said.

"What are we going to do?" said his wife, the lines around her eyes and mouth deepening.

"Don't worry," he said. "I've been planning for us to go to California anyway."

So the two of them took a train across the United States, stopping in Chicago to visit some relatives—they saw more of the United States than they had ever seen of China—and went to live in California, which some say is the real Gold Mountain anyway.

Bing Lee

Bing Lee is a Chinese American artist living in New York City. He makes drawings every night in an ongoing project to compile a pictodiary that reveals personal myths as well as social concerns. He also has created site- specific works of public art, such as murals at Townsend Harris High School and P.S. 88. Lee is a recipient of several grants from the National Endowment for the Arts, the New York State Council on the Arts and the New York Foundation for the Arts. He is director of the Chinese Art Students program at the School of Visual Arts.

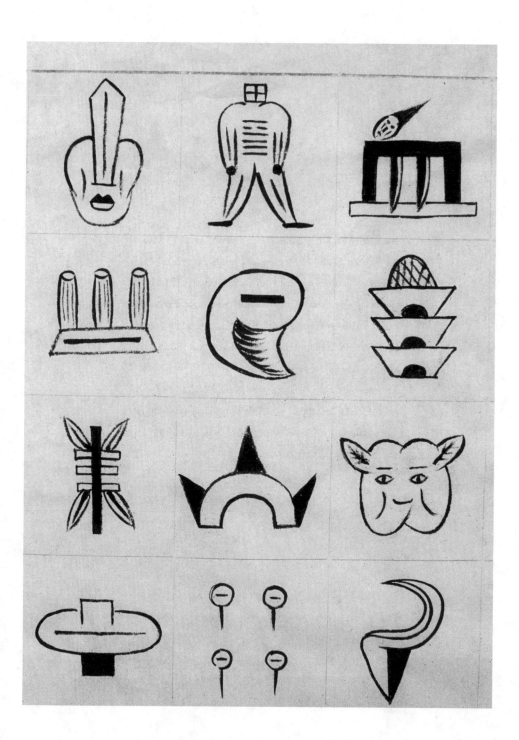

Lan Samantha Chang

My parents met in New York City, so it has always been a powerful
place in the map of my imagination.

Biography

Lan Samantha Chang was born and raised in Appleton, Wisconsin. A New York City resident from 1987 to 1989, she has since received fellowships from the Wallace Stegner
Foundation and the National Endowment for the Arts. Her fiction has been published in
Story, the *Atlantic Monthly*, and twice in *The Best American Short Stories* anthologies. Her
first book, *Hunger*, was published by W. W. Norton in 1998.

San

My father left my mother and me one rainy summer morning, carrying a new umbrella of mine. From our third-floor window I watched him close the front door and pause to glance at the sky. Then he opened my umbrella. I liked the big red flower pattern—it was *fuqi,* prosperous—but in the hands of a man, even a handsome man like my father, the umbrella looked gaudy and ridiculous. Still, he did not hunch underneath but carried it high up, almost jauntily.

As I watched him walk away, I remembered a Chinese superstition. The Mandarin word for umbrella, *san,* also means "to fall apart." If you acquire an umbrella without paying for it, your life will fall apart. My father had scoffed at such beliefs. The umbrella had been a present from him. Now I stood and watched it go, bright and ill-fated like so many of his promises.

Later that morning the roof of our apartment sprang a leak. Two tiles buckled off the kitchen floor, revealing a surprising layer of mud, as if my mother's mopping over the years had merely pushed the dirt beneath the tiles and all along we'd been living over a floor of soot.

My mother knelt with a sponge in one hand. She wouldn't look at me. Her heavy chignon had come undone and a thick lock of hair wavered down her back.

"Can I help?" I asked, standing over her. She did not answer but stroked the tiles with her sponge.

I put the big rice cooker underneath the leak. Then I went to my room. All morning, I studied problems for my summer school math class. I heard my mother, in the kitchen, start to sob. I felt only fear—a dense stone in my chest—but I put even this aside so I could study. My father had taught me to focus on the equations in front of me, and so I spent the hours after he left thinking about trigonometry, a subject he had loved.

My mathematical talent had sprung from an early backwardness. As a child I could not count past three: my father, my mother, and me.

"Caroline is making progress in her English lessons, but she remains baffled by the natural numbers," read an early report card. "She cannot grasp the countability of blocks and other solid objects. For this reason I am recommending that she repeat the first grade."

This comment left my father speechless. He believed I was a brilliant child. And mathematics had been his favorite subject back in China, before political trouble had forced him to quit school and eventually, the country.

"*Counting,*" he said in English, when he was able to talk again. His dark eyebrows swooped over the bridge of his acquiline nose. Despite his drastic ups and downs, bad news always caught him by surprise. But he recovered with typical buoyancy. "Don't worry, Lily," he told my mother. "It's those western teachers. *I'll* teach her how to count."

And so my father, himself an unreliable man, taught me to keep track of things. We counted apples, bean sprouts, grains of rice. I learned to count in pairs, with ivory chopsticks. We stood on the corner of Atlantic Avenue, counting cars to learn big numbers. We spent a lovely afternoon in Prospect Park, counting blades of grass aloud until we both had scratchy throats.

"Keep going," he urged me on as the shadows lengthened. "I want you to be able to count all the money I'm going to make, here in America."

By the time I was seven I had learned the multiplication tables to twenty-times-twenty. In the following year I learned to recite the table of squares and the table of cubes, both so quickly that the words blended together into a single stream, almost meaningless: "Oneeighttwentysevensixtyfouronetwentyfivetwosixteenthreefortythree . . ."

As I chanted, my father would iron the white shirt and black trousers he wore to his waiter's job, a "temporary" job. Or he stood in the kitchen, Mondays off, with three blue balls and one red ball, juggling expertly beneath the low tin ceiling. Each time the red ball reached his hand I was ordered to stress a syllable. Thus "One, *eight*, twenty-*seven*, sixty-*four*."

"Pro*nounce*," said my father, proud of his clear r's. To succeed in America, he was sure, required good pronunciation as well as math. He often teased my mother for pronouncing my name *Calorin*, "like a diet formula," he said. They had named me Caroline after Caroline Kennedy, who was born shortly before their arrival in the States. After all, my father's name was Jack. And if the name was good enough for a president's daughter, then certainly it was good enough for me.

After I learned to count I began, belatedly, to notice things. Signs of hard luck and good fortune moved through our apartment like sudden storms. A pale stripe on my father's tanned wrist revealed where his watch had been. A new pair of aquamarine slippers shimmered on my mother's feet. A beautiful collection of fourteen cacti, each distinct, bloomed on our fire escape for several summer months and then vanished.

I made careful explorations of our apartment. At the back of the foyer closet, inside the faded red suitcase my mother had brought from China, I discovered a cache of little silk purses wrapped in a cotton shirt. When I heard her footsteps I instinctively closed the suitcase and pretended I was looking for a pair of mittens. Then I went to my room and shut the door, slightly dizzy with anticipation and guilt.

A few days later when my mother was out, I opened one purse. Inside was a swirling gold pin with pearl and coral flowers. I made many secret visits to the closet, a series of small sins. Each time I opened one more treasure. There were bright green, milky white, and carmine bracelets. Some of the bracelets were so small I could not fit them over my hand. There was a ring with a pearl as big as a marble. A strand of pearls, each the size of a large pea. A strand of jade beads carved in the shape of small buddhas. A rusty key.

"Do you still have keys to our old house in China?" I asked my father.

"That's the past, Caroline," he said. "*Wanle*. It is gone."

Surrounded by questions, I became intrigued by the answers to things. My report cards showed that I became a good student, a very good student, particularly in math. At twelve, I was the only person from my class to test into a public school for the gifted in Manhattan. My father attended the school event where this news was announced. I remember his pleased expression as we approached the small, crowded auditorium. He had piled all of our overcoats and his fedora over one arm, but with the other he opened the door for my mother and me. As I filed past he raised his eyebrows and nodded—proud, but not at all surprised by my achievement.

He believed in the effortless, in splurging and quick riches. While I studied, bent and dogged, and my mother hoarded things, my father strayed from waitering and turned to something bigger. He had a taste for making deals, he said to us. A nose for good investments. Some friends were helping him. He began to stay out late and come home with surprises. On good nights, he brought us presents: a sewing kit, a pink silk scarf. Once he climbed out of a taxicab with a hundred silver dollars in my old marble bag.

On bad nights, my father whistled his way home. I sometimes woke to his high music floating from the street. I sat up and spied at him through the venetian blind. He no longer wore his waiter's clothes; his overcoat was dark. I could just make out the glitter of his shiny shoes. He stepped lightly, always, on bad nights, although he'd whistled clear across the bridge to save on subway fare. He favored Stephen Foster tunes and Broadway musicals. He flung his head back on a long, pure note. When he reached our door he stood still for a moment and squared his shoulders.

My mother, too, knew what the whistling meant.

"Stayed up for me?"

"I wasn't tired."

I crept to my door to peek at them. My mother staring at her feet. My father's hopeful face, his exaggerated brightness. My mother said, "Go to sleep, Caroline."

But I had trouble sleeping. I could feel him slipping away from us, drifting far in search of some intoxicating music. Each time he wandered off, it seemed to take more effort to recall us. He began to speak with his head cocked, as if listening for something. He often stood at the living room window, staring at the street.

"Does Baba have a new job?" I asked my mother.

"No." She looked away.

I felt sorry I'd asked. Questions caused my mother pain. But I was afraid to ask my father. In his guarded face he held a flaming knowledge: a kind of faith, a glimpse of opportunities that lay beyond my understanding.

All that year I hunted clues, made lists of evidence.

Missing on February 3:
carved endtable
painting of fruit (from front hallway)
jade buddha
camera (mine)

I followed him. One evening after I missed my camera, I heard the front door slam. I grabbed my coat and bolted down the stairs. I dodged across the street half a block back, peering around pedestrians and traffic signs, my eyes fixed on his overcoat and fedora. At the subway station I waited by the token booth and dashed into the bright car behind him, keeping track of his shiny shoes through the swaying windows. I almost missed him when he left the train. Outside it was already dusk. The tall, cold shapes of City Hall and the courthouses loomed over us and I followed at a distance. I felt light as a puff of silk, breathing hard, excited, almost running.

Past the pawn shops, the off-track betting office with its shuffling line of men in old overcoats, toward the dirty, crowded streets of Chinatown, its neon signs winking on for the night. Groups of teenagers, chattering in Cantonese, looked strangely at me and kept walking.

"Incense, candles, incense, *xiaojie*?" A street vendor held a grimy handful toward me.

"No, thanks," I panted. I almost lost him but then ahead I recognized his elegant stride. He turned into a small, shabby building, nodding to an old man who stood at the door. I hung around outside, stamping my shoes on the icy sidewalk.

After a minute the old man walked over to me. "Your father does not know you followed him," he told me in Chinese. "You must go home. Go home, and I will not tell him you were here."

For a minute I couldn't move. He was exactly my height. His short hair was white but his forehead strangely unlined, his clothes well-made. It was his expensive tweed overcoat that made me turn around. That and the decaying, fetid odor of his teeth, and the fact that he knew my father well enough to recognize my features, knew he would not have wanted me to follow him. I reboarded the train at the Canal Street station. Back in the apartment, I stayed up until well past midnight, but I didn't hear him come home.

I didn't need to follow him. I should have known that eventually he would show his secret to me, his one pupil. A few months later, on the night before my fourteenth birthday, he motioned me to stay seated after supper. The hanging lamp cast a circle of light over the worn kitchen table.

"I'm going to teach you some math," he said.

I glanced at his face, but his eyes glowed black and expressionless in their sockets, hollow in the lamplight.

Over his shoulder I saw my mother check to see that we were occupied. Then she walked into the foyer and opened the closet door, where the jewelry was. I felt a tingle of fear, even though I had concealed my visits perfectly.

"Concentrate," said my father. "Here is a penny. Each penny has two sides: heads and tails. You understand me, Caroline?"

I nodded. The dull coin looked like a hole in his palm.

"*Hao*," he said: good. His brown hand danced and the penny flipped onto the table. Heads. "Now, if I throw this coin many many times, how often would I get heads?"

"One-half of the time."

He nodded.

"*Hao*," he said. "That is the *huo ran lu*. The *huo ran lu* for heads is one-half. If you know that, you can figure out the *huo ran lu* that I will get two heads if I throw twice in a row." He waited a minute. "Think of it as a limiting of possibilities. The first throw cuts the possibilities in half."

I looked into the dark tunnel of my father's eyes and, following the discipline of his endless drilling, I began to understand where we had been going. Counting, multiplication, the table of squares. "Half of the half," I said. "A quarter."

He set the coins aside and reached into his shirt pocket. Suddenly, with a gesture of his hand, two dice lay in the middle of the yellow circle of light. Two small chunks of ivory, with tiny black pits in them.

"Count the sides," he said.

The little cube felt cold and heavy. "Six."

My father's hand closed over the second die. "What is the *huo ran lu* that I will get a side with only two dots?"

My mind wavered in surprise at his intensity. But I knew the answer. "One-sixth," I said.

He nodded. "You are a smart daughter," he said.

I discovered that I had been holding on to the table leg with my left hand, and I let go. I heard the creak of the hall closet door but my father did not look away from the die in his hand.

"What is the *huo ran lu* that I can roll the side with two dots twice in a row?" he said.

"One thirty-sixth."

"Three times in a row?"

"One two-hundred-and-sixteenth."

"That is very good!" he said. "Now, the *huo ran lu* that I will be able to roll a two is one-sixth. Would it be a reasonable bet that I will not roll a two?"

I nodded.

"We could say, if I roll a two, you may have both pennies."

I saw it then, deep in his eyes—a spark of excitement, a piece of joy particularly his. It was there for an instant and disappeared. He frowned and nodded toward the table as if to say: pay attention. Then his hand flourished and the die trickled into the light. I bent eagerly over the table, but my father sat perfectly still, impassive. Two dots.

When I looked up at him in astonishment I noticed my mother, standing in the door-way, her two huge eyes burning in her white face.

"Jack."

My father started, but he didn't turn around to look at her. "Yes, Lily," he said.

The die grew wet in my hand.

"What are you doing?"

"Giving the child a lesson."

"And what is she going to learn from this?" My mother's voice trembled but it did not rise. "Where will she go with this?"

"Lily," my father said.

"What will become of us?" my mother almost whispered. She looked around the kitchen. Almost all of the furniture had disappeared. The old kitchen table and the three chairs, plus our rice cooker, were virtually the only things left in the room.

I grabbed the second die and left the table. In my room as I listened to my parents next door in the kitchen I rolled one die two hundred and sixteen times, keeping track by making marks on the back of a school notebook. But I failed to reach a two more than twice in a row.

"The suitcase, Jack. Where is it?"

After a moment my father muttered, "I'll get it back. Don't you believe me?"

"I don't know." She began to cry so loudly that even though I pressed my hands against my ears I could still hear her. My father said nothing. I hunched down over my knees, trying to shut them out.

"You promised me, you promised me you'd never touch them!"

"I was going to bring them back!"

"We have nothing for Caroline's birthday . . ."

Something crashed against the other side of my bedroom wall. I scuttled to the opposite wall and huddled in the corner of my bed.

For a long period after I heard nothing but my mother's sobbing. Then they left the kitchen. The house was utterly silent. I realized I had wrapped my arms around my knees to keep from trembling. I felt strange and light-headed: oh, but I understood now. My father was a gambler, a *dutu*, an apprentice of chance. Of course.

With the understanding came a desperate need to see both of them. I stood up and walked through the living room to my parents' bedroom. The door was ajar. I peered in.

The moonlight, blue and white, shifted and flickered on the bed, on my mother's long black hair twisting over her arm. Her white fingers moved vaguely. I felt terrified for her. He moved against her body in such a consuming way, as if he might pass through her, as if she were incorporeal. I watched for several minutes before my mother made a sound that frightened me so much I had to leave.

The next morning my eyes felt sandy and strange. We strolled down Atlantic Avenue, holding hands, with me in the middle because it was my birthday. My mother's stride was tentative, but my father walked with the calculated lightness and unconcern of one who has nothing in his pockets. Several gulls flew up before us, and he watched with delight as they wheeled into the cloudy sky. The charm of Brooklyn, this wide shabby street bustling with immigrants like ourselves, was enough to make him feel lucky.

He squeezed my hand, a signal that I should squeeze my mother's for him. We'd played this game many times over the years, but today I hesitated. My mother's hand did not feel like something to hold onto. Despite the warm weather her fingers in mine were cold. I squeezed, however, and she turned. He looked at her over the top of my head, and my mother, seeing his expression, lapsed into a smile that caused the Greek delivery boys from the corner pizza parlor to turn their heads as we passed. She and my father didn't notice.

We walked past a display of furniture on the sidewalk—incomplete sets of dining chairs, hat stands, old sewing tables—and I stared for a minute, for I thought I saw something standing behind a battered desk: a rosewood dresser my parents had brought from Taiwan; it used to be in my own bedroom. I once kept my dolls in the bottom left drawer, the one with the little scar where I had nicked it with a roller skate. . . . Perhaps it only had a similar shape. But it could very well be our dresser. I knew better than to point it out. I turned away.

"Oh, Jack, the flowers!" my mother exclaimed in Chinese. She let go of my hand and rushed to DeLorenzio's floral display, sank down to smell the potted gardenias with a grace that brought my father and me to a sudden stop.

My father's black eyebrows came down over his eyes. *"Ni qu gen ni mama tan yi tan*, go talk to your mother," he said, giving me a little push. I frowned. "Go on."

She was speaking with Mr. DeLorenzio, and I stood instinctively on their far side, trying to act cute despite my age in order to distract them from what my father was doing. He stood before the red geraniums. He picked up a plant, considered it, and set it down with a critical shake of his head.

"And how are you today, sweetheart?" Mr. DeLorenzio bent toward me, offering me a close-up of his gray handlebar moustache. Behind him, my father disappeared from view.

"She's shy," said my mother proudly. After a few minutes I tugged her sleeve, and she said goodbye to the florist. We turned, continued walking down the street.

"Where is your father?"

"I think he's somewhere up there."

I pulled her toward the corner. My father stepped out from behind a pet store, smiling broadly, holding the pot of geraniums.

"It's going to rain," he proclaimed, as if he'd planned it himself.

The drops felt light and warm on my face. We ran to the nearest awning, where my mother put on her rain bonnet. Then my father disappeared, leaving us standing on the side-walk. I didn't notice him leave. All of a sudden he was just gone.

"Where's Baba?" I asked my mother.

"I don't know," she said, calmly tucking her hair into the plastic bonnet. The gerani-ums stood at her feet. I looked around us. The sidewalks had become slick and dark; people hurried along. The wind blew cool in my face. Then the revolving doors behind us whirled and my father walked out.

"There you are," my mother said.

"Here, Caroline," said my father to me. He reached into his jacket and pulled out the umbrella. It lay balanced on his palm, its brilliant colors neatly furled, an offering.

I wanted to refuse the umbrella. For a moment I believed that if I did, I could separate myself from both of my parents, and our pains, and everything that bound me to them.

I looked up at my father's face. He was watching me intently. I took the umbrella.

"Thanks," I said. He smiled. The next day, he was gone.

My mother had her hair cut short and dressed in mourning colors; this attitude bestowed on her a haunting, muted beauty. She was hired for the lunch shift at a chic Manhattan Chinese restau-rant. Our lives grew stable and very quiet. In the evenings I studied while my mother sat in the kitchen, waiting, cutting carrots and mushroom caps into elaborate shapes for our small stir-frys, or combining birdseed for the feeder on the fire escape in the exact proportions that my father had claimed would bring the most cardinals and the fewest sparrows. I did the homework for advanced placement courses. I planned to enter Columbia with the academic standing of a sophomore. We spoke gently to each other about harmless, tactful things. "Peanut sauce," we said. "Shopping," "homework." "Apricots."

      I studied trigonometry. I grew skillful in that subject without ever liking it. I learned calculus, linear algebra, and liked them less and less, but I kept studying, seeking the comfort that arithmetic had once provided. Things fall apart, it seems, with terrible slowness. I could not see that true mathematics, rather than keeping track of things, moves toward the unexplainable. A swooping line descends from nowhere, turns, escapes to some infinity. Centuries of scholars work to solve a single puzzle. In mathematics, as in love, the riddles matter most.

In the months when I was failing out of Columbia, I spent a lot of my time on the subway. I rode to Coney Island, to the watery edge of Brooklyn, and stayed on the express train as it changed directions and went back deep under the river, into Manhattan. Around City Hall or 14th Street a few Chinese people always got on the train, and I sometimes saw a particular kind of man, no longer young but his face curiously unlined, wearing an expensive but shabby overcoat and shiny shoes. I would watch until he got off at his stop. Then I would sit back and wait as the train pulsed through the dark tunnels under the long island of Manhattan, and sometimes the light would blink out for a minute and I would see blue sparks shooting off the tracks. I was waiting for the moment around 125th Street where the express train rushed up into daylight. This sudden openness, this coming out of darkness into a new world, helped me understand how he must have felt. I imagined him bent over a pair of dice that glowed like tiny skulls under the yellow kitchen light. I saw him walking out the door with my flowery umbrella, pausing to look up at the sky and the innumerable, luminous possibilities that lay ahead.

Vijay Seshadri

Biography

Vijay Seshadri was born in India and came to America at age five. He grew up in Columbus, Ohio. His work has appeared in the *Threepenny Review*, *The New Yorker*, *Shenandoah*, *Antaeus*, and *Agni.* He is the author of *Wild Kingdom.* He lives in New York City.

Street Scene

The job of redemption, with its angels and lawyers,
runs late into the morning;
the halls are empty, and from sea green foyers
where aquamarine jackets sag unused
no one walks out to be disabused
by the day, so confident and businesslike.
The domiciled, stunned, paralyzed, in mourning

for the vanishing illuminations, radium-edged,
that made their nerve ends glow
in the dark, are secretly pledged
to attenuate themselves in this,
the spirit's nocturnal crisis,
and still twitch with dreamwork,
and won't open their eyes. But although

not enough energy otherwise subsists
for the nurse to pop an antihistamine
and rise from her viral mists,
for the existential tough guy and thief
to wake up to some extra grief,
for the dog to be led to the park,
for the *viejo* to paint his fire escape green,

so that their race might never be caused to perish
from the contradictions of flight,
up above the satellite dish
pigeons of every color but exactly one size
mob, scatter, and reorganize
to practice crash landings on the street
that divides the black neighborhood from the white.

And at a distance rinsed of charity and malice,
their riots are being umpired by

the unmentionable, porticoed phallus
of the Williamsburgh Savings Bank clock tower,
which manufactures the next hour,
serene in an ongoing function
it can never be called on to abjure or justify.

Divination in the Park

1

Under the bursting dogwoods, et cetera,
having just finished a pear for lunch,
I lie over the earth, to feel it swim
inside my posture, and sleep,

while full-bellied women pole home with small children,
and black waves fling
grappling hooks and grab by inches
the torn-off, uplifted rocks

stranded offshore like apple trees in the fog.

2

The upper parts of the earth are slowly thawing.
Less than slowly, the groundwater
rises in the crevices and exposed places,
five strata down where the fossils are.

The winter was mild. In the bulbs and empty hives
spring rubs the velvet from its new brace of horn,
and around the drowning rocks
the feral light of equinox

sheds a pattern on the ocean.

3

To think that before today, of all the days,
I was less than a snake sunning on a rock,
but that now I'm
the lord of the serpents in the temple,

worshipped and adorned in my eloquent lengths.
So what if I fail the test of time?
I cling to the earth as it banks and glides.
Miners enter my abandoned skin

with strings of lights and diagrams.
Gods on couches ring the horizon.

A Werewolf in Brooklyn

Still almost blind in his thinking eye,
the last of the moon, as it zeros in
on the preordained spot, to modify
his downside structures and curry his skin

with its lucent brush, so the dog flares up,
he only can grasp as a metaphor.
A lozenge dissolves in a silver cup
out of which such emptinesses pour

to prove for him the Buddhists right
who say that wolf packs of nothingness stalk
the signature stinks and blood trails of man,

but that to race with them and let them bite
will do for him much better than
Ping-Pong, kind visitors, electroshock.

Amitava Kumar

My New Yorkers are very different from the one's imagined by Henry
James at the turn of the century: the one who, after a visit to Ellis
Island, goes about with a "new chill in his heart" as if he has "seen
a ghost in his supposedly new house."

Biography

Amitava Kumar was born in Ara, India. She is the author of *No Tears for the N.R.I.* and
Passport Photos, and has written for *The Nation, Critical Inquiry, Times of India,* and *The
Economic and Political Weekly.* Kumar teaches in the English Department of the University of
Florida and is a contributor to Impact Visuals. She has also finished a collaborative video-
film, "Pure Chutney."

India Day Parade on Madison Avenue

India is 50!
(Where's my Nehru jacket?)

> —Op-ed column in *The New York Times*

I

You, however,
Soraiya Hasan Ali from Pakistan, whom I've just met,
you are not wearing any Nehru jackets today.
You've cast your *dupatta* aside and come out
wearing an ivory-hued *kameez* with the tiniest
mirrors that make your shape look thirsty like water.

The parade is not going to pass for another hour.
Passing my finger down the pale brown line in the middle,
in a South Indian restaurant two blocks away,
I pretend to read your palm.
The restaurant owner has stuck a sign, "Giuliani for Mayor,"
beside his ornate blue clay cow.
You wait here with a Hindu
communist for the India Day parade.
I'm having trouble reading these lines
in your palm without drawing your hand closer to my heart.

It's been two days since I met you.
The world that was there before seems so old now.
Two days ago,
The New York Times found out
that more and more Indians and Pakistanis
"live peaceably together" in Queens.
It seems love was in the air, for even the right-wing
A. M. Rosenthal wrote a column entitled "India, Mon Amour."

Soraiya Hasan Ali, I am writing this poem for you
because your laughter
was not invented by the man from *The New York Times*.
And because the failure of your poet Faiz—
kuch ishq kiya, kuch kaam kiya
"I loved a little, I labored a little"—
unable either to labor or love alone,
leaving both incomplete in despair,
shares none of the seriousness, worn as a mask,
by Harrison Ford a.k.a. Indiana Jones.
And, in the end,
because even where mines and tall sentry-posts
divide my country from yours
the wind carries words
of a common language, like dried
petals, across the lines of barbed wire.
It is their lightness
that rests in your touch.
The same words
fragrant with the smell of our belonging,
the smell of the same earth, the same trees,
the same seasons of our knowing,

I discover as difference in the slow spiral of your ear
and, turning, in your naked glance.

II

In this month of the summer, during evenings
when lights come on after rain showers, there are new words
being born on the streets of our native cities.

Tell me about us. Will our meaning change
because those words will remain foreign to our memory?
Each time I drew breath today
I took your name but not once

the name of the new bomb called *bidesia*
that has come recently to my town from Calcutta.
There were ads for pressure cookers when I left India
asking you how much you loved your wife.
In all these days, unknown to me and to you,
in so many different ways
new ads must be teaching people how to love.

Standing on the roof of your home,
looking at the Empire State Building
lit up with the saffron, green, and white
of the Indian flag, you tell me of your love
for a woman during your undergraduate years.
On the streets of Lahore,
have they found a name
for lesbians—a name that you'd like?

I have lost India. You have lost Pakistan.
We are now citizens of General Electric.
In this country, there are no new words for exile.
And if you have nothing to sell,
you have nothing to say
that this, or that, is indeed you.

But I still want my words. I still want
to give back to you in the silence
that follows our lovemaking
the words I have gathered
from a part of your body that is dark
like monsoon clouds in July.
The heavy words, like gold coins,
that I can bite with my teeth,
the familiar ones that the vegetable seller
returns to me like small change.
Words, numerous and glittering, drawn like
shiny fish in nets by men with darkened skins.
Words that swing like the new cricket

ball on the pitch surrounded by the hills of Peshawar.
Those words that the women burn in their fires
to keep hearts from shutting with malice.
Words that repeat themselves like the music
in the wheel of the postman's bicycle.
Words that are secret, holding close a hidden love.

If there are no words like that, I want those essential few
that will say north, that will say south.
That will say past, that will say future.
That will say poor, poor, poor, poor.
That will say fight, fight, fight, fight.
That will say hope, hope, hope, hope, hope.

III

When the parade comes down Madison Avenue
it is led by a man who made his fortune playing
the part of the poor in Bombay films.
By the time the lights came on
in the theater, he had succeeded
as the underworld king,
ready to buy the seaside
skyscraper during whose construction
his mother had carried bricks
on her head.

If I fight as hard to be poor as did Amitabh Bachchan,
I too will own a penthouse in Manhattan.

Among the thousands that stand on both sides of the street
there are grandmothers in saris
and an old man in an *achkan* suit
quiet in the shadow of the Citibank office.
At the corner of 32nd Street and Madison
we join the South Asian lesbians and gays.

I stand close to a man, his bright eyes
are lined coal-black and his throat stitched
with ornate silver.

On one float passing by, a man leans
toward the crowd, his voice thick
like sandpaper on the microphone.
Kashmir Hindustan Ka, Nahin Kisi Ke Baap Ka.
"Kashmir is India's, not your father's."
What would this man be doing during a riot?
Women, on hearing his voice
for the first time, outside their bedrooms
where they were hiding with their children,
would not know that it belonged to a face
that had sold them grains and ghee for over a year.
And was now in upstate New York handling real estate.
We caught a cab and the driver said he liked parades:
next Tuesday we are going on strike,
turning Broadway into a sea of yellow cabs.

In the East Village, there are Bangladeshi
restaurants that have names like Indian Delight.
We stepped in one
where the Sikh playing the sitar
smiled at you through our dinner, Soraiya Hasan Ali.
At the next table, an older white man
asked the Bangla waiter if there was anything special
to celebrate the Indian independence. "No, sir," he apologized,
his thick glasses shining, "it is special here every day."

I have this image in my mind of the young
Shashi Kapoor reciting Firaq to the visiting Felicity Kendall:
"Shaam bhi hai dhuan-dhuan,
husn bhi hai udaas-udaas. . . ."
With my hand around your waist, walking on Broadway
I recite those lines because I want to appear
poetic to you, holding on

to something dim and inexpressible:
"The evening is veiled with a haze,
and this beauty touched with sadness;
The many stories in my heart,
trembled just beyond recall."

But you, Soraiya Hasan Ali,
are not cut out to play a role
in a Merchant-Ivory film.
You heard my recital
and followed your applause with the query:
"*Suno*, if you're such a *shaukeen* of translation,
tell me how you will best say in Urdu
Baby, I'll suck your nipples any time."

Trotsky in the Park

I

She screams into the microphone, lips hitting
thin wire mesh of this thing that wants to take in every sound she makes,
and her voice rises, she says I'm not violent, I read poems in public places,
I had promised I'd hold nothing back
      in my poetry,
so this is her name, and she lives on First Avenue near St. Marks Place,
I know dykes, she is no dyke,
and when she moved out she also stole the red lip-liner
that belonged to my roommate.
This poet calls herself Pubic Enemy and we cheer her performance, forever
glad that poetry can offer such sweet revenge.

Poetry gets numbers here. And like Olympic judges
from former East European countries five people in the audience
mark poems on a scale of ten: for that somersault
in the air, 7.8, that shaky start in the cloud of chalk powder,

the score can't be more than a 5.6, for your relentless display
of open vulnerability, risking failure with words,
landing somewhere
between the sixth and seventh stanzas on your feet,
you my darling will get a 9.8. Tell me again
of the time
you heated the olive oil for your pasta
and then rubbed it softly—I think you used the word "slowly"—
you forgot the pasta and rubbed the oil slowly
on your guest's willing body.

A black woman
wearing a Crooklyn baseball shirt proudly like a red dashiki
breathes softly her delicate words about moons bathed in melancholy,
the many moons of unwanted pregnancies and deaths
in poor homes. And even those who tonight have their cars parked
in the suburbs, and if they don't their parents do,
begin to clap and applaud this performance, we're glad,
I guess, that poetry can extract such sweet revenge against white suburbia.
When we come out my friend says it was kind of predictable. Well,
why doesn't America do something new then to black people
so that this woman in the red shirt can start sounding like Woody Allen
—or not?

II

Beneath the green statue in the Tompkins Square Park, a carpenter writes
a letter to put in a packet for his two nieces in Poland, a Madonna tape
and a rubber eraser in the shape of the Statue of Liberty for the younger one.
On the next bench, an art student is learning about an outsider in Paris:
>   "Picasso was a vertical invader. He came up from Spain through
>   the trapdoor of Barcelona onto the stage of Europe."
The Psychic Palm Reader half a block away sits behind that red eye
of neon all-seeing and unblinking like fate. Her shoulders are square
like those of the women Picasso drew; she has had her imagination stretched
across barbed-wire fences that divide rich nations from the poor. Two girls

walk out of an MTV video and step past with lots of grunge sounds
and an old black guy shouts, "I'll give you thirty-five dollars. Fuck,
you should marry me for that . . . . Hey, I know women better-looking than you."
I am writing a note for the *Voice* personals, a public display of affection:

> "Hey babe: Let's snuggle in bed and read the poetry
> of the future or even the missionary-position Marxist writing
> you so greatly admire. XOXOXO."

There is someone reading Trotsky in the park. He is a Pakistani student,
away from home for five years now, thinking of Lahore's streets, the brown, burnt
ancestral land, the men on bicycles as he reads in his book the words:

> "Yet every time a peasant's horse shies in terror before the
> blinding lights of an automobile on the Russian road at night,
> a conflict of two cultures is reflected in the episode."

Puerto Rican kids come out of the laundromat with a ball
and while the ball thrown from one hand turns and turns in the bright air,
the rest of the city that I know so little hurtles inside a subway car;
the white men in dark suits reading *The New York Times*, eyes lingering
over the bodies of humans of a certain gender who've taken
off their clothes for these men, in a row of ads for Bloomingdale's. A man,
class negative, color negative, makes an awkward entry into the car singing
hoarsely about a rainbow, holding in his hand the 2x3 cardboard sign:

> "My mother has multiple sclerosis
> and I can't see out of my left eye.
> Will you help me?"

and there's a middle-aged woman who having carefully rubbed
moisturizing cream on her hands folds them in her lap,
and looks away from the man even though she's on his sightless side.
Before her station comes, she'll have time enough
to quickly read half of the poem on the orange poster above the door:

> "Thank you my dear
> You came, and you did
> well to come. I needed
> you. You have made
>
> love blaze up in my."

III

The man who begins reading
a poem about queer love and clear rage
is clean-shaven and bald, a little
like a Hare Krishna with a Kalashnikov.
This is not poetry for beginners. To his party,
you bring your own anger.
Then someone with Bobby Kennedy's smiling face
printed on her trousers
finishes reading her poem, and an Indian woman in the audience
says she wants a 10 for that one. She says, "I love poems
which have nipples in them."
The emcee tilts his bearded face
and says, "Let's have a tête-à-tête about that, ha-ha."
He is wearing a tweed jacket one size too small
for him, but his satire is in good form
and he knows the audience well.
He quotes William Carlos Williams
and says, "He had a Puerto Rican mother.
Now, they didn't tell you that, did they?"

Poetry is about nipples and Puerto Rican mothers.
It is about being butt-fucked.
It is about Trotsky going mad in the park
because they took it back from the homeless.
Poetry is about the hat that Thelonious Monk wore.
It is about poor nations protecting their land and their languages.
Poetry is the hiss you make
when you don't like the poem someone else is reading.
Poetry is the hiss you make. Period.

I read in a book, baby, that this is the hour
of the immigrant worker—
after the milkman and just before the dustman.
With his immigrant love, the poem that he comes seeking
is not the hiss you make, but a stammer

at your doorstep at dawn,

a terrible, trapped-up hope in this hour of becoming.

It has nothing

of the certainties of those who give names

to bottles of wines in the languages of Europe.

A woman just into her twenties, from Shanghai, alone

at an underground train station

in the middle of New York at night

after working overtime in a garment factory,

looks at her hands

for a long moment

in the bluish light of the station.

Around her is the silence of Trotsky's tomb.

In that silence is born

the silence this poem makes.

S. Shankar

New York reminds us: it is only in the imagination that the barest
outline of an alternative to the tragedy that is the present is visible.

Biography

S. Shankar was born in Salem, India and has lived in New York City since 1993. He is the
author of the novel *A Map of Where I Live* and the collection of poems *I As Man*. He teaches
in the English Department at Rutgers University and is at work on a second novel.

Times Square, New York, 1996 C.E.

I am told they are Guatemalan.
I have heard them before in the square
of time. They were here with their music
beneath the bright and cold geometry
of punctually flashing neon signs.
In my passing, I think I heard them pronounce
my secret name with their unfamiliar sounds.
But I was not human then. I had misplaced
my irresponsibility at home.

If I stop now, let them not mistake me
for something other than what I am.
It may be an unexpected token
has unsquared time and briefly broken
the rectangles in the calendar
I call my life. Is it they who've done this
with the medley of their many drums and strings?
Should I credit them with this great feat?
Or do I, when I ask such questions,
square them with my niggardly need for neat?

Kathmandu in New York

The morning unfurled a cloud-stained sky
over Kathmandu. After a restless night
of storms, we lingered in bed in the shadow
of a moist desire. Later, we set out
on rented cycles to Pashupatinath,
splashing through puddles of water that lay spent
in lanes determined to go everywhere
before finding they had reached nowhere.

So we arrived at last at Shiva's abode.
By the river, the smoke of flesh burning
met us with reeking hands of welcome.
There we watched Fire mount, in heaving embrace,
a body on her flaming bed of wood.
The spectacle of that ravishing
was pornographic. We could not stop.
We fled guiltily from that passion
through the splendid entrance of the temple,
but found no refuge under its gilded roof.

Now I search for you through this New York night,
testing the frail words of a mortal language.

Victoria Eng

Biography

Victoria Eng was born and raised in Chinatown and moved to Elmhurst, Queens, at the age of twelve. After an unfulfilling stint as a public relations director in the fashion industry, she returned to school full-time to concentrate in Asian American Studies and English at Hunter College, where she became a writing tutor. She is currently in the MFA Writing Program at Columbia University. Her work has appeared in *The Olivetree Review, 12 Gauge review,* and *A magazine.*

The Language of Comfort

Chinatown people scare me. I hate running into my relatives on the street, especially the older women that I hardly know, because I can't talk to them. When I'm with Mom, it's not so bad, because she does all the talking. I'm not expected to do anything more than smile and call them by the name that Mom feeds me.

"*Gew Wang Mu-Mu*," she sings, and I reply, "Hullo, Wang Mu-Mu," like a trained parrot, my hands folded demurely in front of me. Then the auntie takes my hand and shakes it, telling Mom in Chinese that I'm a good girl, and Mom beams back at her, wondering if I was good enough to make the woman not see my bleached blond hair. She tries to ignore the way old Mrs. Wang looks me up and down and curls her lip at my very unladylike combat boots. Though my chin is lifted to meet Mrs. Wang's smiling scrutiny, my shoulders are hunched as I reclaim my hand and hide the rest of my body behind Mom's. They chatter in Chinese while I watch people grumble and step around us on the sidewalk. I keep a close-lipped smile on my face until I hear Mom's voice winding down to a good-bye, and then I turn up the wattage again, waving cheerily.

I can smile and be a cute, well-mannered daughter because I'm with Mom. But if I'm alone, I do whatever I can to avoid the old ladies. It's usually not very hard to spot one. My nightmares all have the same perm. It's as if every Chinatown lady over the age of sixty goes to the same beauty salon. They stand in line with wet strands of black hair sticking to their faces and wait to sit under rows of huge egg-shaped hairdryers, straight-backed and face forward. After an hour of vacuuming and frying, the eggshells pop them out with freshly coiffured afros. They smooth their lacquered hair and wrinkled black handbags and step outside to blend into the crowd and one another.

On Bayard Street, I can recognize one bending over the cartons of a fruit and vegetable stand, squeezing oranges or examining bunches of rubber-banded bok choy. And if she doesn't see me, I dip behind the person walking ahead of me, speed up a little alongside him and twist myself around in front of him so that the stranger is always between me and my nemesis as I pass to safety. I continue on to Bowery, wary of another near-encounter.

I wish I didn't have to run away from them, but I always tell myself afterward that I'd feel worse if I let them see me. I can't talk to them. I'm embarrassed at my scant knowledge of Chinese. I can't answer simple questions like "How's school, what are you learning now?" Can hardly even recognize anything beyond "Where's your mother?"

Mom was pleased when I told her that I was taking a Chinese course here in college, but it was Mandarin, a dialect I'd never known. Even though both dialects share the same written characters, I had never learned to read and write them, so I had to start from scratch, with none of the advantage I thought I would have from my childhood exposure to Cantonese. I was swamped in a matter of weeks. The strokes, slashes and dots of the different Chinese characters refused to print themselves in my head. I made it through the first semester, but I dropped out of the second right before the mid-term exam. And it didn't make my Cantonese any better at all.

Mom talks to me more often in Chinese now that I'm an adult. I still answer her in English, the way I've always done. Sometimes I feel like it was her fault for not enrolling me in Chinese school, and that she's trying to make up for it now, but I remember that when she had asked, I had refused to go, wanting my afternoons free so I could watch "Looney Tunes" on TV. She didn't make me go like some of the other kids' parents did, and I thought that was pretty cool. My older sister, Gloria, snickered that she had broken Mom in for me, because when Gloria was six, she had been forced to go to Chinese school until she got herself expelled.

And now, twenty years later, I keep surprising myself with my growing dumbness. When I have to speak or even hear Chinese, I reach into my head for translations and grab nothing but air. Lilts and inflections of voices, dipping combinations of vowels tell me whether Cantonese or Toisanese, the country dialect Granma speaks, is being used, but when put on the spot, I am instantly deaf and mute in both.

Meaning is so close that I'm convinced the words are on the tip of my tongue. My throat bobs to capture them before they spin away, and that's when I realize that something is suddenly gone, like a tablecloth that has just been pulled out from under me. Actually, me trying to speak Chinese is a Looney Tune moment. I'm Wile E. Coyote chasing after the Roadrunner. My fangs are bared and I'm just about to grab the scruff of his neck, when he leads me right off a cliff and disappears. I freeze, suspended, my legs bent in running position, my arms stretched out in front of me, fingers splayed. Clarity washes over my face as I realize there is no longer any ground beneath me, and I zip straight down to end the cartoon with a musical flourish. Except, in real life, there is no Porky Pig's "Bedee-bedee-bedee-that's all folks!" to excuse me. There is just the awkward silence of me fumbling for words with a grin on my face that's only charming when I'm with Mom.

I'm losing my Chinese slowly but surely. I gauge it by my growing silences and timidity at speaking when I'm with Granma. Soon I won't be able to talk to her at all. That's why I started massaging her more often. Whenever I go back to Queens, I go with my hands strong and ready to knead at her skinny neck and pound on the sharp bone of her shoulder blade, where the arthritis is setting in as a dull throbbing ache she carries with her every day.

When we settle in front of the television together after dinner, she beckons to me from the couch with the homemade orange-flowered slipcovers. *"Hoong ngau opp guit,"* she says, and I take a seat next to her, turn her around so I can pound her bones like she wants. I don't ask what's wrong; I know that she would just answer, *"Mm shee fook,"* an all-purpose ailment that translates simply to "not comfortable."

We can't converse while I'm thumping my knuckles on her back. At those moments, with her head bowed low and our eyes closed, we don't have to. I can feel where she hurts, can tell which spots I should press my thumb into, because I am just like her. The places that bother her will bother me too, eventually, if I live to her age of seventy-seven. "Ai yaaa," she exhales, a deep sigh that tells me more about her everyday life than any words can say. That's what makes me feel so close to her. I touch her.

I can hug her, completely enclose her frame within my arms as she stands in front of the stove, measuring the bean sprouts she's about to toss into the wok. The stovetop range casts an amber light that illuminates the fine wrinkles on her face, lines that are beginning to sketch Mom's face, lines that will one day define my own. She stays still, not hugging me back, but she doesn't recoil either, and that encourages me to plant five kisses on her cheek while I tell her that I miss her, and *"Ngau hon nei sai."* She laughs at that, because I am mangling the simple phrase "I really love you" by inverting the words "you" and "all" to mean "I love all of you." I've always done that, since I was a kid, and she doesn't correct me anymore because she knows I know it's wrong. It's become our private joke.

"Ya know what she's tellin' ya?" Granpa asked one time in Queens, Granma looking over his shoulder at me. I shook my head and tried not to notice her smile fade. "A course ya can't understand," he said. "Ya Jook Seng." He wasn't trying to insult me, but I'd been called "hollow bamboo" too often not to take it that way. I just shrugged it off and I didn't press him to translate; he doesn't have the patience to anymore. He learned English in the "ahmy" during World War II, where he didn't have to translate; he just had to speak. The last few times he did translate for me, he gave me a three-word synopsis of what Granma had been rambling on about for minutes. And without his teeth in, I could hardly understand his English. So I let it go. I figured they understood.

But not the ladies on the street. They don't know how Mom tried to enroll us in Chinese school when we were little. They don't know that Gloria got kicked out for passing notes when she was supposed to be practicing her characters, and they don't know how disappointed Mom was when I said I wouldn't even consider going.

And they don't remember that Mom had raised us without our father, who had died of cancer months before I was born, and so she couldn't be as strict with us. I think she must have been too tired from working full-time as a receptionist in a busy Chinatown clinic to make sure we were understanding her Chinese. They don't know that at seven in the morning or at seven at night, it was probably just easier for her to tell us in English. Maybe she made it a point to speak to us in English-only so we'd have an easier time in school than she did, juggling two languages, but they don't know that, either. All they see is me trying to dodge them in the streets of Chinatown so I won't have to talk to them.

I get caught by sharp-eyed aunties sometimes, and I'm spun back to myself at sixteen, a captured specimen suddenly on display. They stand back, clutching plastic bags full of oranges, looking me up and down, taking in my teased hair and noticing how my black T-shirt is stretched out and wrinkled from being left on the floor of my room for days. At sixteen I have a busy social life and I avoid doing laundry; my philosophy is that if the armpits don't stink, I can wear it.

Mom grimaces when she sees me getting dressed. *"Hom choy,"* she mutters, shaking her head. "You dress like a bum." I don't care what she thinks, but at that moment I wonder if that is what is running through my aunties' minds. I try to look beyond their pearly smiles to see if they really do think that we are too poor to buy "good" clothing, as Mom puts it. They might not understand that I prefer buying fifties vintage dresses and jackets from the Salvation Army. I love the tackiness of brightly colored geometric patterns on the fabrics so much that I can overlook the musty mothballish smell that sometimes lingers on them after washing. But that day, I wonder if they can detect it on the iridescent blue men's jacket I have thrown on to complete my outfit.

Mom can't understand it either. "These clothes are used," she sniffs. "Why would you want them?" It becomes useless to explain that too many kids are wearing the baggy Benetton pastel sweatshirts she prefers for me, and that I want to stand out. I continue to rummage through thrift store racks even when I can afford to move out into my own apartment, and instead of picking things up from the floor, I pull out favorite shirts from my wicker laundry hamper, convinced that they are clean enough to wear one more time.

I feel paranoid when I'm in Chinatown. No matter how crowded the streets are, the people weaving around one another to get home or to the next grocery store, I feel like someone is staring at me, judging me. There are some places that I have tried to avoid since I was a teen, like the OTB on Chatham Square. I haven't been on that block for years; when I need to go to the Citibank on the corner of Mott and Chatham, I take the long way around to avoid walking by it. I don't even know if it's still there, but the feeling stays permanently etched in my memory and I remember how I would scurry along the block, trying not to feel the stares of the old men squatting on their haunches outside, smoking.

The letters stand for Off-Track Betting, but I didn't know that at the time. I had always thought it to be some sort of strange social club, where all the old men of Chinatown gathered, yet never spoke to one another. No matter what the weather was, the double doors were kept wide open and the place was packed with old men smoking cigarettes. They all seemed to be wearing the same outfit, dark worn wool suit jackets, dark pants shiny with wear, and white button-down polyester-cotton-blend shirts opened enough to show the yellowing neckbands of Fruit of the Loom T-shirts. Rows of them, crowds of them blending into but not facing one another. They were all looking up at television screens suspended from the ceiling in different corners of the place. On the screens were circles of muddy brown racetracks which had lines of horses wavering across them.

I hated walking by that place because of the smoke. The old men hanging out outside, sitting on the fire hydrants, bugged me because of the way they stared at me walking by. They never said anything to me, but they would stare at my clothes, my hair, while pulling on their cigarettes. Even as I passed, I could feel eyes that would never meet mine boring into my back.

One time, when I was sixteen, I nodded hello to one of the OTB men. It was winter, and the OTB was less crowded than usual. He was sitting on the fire hydrant outside alone, hunched into his blue padded silk jacket and balancing a Winston between his thumb and fore-finger, which protruded from holes in his woolen glove. He had been watching me since I had turned the corner from Mott Street.

I had on a leather motorcycle jacket that I had customized by painting it bright green. I thought it looked pretty good; since I had painted it, I had been getting compliments from people I didn't even know at Brooklyn Tech, my high school. Conversations would always progress from how I dyed my jacket to how I dyed my hair blue, red and yellow, and before I knew it, I had a new friend to wave at in the halls. I was hot shit, no longer considered weird like I had been at Transfiguration. I'd feel a grim glee every time I walked past my old elementary school on Mott Street, and I made it a point to do so whenever I was back in Chinatown, especially after three, when I'd still see kids hanging around the schoolyard in the blue plaid uniforms I had detested for so long.

I had turned the corner, strutting, when I noticed him looking at me. He reminded me of Yeh Yeh, my paternal grandfather who had passed away when I was nine, the way his wrin-kled neck stuck out from the stiff mandarin collar of his menop. I wanted to smile at him, and I wanted him to smile at me, too, give me a smile that could only come from a grandfather.

As I got closer, his eyes darted away to look at a point beyond me. I was determined to get his attention. I slowed down, so he would have to look at me. He did, and I nodded with a shy smile. I would have said hello, but he turned his whole body away suddenly, so he faced the direction I had just come from. My pace faltered at the sudden rejection, but I kept walking.

Then I heard it.

The distinctive *hghawwkkk* of nicotine phlegm being conjured to the lips. And a *ptoo*. Right on the pavement. Right on my footsteps, so close that I could almost feel the spit drops spread across my back through the leather.

I don't know why I stopped to turn around; after all, people spat on the ground all the time, especially in Chinatown. But I did, and I caught his stare, which bored right through me. "Impostor," they said. "Jook Seng." All of a sudden my clothes felt wrong. I should have been wearing something less conspicuous, like a simple pair of jeans and a pink cable-knit sweater. The perfect spikiness of my hair, achieved after half an hour of blowdrying, teasing and shpritzing, now seemed garish. I was a fake and this man knew it. Chinese on the outside, but not inside, where it counts. Inside, I had wanted him to acknowledge me, to give me the acceptance I was becoming used to getting from my schoolmates. But it was my clothing on the very outside that gave me away, and from that moment, I resolved never to make the old ones see me again.

I'm twenty-six now. I still hug the walls when I'm in Chinatown, and I still scan puffy hairdos for recognizable faces to hide from. But now I am running away for another reason. There is still the language barrier, and maybe I'm getting to a point where I can be more comfortable with my ignorance. Or maybe I'm just a little bit more adept at hiding it. Now, I am more aware of the fact that I am the age my mother was when she got married to my father in Chinatown, and older than Granma was when she married Granpa in China.

But things are different for me, I keep telling myself. I'm not my mother or my grandmother, and I'm not Chinese the way they were. I'm not even *Chinese American* the way they are, the way the older people of Chinatown are, balancing traditions and a language of a country I've never known with what I take for granted. If I hold myself to their standards and judge my loss of language as a loss of identity, I'll never be *shee fook*. No, I'm something else, a new breed, hybridized by New York inside and out of Chinatown. I'm trying to get comfortable with that.

Throughout the years, with the aunties, I steel myself against the silent criticism. Holding my own sacks of groceries, I stick on the same fake smile, the same mechanical nod, to hide the fact that I know hardly any Chinese. I don't need much, though, to understand the one question they always ask me: "You're so young. Why don't you live with your mother?" The accusation beneath the concern transcends our language barrier, and I hear, "You're not married. You can't live on your own. Go back to your mother's house like a good daughter should." I try not to let it bother me. After all, I know that inside, they aren't being malicious. That's just the way they think life should be. I just keep nodding and smiling, imagining plastic bags wound around well-meaning necks and weighted down with oranges.

Carol Sun

Carol Sun is a native New Yorker who grew up in the Bronx in a predominantly Irish and Italian neighborhood. Through joining Godzilla she began to explore her cultural identity as she met and interacted with other Asian American artists and became exposed to their work.

Richard Oyama

Biography

Richard Oyama was born and raised in New York City. He has an MA in English: Creative Writing from San Francisco State University. In 1979, he coedited *American Born and Foreign*. His work has appeared in literary magazines and anthologies, including *Asian America*, *Dissident Song*, *Breaking Silence* and *Ayumi*. He is an adjunct professor of Ethnic Studies and English at the California College of Arts and Crafts in Oakland. He is currently working on a novel.

The Lost

David Shimamura listens to the muffled noise and motion of the noon city. He has slept badly. Thin bands of sunlight fall faintly through cheap bamboo blinds across the checkered linoleum. The forty-dollars-a-month West Village studio walk-up, where he has lived for a year, has few amenities. Wooden boards conceal a sunken place where the linoleum warped. The July sun beats dully and the air hangs heavy and still as an exhausted flag.

David hears garbagemen scrape aluminum cans brimming with trash along the sidewalk, then dump the refuse into the churning iron mouth of the sanitation truck. Storekeepers unlock metal grates that bar the fronts of their shops. Across the street a bakery worker pitches unsold French rolls into large metal bins which are left out overnight. When it grows dark, David will furtively pick out a few choice rolls from one of the bins for the next day's breakfast.

The streets are crowded with workers on their way to Midtown, men in light linen suits, women in dark skirts, white blouses and tennis shoes. Their faces assume masks of protective hardness, flesh gone gray, eyes stunned by the marine light of a video terminal. The crowd surges forward in the city of the shadow of death, which had undone so many. The morning commute is jittery with anxiety that tightens a gaseous knot in the stomach.

At dawn, the sky is blue-black, but by midmorning, the sun's high glare filters through pestilential clouds of black smoke floating from Jersey factories and drains it of color, a whitish haze. The traffic inches along the Avenue of the Americas.

David listens to the sound of the world outside his window and feels that he should be taking part. While at the university, he started reading novels of his own choosing rather than the assigned texts and regularly cut classes. Sometimes he got drunk on quarts of Johnnie Walker, dozing on the patchy brown grass of the college lawn.

I could invent tasks for myself to give my life the illusion of order and purpose and meaning. I could walk around these familiar Village streets, hunting odd and beautiful faces.

I could play b-ball on the West Fourth Street court, pick up a game with local Italian punks who think they're hot shit, out-of-work heads high on wine or weed or crack, looking red- or dull- or dead-eyed, scratching their scarred arms, dressed in torn jeans and ragged tie-dyed shirts. The hippies appear clumsy and awkward, twitching jerkily like actors in a Chaplin silent, rapping silly shit, heaving the ball over the backboard. They nod out, heads pillowed on folded arms on the park's stone chess tables.

I could nurse a beer alone in a neighborhood bar, while the bartender washes out last night's glasses, wipes down the counter with a wet rag, grabs a bucket of crushed ice from the cooler, and arranges the translucent altar of bottles against the back mirror. Sunlight washes the burnished wood interior like a church, blue glow of the TV over the bar some signal fire to the lost, rain of dust sifting slantwise through the hallowed light.

David recalls all of the mind-numbing clerical jobs he has been fired from in the past year, the newly painted white corridors, the temporary offices constructed of pasteboard without ceilings. He remembers one supervisor, Bertha, an enormous white woman with close-cropped silvery hair and aviator glasses concealing reddened eyes, who looks like a woefully overweight version of Gertrude Stein. Her cohort, Louella, is an older Southern woman whose face is a complex mass of wrinkles and folds, her cheeks sagging, her color sallow.

Next to David sits Mamie, a Chinese woman whose eyesight is slowly failing, her left eye beginning to close. She tells David to use garlic as a cold cure. "Chinese use it for thousands of years. Some things you have to keep secret, you know," she says and winks. She advises him to visit his parents and buy them a small gift. "You see them, bring them something. It sweeten their soul."

The jobs mean nothing to David. None of them ever made him feel like "a productive member of society." He has no idea what that phrase means.

And so he lies in bed, his mind a sucking whirlpool, summoning the will to face the day.

2

David walks through Times Square in the August heat. His throat feels dry, but this is a place of stone. He walks past the movie theaters and porn peepshows. Blood pounds in his ears. His eyes have a shocked look. If he stops walking, he will die.

Pausing before the ticket booth of a theater, he pays for a ticket and walks inside. The lobby is painted bordello red and poorly lit. David walks into the theater and quickly takes a seat in the back.

Cleopatra Jones, a black woman in a blond wig, sits crosslegged on the bare stage. Her muscular buttocks twitch beneath her tight red dress. She talks to the audience of older white businessmen, unemployed black men, sailors on leave. "If your wife only knew," she says to one white man, who confesses that this is the first time for him. "You're too big for me!" she says to a sailor, paying him the standard compliment. David wonders how many times she has repeated these lines. He slumps down in his seat.

The performance begins without ceremony. Cleopatra's breasts hang pendulously like coffee-colored gourds and her wiry pubic hair looks white under the blue stage lights. She sits down on the stage, sidles close to the edge and opens her legs. When none of the customers oblige, she says, exasperated, "Don't anybody here like pussy?" The parade of women follow without fanfare or introduction. They are black or Latin, some are fat or homely looking. None smile.

The lights dim and a movie begins. The images are vague and out of focus. Cigarette smoke flows ghostly in the projected light. The audience is silent except for lipsucking noises and sexual boasts. "Take your hands outta your pockets," a comedian cracks. "This is for freaks, I come to see the real thing," a critic objects. "This is disgusting!" someone in the back row shouts, assuring the others that he has moral qualms. In the first row, a drunk smacks his wet lips and mutters incoherently.

David leaves the theater, momentarily blinded by the flash of sun, then ducks into a storefront peepshow. The store displays videotapes, books and sex toys, and black curtains line the walls. He pulls aside one of the curtains, drops a quarter into a slot and a black screen slides away from a window. David thinks of bloody slabs of meat hanging from metal hooks.

3

The October air is chilly, but David's face is damp with sweat. The street gives off a weird silver light. He walks across the campus to the open plaza of redbrick buildings, marble fountains and wide stone stairway. His heart beats dully, his breathing is shallow as if his rib cage is bound tight with bandages. He feels faint.

He has not slept for three days. The muscles of his body emit a shrill soundless scream. He staggers awkwardly down the street, hands thrust in his pockets, shoulders rigid, taking long rapid strides as though he cannot walk as fast as his brain commands, cannot arrive soon enough at his destination, which is undetermined. This walk is a test of his shattered courage. This bonegrinding, nerve-destroying tension. This utter emptiness. This is what death must be like.

Music is his only solace. In his lightless room, he listens to the sound of a tenor saxophone and imagines that his body dissolves into its cry, its molten core, its spiraling ascent. The music seems to touch the bottom of his soul, the darkest sources of his being: wet, smeared, radiant.

4

Snow falls in waves across the dark shapes of the city. As David walks alone on the street, the cold seeps through his blue down jacket into his bones. He bends his head to his chest. Under the streetlamp's soft glow, snow eddies along the sidewalk.

David pulls a business card out of his pocket and looks for the woman's name on the card. He finds the name in the directory of a brownstone building on West Eighty-eighth Street and rings the bell. When the downstairs bell answers, he opens the front door and takes elevator to the sixth floor.

The woman opens the apartment door. She is a fortyish white woman in an Indian madras dress. Her shoulder-length hair is straw-colored and unkempt. Her face is plain and angular with an emotional remoteness or absence as if she had reconciled herself to the diminution of pleasure and surprise. She smiles wanly. Through a beaded curtain hanging across an open hallway, he sees a small group kneeling before a golden altar on which incense smoke spirals.

At first he hears only the dull murmur, then realizes that they are chanting rapidly in low voices. The woman ushers him into the apartment, takes his jacket and scarf and leads him into the next room. She hands him a string of prayer beads and tells him that if he chants for whatever he wants he will obtain it. David feels foolish and wonders why he came.

As he kneels, he glances quickly at the other people in the room. None acknowledge his presence. They are white, young or middleaged, all with eyes closed. After an embarrassed pause, he picks up the chant. He closes his eyes, chants, allows the other voices to flow into his consciousness. David tries to forget, to nullify his mind, to chant and surrender to the mechanical drone of the voices . . . He chants, drifts, awakens to consciousness again. It feels as if much time has passed. He feels ridiculous and ashamed. What would he wish for? What would save him?

He stops chanting, opens his eyes and rises. The woman pleads with him to stay. He gently refuses her and slips into his jacket. A knowing look crosses over her face, which settles into a mask of certitude. She has destroyed the ego, transcended desire and penetrated the mysteries. She knows his inner self better than he knows himself.

"It's because you're Japanese," she says with authority. David walks out of the building, numb to sensation, and vanishes into dark waves of snow.

Black Hungers

Her huge hands grip the table edge, bracing against the catastrophe of the day, amid a disorder of forks knives aluminum coffee pot, its lid a hat tilted rakishly. Who serves? Who is served? they ask. Hungers we cheat deny dissemble; we call them impure "black" hungers. Her hair a hot-combed wave, chin jutting, her mouth pugnacious, closed: steel-edged recriminations withheld, tongue-spit curses locked in her heart. And her eyes, heavily circled, her wide watchful eyes have seen horrors that stop the mind. She is "through with lust and lactation, tears and terror."

To this white man, this interloper, she will give nothing but her stony dignity. It is her face that has the stigmata of the blessed, not the wall portrait of Saint Thérèse de Lisieux in re-nunciation of the world, the cleansed oval of her face, the unformed face of a child: its mercy, its innocence, its seeming immunity to hurt. Her shapely hands press a spray of lilies to her breast. This is the heaven to which we must rise, her face says, and inevitably fail, and fail again. Behind her the broken mosaic of the wall her portrait fails to bind.

Through an open window the morning light through the sooty paper shade, through the striped transparent curtains redeems nothing, not even the clean folded sheets on which it falls like an illuminated manuscript. It is only light.

(After a photograph from Bruce Davidson's *East 100th Street.* The quote, "through with lust and lactation, tears and terror," is from *The Bluest Eye,* by Toni Morrison.)

Salad Days

This sultry Sunday afternoon before Bon Odori, the Festival of the Dead, the windows are raised. A high-contrast haze obliterates wavy iron bars, pots of African violets, fortress of Harlem tenements, roofs an unbroken sea of tar. My father presides over the low table, fastidious and impeccable: white shirt, thin black tie, black pants, arms ringed around his right knee. He is handsome still, his bristly hair trimmed short, hairline retreating. His gaze falls on my sister's clownish face, his upper lip curling in an enigmatic smile: hint of a smirk? My brother crouches at the head of the table in a cotton kimono, stoic, contained, the first son to refuse his role.

Hannah, my sister's best friend, peers shyly, demurely. Hers is the proper face for the camera's fixed gaze. Her hair cascades perfectly, framing the face one sees in a gold cameo, not my sister's monstrous openmouthed imp. Mine is the guarded look of the good child, his acute awareness of form. Sporting a rice-bowl haircut, my big head lolls on my thin shoulders. A cloud of steam ascends from the *mizutaki* in the electric skillet, a large Chinese porcelain dish brimming with pieces of raw chicken, shiitake, greens, bamboo shoots, thin sheets of nori, transparent noodles. Uncomfortable in a stiff square-patterned kimono, I wait for the feeding frenzy to break loose once the camera's eye turns away.

This is a portrait of salad days.

None of that will seem true.

Ishle Yi Park

"There is no air in the City, but there is breath . . ."
        - Toni Morrison

Biography

Ishle Yi Park was born and raised in New York. She has been published in *Koream*, *Asiam*, and *Dark Phrases*. She teaches writing workshops in a women's prison.

Maritza on Sunday

If it's a girl I'll call her Sky, she thinks
walking down Crescent; brownstones upon brownstones
melting in an aerial view as she gyres and tumbles over sidewalk
over stomach, her universe bending to a   *soft thing*

like mittens, like good hair, like earlobes, like mewing need.
She blinks through white sun to Saint Bartholomew the Divine on Marcy,

remembers summer's fire pump laughter and rhythmic beat of laundry rope on rock,
wild kites of music flying out cars and corners' shady gossip
cooing, cooing through the heavy wooden door, barely reaching
the stiff pews where she sat, a small sack of unforgiving bones wrapped in lace.
the desire to wear pink glitter jellies instead of church shoes
pulled her hard as the comb yanked through her   *bad*   hair

She remembers thinking they created myths
out there while she sat through false ones . . .

It would be better to eat our daughters like communion
than do what we do now, she thinks.
But holding her womb, she keeps walking
toward the weedspot, because winter is still far

and useless to ponder as the jar of pesos
from *Aibonito* collecting dust in her kitchen.

Secret

Orchid only grows in wood
Palms held a circle of heat on sand.
In three months I'll be able to float, she thought feverishly.
Your cousin from China made your middle finger grow longer with his
chi gong, and only wants a Visa in return.

Aloe is resilient.
I split it here, and still.
Oh nyah. Your *daegu* dialect a balm to my ears.
Strange music.

Buy a 1950s silver clock
from Rainbow Thrift Shop so grandpa can feel useful
until dinner. Green tea and brie cheese melt a throat.

Two elements. What is more truthful than
a bare tree in winter?
Your fingers still twitch remembering
the Japanese, a lost stitch in gray wool.

Elda Rotor

"Cherish this city/left you by default/include it in your daydreams/there are still/secrets/in the streets/even I have not discovered."

- Audre Lorde

Biography

Elda Rotor was born a caesarean section at Makati Medical Center in Metro Manila, Philippines. She grew up in Manhattan, where she still lives, keyless yet inspired, near Gramercy Park. She publishes and edits *New Digressions,* an art and literary magazine that encourages but is not exclusive to emerging writers and artists under thirty. Her poems have appeared in *The Asian Pacific American Journal*, *New Digressions*, and the anthology *Flippin': Filipinos on America.*

Home

I

How much we keep hold of our cocoons
our rent-controlled rules, asbestos silk wraps around us
dirty thick-stained windows look out
to the same old skyline of buildings,
a few new half-empty condos
At night the lights flick off and on,
never really the same lights every year
the same but different
like dead bulbs on our Christmas tree
rearranging the outline of the familiar
these walls wrinkle and pucker like my father's face
paint and plaster crack to the touch as they protect me
I breathe in ghosts I love and miss

II

I could leave small china plates of food for spirits
like my mother did at every birthday party
one candle, one small plate
a spoonful of rice with chicken
strands of cellophane noodles
a taste of all that was on our table
so that by the end of the night we would
all share the same breath
Mom enters the empty bedroom
escapes the chatter of our guests
mothers gossip and hold plates like altar boys
beneath the mouths of shouting children
fathers storytell in doorways
trying to outmatch each other
with *cerveza* in hand

Inside with a soft greeting
she places the plate and candle
on a plastic lace doily on her dresser
she reappears and closes the door with a warning
we were not to touch
this was for her sisters, my grandmother

III

But I have never offered her food
just blow kisses at the night, give some change
to the church once a year
father arranges for seasonal flowers on her grave
Not too often we talk of her thriftiness,
her temper, her secret dislike for work friends and relatives
her subtle taste in jewelry
we try to outmatch each other
using these old walls as markers
as inspiration
flickering unevenly across our familiar
so that by the end
we all share the same breath

Mars into the Hudson

(after Matthew Arnold's *Dover Beach*)

the downpour pushes coolness through the window
our arms and faces smell like the city
the stick of sour ripeness from gardens in empty lots
I can almost tell how many inches of rain have fallen
by the sound of taxis rushing through street puddles

then sunlight exposes black soot on windowsills
children smell like sweat and lead
after day camp under public sprinklers

nothing too fresh about this all
no dew, no bird-feeders, no pinewood
nothing bed-and-breakfast about this place

but sometimes the July sun
is indiscriminate and brilliantly red
even from our fine-toothed comb view between buildings

and in a cab west down 21st street
I saw its wholeness and thought Mars
was slowly crashing into the Hudson
sensing a fear so good of a place
much greater than I could ever own
relearning the difference
between what is natural and
what is familiar

nature plays a small performance
but enough to remind me
we measure ourselves here
by greatness
always less
than the sun

Early Morning

Tai Chi hands
carve out endings to our dreams
silent move of right angles in morning dew
half-stories waking lovers share in their beds

in a far place
cowboys and farmers are already at work
pushing the crack of sunlight
from under night's door

as we stretch and
suck in the crisp air before dawn

these are the hours we have the city alone
awake with a thousand thoughts rubbed from sleep in our eyes
here we lie weightless
not yet distracted by the hunger in our bones
so close to those answers
we will search for
the rest of the day

Xu Xi

I wanted to transport my Hong Kong, with all its anger and energy, its ugliness and beauty, its clash and crossings of cultures, so that I could open its soul, unburden its song and make its voice heard around the world. I can do it at last in New York.

Biography

Xu Xi (Sussy Chako Komala) was born in Hong Kong and now divides her time between that city, which has been her home intermittently for almost thirty years, and her adopted home in New York. She is Chinese Indonesian; her languages include Cantonese, Mandarin, French and baby Bahasa. Her most recent books include a novel, *Hong Kong Rose* and a collection of short fiction, *Daughters of Hui*. Her work has appeared in *Manoa* and *Home to Stay* (an anthology of Asian American women's fiction), among other publications, and has been broadcast on the BBC and elsewhere. She was a New York State Foundation for the Arts fiction fellow. She holds an MFA in fiction from the University of Massachusetts at Amherst.

From *Hong Kong Rose*

Shortly after my return, Paul asked if I was ready to go to New York. He reminded me of Albert's invitation to Provincetown.

"Together?" I was dubious. A new kind of cautiousness had entered our relationship, and I had begun to distance myself mentally from him. He hadn't raised the question of pregnancy again, or divorce. I hadn't raised the issue of leaving him, although I found myself thinking about it daily.

"It's business. Gordon Ashberry and Albert Ho. I though it might be helpful if we could entertain together, since your dad knows Gordon well."

"I'll think about it," I said.

Man Yee was jealous when I told him. He had recently been reinstated as Paul's first-choice lover.

"And you say he doesn't love you? At least you share his life? At least you share his life." He looked mournfully at me from across our table at the ABC.

"You share what's important, what's real in his life," I responded.

He gazed thoughtfully into his iced coffee. "Paul cries after sex with me, did you know that?"

I thought about Paul's alternating moods of anger and joy over our sexual encounters, although these days he had stopped making love to me. "Always?"

"Always. He becomes like a child. I try to tell him not to be afraid, but he cries until he can't anymore, and then he becomes his usual mean self."

Between Man Yee and my husband, there appeared to be little tenderness. Paul must have reserved all of that for me, because he still treated me with gentle and generous care, as if I were fragile and precious. And I relished that feeling, even after everything that had happened. Now, I was ready to face who he really was, even if I had to do it through his lover. "Tell me how you and Paul met."

"Oh that was years ago." His face dissolved into a happy smile. "You know that Ambassador Hotel in Tsimshatsui? There's a bar in the basement which is a gay hangout. He was still at Hong Kong U and I picked him up there one night."

"When exactly was it?"

"Nineteen seventy-two. January eighth, precisely. Over eight years ago."

The day after I left for college! I swallowed a large gulp of my drink. Confronting Paul's reality was going to be harder that I expected.

"Take it easy." Man Yee laid his hand on my arm. "I know it's difficult, but you better know and then decide what he means to you. Look, he started as a young boy, in South Africa, with his cousin Robert. They were just playing around as kids, but one time Robert masturbated him, and, well, it kind of went on from there. It stopped abruptly though, when his mother found out. But Paul's real problem is that he's AC-DC, you know about that?"

I nodded. Alternating and direct current. Standard slang from my teenage life. Yet back then I had giggled along with my friends, never dreaming how it would one day apply to me.

"Anyway, at the beginning, I was boss. Until I took him home with me that night, he hadn't touched another man since Robert. He used to be such a sweet boy. And then he grew up, became more sure of himself, became mean. After the first few years, especially after you came back, he would be absolutely cruel to me, because he knew he wielded the power."

I took it all in. Was this why Paul finally let both of us off the hook over our friendship? He knew we continued to meet and didn't object.

"How long will you be away? Paul didn't tell me, you know."

"Three weeks."

His face turned sour. "Lucky you."

I let him believe what he wanted, but it wasn't the complete truth. Paul and I would only be together three or four days, after which I'd spend time with Regina while he headed off to Provincetown to Albert's house. Albert was Robert's replacement, that was becoming clearer to me all the time. Man Yee appeared to envy Albert, but did not harbor the kind of jealousy he leveled at me, or, for that matter, I at him. So perhaps Paul had been telling me the truth when he said Albert was just a friend.

Man Yee left a few minutes later. I wanted to sit for a while, which I did over a second iced coffee. My mind was muddled from what I'd just learned. From some place in my brain, Kenton's voice saying, "fifteen words or less, Rose, bottom line." He said that whenever he wanted to make me tell him the crux of an issue. A good habit, because business problems often got clouded by loads of irrelevant details. Wasn't it the same with life? As confused as my life seemed, with bits and pieces floating all through space, crash landing in scattered places everywhere, assuming problematic shapes that appeared insoluble—I had to get to my bottom line. Which boiled down to this: I was going to New York with Paul to reassert my rights as his wife.

"You aren't going, are you?" Elite's response, predictable enough, was caustic in tone. "I mean, Provincetown, really. Are he and Albert also planning a tête-à-tête on Fire Island?"

We were lying in bed after making love. The funny thing about being Elite's lover was that it was inextricably tied to my being Paul's wife. My desire, if not my affection for Elliot seemed to grow with my new-found resolution to assert certain marital, if not conjugal, rights with Paul.

"What do you mean?"

"You really don't know?"

I made an impatient sound. "Would I ask if I did know?"

"Okay, sorry. I keep forgetting you don't really know much about America. I meant gay life. Provincetown and Fire Island are popular gay hangouts."

"Oh." Elliot's earlier sarcasm made no impact. "Well, that's just his life, isn't it? Anyway, it'll give me time with Regina. What's wrong with that?"

"He's using you."

"It's business too."

"So that makes everything all right? Sometimes, Rose, your slavish attitude to convention amazes me. Hong Kong convention I mean. You're better than that."

Talking to Elliot was always easier in a horizontal position. It struck me that he was slavishly susceptible to sexual conventions. "But, Elliot, I'm a Hong Kong girl."

He suddenly got out of bed and pulled me roughly up by my arms. "Stand up," he commanded. I obliged. "Now, Rose Kho, Rose Lie, whoever you are, listen to me. You're special to me. For someone so competent, you can be such a coward. For whatever reason, you insist on remaining married to—what is it that Regina calls him?—that stuffed penguin? And putting up with incredible hypocrisy from your family, his family and god knows what else you haven't told me about.

"It's got nothing to do with being a Hong Kong girl. You're a liar, plain and simple, and the worst part is when you lie to yourself. It's bad enough when you lie to me—don't put on that innocent expression, I've always known you do—but I don't care. I love you, Rose. But be honest with yourself, that's all I'm asking you to do. I'm willing to pledge all of me to you. Let go and love me. Can't you do that?"

He stopped abruptly and let go of my arms. His grip had been rough, and my arms hurt. I looked at him, trying to read his expression, but was confronted by his slightly myopic gaze. It was disconcerting looking at Elliot without his glasses.

"I'm sorry," he said. "That was uncalled for."

I put a finger to his lips. "Don't apologize." I kissed him, feeling at last as if I were in control, willing myself to love him for the moment as deeply as I could. I felt the heady rush of emotion which so elated me whenever Paul used declare his love for me. It was a feeling I wanted to hold onto, because it stabilized my emotional state. What did it matter if I'd already decided to go, regardless of what he thought? By now, I know I didn't really look to Elliot for decisions regarding my marriage. Unfair? Perhaps. But life wasn't really about playing fair.

We made love again that night, and I didn't leave his flat until the early morning hours.

"Let's meet in New York." Elliot's proposition, two days before my trip, threw me. "Why not?" he continued. "It's not like Paul will be around, and your sister will cover for you, won't she?"

I hadn't bargained for this. Elliot was the secret I deliberately kept from Regina.

"In fact, I'd like to meet her."

"No!" The violence of my response shook me. Suddenly, the playing field had tilted in his favor, and I didn't like it. I saw Teresa looking at me and realized I had spoken more loudly than I intended. I got up and shut my office door.

"Okay, Rose. Relax."

The silence on the other end lasted several minutes. I was trying to control the tears. The foundation upon which I'd built my life was swallowing me like quicksand. The trouble with Elliot was that he was now almost as dominant a force as Paul, with the power to upset my balance too often. In fact, Paul was now the calmer force.

He was the first to speak. "I want you to find me exciting enough."

"Is that what you think I want? Excitement?"

"Sometimes."

"How little you know me." How little, I repeated to myself, we all know ourselves.

"I didn't hear . . . "

"It was nothing."

Another pause. And then, right on the beat, "Maybe New York's not such a good idea."

How well he did know me! Elliot made me reach into parts of myself I never ventured to on my own, and then I would be irresistibly drawn to him again. It was becoming a recognizable pattern. "Of course I'll see you, Elliot. I can't bear to be without you. You know that."

I could hear the smile in his voice. "Oh Rose, I'm sorry I've hurt you. I didn't mean to. You can stay with me once Paul leaves, as much or as little as you want. And you spend as much time with Regina as you want. It'll be wonderful . . . ."

He rambled on happily, making plans to take me all over New York. I listened to him, swept up by his excitement. The tense anticipation of the past two weeks as Paul and I treaded warily around each other in preparation for the trip, began to dissipate at the sound of Elliot's voice. But a small part of me retreated inside its shell, safe in the world I understood about Paul and Man Yee and me, where Elliot never arrived.

Over the last couple of years, I've wanted to apologize to Elliot for lying to him. I articulated this thought to Gordie earlier this year.

"No apologies needed," Gordie declared. "He's a big boy. Besides, truth is fiction and fiction truth—didn't someone Chinese say that?"

It's difficult to argue with Gordie's logic. He understands me. What Elliot didn't understand was that my need for privacy surpasses any compunction I might have felt about lying. It was the way my father was, the way Paul was—people with obsessions and familial incongruities to hide. Gordie would know.

Wouldn't you know, it was Elliot who first quoted me that truth-fiction couplet, the one from Red Chamber? *He'd read it of course, in Chinese. I never even made it through the English translation.*

Scotch and my night watch. A safe enough place for the moment.

"I'm taking you to Frank's," Gordie declared when he picked Paul and I up our first evening in New York.

"It should be the other way around," Paul remarked.

"Wait till I'm in Hong Kong again."

Frank's the perfect place for carnivores like me. Gordie drove us down to the lower West side in his Jaguar to the meat market on twelfth street. In the dank and rough neighborhood, we walked into a steak house with sawdust on the floor.

"It's unpretentious," Gordie declared. "And you'll love the food. Rose, your dad tells me you 'adore' steaks. These are the best in town, only in my humble opinion, of course."

A portly and exceedingly polite maitre d' showed us to our table.

Gordie never stopped talking. "You both look like you metabolize fast," he said as we sat down. "I'll be you can eat a lot. Wait, don't say it. I'm being far too personal, right? Here I am, setting back Sino-American relations a century right after our peanut farmer's done his thing."

I suppressed a smile. "Peanuts are a remarkably universal crop."

"Yes they are. Paul, take note and draw up an offer to purchase every peanut farm south of the Yangtze."

It was impossible not to like Gordie. Even Paul relaxed around him and drank more than he normally would in a business-cum-social context. He had a quick mind, and flitted from topic to topic like a moth drawn to the center of light. It was intriguing, how frivolous he seemed. But every now and then, he'd make a shrewd observation I wasn't expecting. It was easy to see why Kenton liked him.

But all through dinner I caught myself staring at his mouth a lot, thinking, he has the nicest lips. When he smiled, which he did often, I smiled back.

"He talks a lot," I remarked to Paul that night. "And he seems young to have done as much as he claims."

"What ever he is, he has the financial backing."

"Really? Where from?"

"Family, I think. East Coast old money. He went to Yale."

"So he's genuinely going to open offices in Hong Kong and Beijing?"

"Looks like it. You'd be surprised; he speaks fluent Mandarin."

I lay awake long after Paul fell asleep that night. Paul had been behaving like such a perfect husband. Even before the trip, he had come home one day with a lovely lightweight jacket for me to "wear in New York's summer evening chill." On the long flight out, he had been solicitous, getting a blanket for me and making sure I was comfortable. And he had talked, trapped together as we were during those hours, about why he really wanted to go on this trip. It was the way we used to talk a long time ago, as teenage lovers, as a young courting couple, planning the perfect life ahead, being, as we strived so hard to be, perfect. False hopes and comforts. Good for their time.

"I need to know, Rose, who I am. Albert said I'd find out in Provincetown. I think I know what he means, but I won't know until I try. It's difficult to explain. I know I've been cruel to you, Rose. Albert helps me, the way . . . Robert used to. Believe me, Rose, I'll always love you, no matter who I am."

His words came back to me, as I sat next to his sleeping form. Maybe it was the wine and the altitude, but he opened his heart to me, the way I used to with him when we had first met. I believed in his love. It wasn't about what was right or wrong, but simply what was. If our life did not become what I once envisaged, that didn't make it wrong. The same was true of our love.

I thought about Elliot, who awaited my summoning. And about Teresa, whose daughter was entering kindergarten. And about Lars, Myrna and Kristin. Lars had recently sent me a photo of the three of them. They looked so happy together, like a family at peace with life. The note in his card had said, "Kristin asks when you'll have a little girl she can play with!"

I thought about all these people who had what I couldn't have, because no matter how I looked at my life, when I pushed aside the clouds that blurred my vision, the only thing I knew with absolute clarity was that I still didn't understand very much about myself at all.

Paul and I stuck to our original plan and went our separate ways for the rest of our trip. I arrived at Regina's doorstep somewhat apprehensively, promising myself I would call up Elliot right away if her place proved more than I could stand.

Regina wasn't home. The Stan that opened the door was shorter and tougher than the

Stan I imagined. His complexion and features were very southern European, probably Italian. I had been unprepared for that, having never even known his last name. On the phone, his voice was blandly American, but with a slight lisp, and I had pictured an effete, probably blond, artistic-looking Midwesterner. Stan could almost have been a jock.

"Oh hi, Rose," he said. "Long time no see. Good thing you arrived when you did—I was on my way out. Make yourself at home."

I wondered what I would have done if he had left before I arrived. But this casualness about everything was typical of Regina and her friends. "You must be Stan. I recognize your voice. We haven't met."

He frowned slightly, but did not seem particularly disconcerted. "No, I suppose not. Guess I've seen enough pictures of you though. Seems like we have met because we've had the kind of conversations we've had, and Regina talks about you often."

"Does she?"

"All the time. She adores you. Anyway, make yourself at home," he repeated. "I'll see you later."

Regina's place was less messy than I expected. She lived in a loft on Greene Street, half of which Stan used as his studio. From what I could piece together over the years, Stan lived there as well half the year. The other half he spent elsewhere, although where Regina never said.

The loft was enormous. Five thousand square feet of raw industrial space confronted me. It was on the second floor of an old garment factory. Stacked in the north corner were several old sewing machines, black workhorses, the likes of which I'd never seen before. There were windows along only two of the walls opposite each other, rows of tall oblongs each made up of smaller, square panes. And the ceilings were high, at least fifteen feet.

Near one of the windows, there was a large painting on an easel in the section which appeared to be Regina's studio and living area. I stared at the picture of the reclining naked woman for several minutes, uncertain what to make of it. There was something familiar about the face, the lips, the teeth. With a start, I suddenly realized I was looking at a portrait of myself.

The contours of my body were exactly right, even the slight arch of my left hip which Mum called my crooked hip. On my right thigh was the scar that never completely faded form the time a neighbor's dog bit me when I was eight. And she had painted my unmatching breasts—my left nipple smaller than the right. Only the hair was different. It was long like hers. I had never worn it that way. I felt strange looking at it, as if something had been stolen form inside me.

The door opened and Regina entered loaded with two full grocery bags.

"Hey, you made it!" She dropped everything she was holding on the floor, ran toward me and gave me a big hug.

"Regina, you haven't even closed the door."

"Fuck the door. You're more important that some silly door."

It had been over two years since I'd seen her; I was unprepared for the sight of her, so thin and undernourished. Her skin was dry and flaky, and her hands and skin felt rough to my touch. But Regina was still beautiful, a radiant glow on her face that came from somewhere deep inside her, despite the wear and tear of life. I wondered if she would always be that way.

"Let's do everything!" she declared. "The museums, restaurants, even shopping, a trip upstate to Plattsburgh—whatever you want you name it. I'm not working one bit while you're here."

"Can we talk? Can I brush your hair?" I wanted to know.

She kissed me on my forehead, the way she used to when we were kids. "Anything the princess wants."

I thought about Elliot, patiently waiting until I was ready to call, and put him out of my mind for the moment. He knew not to expect me for at least a couple of days.

We spent the first afternoon and evening talking and eating. Regina cooked me one of her amazingly delicious fried noodle dishes.

"Whatever happened to Tristan?" I asked while we ate.

She frowned, as if trying to recollect who I meant.

"You know, the love of your life? The one you came to New York for?"

"Oh him! He never made it. Naah, he was a washout."

"So you're no in love?"

"Only with art." She stretched, flinging her long arms back behind her chair. "What's love anyway?"

"You should know, you're the poet."

She lit a cigarette. "I don't know a thing, Rose. Nobody does. We just think we do during the illusion of being alive."

"You and your philosophizing. You don't change."

I polished off the rest of my noodles. It was easy being with Regina. I actually enjoyed not being neat, now that Regina wasn't as much of a slob as she used to be. She confessed that it was Stan's condition of her living there, since it was his loft.

"Stan's a good friend, isn't he?" I asked.

"He keeps me going. When I've been low on funds, he's subsidized me."

I pondered that a moment. "Doesn't sound like you."

"It's different with Stan."

"How come?"

"He's gay."

I wanted to shoot back a rejoinder about Paul, but thought better of it. As far as Regina was concerned, Paul would always be a stuffed penguin.

"You know, Aunt Helen thinks you and David Ho should get together. He's back in Hong Kong now."

"Yeah, I know." She made a funny face, sucking in both her cheeks and pulling wide her eyes. "He only likes white bread, know what I mean?"

"You're wrong, you know. Helen says he's sweet on some local girl, a recent graduate form Hong Kong U. One of Chong's protégés. You know how Uncle is, always 'adopting' people. I think she worked at the hotel to get through school."

She registered this. Her expression didn't change for a few seconds. And then, she picked up her wine glass and sent it flying across the room. It smashed against the base of the easel on which rested the painting of me. "Damn the man," she said calmly, never raising her voice. And then, as if she'd only just realized what she'd done, "oh shit, I'll have to replace another of Stan's wine glasses."

I always thought David was just a friend. Perhaps that was the problem.

Regina cleaned up the mess from the wine glass. She swept the shattered pieces into a dustpan and dried the floor with a towel. Her long hair hung round her shoulders as she stooped down. She looked pathetic and frail. That image took me aback.

"What made you paint me?"

She spun her head round form her stooping posture and stared at me. "It was that recognizable, huh?"

"Of course. I felt like I was looking in the mirror."

"Memory, I suppose. I didn't want to forget." She turned back and continued cleaning up.

"Why's it so important to remember?"

"I'm not sure."

We slept together that night on her large, queen size futon. Regina fought battles in her sleep, her grinding teeth loud enough to wake the dead. And her arms flailed, warring with imaginary monsters. I tried to still the arms of my warrior maiden sister. She grunted whenever I touched her, and then rolled over for a while in peace.

The grinding lasted all through the night.

"I haven't told her yet."

It was three days later, and Regina had gone out to the store. I called Elliot, feeling guilty for the lapse.

"God, Rose, it's good to hear your voice." he paused and continued in a low, persuasive tone. "No pressure, you know, but it's hard sleeping nights knowing you're here in New York."

Early signs of desire. Elliot had an irresistible phone sex manner.

"I'll tell her today."

"If that's what you want. Otherwise, I do understand. I have to be here anyway. It's just that I'd rather not sleep alone."

Spending several nights with Elliot held a magnetic attraction. I had avoided calling, because I knew the sound of his voice would make me abandon Regina, which she would hate. I hadn't promised Elliot anything before I came, but implicit in my non-commitment was promise enough for him. Besides, as he said, he would be headed this way in any event; it was just a question of timing. That mitigated my guilt a little.

I heard the sound of a key in the door, and quickly ended the call.

Regina came in loaded with groceries. "Who were you talking to?"

"How did you know?" She had found me out, the way she'd always find me when we played hide and seek as children.

"Intuition."

"Come on, Regina, tell me. I hate it when you do that."

She gave me a sly smile. "You make a prominent shadow in the window."

I gave her my best offended look.

"Okay, so I've told you. Now tell me. No secrets, remember?"

Of course I remembered. Once, when we were seven or so, we had run away from home together. We had gotten as far as three blocks away and stopped at the bus stop where Regina had said we should wait for the bus. It was on Prince Edward Road, and a number nine bus stopped in front of us. I looked at it, not knowing where it would take us, and panicked, saying I couldn't go, I was afraid. Regina had comforted me and said she would take me home. "You can't tell Mum," I begged her, because I was terrified our mother would ask Dad to spank us for doing this. "You can't let her find out. And you can't tell anyone else."

Regina had promised me. "It's our secret, and I won't tell a soul. But you have to promise me you'll never have any secrets from me." And then Regina threatened that she would tell Mum and also all our friends what a coward I was and I cried and begged Regina not to do that, and promised her I would never keep any secrets from her.

Until Elliot, I had told Regina everything.

I looked her straight in the eye. "I'm not staying with you the rest of my trip."

She dumped the grocery bags on the floor. "So who're you staying with?"

"No one you know."

Regina appeared relatively calm. "Okay. You want to take off after we go to the MOMA this afternoon?"

"That would be," I hesitated, "convenient."

She kicked off her shoes, and brought the groceries into the kitchen.

"Well, life should be that way, shouldn't it?"

I cringed at the sarcasm in her voice, but was relieved by her otherwise ready acceptance. Before we left for the MOMA, she said that if Paul called she would say I was out. I promised to check in with her daily.

At the MOMA, Regina dragged me to see the Munch. I didn't particularly like that painting— it was gloomy and dismal, and depressed me. Regina had insisted, saying it was time I learned what real art was about instead of boxing myself into Escher.

"I love Munch," she said, looking straight ahead at the painting. "He keeps me from killing myself."

"That's morbid of you."

"It's what your type would say, isn't it?" Her eyes flashed angrily.

I started a little at her sudden change of tone. "What do you mean, 'my type'?"

"Oh, you and Paul, Mum and Dad. You know, the bourgeois compromise."

"Honestly, Regina. You make us sound like something out of a French novel."

"Oh go away and leave me alone!"

Her words came out in a sort of shriek, and I saw several people turn and look at us. I was embarrassed at my sister's strange behavior. At the same time, a warning signal in my brain made me realize that something was extremely wrong. This wasn't the Regina I understood.

"You come here," she went on, "with your fancy clothes and money and self-satisfied life, even though your marriage is a complete farce. What makes you think you've got a right to live like that? What gives anyone that right to live like that?"

"Calm down, Regina. I didn't mean anything." I put my hand on her arm. She shoved it and began to walk towards the exit.

"Regina, wait," I called after her. But she strode off, at such a rapid pace I could barely keep up with her. "I'm not like you and Paul. I don't understand make-believe love. You needn't have stayed with me at all you know," she called back through the crowds. I tried to keep sight of her, but she marched off into the streets towards the subway. Before I knew it, she had disappeared.

There I was, a block or so away from the MOMA, quite baffled. His outburst had been unexpected. We had had a wonderful time, or so I though, eating in Chinatown and the village, shopping, sightseeing everywhere, nattering all night and not getting enough sleep. I stood there in midtown, trying to figure out what had gone wrong, and what to do next. My first thought had been to follow her into the subway. But the subways intimidated me, since I didn't know my way around the system. During my stay so far, I'd only taken taxis and had always been with Regina. On my own, with no map or reference point, I felt slightly marooned.

I went to the nearest phone and called Elliot.

"I'll be right there."

And he was, and I kissed him on the streets in full daylight, unafraid. It was a wonderful feeling, being anonymous in a strange city and knowing Paul was miles away in Massachusetts. He hadn't called once since I'd been with Regina. He probably wouldn't.

Elliot took my bag, and we walked away from the museum, his arm around my shoulder.

"I love this," he exclaimed. "I'm on home turf for a change."

I laughed. "God, I've missed you, Elliot."

"It's Thursday."

"So it is."

Elliot drank that afternoon. I watched him become silly, very different from his cool, business-like self in Hong Kong. "You're not home," I said to him at some point, "you're on vacation!" to which he responded, "New York will always be the home."

We had nine, glorious days. Elliot commandeered all the arrangements, right down to choosing what I should wear, which was baffling. Normally, he never paid attention to my clothes. We were staying in an apartments on East 96th which belonged to some friends of his who lived in Athens. "He's been posted there for a couple of years, but they bought this place cheap and didn't want to let it go," he told me. "Now, they lend it to itinerant wanderers like me." I finally remembered to call Regina three days after I left her, and she sounded fine. She told me Paul hadn't called, and asked if I was getting enough to last me till I had to go to "prison with the penguin" again, but I ignored that remark, knowing that at least I got more than she did, and happy that she had forgiven me enough to talk to me.

He took me to a concert in Saratoga. We spent the night there where the air was still chilly after sunset. It reminded me of Plattsburgh with its open outdoor space.

"You can breathe here," Elliot said, as we checked into our cabin motel room. "I used to come here in the summers when I was in high school, and worked my summers here in college."

"College," I repeated.

He closed the door of the cabin and placed our bags by the dresser. "Yeah. College. Somethin' wrong with that?"

Most of the time, Elliot spoke generic American English, sounding almost like a Midwesterner. Only a slight East Coast inflection crept into his accent. On extremely rare occasions, he sounded very New York. This was one of those times. "I guess I never stop to think about you in college."

He laughed. "Or that I had a life before Rose. I know I know, I only exist because of you."

We went for a walk before the concert that evening. Elliot had insisted on getting up at five in the morning to "beat the traffic", although as far as I was concerned, upstate New York didn't know the meaning of traffic compared to Hong Kong. I realized how little I though of the American side of Elliot, so used was I to seeing him in Asia.

"So where do your parents live?" I asked.

"Saratoga," he replied. "Don't' worry," he added, seeing my surprised look, "they're in Israel."

"Israel?"

"You have a penchant for repeating what I say lately."

"I can't go to Israel on my Indonesian passport."

He smiled. "I know. But my family is Jewish, you knmow."

I knew that, but it hadn't ever registered. I supposed there was no reason it should, especially in Hong Kong. but my political and racial background clearly had registered with Elliot. It struck me, as it often did when I was around him, how ignorant I was.

I found myself kissing Elliot a lot during those nine days. Whether we were on a sub-way together, on in a restaurant or in Lincoln Center, I would turn to him and kiss his cheek, his hands, his lips. It was almost as if I wanted to reassure myself he was tangible, really there. It was almost as if I wanted to reassure myself how much I loved him.

On the afternoon of the tenth day, he said, "Would you like a steak tonight?"

"Steak?" I stared at him in amazement. Elliot hardly ever touched red meat.

"There you go with the echo effect again." He laughed at my surprise. "There's a lot you still don't know about me. So, what about Sparks?" he continued. "And wear something really really really sexy because red meat makes me positively horny."

"Elliot!" I gave him a look of amused indignation.

He looked faintly, but not believably, sheepish. "Sorry."

This wasn't the Elliot I knew in Hong Kong, restrained and overly formal for the most part, and almost shy in his politeness. "Anyway, Sparks is the best steak place in New York."

"I thought Frank's was."

"Frank's?" His eyes widened in disbelief. "Someone's been feeding you a pack of lies. Did you go there with Paul?"

"His client took us."

He shook his head disparagingly. "No class. Doll, with me, it's only the best."

No, I definitely didn't recognize this Elliot, I thought as I got dressed. He never called me "doll" or carried on in this manner. He was starting to sound like Gordie. I actually liked it, because it was unexpected. But I had a nagging feeling it was out of character, that it was a show for my benefit because he suspected I thought of him as weak. I suppose I did, because he too readily took a back seat for my affections, patiently accepting the few crumbs I threw him.

As we pulled up to Sparks in our taxi I caught a glimpse of the valet parking attendant driving a sleek Jaguar away. Had I been more alert, I would have recognized it and avoided what happened next.

The man in front of us inside the restaurant was upset at the maitre d'. "What do you mean my reservation's for eight thirty? I made it for seven thirty."

"I'm sorry, Mr. Ashberry. We must have made a mistake because I show your party of six at eight thirty. I'm afraid . . . ."

I knew immediately, but there was nothing I could do.

"That's it, we're out of here! I'm taking my group elsewhere." He turned around and crashed right into us. "Why the . . . don't you watch where . . . oh goodness," and he stared with the shock of recognition, "Rose Lie! I'm terribly sorry, I didn't mean . . ." He stopped as he caught sight of Elliot, who had his arm around me.

I could feel my face turning bright red as I tried to disengage myself from Elliot. He kept his arm firmly planted on my shoulder. A desperately sinking feeling assailed me. "Gordon, Gordie. What a coincidence," I held out my hand, which he raised to his lips, a mischievous glint in his eye.

He turned to Elliot. "I'm at a disadvantage since you know who I am. You are?" His look of polite inquiry held the faintest mockery of a smile.

I quickly interjected. "Gordon Ashberry, Elliot Cohen. Elliot's a friend of my family's."

"An old friend," Elliot added, trying unsuccessfully to stare him down, since Gordie stood almost a head above him. Elliot gave the small of my back a sharp poke. "In fact, you might say we're extraordinarily well acquainted." There was a defiant edge in his tone. "So, how do you two know each other?" His tone became distinctly Jewish New York as he said it.

Gordie winked at me. "Rose and I go back a long way, right doll? You could say she came to New York to meet me, with her father's approval of course."

Elliot drew me lightly towards him.

Gordie's eyes laughed. "You look even more ravishing tonight, by he way. Of course, you always do." His eyes took in my low neckline. I felt goose bumps on my breasts.

This was how a cornered animal felt! I wanted to brazen my way out the way the two of them were doing, but couldn't. I felt naked in the "really really really sexy" crimson wisp of a dress I was wearing, the same one my mother-in-law bought me years ago.

"But, mustn't hold you up. I still have to find another restaurant tonight. Good to have met you, Cohen. I'm sure we'll be running into each other again." He pumped Elliot's hand in a hearty handshake. "And Rose," he leaned over and kissed my cheek, his hand lightly brushing my arm as he did so, "I'll see you in Hong Kong." He whisked off, and I breathed a quiet sigh of relief. "By the way, Elliot," he called out as we entered the doorway, "she likes hers rare."

Elliot was chuckling all the way to our table. I was furious.

In our booth, he leaned against me and gently kissed my neck. "So it's 'Gordie' huh? Don't say it, he prefers to be called that, right? What was that remark about your father all about? Who the hell is he?"

"Family friend. Also a business connection for Paul."

"Did I catch you with you panties down, doll?" he whispered in my ear.

"Shut up!" I was trembling slightly.

"Well well well, so even the unflappable Rose does get shaken. That's so unlike you. Maybe you've met your march?" He pulled away and opened the menu. "I'm starved."

"Elliot, it's not what you think."

He was calmly perusing the wine list. "You don't have to explain. Want to get absolutely smashed? That's what you like to do, right?"

I gritted my teeth. "He's Paul client and a long-time friend of my father's."

"So we've both been caught with our pants down, right doll?"

"Why do you keep calling me that?"

"What?"

"Doll. I don't like it."

He closed the menu and looked at me. "Why? Because Gor-die," and he stretched out his name in a silly, schoolboy voice, "calls you that? And what else doesn't my delicate little Rose like, hmmm?"

"Why are you being like this?" I was off-balance and despairing of regaining control. It was such an unaccustomed feeling around Elliot.

He reopened the menu and trained his eyes on the page. "I'm jealous. So sue me. Even if you did leave Paul there'd always be some other, younger guy lusting. Do you really like your steaks rare?"

The deliberate calm of his voice was so comical that I began to giggles. Elliot shot a sidelong glance at me.

"First she's almost hysterical, and then she laughs. What's with you anyway?'

I put my hand over my mouth to stop the giggles. They turned into hiccups.

"Elliot, I . . . this . . . is just too silly . . . for words." I said in between hics and sips of water.

"You sound ridiculous."

"I . . . know."

"We're both ridiculous, aren't we?" His voice had softened into the Elliot I knew. I gulped down the last of my hiccups. "I'm just as bad as you," he went on, "trying to be the lover I think you want."

I rested my elbows on the table and leaned towards him. "You are."

"What?"

"The lover I want."

We gazed at each other for a moment.

"Don't need the red meat," we said in unison.

"Or the wine," I added.

We didn't eat dinner that night.

I flew home with a reticent and sullen husband, the complete opposite of the man who had accompanied me on the trip out. Once during the long flight, he abruptly said, "I wish we could live in America."

"You don't like America."

"We could be free there, Rose." He looked pleadingly at me.

"You mean, you could be."

"I wouldn't be as jealous there."

"Wouldn't you?"

"I don't think so."

"Wouldn't it be simpler if we just stopped pretending, and give up what we have?"

"No!" He was emphatic. And then, gentler. "No, it would destroy my parents."

"Your parents or you?"

"What about your family Rose? Your father?"

I didn't reply. Paul knew he had pushed the right button and turned smugly away. He resumed reading and we didn't speak again the rest of the flight.

Except for the first night, when we both collapsed gratefully into bed, Paul didn't spend any nights at home all the next week.

Marion called me once, at four in the morning, apologizing for the hour but saying she couldn't sleep. It was a Thursday night. Paul wasn't home. Without her even telling me, I knew Paul Sr. wasn't home either.

It was midwinter and cold. She picked me up in her car half an hour later, and we drove out, far out, to the furthest beach on Castle Peak Road, marked on the road at nineteen and a half miles. And then we walked on the sand, just talking, until the sun rose.

This was what family meant, she said, the privilege to share a private moment, a moment that no one else would ever know about. She put her arm around me; it was one of the rare times she displayed any emotion. You're as dear as a daughter to me, Rose, she said. You understand about Paul, about us. I had put my arm around my mother-in-law's waist and said, very softly, you mean the world to me, Marion. I'll never do anything to hurt you.

In a perfect world, Marion would have been my mother, and my father would be happily married. Even now, when none of this really matters anymore, I look back and see a kind of happiness and peace in the midst of the turmoil of my life back then. Family. What would my life have been with out family?

I talk to Gordie about many things in my life, but not about Marion, never about Marion.

Pico Iyer

New York, for me, is a great downsizing mechanism, bringing you down to earth, and size, and refusing to put anything on a pedestal, even itself. It's the only city I know that sells postcards of policemen performing arrests and homeless souls holding up their placards.

Biography

Pico Iyer was born in Oxford, England, and lived in New York from 1982 to 1986 (anxious to get out, he now can't wait to return, albeit briefly). A longtime essayist for *Time* magazine, he is the author of several books, including *Video Night in Kathmandu* and *The Lady and the Monk*.

New York: A City in Black and White

From my perch above the sea in California, New York seems a crepuscular place, Stygian almost, smoke hissing out of its manholes, long, dark streets narrowing one's horizons, infernal tremors rumbling beneath one's feet. Light is what gets lost in translation. The golden light slanting off the tall glass towers on early summer evenings; the leafy calm of October afternoons; the hush of first light after early snowfall, when even the avenues are deserted and still—all these are erased, in memory, or translated into Stieglitz monochrome. In memory, at least, and imagination, it is always 2 a.m. in New York, and you don't know what you're doing there.

From Santa Barbara, in fact, an escape as lazy and unreal as Helmut Newton's Monte Carlo, New York seems almost a Newtonian invention, made to illustrate Newton's three laws: that the world is a fashion show set in a jungle, peopled by creatures dark with a stalking glamour; that characters define themselves boldly against the landscape staring back without apology at the camera's unsettling eye; that life, in fact, is theatrical, sinister, and a touch debauched. When Newton turns his eye on such polyester idylls as L.A. or the Côte d'Azur, it can be a shock almost to see what Pinter calls the weasel beneath the cocktail cabinet; in New York, though, his pictures feel like documentaries. L.A., after all, unrolls like a situation comedy, a life of no moment played out against the synthetic blue of sunny two-D backdrops; New York is cinema verité round the clock and in the round. "Londoners live *in* streets," as Peter Conrad notes, "New Yorkers live *on* them." And on every street in New York City, people are forever clamoring to push themselves forward from the milling masses, auditioning for a part in the city's nonstop drama, calling, "Take me! I'm different! I'm unpassbyable!" Seen from afar, at least, in the vicinity of Hollywood, New York is one nocturnal carnival of ashen faces and outré poses, lined up along an unlit, forbidding street, sometime after midnight, in the shadow of those dark satanic turrets that Barry Hannah likened to the fingernails of corpses.

From afar, indeed, in memory and imagination, all one's images of New York are negative: not just in the sense that they are unflattering, full of threat, shadowed by unease, but mostly because it is a city seen in black and white. The lighting is harsh, the contrasts are stark, and the effects are as loud as a tabloid headline in your face. When I think of New York, I think of people with an unearthly pallor, dressed all in black; of black jackets and white ties; black limos and white lies. New York comes to mind like grainy images on a contact sheet; dark tower blocks along the Great White Way; Art Deco buildings and King Kong; underground catacombs and Tom Wolfe–white suits. New York is the black and white of a Jules Feiffer cartoon, the black and white of the Great Gray Lady, the black and white of the editorial pages of *The New Yorker*, from which all color has been tactfully removed. It is also, in the end, the black and white of Warhol's sepulcher stare (so different from the cheery smile of that other pale blond artist, Hockney).

New York, in the mind, is the black and white of film-school projects, of *She's Gotta Have It* and *Sidewalk Stories*, of Jarmusch's arty squalor, and the skyline that inspired *Metropolis*; it is the black and white, in every sense, of Spike Lee. New York is the black and white of Lou Reed, Suzanne Vega, and the Talking Heads; the black and white, in fact, of all downtown (which in New York connotes not bright high-rises and municipal plazas but long sunless avenues and abandoned lots). New York is, above all, the black and white of Weegee photographs, clinical X-rays of the naked body, entwined on park benches or caught in a postmortem flash. New York, like Berlin, always suggests the dark: black and white and dread all over.

If black-and-white is the color of stridency and assertion, it is also, however, the shade of nostalgia, and it was the inspiration of that great anticolorist Woody Allen to compose his valentine to *Manhattan* in elegiac black and white. For all one's happiest memories of New York come from the era of black-and-white, when it was the world's bright promise. Allen chose to pay homage to the vanished elegance of George Gershwin and Willie Mays. But he could as easily have chosen other black-and-white mementos: Yankee pinstripes and the Stork Club; the Chrysler Building and the Cotton Club; newsreels, ticker tape, and Eisenstaedt's famous picture of the D-day kiss. What colors come to mind when one mentions Macy's? Or the Lower East Side? Or the South Bronx? Black and white and white and black. Say "Ellis Island," and the mind resolves into a framed snapshot done in black and white.

The only apartment I ever rented in New York—when I was doing time there—I rented because its proprietress rejoiced in the name Aida Descartes. Later, alas, I discovered that neither opera nor straight reasoning was her forte. That same apartment, when I fled New York, I left in the care of a thick-voiced, large-bodied pool player from the Bronx, who paid two months deposit in cash and looked, to my delight, like a recent refugee from *Prizzi's Honor*. In New York, though, things are often what they seem, and life seems determined to incriminate art. And so, sure enough, just a few months later, the picture-perfect gangster proved as bad as I had hoped. In New York, even the humor is black.

When I returned to my apartment, I found it laid waste amidst a blizzard of eviction notices. Unpaid bills were stacked inside the bookcases, and Polaroids of my sublessee, half naked, were displayed along the fridge. And yet, in the middle of the debris, there were piles of *Gourmet* magazines, and recipes carefully clipped; books on how to be slimmer, and books on how to talk better; a portrait of an elephant, inscribed, by "Barbara," "Come Back Soon." A miniature pool table rested on my shelf, and underneath my record player, twenty-year-old copies of Peter, Paul and Mary. A mobster, yes, but one with human aspirations. New York is the place where Horatio Alger stories come with afterwords, or dark twists at their conclusions; surrounded by unconquerable verticals two hundred times taller than oneself, one's body and one's dreams are brought quickly down to size. No one makes a mark on New York, and New

York leaves its mark on everyone (where the accommodating, annihilating West is literally recumbent, a laid-back promise saying, "Do with me what you will").

New York, then, is also the black and white of screaming newsprint. Reality gets everywhere in New York. It pounds through the walls and seeps up through the gratings and tugs at one's sleeve and asks for a quarter. New York is a world unedited, unbowdlerized, with expletives repleted: not just Manhattans, but Bronx cheers and Bowery Bums. New York is a decidedly grown-up city, elevated in all senses of the word; I cannot remember seeing children there, or places for children to play, and innocence seems as implausible as solitude along its adult streets. "New York is too real," writes Don DeLillo in *Great Jones Street*. "It's just about the realest thing there is in the observable universe." New York is also, in fact, the terminal, hearse-polished sentences of DeLillo, with their slatted, venetian-blind effects, cold bodies arranged in cool positions.

Part of this, no doubt, is just because New York is such an angular place, geometrical and pointed. The city is a rationalist's conceit of sharp edges and straight lines, the 2,028-block grid that so obsessed Leger and Le Corbusier; a crossword puzzle of a place, its black-and-white blocks marked by numbers and letters. Alphabet City indeed. Skyscrapers sharpen to a point; Wall Street canyons foreshorten all perspective; the old subway maps are Mondrian patterns. New York seems often, in fact, like a city without curves. In memory, at least, it becomes a kind of boxed cosmopolis in the dark: office workers awakening in tiny cubicles, descending into the tunnels and compartments of the subway, coming up into their boxlike, fluorescent offices and then, after dark, descending again into the underground. A city on speed, as crowded in time as in space. And a mathematical diagram of a city, where quantities have a police-blotter precision—Jan Morris noting, ten years ago, that more cases of human bites were recorded each year than rat bites; the photographer Jacob Riis, one hundred years ago, remarking, of Baxter Alley, "I counted seventeen deeds of blood."

Much of this, of course, is what has made New York electric. It is the great man-made artifact of the Machine Age, a drawing board for every kind of absurdist utopian blueprint. Madmen have always had outsize designs upon the place, as Rem Koolhaas shows in his very mad, and brilliantly vertiginous, *Delirious New York*: Frederic Thompson's literally lunatic construction of Luna Park, studded with 1,326 snow-white towers and rewired each night with 1,300,000 lights; Senator William H. Reynolds's notion of a Dreamland, a huge water park complete with small boys dressed as Mephistopheles, reciting nonsense, and an experimental community of lascivious midgets, where terrain was to be defined by the absence of color; Henri Erkins's Dream Street, built on Forty-second Street, which sought, through mirrors, artificial moons, and a hidden orchestra, to re-create the splendor of Caesarean Rome, assisted by a "semi-nude female figure" blowing bubbles from a pipe; the Radio City of Samuel Lionel Rothafel, into which hallucinogenic gases were to be seeped to enhance the euphoria induced by its golden sunset arches. Plato's Retreat has a noble pedigree.

When Dalí was invited by Bonwit Teller to decorate a window on Fifth Avenue, he erected a nightmarish surrealist manifesto of naked mannequins shrouded in dust, and chaperoned by a bloody pigeon. Its theme was "Day and Night." Black and White again, in short. ("The lunatic asylum which I saw was perfect," observed Anthony Trollope after visiting New York. Perfect indeed, one thinks.)

Those of us who have escaped New York gather sometimes like semi-hysterical graduates of some internment camp and, amidst pastel greetings and crayon skies, blacken the city in our minds. Discussions begin, inevitably, with parlor-game dialectics. New York makes one hard, California makes one soft. California is about Being, New York about Doing. The East Coast is a race, the West Coast an exploration. Soon, though, the grievances strike deeper. New York, we say, is a place where day-dreaming is obsolete, an antitropic that condemns everyone it touches to a life of grime (New York has at least taught us sarcasm). New York never, even at break of day, we agree, feels like a city reborn. "In New York recently," wrote Emerson, "one seems to lose all substance, and to become a surface in a world of surfaces." In New York City, we commiserate, we could never see the stars.

And the only way to preserve this image is, of course, never to visit the place itself. For as soon as one does, one finds, to one's horror, that the city is much brighter than one imagined, looser than one recalled, marginally less evil. The museums, one sees, are flooded with images of light (even Hockney); the sidewalk cafés in summer almost feel like California; the music of the streets blazes with neon energy. And as the colors come flooding back, one begins, very slowly, to realize how many shadows are lost, how much dimension fades, in the bleaching, never-ending California sun.

New York, in memory and imagination, seems almost like a hallucination—a rush of strange faces, twisted shapes, flashes of the unexpected; a cultural pawnshop cluttered with bric-a-brac; a reality so exaggerated that it becomes a kind of surreality. And, from a porch above the sea in California, that can almost seem like something to yearn for.

Arlan Huang

As a young boy Arlan Huang's grandfather told him a story about his youth in China, which had to do with smooth stones, eels and latrines. It was a special story that was saved especially for Arlan, and it became a symbol of their relationship. This was the inspiration for his piece "100 Smooth Stones for Grandfather." These "stones," hand-blown glass each etched with a Chinese character, are numbered and coded to a thought, memory or reminder of their relationship.

Wang Ping

Biography

Wang Ping was born in Shanghai, came to New York in 1985, and hasn't left since. She is the author of *American Visa*, *Foreign Devil*, and *Of Flesh and Spirit*. She has received awards from the National Endowment for the Arts and the New York Foundation for the Arts.

Song of Calling Souls

THE DROWNED VOICES FROM THE *GOLDEN VENTURE*

So here we are
     in the evening darkness
     of Rose Hill Cemetery
gazing out from our ghosts
     like the homeless outside windows.
No moon,
     the spring not the spring of the old days.
Our bodies not ours,
     but only bodies rotting
     in the grave of lao fan.
We look at the sky
     the earth
     and the four directions.
The storm gathers in
     from all sides.
How shall we pass through this night?

The wind comes blowing.
     We six
in deep shadow
     stand at the end of time,
stand in the night
     that is not just an absence of light,
but a persistent voice,
     unsteady and formless,
hum of summer crickets.

Something wants to be said,
     even if our words
grasp the air in vain
     and nothing remains.

Our story has set a fact
    beyond fable
Our story
    has no beginning or end

"Home," we say,
and before we utter the word,
our voices choke with longing:

    The cliff of Fuzhou
        studded with stiff pines
    The water of Changle
        shadowed in the sway of bamboo.
    Sea and sky fused.
        Mystic fires along the shore.
    Fishermen's dwellings everywhere.

        How lovely!
        How familiar!

    When dusk falls,
        faint seagull cries.
    Blue smoke rises
        from red-tiled roofs.
    Small boats offshore
        and fishhawks in silhouette.
    Salty winds
        carrying the murmur of reeds.
    Tide roads of the sea.

The scenes grow in memory,
scenes we lived day by day,
paying no mind:
    Generation after generation,
        nets cast into the lingering light,
        seeds planted in the morning mist.
    Fishing kept us out of the waves.

Farming bound our women to the soil.

But at times
　　we heard a voice, a promise,
　　　　a golden dream.
Things seen and heard
　　turned to confusion.
We pulled our boats onto shore,
　　left our wives and children
　　behind the mountain's shadow.

From village to village
　　we bought and sold
anything at hand
　　socks underwear suits dresses gold even drugs
seven days a week
　　three hundred sixty-five days a year
and not just for the money:
　　the yearning for adventure
　　ran deep in our veins.
We played hide-and-seek
　　with the government and police.
When we got caught and lost all our earnings
　　we called ourselves "Norman Bethune."
If Mao were still alive
　　he'd have surely praised us
　　as he did that Canadian doctor
　　who gave his life
　　helping us fight the Japanese ghosts.
We were glad
　　to help build a "socialist" China
　　with our illegal gains.
Anyway we had a good laugh
　　over our losses,
Still, waves of desire
　　rose daily,
this voice luring

from the far side of the sea.
Not that we yearned for gold
or worldly delights,
but this voice
first muttering
then roaring in our heads.

So in hope and fear we fared.
In tears we fared.
Mist spread a veil
till ocean-bound.
Pinewood mirrored
in deep green.
At the bottom of the *Golden Venture*
we did not see our women weeping
did not hear our children calling.
Only the voice
"Kari, kari . . ."
of wild geese.

We sailed the ocean
in the hold of the *Golden Venture*
pigs chickens dogs snakes,
whatever it was they called us.
Our bodies not ours,
sold to the "snakeheads" for the trip.
You ask why we did this?
Ask the geese why they migrate
from north to south
why the eels swim thousands of miles
to spawn in the sea.
Tides of desire
rise for no reason.
so we fared with the faith
New York had more *fu* than Fuzhou,
people there enjoyed "perpetual happiness"
like the name of *Changle*.

So we sailed with the belief
    we could buy ourselves back for $30,000
        within three years.
    Our hard work would bring freedom
        to the next generation.
    Our sons would be prosperous and happy,
        not like us, cursed
        by our own country, cursed
        by the "old barbarians."
    America needed our labor and skills
        as much as we needed its dreams . . .

And here we are,
    hovering around this New Jersey cemetery.
Or bodies gone,
    but our blind souls still hanging
        like curtains soaked in rain.

        Our summer clothes so thin!
        So thin our dreams!

Hovering,
    that dark night near Rockaway,
our ship finally heaving into sight of New York.
In thirst and hunger we waited.
In fear and hope we waited
    to be lifted from the ship's hold
    and alight on the land of paradise.

"Jump," we'd been told,
"once your feet touch American soil
    you'll be free." In the dark rain we waited.
"Jump," someone shouted,
"the ship is sinking, the police are coming!"
so we jumped
    into the night
    into the raging sea,

our breasts smothered
    by foam and weeds,
our passions tangled,
    the breath beaten from our bodies
by despair and hate.

          Oh, we've sunk so low!
          We've sunk so low!

Only to rise again,
    for clinging to wrongful things.
Easy to sink
    in the fire of desire.
Regret comes after the deed.
    Sorrow!
Our former days now changed,
    leaving no trace.
The distant mountain lies alone.
Shadows of the city so far away.
    Sorrow!
We can speak only in weeping,
memory nothing but white hair on the heart.
Condemned to wander,
lost among the roots of our six senses,
gazing at New York,
gazing homeward.
Fuzhou's mighty waves roiling through the night,
bride in green unveiled in scarlet chamber,
lovers' pillows joined like Siamese twins.

Who can avoid sorrow in this world?

Our legs lingering
    in the dew-drenched grass
here and there, still clinging.
This deep night,
    is it outside-this-world?

Our women and children
     still awaiting our return.
But here we are,
     nameless,
in life and after life,
     apart.
Our song is the crane
     calling in her cage
when she thinks of her young
     toward nightfall.
Will it reach Fuzhou and Changle
     and stir souls from their sleep?
On the boat
     we were close,
hundreds of us in the hold
     jammed in and in.
Here we live even closer,
     six bodies in one hole,
the earth sifting into
     our common grave,
unmarked,
     no stone erected
then crumbling.
     Stands of the shore
may reach an end,
     but not our grief.

Home, oh go home!
     An empty wave.
Ten thousand voices,
     broadcast the pain.
Please, oh please
     call our names
          Chen Xinhan, Zhen Shimin
even if you can't say them right
          Lin Guoshui, Chen Dajie
even if you don't know

our origin or age

        Wang Xin, Huang Changpin

Please, oh please

    call us.

Raise our shadows

    from the moss.

Be gentle

    as you call our names.

Do not wake us by force.

    But call us.

Do not let us fade

    from this place,

unlit and unfulfilled.

Yukihide Maeshima Hartman

Biography

Yukihide Maeshima Hartman was born in Tokyo and emigrated to the United States when he was eighteen. His poems have appeared in many magazines and anthologies, including *New Directions*, *Broadway*, *Hanging Loose* and *American Born and Foreign*. He lives in Manhattan with his wife.

Illustrated Version

A mute figure is gesturing to you
in the damp and gray sky:
There is a brief and almost imperceptible flare
above the thick growth of tall pine trees.
Then it is back to darkness. A distant echo
of cannonball thunder. Then silence again.

You touch the ancient traveler
by the hand, pointing
to the dense fog ahead.
You are about to speak,
but no word comes to you.

The traveler trudges on
(rather poor of sight)
where you join him
on the twilight journey
deeper into the dense woods.
You are feeling lighter.
A deer looks up.
Another layer of surface
is added to the picture.

It begins to pour.
Then it stops.
You wake up invigorated.

Soon, a procession
comes into the light
(the original lapse of time)
accompanied by lively plucking
of musical instruments and children
in bright costumes clapping
their small hands and turning.

The vague figure in the dark
becomes more indistinct: Now you see him;
now you have lost him.

You study the annotations deliberately,
scrutinizing some of your awkward and untimely
decisions along the way. It helps
with the translation.
A sense of awe
(the steadily manifesting nature)
is brought back to each one of us
in a moderately modern version.
A whim. A kind of shorthand
that permeates the damp soil.

The spine of the book is crumbling
before it is complete.
The binding is made of hemp
and rice glue. The ink is handmade
on the spot by smashing charcoal
and mixing it with water
from a stream nearby.

Behind the tall pine trees,
thunder is ready.
The book flies open.
An insect is crawling across it.
The moon is shining steadily.
The traveler, as he takes another step,
bores holes in the book
with his worn sandals.
You follow him through the darkness,
his traveling pouch on your back.
The forest closes behind you.
You return to his vague memory
as he turns in his sleep

making a motion
as if to grasp for the moon.

Breaking Off

I crane my neck
to one side and crack it.
Others step back.
That is about all.
I sketch in the rest of the scenery
where an anonymous couple is seen
in a dense but pedestrian atmosphere:
—a sleepy retrospective.

You are throwing mortal blows
at dead issues. Strangely,
in a looking glass, you abscond
like a common thief. In the fog,
life is reinvented for another review.

I arrange flowers on a dinner table.
A huge part of the menu is left blank.
Octopus to start, followed by salad
and new potatoes. Stilton and choice wine.
Port and pear. However, blooming life
comes under another title.

No wonder. A vague line is drawn
between reason and cantankerousness,
and I cross it, willingly,
keeping late hours, from café to café:
simply, I must consume to exist.
That Buddhist looks scrumptious,
and this Christian, so alluring.
I exercise my culinary skills famously.

Heavy rain comes pouring down.
While nursing a headache,
I am lauded for my restraint.

A cat wanders in,
casts a sharp look around
where paint is peeling off the wall.
My thoughts keep stepping out of bounds.

The ancients knew: you turn to stone
if you look backward for brightness.
I get back on track,
staring intently at the Florida peninsula.
I am its clichés: they taunt me terribly.
I grow thicker skin, become phlegmatic.

On top of each other,
like kittens at play,
diagonal lines are collapsing
on my chest. Drawing fresh water
from below, I untangle
a bright fairy tale.
The sky revolves around my head
like a dizzy dame.
No one knows, but I know
she is a peerless thinker.

In Central Park, a policewoman is bouncing
atop a stallion, whose penis swings
under his belly like a fat rudder,
directing traffic. The leaves swell,
oozing sodden colors.

I sniff your nape
before biting into it.
My heart is pounding.
The leaves begin to fall precipitously.

That was long ago.
Going backward, and coming upon
a wishing well, I hide behind a tree.
The snow comes down lightly.
I am feeling rather compromised.
An obvious metaphor comes to mind,
but "cheering and hooting"
is not it.

You freeze, and then jaywalk.
You trot about like a white fox
in white snow, casting your eyes
downward, feeling weighed down
by the sheer whiteness of the blank page.

I invite a statue in a museum
for a drink. I intend to twist his tail.
The statue steps down
from the pedestal and slaps me
across the face. I must have
misjudged the situation.
I have made the premise too broad.

The dough is punched down,
and left in the refrigerator
overnight. The last minute
stuff: a note is tacked on
the front door downstairs,
directing folks
to the right apartment.
I wake up exhausted
with scratch marks on my body
that I do not recognize.
My eyes water
in the morning light.

Someone is brewing a sandstorm
close by. She touches your body
with a sudden gust.

I make a loop
and jump through it.
I seem to have given birth
to a pooch.

Patrick Rosal

```
... allow me
this-to walk
the path of wood
with both eyes open.
                - Paul Genega, "Walking the Plank"
```

Biography

Patrick Rosal, born and raised in New Jersey, is the son of Filipino immigrants from Ilokos. He has been published in the *Paterson Literary Review* and was a winner of the Allen Ginsberg Award.

Infinity of Reflection

There I am, regarding myself in a blacked-out
shop window on Second Ave.—must have closed down
just days ago. In my reflection I'm mostly shorter
than the men passing behind me in suits
and I'm sometimes taller than the women,
except for the blonde with the matching bracelets,
clacking her way uptown, sounding like a nail
being tapped into a jewelry box. I'm astonished
by how little I look like the me I think I know:
cheeks full, slanted eyes, paunch and posture of a martyr
(I think of Stephen as the saint with shoulders hunched).
Whatever happened to the jawline I wanted—square,
wide, rippling even as I'd smile? And my physique—
like a Chinese acrobat—the one I'd promised to keep?
At least I have my legs—or maybe I just think I do,
since they're always hidden by these baggy jeans.
The closer I get to the glass, the bigger
my brows, my nose—suddenly I'm all fogged up.
How much can I really learn from looking
at myself looking at myself looking?
I walk to a bodega downtown that sells
the best apples in the city—glazed in chocolate, big as mangoes,
so sweet after a bag of potato chips and a smoke.
And shiny—so I can see the streetlight glinting
on the end I'm about to bite into.
It makes me think I can see my eye.

Late Night Traffic Jam

I'm stuck again on the BQE
watching the airplanes budge
overhead. Not one fuselage.

Just the stiff bright crawl
of each against the night,
all dark except for the stars
vaulting into view:
the Pleiades, Serpens, Polaris.

What is distance
but a way of noticing
the late-coming astronomical burn
despite the immediate light,
the close glower of highway lamps,
the road signs?

Headlights collect in the rearview.
Planes clustered
above the runway
remove themselves
one by one.
(Their beaded length
the slow wag of a dragon's tail.)
Against the sky's steep arch

those stippled myths,
those declining flecks of white cinder—
Andromeda, Perseus, Orion—
they flaw the celestial vacuum,
still searing
the rampant immaculate black.

When Death Approaches the Room

Like a tattered black blanket,
loose from the fire escape clothesline,
some silhouette of a flock takes off—
the bony applause of wings.

Wind purls spirals of dust and paper
up our brownstone steps.
A neighbor's child, gnawing an apple,
toddles in the stain-lit hallway.

Our sink's toppled with dishes.
The TV flickers blue.
My father—
late from the races again.

Slats of streetlight puncture this room,
thick with the odor of iodine,
dialysis bags, the chronic groan
under the sheets. Tonight,

I'm beside my mother's bed.
She almost smells like urine.
How many times must she have sponged
my skin, drenched with fever?

I'm turning her heavy body,
soft from little use,
yellowing, naked.
I cradle her against my chest.

My aunt begins to wipe her clean.
I want to turn my head. I want
to burrow my nose in my palms.
For this, I want to free my hands.

Patricia Chao

Biography

Patricia Chao was born in Carmel-by-the-Sea, California, the daughter of a Chinese father and Japanese mother. She earned her M.A. in creative writing from New York University in 1992. It was at NYU, while studying with studying with Mona Simpson and E.L. Doctorow, that Chao completed the first draft of what would become her first novel, *Monkey King.*

From *Monkey King*

Like most people I have many names. My father gave me "Delicate Virtue" in Chinese, but for the tough American world my parents decided that "Sarah Collisson Wang" had a ring to it. Herbert Collisson was the chairman of the Asian department at the Army Languages School in Monterey, where my parents were teaching then. But Sally is what I'm known as, Sally Wang-Acheson for the six years of my marriage, and since then I'm back to Sally Wang, those two flat a's knocking against each other when Americans pronounce it, so graceless and so far off from what Daddy intended.

"What does it matter what Daddy intended?" I can hear my sister, Marty, saying. "He never gave a flying fuck about who we really were."

You should understand this: I am not the kind of person anyone ever expected to go crazy. That's more my sister's department. The only extreme thing I'd ever done in my life was to drop out of college to get married. I thought I'd never have to make a big decision again, except maybe whether or not to have children.

It's in my nature to hoard, and this turned out to be a god-send. My ex-husband, Carey, and I kept separate bank accounts, so when we got divorced the division of finances was simple. After I quit my job—telling my boss I wanted to freelance so I'd have more time to paint—I had enough savings to survive on for several months.

My new apartment in the East Village had a northeastern exposure and no coverings on the windows, so that I could sit in the baby rocking chair nights with the lights off and stare straight uptown to the silver spire of the Chrysler Building. Carey had kept most of the furniture, since it was originally from his family. My clothes were hung on exposed racks like a department store and I slept on a mattress on the floor. I had one mug, one glass, one plate, one set of cutlery, a single pair of chopsticks. Spare, the way I like things.

I actually did try working at home for a while, but it was just as excruciating as the office. Mornings I'd switch on the TV and just lie there, not getting to my drafting board until early afternoon, sometimes not at all. They fascinated me, those talk-show guests, bad skin slicked over with pancake makeup, as they related their dramas in quavering tones. I'd have to remind myself they were getting paid to do this.

I decided that what I needed to do was make my life extremely simple. Every Friday afternoon I went grocery shopping, always with the same list: a whole chicken, brown rice, and frozen vegetables. I'd stew up the chicken and live on it for a week. That was an old Wang tradition—even my sister, who can't boil an egg, has been known to call my mother long-distance for the recipe. One day at D'Agostino's a stock guy came up to me. "Hey, lady, are you all right?" I guess I'd been loitering in an aisle or something. Looking into his face, I realized he thought there was something wrong with me, maybe that I was mentally retarded.

I was cracking up and I knew it and I couldn't stop it.

It got worse. I couldn't tell anyone what I was seeing then. For one thing, my father was everywhere, a shock of white hair in the periphery of my vision, and then I'd turn and it would be a stranger, even a woman, or worse, nothing at all. Footsteps up the stairs at night, although I lived on the top floor and there shouldn't have been any.

I took the bus to Chinatown and wandered around scrutinizing every single little old man on the stoops, hoping this would break the spell. They mostly spoke Cantonese. Daddy's language had been a pure, educated Mandarin. Walking those teeming sidewalks, I felt totally alien although the tourists thought I was part of the scenery. When they stopped me to ask directions and I told them I didn't know, they were always amazed and put off by the fact that I spoke perfect English.

I found the old *bao zi* shop where my parents would take Marty and me. Chinese McDonald's Ma called it. I sat on a cracked green stool at the Formica counter and ordered a pork—*cha shao*—with an orange soda, like I used to. But when the steamed bun came I couldn't eat it. I drank my soda from the can through a bendable straw and watched old peasant women come in and order dozens of buns stacked in boxes tied with string. The women scolded the bakery man if he didn't have exactly what they wanted. He just smiled and was cheerfully rude back to them.

Chinese man the best to marry, Ma would tell Marty and me. Like American, basically tenderhearted.

Except Daddy. I had killed him in my head long ago, long before he actually died. What he had done to me was horrific. Still, I'd recovered. I'd even gotten married. So what was the problem? Why was he plaguing me now?

USELESS GIRL. WALKING PIECE OF MEAT.

I crossed Canal and went into Pearl Paint. It was mobbed, as usual, with serious and not-so-serious artists. On the second floor I meandered into the mezzanine, where the priciest oils were. Without thinking I picked up a couple of tubes of Old Holland cobalt violet light and slipped them into the pocket of my parka. My heart began to thud so hard I was sure it showed, but as far as I could see no one looked at me twice. I just clomped down those rickety loft stairs and strolled out of the store with eighty bucks worth of paint in my coat. No electronic beeper, no security guard grabbing my elbow.

In a store window I happened to catch a glance of myself and saw what a lowlife I looked, hair hanging down in a tangle. I hadn't even bothered to wash my face that morning. Amazing that I hadn't gotten stopped.

At a street vendor, I bought produce: pale chartreuse star fruit, persimmons, giant globes of winter melon. Then I went home and piled it all on a card table and tacked up a stretched canvas on my wall. Using a new palette, including the paint I'd stolen, I made several false starts. Nothing was happening—it was too static. I rearranged the fruit more gracefully, but this time it looked pockmarked and malevolent. I adjusted the light down and then the fruit looked dead again. *Nature morte.* Over the next couple of weeks I watched it all rot. It became a kind of pleasure to wake up and examine each new stage of decomposition. I almost couldn't bear to throw it out.

Fran suggested I try Chopin nocturnes. "Remember at school, when we'd get depressed? They always worked for you then." I dug out the tape and played it over and over, but the only thing it did was make me cry.

The bare night against the panes started to spook me. I unpacked one of my few boxes of marriage stuff, the steel blue Porthault sheets we'd never used, and stapled them up over the windows. The shroudlike heaviness of the drapery spilling down and pooling over the dusty floor was comforting. Now my apartment had two levels of brightness: dark or dim. I rarely turned on the lights.

I tried calling my sister. She was always out—at her job as a clown at the South Street Seaport, acting class, auditions, or the kinds of parties you read about in *New York* magazine. When I finally got hold of her she told me that her new boyfriend, a producer, had invited her to his villa in the south of France. The next thing I knew she was gone.

"Career connections," Ma explained to me from New Haven. By then I was hiding behind my machine, listening to the disembodied voices of the few friends who still called echoing in the empty apartment. My mother hates leaving messages and will just hang up and dial again, as if she could wear down the machine that way. She did this so many times in a row that one night I finally picked up, just so she would stop.

I told her I wasn't feeling well.

"New York City air," my mother diagnosed. "You come up to the country to rest. Stay as long as you want." Ma considers anything not Manhattan to be the country.

I decided it couldn't hurt. Although I had a set of perfectly good luggage Uncle Richard and Aunty Mabel had given me as a wedding present, I just threw some stuff into an old Macy's shopping bag. Maybe I wanted to make sure I wouldn't stay in New Haven long, which was a joke considering how soon after I arrived it became obvious that I would never leave.

Ma picked me up at the train station and then went back to Yale for a department meeting. We were in the middle of a January thaw and I sat outside on the front steps and watched the snow melting off the eaves, plopping onto the gravel border. When you're clinically depressed something like drops falling can mesmerize you for hours. Then I wanted a cigarette and I'd forgotten to buy some before I left the city, so I went inside and up to my sister's room. Her desk was uncharacteristically bare, but in the top drawer I found used checkbooks, a letter from an old boyfriend ("My Winky" he called her), a ruffle-edged snapshot of the two of us on the swing set at our old house, and finally a pack of stale Larks.

The backyard was separated from the driveway by a concrete curb, beyond which the terrain sloped steeply into a flat meadow. I sat on the curb with my back to the house and lit up. Even in this season, through the acrid taste of old tobacco, I could smell the clean must of the evergreens. I felt a spark of hope. Perhaps after all it had been a good idea to come home. I could see myself leading a dull, comfortable life for a few weeks, doing errands for my mother until I got my brain back. I exhaled, watching the last of the smoke from my cigarette curl up in slow motion.

When I was still able to, I took the Honda over to our old house on Coram Drive. In physical distance, it was nothing, about five miles. When we lived there, the house, the last on a dead end, had been painted forest green with black shutters. It had changed hands a couple of times since my parents had sold it, and now it was buttercup yellow, with a neat white trim replacing the shutters. At some point the side porch had been insulated to serve as another room, because I saw white curtains at the windows. Thick ruffled curtains, not the delicate lace-trimmed ones my mother favors. The cozy effect was completed by a calico cat sitting on the sill, something that made me realize just how completely wiped out our presence there was. We never had any pets. Daddy said that animals belonged on farms, where they could pull their own weight and weren't just another mouth to feed.

The bedroom Marty and I had shared had a closet with a window. This had been my hiding place. From the window you could see past the grass island with its hawthorn bush and straight down the block to where the road made a sharp bend, by Witch Dugan's. You could check out who was out riding their bike, who was playing kickball, who was getting yelled at by their mother on their front steps. I peered up at the window but couldn't tell whether it was still being used as a closet or whether they had decided to make it into another tiny room.

It was too early in the season to tell if the daffodil bulbs my mother had planted along the front walk had survived. The hawthorn bush had been cut way back, almost to a stubble, and I couldn't see any berries. I looped the car slowly around the circle several times, wondering whether I should park in front and knock. Someone who'd paint their house yellow and owned a cat would certainly be friendly. Maybe they'd even give me a tour. I hoped my circling wasn't conspicuous. People were always getting lost on Coram Drive, it was such an odd little street, with its dramatic L-shaped bend and then suddenly the circle, which belonged to us, the neighborhood kids. We'd be out playing and have to scatter to the sidewalks or up onto the island when a stray car came by. "It's a dead end, stupid!" we'd hoot at the driver, who would either glare or look humiliated, depending on whether it was a man or a woman.

There were no kids out this time, not surprising on a bleak, tail-of-winter day. The

Katzes' house next door had been knocked down a long time ago and someone had put up an ugly rawboned ranch that didn't go with the modest fake Colonials on the rest of the street. No doubt the goldfish pond out back had long since been filled in. I ended up not stopping at all but instead retraced my route out to Whitney Avenue, past St. Cecilia's and lake Whitney and the wicked curve that was the last thing Darcy Katz saw in this life, and back home to the fancy house on the hill that contained only my mother, bent over the desk in daddy's old study, paying bills. When she asked me where I'd been I told her out by the lake.

My lie gave me an idea. I needed to draw again. I couldn't read, and I couldn't paint, but there hadn't been a time in my life when I couldn't depend on that most elementary of connections between my eyes and the paper. I went up to the attic to look for the old box of drawing pencils and a half-filled sketch pad I knew were there from high school. The place was a mess: boxes brimming with schoolbooks, crates of Nai-nai's Limoges, which my mother thought was too good to use, packed in straw, ancient black fans with wicked-looking blades, bulging garment bags on hooks, moving cartons containing Daddy's old Chinese newspapers. Everything I touched brought up a puff of dust, making me sneeze.

And then I saw it, behind an old black trunk from China: the green plastic laundry basket filled with stuffed animals. They were battered almost beyond recognition, but I remembered them all: Buzzy the bear, Charlie the giraffe, Wilbur the donkey. I reached into the pile and pulled out the most raggedy one of all: Piggy. His fur, what was left of it, had been worn to a kind of sickly flesh color, the plastic snout with its two indentations still a garish orange. When his dark beady eyes caught the light from the overhead bulb, I felt a repulsion so great I almost dropped him.

In the next instant he looked benign, dirty and scarred, an old warrior.

I brushed him off and took him downstairs with me. For a while it would give me a jolt to see him sitting there on my pillow, plain and alone, but then I got used to it.

I had completely forgotten about my plan to go out by the reservoir and draw. By the time I remembered, it didn't seem worth it.

I began staying in bed all day. Every afternoon at one exactly Ma would come home from teaching, roaring up the driveway, clanging in the kitchen, and then rapping at my door. Without waiting for an answer, she'd push it open.

"You want cottage cheese? I make a nice salad, put fruit cocktail on it."

"No, Ma, I had something."

She knew I was lying and I knew she knew it, but we had to go through this ritual every day.

"Where all your grade school friends?" she asked me. "Maybe you call them, have party here."

"There's no one left," I said vaguely, and then I realized I had made it sound as if they were all dead.

I ventured out of my room only when I heard the door between the master bedroom and bathroom open as Ma went to bed and I could smell the soap from her bath in the hall.

Night was when I felt most comfortable. The house looked different then, the stark furnishings and Tudor arches friendlier in chiaroscuro. I wandered down to the kitchen and found food laid out on the counter: Chinese plum candies in blue and red wax papers, sesame crackers shaped like chickens, swollen-bellied pears in browns, greens, and yellows, tucked into the Rembrandt shadows of an earthenware bowl. Ma's own still life, to tempt me. The refrigerator was stocked with cottage cheese and plain yogurt, things that my mother herself never ate, but she must have remembered my vegetarian phase in boarding school. I sat down at the kitchen table and like an animal devoured what I had picked out, not knowing or remembering what I was cramming into my mouth, staring out at the black beyond the tiny window over the sink. Sometimes I'd take the food into the living room and consume it sitting on the floor with the TV on, sound off, even though I had no idea what was going on, watching simply in order to concentrate on something besides the static in my own head.

When even silent TV became unbearable, I went down into the basement and sat there in a dream until the sun came up.

My one-month visit had spilled into two. Ma made me an appointment with her doctor, who ordered a bunch of tests. The tests turned up nothing. I was underweight, but not seriously so. The doctor suggested that I see a psychotherapist.

My mother thought this was nonsense. "All you need is career. That takes your mind off personal problems. You seen my sewing scissors?"

"No," I said.

One afternoon Ma came to my room and announced that she had invited Lally Escobar to tea. "She especially wants to see you."

"I don't want to see her." I was lying in bed as usual, still in my pajamas.

"But she knows you're home. What am I suppose to say when she ask for you?"

"Tell her I'm asleep."

My mother said firmly, "You come down," and shut the door.

The only place I could think of to hide was the basement. I made it down to the first floor without Ma hearing. The teakettle began to whistle at the exact moment I opened the basement door and shut it behind me in a single motion. At the bottom of the stairs I held my breath. The kitchen floorboards creaked as my mother moved about above me. Then I heard the chimes of the doorbell and short quick creaks as she went to answer it.

I didn't dare turn on the light. When my eyes got used to the dark I edged my way deeper in through the maze of boxes and old furniture, the oil furnace growling in the middle, and finally reached the corner where I'd made a kind of nest for myself out of an old stadium blanket on top of several rolled-up rugs. I drew my bare feet up and tucked the bottom of the blanket around them.

Lally and my mother were talking. There was a package of Pepperidge Farm lemon nut cookies on the table between them. Because they were having Western tea, Ma was using her tulip tea set that had cups with handles. There was a bizarre rasping noise that I recognized as Lally's laugh. I pictured her in her gardening outfit—a pink-and-green-striped turtleneck and overalls—although she probably wouldn't be wearing that today.

I waited, growing colder. The dark pressed against my ears, so that I could hear my blood pounding. I covered the sides of my head and tried to slow down my breathing. The furnace rumbled. Lally wasn't laughing anymore. In fact, it was perfectly silent above. I imagined slowing down my breathing more, suppressing my heartbeat, like the yogis in India. Only I'd will it past suspended animation. I'd make myself die.

I reached down between the rolled-up rugs and felt for Ma's sewing shears. It wasn't the easiest thing to do in the dark, but I knew where there was virgin skin, up near the crook of my elbow. The feeling came, not as sharp as it would have been if it hadn't been so cold, and it didn't last nearly long enough. There was one window high up in a corner that let in a bit of daylight, and I made myself concentrate on that. My cut began to throb. I pressed a corner of the blanket against it.

PIECE OF MEAT.

The window had gone completely dark by the time I finally decided it was safe. I unfolded myself from the rugs, stamped around a bit to get the circulation back in my legs, and then went up the basement stairs, slowly and deliberately this time. When I opened the door there was my mother sitting alone at the kitchen table, looking directly at me. The tea things had been cleared away, and the dishwasher was humming. I blinked hard, getting used to the light, and saw that my arm looked much worse than I'd imagined. I hadn't been so neat this time.

For a moment I thought she wasn't going to say anything at all. I turned to go on upstairs to my room.

"Lally gave me the name of someone. A woman doctor." I must have looked blank, for she added: "A doctor for your brain."

"A psychiatrist?"

"She has a medical degree from Yale. Good reputation."

So this was it. If my mother admitted it, I really was crazy.

I knew in my bones that no matter how brilliant this person was, she'd never be able to cure me.

Lawrence Chua

Biography

Lawrence Chua is the author of the novel *Gold by the Inch* and the editor of the anthology, *Collapsing New Buildings*. His writing has appeared in *Rolling Stone*, *Vibe*, *The Nation*, *Artforum* and many other publications.

From *Gold by the Inch*

An Organized Practical Understanding of the True Nature of Things, or What Is What

Tabula Rasa. Start from there: a clean slate. Rebuild the home from scratch. It's not Uncle but the muezzin who welcomes me back to ground zero on the first morning back in Penang. The announcement comes from the minaret on the television in Uncle's living room just as the sun rises and my cousins get ready for school and the factory. Uncle has been up for an hour already, ready to report to his building site. Only I am left out of the morning rituals. Only I have the luxury to sit and listen to the *azhan* compete with the sound of Uncle coughing up phlegm in the sink. Last night's tobacco. This morning's religion. *The expression of real distress. The protest of real distress. Allah yang maha besar. The sigh of the oppressed. The soul of a soulless world. The spirit of social conditions from which any spirit has been excluded. The opium of the masses.* The call fades into the morning news: a story about Khmer Rouge orphans, twelve-year-old children of the Year Zero who killed their parents for a better world.

Growing up in New York, I would never have known Ba had parents. He would never talk about them. Occasionally, a letter would arrive from home, written in someone else's hand because no one back here could read or write. history drifted from these impossibly thin sheets of paper to become abstract traces on concrete walls, eventually overwritten by a stronger hand. A few days before my first Christmas in New York, Ba took me to a Roman Catholic church down the street. After he taught me to kiss my hand when I had finished crossing myself, we stood there in the pews for a second, looking at the empty building. Then, suddenly, Ba seized my hand, the one I had just kissed, and we left to go shopping. We arrived in quiet awe at a store two city blocks long, thronged with customers and goods. Swirling plastic race cars. Bicycles. Fishing gear. What I really wanted was a dog but I settled for a race car set with cars that fly across the floor. Ba pulled a red PAID sticker from his pocket and slapped it on the box.

—Don't tell your mother.

His grip tightened around my hand. His eyes lit me up with terror. I wanted to cry, but instead we walked out the front entrance; my ten-year-old heart missed one full beat passing the security guard. I was confused, but Ba wasn't. He walked out of the store like those goodies we stole belonged to him.

Only a few years after that, Ba left Ma, and then left New York. He bounced around from city to city, deeper into obscurity. He remarried—an American woman—and then finally settled for a few years in Los Angeles. I saw him there, broken, and encouraged him to move back home. He took my advice, returning to his birthplace to terrorize his remaining family.

Then, finally, he took his last residence in Honolulu. I couldn't bring myself to visit, waited five years until I heard he was dying. That made me feel better, knowing the act wouldn't have to be repeated. But it wasn't his pending death that was so unnerving. It was his life. The dirt and the jetsam crammed into the tiny apartment he shared with his new wife behind the shopping center. How many useless gadgets, appliances, and unnecessary furnishings shadowed the small place.

Shadowed him.

Television sets. Food processors. Commemorative plates for the lunar landing and the Challenger disaster. Tote bags ordered from the sides of cigarette cartons. Cheap costume jewelry and worthless watches. Certificates Luk and I won as children (mostly Luk). Honor roll. Luk's diploma from high school. Ba clutched his memories in objects. An endless parade of stray cats wandered aimlessly in and out of his apartment. There was a large crucifix hanging on the wall, above the portraits of my great-grandparents he had stolen from Uncle's house in Penang. But a carpet on the floor, moldy and caked with insect limbs and filth, repelled me more. When I tried to convince him to get rid of it, he became incensed.

—I'm not happy with the way you are living your life.

I ignored him until he repeated himself. Then I spoke.

—That's fine. I'm not happy with the way you live yours.

—There is no life for me, he said. —Only death.

I laughed. It was a slow, unsteady laugh that did not alter Ba's features.

—You know what your problem is? He didn't wait for me to answer. —Your problem is you don't believe in anything.

The dream of starving is to be fed. The dream of the children of the starving is to have appliances. He was dwarfed by the acquisitions in his apartment. Defeated. His ashen skin hidden by a baseball cap. Chain-smoking Kools. No color. No blood. No life. He lived long enough to complain about the Filipino who tried to take away his night shift at work. Ba had been working all his life toward a goal he could no longer describe. I stood there in the doorway, wanting to flee. Not listening to his words. Wondering at this man who used to terrify me. Who used to beat me when I wouldn't clean my plate. Who called me spoiled when I left over a grain of rice. Wondered at how this small, lifeless man could have ever intimidated me. I almost missed the terror. I watched his body sleeping on the floor early in the morning. The body of my father. Broken. Pained. Aching to be remembered.

Morning market. Taman Fettes. Everyone is here. I can trace every member of my calabash family here. Auntie running the *kedai kopi*, where I order my coffee *o kosong* and get a cup of frothy unsweetened pitch. Uncle Ah Seng pressing a few extra *buah cikgu* in my hands when I tell him how long it's been since that fruit has crossed my lips. My cousin bringing over a copy of the *Star* to read over breakfast. They all know me before I introduce myself: the son come back. I go to pay respects to uncle Ah Sem. A squat dun man standing at a soup cart cutting squiggly *kway teow* from a nearly translucent white block. He barely looks up when I say his name. He sighs.

—Uncle told you about the trouble your father—

Before he can continue he looks up and sees my face. Stops.

—Yeah, yeah, he told me all about it.

Ba came back here after losing his job in Los Angeles, his savings, and his right to residence in America. He came back with a ticket Luk bought him. Within a month, my cousins were writing short, urgent letters for their parents, begging us to come take him back to America. *We have known no peace since he came*, they wrote. When BA arrived, he looked for the house I was born in, a house built on land leased by the Catholic Church. But it had been reclaimed to build a seminary. The church—the Sacred Heart of Jesus Limited—gave Uncle a small fee to resettle. Ba claimed Uncle's new house as his own, his due as the family's eldest son, regardless of his absence. When Uncle smiled ambivalently instead of acknowledging Ba's claim, Ba tried to burn down the house.

Now I can not bring myself to tell them. He is dead.

Was it his rage he finally choked on? His body looked as if it had burned from within. Scalded white. I marveled at its collapse.

Uncle insists Ba's actions have no bearing on me. We can make a family without him, he says. I feel secure hearing that. But still, I half wonder if this reconstituted family expects me to be the proof of the better life he made for himself. They observe me. Smile at my awkwardness, my stumbling through the language. As if they are looking at something inhabited by more than one self. More and less than one. Me and you. In the mess but not of it.

I died when I was ten and that's when you were born. Confused. Hungry. Nostalgic. Crying for attention. That's how you came into the world when the plane took off, circled Subang International Airport, and then tore off into the clouds. There was no airport in Penang then. My great-grandmother and some aunties took the overnight train with us through the forest to Kuala Lumpur. We arrived bleary-eyed and confused. I spent an hour or two sleeping in my brother's lap, before waking up to the call of the muezzin bouncing off the railway station's roof. A big Peugeot taxi carried us to the airport. I cannot remember the rituals at the airport, or the waiting, not even the goodbyes, the formality, and then the tears, mostly from the family that wasn't leaving. I remember my great-grandmother, sticking a bag of oranges or mangosteens in my hand before we left.

—Listen, don't be arrogant there. Be humble, because we are humble people. Remember us here back in the . . .

Or perhaps she didn't say anything.

Just smiled weakly as we left her behind.

I was too bewildered to feel anything but excitement and then, perhaps, relief as I boarded the plane, forgetfully leaving the bag of red fruit in the airport. Yes. I remember feeling relief as we climbed the steps to the plane, not looking behind me, feeling my great-grandmother's eyes on my shoulders. Feeling as if a burden had been lifted from me as I receded into the depth of the plane. But still too young to know what that burden was.

Dark Shore Just Seen It Was Rich

There is no meaning at the end of the superhighway. Its surfaces, conceited as skin, lead effortlessly down the trail of an impossible and terrifying final reality. The signs along the edge all point to its imminent collapse. Signs more often than not whispered in splinters of postcoital anxiety. Signs so beguiling as to seem seductive. Sign as familiar as the pillows worn to clouds by our bodies. Signs like:

—Why do you love me?

I wasn't sure I heard it the first time Jim said it. I asked him to repeat it, to be sure there was no mistaking the question. He repeated slowly, taking care to shape his mouth precisely around each syllable.

—Why do you love me?

In the moment after he spoke, I became suddenly aware of my hand resting on his side, of the impossible way our bodies were contorted, and of how we could lie to ourselves that this position was comfortable.

—I love you—

I began, stopped. Started all over.

—I love you because you love me.

The first layer consists of what we had in common. We were the same age. Is that enough to establish the beginnings of a friendship? A relationship? Love? Whatever. Jim was an interior designer. Luk introduced us. Jim wasn't handsome or bright, but he was well paid and he had a profound sense of decoration. He was always surrounding himself with things he considered "beautiful." The coke he funneled up his sinuses merely heightened his appreciation of that beauty. Jim's voice had assumed the soft, nasal twang of Winnie the Pooh after having his nose reconstructed twice. A nose that slid down narrow between gray eyes and tight, pale skin. Skin as unconcerned as it was unapproachable.

I noticed how different we looked one morning, standing together in front of the bathroom mirror, his arms draped around me.

—You look like an angel.

I looked again.

—And I look like the devil.

It is not good for a person to look like an angel. It fucks with his character.

The second layer is about equity. Depending on how the word is used, it can mean cash value or justice. Anyone observing us from a distance might believe there was a certain amount of both involved in being his decorative companion. If nothing else, and I know this sounds mercenary, I got a lot of free plane tickets out of it. He was constantly trawling for antiques: Florence, Tokyo, Prague. On our first-month anniversary, he handed me a plane ticket to Paris. It was, he said, his favorite place. The Radiant City. We stayed in our hotel room for most of the weekend, finishing off the two grams of cocaine he had brought in his jacket pocket. (*They never check there, they always search the suitcases*, he said, and insisted that we walk through customs as if we didn't know each other.) Once I ventured out alone while he was sleeping. I think it was probably the only time he slept during that trip. He was lying easy in the milky light of our pension, crumpled around a pillow when I left, his eyes shut in grateful repose.

It had been a long time since I had walked anywhere so consciously alone. It was the end of spring, and the warm night air teased the slimy coating of complacence that had settled on my skin. I wandered down the city's open boulevards, passing as close to other pedestrians as I could without knocking them over. I felt them brush against me. Touch my new skin. Inhaled the violence left in their wake as they passed. I wandered, with the barest direction in mind, toward Les Halles. It was my first time in this blue city, but each street and monument fell into my view with familiar precision. I felt strangely at home here, amid the trophies of civilization. At first I thought I was in the midst of someone else's civilization. I couldn't easily be called Thai or Chinese or Malaysian or American, but I certainly wasn't French. Still, every edifice and corner announced it was mine. My shoulders fell back and my legs took the lead. I ventured into the Metro with what could loosely be termed pride.

It was the wrong fare. Even before I had walked through the turnstiles, I was sur-rounded by ten men in black paramilitary uniforms who threw me violently against a wall and put their hands all over me. Without explanation, one held the back of my neck, quietly press-ing my forehead against the wall. I felt the cool of the tile against my head, then, his hand start-ing to warm against me. I became aware of my skin under his grip, prickling with frustrated heat. I felt the policeman look down the collar of my shirt, felt him exhale on my back. Against his breath, my skin became a decaying act of resistance, a virus marking me as an illness. Something to contain. Something to cherish. He fished my passport out of my pocket and laughed softly in my ear.

—*Américain?*

His colleagues seemed amused and unimpressed. They brushed off my shoulders. Patted me on the back.

—*Vous êtes très gentil, monsieur.*

I didn't turn to see if their faces read smug when they said that. I went on my way.

When I told Jim what had happened, he didn't believe me. He was certain I had made up the story just to amuse him.

—Things like that never happen when we are together.

He snickered and promptly forgot the incident. I knew from then on what purpose Jim served in my life. Jim gave me the appearance of belonging: to a place, to a time, to him. As decorations, I wasn't always able to articulate my value, but Jim knew it intrinsically.

In those days, I was almost obsessed with my value. If I could have asked strangers what they thought it was without sounding indelicate, I would have. I had just started school and was studying economics. I made it through the first year and then dropped out. I remember getting through Adam Smith's *Wealth of Nations* but really wanting to read his *Theory of Moral Sentiments*. Economists explain how production takes place in those relations between classes of people. But they never explain how those relationships evolve in the first place. The Holy Qur'an says no man should bear the burden of another. Man can have only what he strives for. Maybe it is as simple as that: Don't write checks with your mouth that your ass can't cash. But I was never really a prostitute. No. I would never count the money left on top of my clothes. I was more of a worthy companion, someone who knew the prices and the categories had already been fixed. Someone who couldn't be bothered to haggle over spare change.

The third layer is that a relationship between people is exclusively a thing. Ours took on a ghoulish objectivity. It acquired a rational and all-embracing patina of autonomy that concealed its nature: a relation between people, a hectic frequency across differences, an exchange of capital and services. The thing it became was an investment, and I was frustrated when I came to collect. The dividends were getting smaller. Maturity seemed further away than ever before. It was depressing, watching all that money squandered up Jim's nose. I threatened to leave him. He promised to clean up. I believed him, and believing him meant putting it out of my mind.

In the meantime, his addiction bloomed.

We were out at a club one night, and I saw him go off into a bathroom stall with a drug dealer we had both fucked once. I could tell what he was going to do the minute I saw him disappear behind that door. I was waiting for him when he came out. He looked surprised to see me.

—You have something under your nose.

I don't know if I sounded calm when I said that. Probably not. Probably my voice was shaking. I'm not sure if I was angrier that he had broken another promise to me or that he hadn't offered to share his candy with me. Probably the latter. He rubbed the frosting off nervously. Then he slapped me. It was the first time a man other than my father had hit me. I watched him run out of the club before I could even feel the blood rising to my cheek. When I got back to our apartment that night, my clothes were all over the street, hanging off the building. I saw a woman pick up a shirt he had brought me, hold it up, and then drop it back on the sidewalk, like it was too heavy or ugly to carry away. I yelled up at our window, twenty-three stories above the street.

When I opened the door to the apartment, he was sleeping in bed. I sat there in the dark for a short time, breathing heavily, wondering what I should do now. Wondering where I could go. He finally woke up. I told him I was leaving. Had enough. He kept on saying how he didn't want me to go. I said nothing. He took my silence for an argument and became enraged. Turned. Said he wanted me out. He picked up the telephone and smashed it against my face. I felt its cold thickness disappear into a warm bath. Looked down to see blood all over the place. Knew it was my blood because it was red.

The police came. He told them I was trespassing. That they should arrest me. I begged them to let me call our next-door neighbor, who could vouch for my identity. One of them started to giggle when he put the handcuffs on me. I couldn't blame him.

I spent the night in jail. A cell about the size of my bedroom, it was built out of white cinder block smudged with the memorials of previous residents. That cinder block stuck a long time in my head. I knew right away where I had seen it before. It was the same bulwark of cement that contained us the first years I lived here with my parents and Luk in municipal housing projects. Some crazy fool had written, in ink still fresh on their fingers from the print pad, *I don't belong here.* It made me laugh. I knew better. I knew the absence between home and prison. That everything in the cell had been made specifically for it. Specifically. Including me. It's those vines. They always bring you back to the forest.

I fell asleep for fifteen minutes on that familiar concrete. Woke up with my dick hard and my body knotted over with pain. I tried washing the night's grease off in the cell's small steel sink, but there was no soap. I stood with my face by the faucet, scratching oily pieces of flesh into the basin, listening to the drain beneath me gulping in satisfaction. For breakfast, they fed me a tasteless ham and American cheese sandwich on soggy Wonder bread. They also fed me an apple that was already turning brown and I remember biting into it, thinking how sweet and worthless it was.

Jim finally came to the station to dismiss charges against me. He had thought it over and realized it wasn't worth it. The police returned the contents of my pockets. The had scrupulously catalogued it all, right down to the denominations of bills and coins. $24.52. Jim was there when they released me. He looked me over hard. His eyes breathing me. Appraising me. Fixing value like he always did. Like it was his job. But it was value I now knew was less than the worth of my skin. Skin the color of decay. Another layer crumbling in the rinse.

Chanika Svetvilas

Chanika Svetvilas' "My English" transforms the text of 1950's American English textbook page by page using collage and mixed media. The layering of images and grammar text creates a personal statement and satirizes how information is received and consumed and how information conditions society.

14

MY ENGLISH · BOOK THREE

Forum Discussions

Our Democratic Way. As citizens of a democracy, all of us have the right to meet publicly and discuss questions of general current interest. Free discussion plays an important part in the social and economic life of our entire population. It contributes to the informal education of millions of persons both in and out of school. It helps to direct our community and national thinking. It has a tremendous influence in the formation of more enlightened private and public opinion.

Most of u   Meeting of the Air and to   sten to them regularly. T   programs th best on the a   ed school an community   articipated in them by exp

Our Class   questions that we can disc   Here are some pointers to g   a forum and in conducting

Several d   ur class should decide on a   which everyone is eager to d   tion on which opinion is   have a committee, w   can hand in good qu   by the commi   ssion.

Whe   estion, you should s   ese leaders (one to   teer, be cho b   ch   he

               at the   ssion.   at the meeting

$1 Massachusetts State Lottery

FIVE CHANCES TO WIN ON EACH TICKET
OVER $66 MILLION IN CASH PRIZES.

CASH IN A FLASH

5   4   3

7   9   OR   2

Match "YOUR NUMBER" to any of the other flash numbers and win prize shown. Get a Flash symbol " ☐ " and win that prize automatically.

VOID IF REMOVED

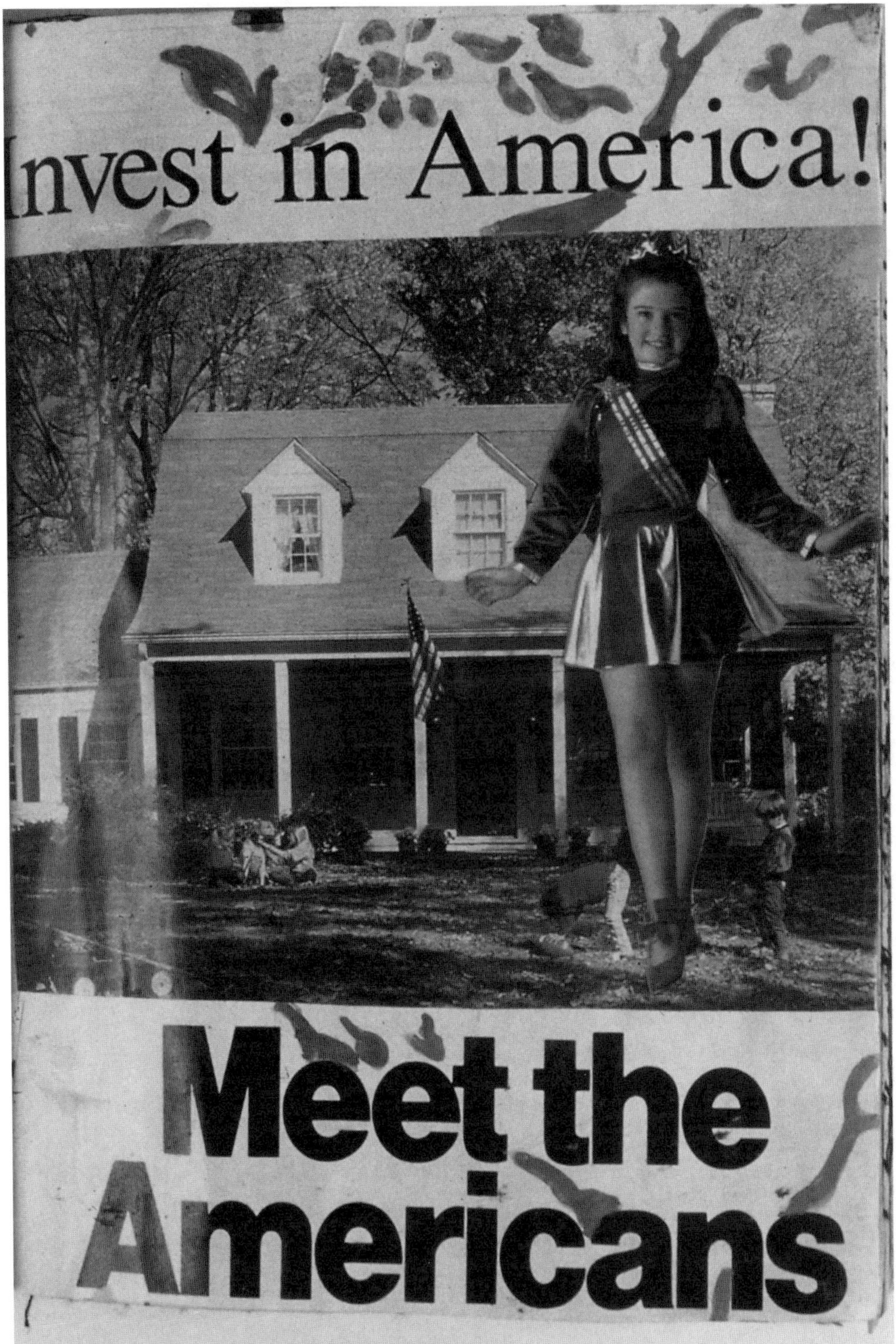
Invest in America!
Meet the Americans

Luis H. Francia

Biography

Luis H. Francia grew up in Manila and has lived in New York for more than two decades. He is the author of two books of poetry, including *The Arctic Archipelago and Other Poems*, and a collection of essays and reviews, *Memories of Overdevelopment*. He is the editor of two anthologies of Philippine literature, including *Flippin': Filipinos on America* (with Eric Gamalinda). His poems and nonfiction have appeared in numerous publications, including *Returning a Borrowed Tongue*, *Bomb* and *Manoa*. In 1978 he received Manila's most prestigious literary award, the Palanca Memorial Award for Poetry.

Memories of Overdevelopment

Growing up in Manila I saw the future and it was New York. More accurately, the future was shown to me, its horizons dominated by skyscrapers and populated by witty and cynical beings. It was the only future that could have been shown to me then, given my education, given the milieu I grew up in, given, in short, the kit-and-caboodle of post-American colonialization. My peers and I were sun-browned Coca-Cola kids, albeit with Catholic prayers on our lips, and pagan desires stalking our hearts and loins.

In 1898, when the United States took over from Spain as the Philippines' colonial masters, we managed the voyage to the New World without having to leave tropical waters. We became intimates of Hollywood; felt the pulse of the mighty automobile beneath our feet; inspected the New World species in the form of Yankee administrators as closely as they inspected us; learnt a new tongue; and set our gaze upon the sacrosanct ideals of Jeffersonian democracy while being deprived of our own. Of all the groups immigrating here, only the Filipinos' voyage takes on the added dimension of pure nostalgia.

True children of the electronic age, objects of America's Asiatic thrusts, we know all about America even before we come. Remembering the future, we arrive here strangers in a familiar land, revisiting places we had never set foot on, renewing friendships that had never begun. All the sacred totems appear and reappear, as we expect them to: the sky-high metropolis, the cowboy, the holy superhighways, the icons of blue jeans, fast cars, and the cinema.

In the early part of my voluntary exile, the myriad sensations and impression I had relating to my new environment were essentially variations on the theme of déjà vu. It was as though I had been sucked from my living room right onto the TV screen and had now become a participant in a program I had watched for most of my life.

At the age of twenty-three, I had landed in the Land of Having, where there was the illusion of even the have-nots having. Yet economics was never the impetus for my move—I could have had quite a comfortable life had I stayed in Manila. I come from a middle-class family where I was the fourth of five children. "Middle-class" might not be an appropriate term, for there it means a lifestyle which in many ways resembles that of the rich here. There were always a maid to do the housework and to cook, a washerwoman, and even a chauffeur from time to time. Rich families had even more servants—platoons—all live-in, which was true of most servants. It rarely occurred to me to wear the same set of clothes two days in a row: after all, there was someone to do the wash. I never knew, till I moved abroad, how to cook rice-there was someone to cook. I was educated at a venerable, prestigious, and exclusive university run by American Jesuits, whose graduates, along with those of the country's other elite universities, were supposed to run the country. Right after graduation, with a BA in Humanities, my first (and only) job in Manila was as a management trainee with a management services firm. My job was to teach employees of various companies such subjects as business correspondence, management, speech, life and nonlife insurance, and even etiquette!

As far as politics went, I was involved peripherally with a party of liberal-democratic leanings which sought to establish itself in the late 1960s as a viable alternative to the two-party system (aping the system here). But it was never a passion. The rest of my time was spent cultivating sexual and alcoholic pleasure, and in writing.

The replay of all things American, triggered by my arrival, was now richer in detail, and initially intoxicating in its immediacy. It was an intoxication primarily with things and resources—the availability and sheer abundance was, I thought then, enough to make an ascetic foreswear his ways. I was amazed, for instance, that apartments came equipped with appliances and hot water. Or that one could have a telephone line all to one's self, no "party line," a common occurrence in Manila where a line is often shared by two households (strangers to one another), which can lead to either acrimonious exchanges or to accommodation.

Inevitably, there was a part that was threatened by my departure, for discovery comes with its Pollux: a sense of loss and regret. Revelation is never cheap, especially when it is self-revelation. Ostensibly I had left for further formal education, but that was just an excuse. There really was no one precise feeling or reason that prompted my leave-taking of the dear and the familiar, only vague but strong stirrings, like those of a fetus signaling its bearer that its time had come. My spirit ever since childhood had been suffused and impregnated by Western mores and ideas; the Eastern self was very much there, but subdued, a wallflower content to watch its mate waltz merrily. There were fermentations of conflicts, of ideas; modern seemed ancient, passé, and ancient was far off, gleaming, like a distant star about to be named. What better thing to do than to be a magus in reverse and journey west, to deliver myself from myselves? Here in a frontier society unsettled by custom, perhaps the ancient within me would rise to reaffirm its existence, if only to protest.

In a culture where the distinctions between what is "foreign" and what is "indigenous" have long been blurred, the education I received—patterned after the American system—further eroded these thin lines of distinction. In retrospect, for instance, it seems a bit comical and absurd to have busied ourselves in search of existential angst and the Meaning of Despair, when tropical weather never did seem right for such soul searching. Having known winter, I realize that Raskolnikov could never be in Bali and that it would be unimaginable for *Das Kapital* to have surfaced in the Sulu Archipelago. On the other hand, it is just as inconceivable for the Royamana to have originated in Sweden.

Nor did starting university as sixteen (as did many of my classmates) help any: too immature, too sheltered in the family bosom to question anything seriously. Only in my junior and senior years did I begin to realize how many strata there were in the Philippine society.

Also came the realization that perhaps the first step in discovering what Philippine culture was like, *in toto*, was to run away from it.

The only constant in the last twelve years of sojourning has been the mute, immutable, ineffable self, the eye of the hurricane, the man-fathering child. It is that self that looks amusedly upon any attempt to explain a duality that it is illusory. To it, I suppose, East and West do not matter—all that matters is a unity of thought, action and feeling. I hesitate to use the word "consciousness" in a time when it has become common currency, but my stay here makes most sense to me when I view it in terms of a stage on the way to higher consciousness, to self-realization.

Where the Iberians were arrogant and autocratic (therefore less deceptive), the Americans seemed eager to engage in dialogue, to share their knowledge, to be "democratic" in their tutelage of the "Little Brown Brother," as the Filipino was patronizingly referred to. This altruism, however, was a salve for the conscience of a nation engaged in sustained and orderly plunder. (For Spain, that salve was acting as the bearer of God's word.) And so, even as a half-century of discourse on the wonders and saving graces of the New World started, the stage was being set for the military protection and economic sustenance even after the dissolution of colonial rule in 1946.

The U.S. being the last plantation owner, English was (and still is, though this is changing) the language of commerce, culture, and government. At home, three languages were spoken: English (among family members), Pilipino (mainly to the household help,) and Spanish (between my parents, and between them and many of their friends). In retrospect, one can see how this multilinguality and its hierarchical use reflected the legacies of America and of Spain, for though we were independent, our tongues were not.

In school, we were strictly forbidden, under pain of corporal punishment, to speak Pilipino, patronizingly referred to by the school authorities as "dialect." This rule (at the cost of syntactical mastery of Pilipino—it was treated as a foreign tongue) coupled with endless hours of parsing, rhetoric, and composition, *did* result in our getting to know the formal structure of English quite well.

Many Americans are often surprised that we should speak English quite well. They are of course unacquainted with the fact that for many of us it is a native tongue, one of at least two. Sometimes, the surprise veils a certain degree of resentment, as though some cultural territorial imperative had been transgressed. During my first years in New York, there were invariably people who, upon hearing that I was new to the city, would exclaim, "And you speak English so well." Some meant it patronizingly, others were just ignorant. After a while I learned to slip the blows and counter only those aimed at the gut.

Our education was thoroughly Western, classical, and scholastic, i.e., Jesuit. Discussing Aristotelian concepts, analyzing the humourless treatises of Aquinas, we fancied ourselves to be modern counterparts of the original Peripatetics exploring the realms of reason under the incomparable Aegean light. (Coincidentally, the university I attended was called *Ateneo de Manila*, Spanish for Athens of Manila.) Just so we wouldn't forget the role of Reason as handmaiden to Faith, we had courses in Theology (Reason buttering Faith), weekly Masses (Faith buttressed by Grace), and annual retreats. A retreat was usually a three-day period of silence, isolation, and religious contemplation, spent, more often than not, at a seminary. It was also a three-day re-creation of the joys of cooking in Hell, the lowest basement in the cosmic hotel, where God was a cross (no pun intended) between a rather cold hotel owner and a vindictive maitre d' who'd demote you to scullery boy if you so much as enjoyed the sudden appearance (quite frequent in Catholic schools) of erotic thoughts.

Female presence on campus was a strictly regulated phenomenon, the regulatory bodies being those of Spanish tradition and of the ultra-conservative then archbishop of Manila (this was in the sixties), who firmly believed that the frequency of one sex's appearance was directly and proportionately related to an increase in sin in the other. Inevitably, the state of one's libido was heightened, rather than diminished, by such pontifications.

This separation meant, among other things, that we got to play both male and female roles in school presentations. I remember my eldest brother once had the role of Queen Elizabeth in a play about Edmund Campion. I myself was a member of the female chorus in Gilbert and Sullivan's *The Mikado*, complete with kimono, geisha wig and makeup. These stages in some ways were apt metaphors for the Filipino's transcultural hybridization: We were Filipinos. The lines we spouted were English, and the ban on women on stage was definitely a Spanish Catholic prejudice. Friends here have often asked me why it is that they rarely hear of Filipino immigrants. Perhaps it is partly because we're transcultural creatures and have become so adaptable to whatever circumstances we find ourselves in. Like the proverbial bamboo, we sway with the wind, rather than against it. In a country that has historically and geographically been a crossroad in Southeast Asia, East and West have met and mated countless times.

So here we are in New York, would-be princes, abdicating royalty, fugitives, vagrants, lovers, odd men and women, come seeking kingdoms or fleeing them; come to repay the favours of our childhood; come, eager to barter old lives for new and remembered ones. If many of us come here in search of new lives, then it stands to reason that our identities become subject to some sort of metamorphosis. (Many of course remain anamorphic.) And New York is very good for metamorphosis-this city is nothing if not a colossal auctioneer's lot. Whoever you wish to be, or identify with—Van Gogh? Theda Bara? Billy the Kid?—the trappings, and room enough to put them on, are available. At this very minute, throughout the city, people are busy assassinating their old selves in preparation for their new persona.

Some come with no second thoughts, making their choice of this country seem preordained—they never look back. And there are those who, with feet firmly implanted here, are forever, like Lot's wife, looking back across the Pacific or Atlantic, waiting perhaps for the word that, finally, things are much better back home. Too often, when that word comes (if it comes at all), they've become too comfortable here and never return, though the worm that live in all exiles' memories pesters them forever.

Today, as then, as tomorrow, the majority of immigrants seek to have freedom *from*: from poverty and its attendant horrors , for religious and racial persecution, from political oppression. Their sons and daughters, having had their niches secured, seek freedom *for*. Where their parents stressed—all too often, it seemed—the need for communal expression, mainly as reaction, the first-generation Americans look more to individuality. No longer strangers at the gathering, they feel free to act, and to entertain illusion.

Inevitably, the brave soul that ventures here from foreign places must be a St. George and slay the dragon of stereotypes. In my case, I must be St. George twice over, for I have to contend with the stereotype not only of the Filipino but of the Hispanic (in New York, read Puerto Rican), due to my partly Spanish ancestry and my Spanish name. I must say the stereotype of the Oriental is a little bit easier to contend with, though no less discomforting and infuriating.

The whole question of stereotypes has made me acutely aware of how much there is to a name. Some smell sweeter, the bard's immortal lines not withstanding. I find my name transformed invariably whenever I get junk mail: Francia becomes Francis, or Franco, or Francisco; Luis becomes Louis or Louise or Lois. To Con Ed, after all these years, I am still "Louis," though I have spelled out my name for their representative on a number of occasions.

So we wait, whether poets, painters, engineers, doctors, or secretaries, like so many New Yorkers, for the right moment. This indubitably means *recognition*, recognition of us as individuals with unique contributions to make to the fabric of society. Such contributions may be an infectious sense of the absurd, the ability for meticulously done oils, or a divine culinary touch.

While the spiritually advanced may be content with self-recognition, the rest of us, having mortal egos, desire recognition from beyond our circles, of what we are and of what we have done and can do. Recognition that, for instance, transcends the quota system—a system that is as far away as you can get form recognizing the individual. While, in a minimal way, this system has its use, it is more accurately an indication of how ethnicity is used, or misused, by the powers-that-be. Ethnicity becomes a double-edged sword: While its current fashionable status might seem to acknowledge unique cultural richness, it also, unwittingly or not, establishes a demarcation line that is taboo to cross. Englishmen may play neurotic Russians or messianic Arabs, but for a black-Hispanic group, or an Asian American ensemble to attempt, say, Brecht or Shakespeare, is enough to drive some critics into paroxysms of righteousness.

The word "ethnic" has become just another term for "exotic," particularly when it comes to Asian Americans. And "exotic," of course, is a gilded cage within which are meant to preen our feathers. Often, the enjoyment of an audience at an "ethnic" event may not come form the substance or the form, but from the strangeness, the novelty of it all. In the process, aesthetic judgement evaporates, replaced by a confused sentimentality and increased tolerance for shoddy artistry.

In the popular eye, the Asian/American is a quiet, accommodating individual who tends to smile a lot. Or a dark-tressed, willowy, and submissive beauty. Let it be established that Asian Americans don't smile all the time. They frown, fart, kill, create, fornicate, go insane, rebel, display genius and imbecility and generally die before they reach one hundred.

One may cross-reference, tabulate, measure, and index the Asian/American, or for that matter, Jew, Gentile, Arab, as though these were migratory birds, but to do so is to misinterpret the immigrant phenomenon. It is first and last a human experience basic to our condition—all of us are, after all, like wildlife and flora, ravening after light and life, wherever these may be obtained and under such conditions as approximate most closely those we consider optimum. In such a search, myth and fantasy become prominent landmarks. But, there is the *myth* of America, and there is the *fantasy* of America. If one confuses the two (rather easy to do, as many have), one can wind up disillusioned and bitter.

America the myth embodies the Puritan, work-oriented ethic, and the capitalist vision spinning on the wheels of free enterprise. A catalyst toward an affluent society, it balances its materialistic premises by prodding its subscribers to build a just and free society, or at least to endow it with appropriate semblances. As an operative notion, "America" has acquired the stature of a Platonic ideal, never realized, of which what we see here is just a pauper aping the king.

America as fantasy functions as a *religious* belief, and no one is more zealous and full of proselytizing cheers than the immigrant who has made it. Nothing surpasses the display of faith put on by the convert, for still imprinted in his mind are the vicissitudes of the Old World.

The convert's zeal is often characterized by a monolithic mentality, best expressed by "America: Love it or Leave It." Such zealousness invariably has its comic, absurd side. There was, for instance, some four years ago a wrongheaded but fortunately shortlived movement within the Filipino community in New York to have the Philippines become once again a territory of the United States. When I first heard of the movement, I was dumbfounded, angry, then greatly amused. Just think of it: Had the movement succeeded, we would have had the dubious distinction of being the first country to petition the United Nations for *dependence* on another country!

There are days when the pall of disillusionment hangs heavy over the city, when even the most incorrigibly cheerful believer pales a little. In such weather one is bound to hear murmurs, indicating a view of immigrants as a pullulating mass soon to impoverish the

American Dream—they will burn it, rape it, desecrate it. Then I feel the myth shrink dangerously close to nothingness, and fantasy correspondingly increases, to cushion against the claws of
resentment. On such days, I tell myself, the trick is to incorporate the myth and not let it
incorporate you. The trick is to see it as a human construct, after all; the trick is to keep your
distance from it, even spit at it from time to time while delivering a few good kicks to its butt,
as you would to an erring pet.

One can think of America as the longest-running and most successful movie in the
history of cinema. The advertising campaign has been one of amazing effectiveness, and the
teasers, in their use of the superlative, have been exceedingly convincing. This is indeed the
land of "EST"—the "greatest," "richest," "freeest," "strongest," etc. All those queues at U.S.
embassies throughout underdeveloped countries—they're really lines of cinema-goers at box-
offices, waiting to see "America."

America becomes an occasion for recreating (myth) or parodying (fantasy) ourselves.
The very contradictions and tensions that seem to plague this society are really what make it.
Paradoxically, immigrants are a source of strength precisely because they are a perceived source
of tension. Unwittingly or not, antiforeign sentiment only firms up the immigrants' resolve to
stay, makes them work so much harder, makes them willing to bear a substantial amount of
abuse. No need to recite the litany of immigrant accomplishment. It is a familiar tale, full of
sound and fury, signifying something: entry, opposition, struggle, achievement, assimilation.

Historically, the immigrant saga has always rested on the necessary existence of hetero-
geneity and paradox in a protean society. Should the possibility of paradox disappear, whether
apocalyptically or through plain atrophy—should homogeneity become king—then this
country's evolution will be quite impoverished. Then a fundamental part of the myth will pass
away. America will sing, not in a Whitmanesque way of the future, and only mutedly of the
present, but mostly and loudly of the past, a child grown stodgy and suddenly very old, content
only in its memories of overdevelopment.

Leonard Chang

Biography

Leonard Chang was born in New York City. His first novel, *The Fruit 'N Food*, won the Black Heron Press Award for Social Fiction in 1996 and is now taught in colleges around the country. His second novel, *Dispatches from the Cold,* was published in 1998. His short stories, essays and book reviews have appeared in numerous periodicals, including *The Crescent Review*, *Prairie Schooner* and *Confluence*. He teaches in the MFA program at Antioch University.

Break a Leg Travel

It was New Year's Eve in New York City, and Jay and I were breaking into my father's travel agency by pushing in the air conditioner. He boosted me up by lacing his fingers together like a stirrup, and I stepped into his hands even though my sneakers were wet and slightly muddy since the rain hadn't let up all night. Dick Clark was getting soaked. I climbed over Jay, quickly yanked out the two old screws holding the air conditioner in place with the pliers I had brought, and began pushing the air conditioner along the small platform my father had installed a couple of years ago. I knew about this because I had visited him when he had been doing this, and I had to help him by holding the ladder steady and handing tools up to him. He had lectured me about college. I had barely passed my freshman year and he wanted my sophomore year to go better. It didn't. I got kicked out.

As I pushed the airconditioner farther in, Jay told me to hurry up. "Christ. There're people down the street."

Rain had dotted my glasses, and I had trouble focusing. Reflections of lights distracted me. We were drunk. The air conditioner was sitting near the edge of the platform, and there didn't seem to be room for me to climb through. I told Jay this.

"It's freezing," he said. "Just try."

I slowly pushed the air conditioner as far as it could go, and began climbing up through the small opening, using Jay's shoulder and the door handle as steps. I cursed as I struggled up and caught my jeans on a corner. I was sweating, dizzy. "Is anyone coming?" I asked.

"I don't think so. Can you make a little more noise? Can you attract more attention?"

"Fuck you." I managed to climb through the opening and almost knocked the air conditioner off the small ledge. I scrambled to keep it steady and banged my shoulder against the plexiglass, making it shudder.

"Shit! What are you doing?" Jay asked.

I jumped down. I looked at him through the door and pointed to the back. "I'll open the back."

"Open the door."

"The alarm will go off if this door opens."

"Great." He looked around furtively and ran to the back of the building. I walked across the carpet, around the front desks, glad to be somewhere dry. The back door was in my father's private office. I undid all the bolts and locks, and opened the door. Jay was standing there, wet and shivering. "Finally," he said, and stepped in. I shut the door and tried to shake some of the rain out of my hair. Jay had already begun snooping through the desks.

"The petty cash should be in here somewhere," I said, searching the file cabinet by the desk. In the top drawer was the small index-card box with a roll of bills and some change. I counted thirty dollars and pocketed it.

"Kind of small for a travel agency," Jay said from the other room.

"It's my dad and three others."

"What's with the name?"

"Good Luck Travel? Isn't it obvious?"

"Well, yeah. But isn't it bad luck to say 'good luck'?" he asked, coming back into my father's office. "Aren't you jinxing the travel?"

I stared at him. "That's in show business."

"Oh, yeah." He started laughing. "I'm so fucked up. Can I smoke in here?"

"I don't care."

Jay sat in my father's chair and pulled out a joint. He noticed the computer on the desk. "Hey, this thing is still on." He reached over and turned it off before I could stop him.

"Shit. It's supposed to be on all the time. It's linked to the main computer, the main travel thing."

"Oops. I broke the link to the mother computer. Is that like a mother ship?"

"What?"

"What if your father named this place Break a Leg Travel?" He passed me the joint. "You know, the show business thing? Would customers get it?"

"Probably not." I sat back in one of the chairs, the same chair I had sat in when my father yelled at me last month during the Thanksgiving break. He was angry that I had been kicked out on Academic Leave.

"What time is it? Is it time for the ball to drop?"

"Not yet. Another hour or so."

"Perfecto." He pulled out a new bottle of Southern Comfort and took a few sips. "You think these computers are worth anything?"

"Yeah. But forget it. I'll take the money, but I won't steal anything."

"Just asking." He held out his fingers for the joint. I gave it to him and took the bottle. He said, "So what're you going to do now?"

"I don't know."

"I told you that *mi casa es su casa*. The apartment's a dump, but you can crash there."

"Thanks. I might have to until I find a job and a place."

"You short of cash?"

"That's why we're here."

"Yeah, right. You mean we're not buying more drinks?"

"Just a few more."

"I'm so fucked up. I can't feel my face. Go ahead and slap me."

"I don't want to slap you."

"No, really. Go ahead. I can't feel my face."

"I'm not going to slap you."

He sighed. "Fine." He kept poking his cheek with his finger. "My mom called yesterday and was surprised that you're staying with me."

"She calls a lot."

"Every Sunday. She's a pain in the ass." He suddenly looked uncomfortable. "Hey, sorry about your mom. I never got to say how—"

"Forget it. She's been sick a long time. I think my father was glad she croaked."

"My mom got all upset when she heard. She wanted to go over to your house and talk to your dad and all. I told her to lay off."

"That was good. My father had to deal with the whole fucking Korean church showing up at the house."

"How was the funeral?"

"I didn't go."

That stopped Jay. "Oh. Whatever."

I shrugged.

Jay looked at the typewriter cover and pulled it off. He said, "God, remember that time we broke into the school and checked out our files? That was genius."

"Mr. Stanton wrote that you were an underachiever."

Jay laughed. "What a fucking idiot. How do you become a guidance counselor? Maybe I can do that." He looked at the joint. "Shit, you want some?" We switched again. He took three big sips of the Southern Comfort and made a face. He sat up in the chair and pulled himself forward. "Well, Mr. Kim. What do you want to do with your life?"

I smiled. "I want another sip of that Southern Comfort."

He passed me the bottle. "Let me check my charts." He flipped through a travel brochure. "Well, your choices are limited. Let's see: you can be a drunk, a thief or a bond trader. No, wait. If you're a bond trader, you'll have to be sober. Scratch that."

"A sober bond trader?"

"Maybe not."

I laughed. He slipped a piece of stationery into the typewriter, turned it on and began typing something. The humming and clicking filled the office. I took a big hit from the joint. He started reading as he typed: "Christopher Kim is a personable, likeable young man with lofty ambitions." He stopped. "Shit. Where's the erase key? Can't even spell *ambitions* right."

"*Ambitions* has two e's."

He looked up, startled, and stared at me for a moment. Then he smiled. "Ha, very funny."

The joint was getting low, and I tried to get that last bit without burning myself. I held it out to him. He squeezed out the ember, then ate the rest. He continued typing and reading: "His desire to not deal with anyone, amid drinking booze and smoking pot, is extraordinarily mature for his age, and, in my opinion, is quite attainable, and he need only apply himself in the manner of other prominent booze drinkers and pot smokers, and he will succeed. I am confident in his abilities. Signed, Harvey Stanton, Guidance Counselor."

He whipped the paper out of the typewriter, and signed it with a flourish. He laid it in front of me. "Go west, young man. Go west." He gulped down more of the Southern Comfort. "Is it almost time yet?"

"Not yet. It's only a couple of blocks away."

"Yeah, but it's packed. We'll never get near Dick Clark."

"Dick Clark is a weeny."

Jay started laughing, then coughing. "Shit. My lungs are probably mush."

I looked around the office, wondering if there was any more money lying around. I said, "Check the desk if it's not locked. Is there anything in there?"

Jay did this, while I got up and looked through the other cabinets. I saw customer information, bills and receipts, but nothing interesting. As I was looking though the bookshelves, Jay said, "Oh, man. Oh, Chris. Check this out."

I squinted and moved closer. He was holding up a credit card. I hurried to him and looked at it. It was in my father's name. We looked at each other, and he raised an eyebrow. "What's a card doing here?" he asked.

"I have no idea. Expiration date?"

"Not for a year," he said, reading the card.

"Maybe it's a business account," I said, taking it and examining the signature. "What do you think?"

"I think there are plenty of bars and restaurants open right now. A lot of parties."

"What if it doesn't work?"

He shrugged. "We act innocent."

I was suddenly hungry. "Let's go to a real expensive restaurant. I want some steak."

"What about the ball? I want to see the ball drop."

"Yeah, yeah, let's book," I said. "I want a big steak."

He hurried after me. "We can go to a nightclub!" he said. "They're all having parties!"

We quickly ran out into the back alley. The door slammed shut and locked by itself. He stopped. "Wait! We left that stupid letter on the desk!"

"What? Are you kidding?"

He ran back to the door, but it wouldn't budge. "Shit," he said.

I thought about my father finding the letter on Monday morning, the cash missing, the credit card gone. Would he call the police? I wasn't sure. I wouldn't put it past him.

"We have to climb through the air conditioner opening again," he said. "Let's hurry."

"Fuck it."

"What?"

"Fuck it," I said. "Let's see the ball drop."

"Your name's on the sheet. Shit, I was so stupid to write that."

"Jay, I don't care. Let's go."

He hesitated. "Are you sure? Your dad will be so pissed."

"Let him."

Jay shook his head and slapped me on the back. "Your funeral." He stopped, and seemed almost to wince.

I waved it off and said, "Let's have a little fun."

As we ran toward Times Square, the crowds growing thicker, the freezing light rain coating my glasses and blurring the streets, I tried to make out the different lights around us. The raindrops stretched and warped my vision. I really wanted that steak. I checked my watch. Eleven-forty. Dick Clark waiting for us. I patted my pockets, making sure my father's credit card was still there. I tried to imagine what my father would do once he found the letter. He wouldn't be surprised. He knew I was a screwup. That was one of the reasons he threw me out. No job, no school. Staying out late with Jay. Would he crumple up the letter, throw it out, then buzz his secretary and tell her to cancel the credit card? Would he call the police? I pushed it out of my mind and grabbed a spin noisemaker off the street, the kind that rattled loudly as you twirled it. My lucky night. It was getting closer to the New Year. I spun the noisemaker while we ran.

Ava Chin

". . . New York was a wild metropolis, wherein we were disappointed if we had not two or three murders or a spicy riot or two for breakfast entertainment."

　　　　　- 1856 Campaign Literature for Mayor Fernando Wood, written by Daniel Mcleod.

Biography

Ava Chin, a Queens native, has written poetic lyrics for the alternative rock band Soul Coughing ("despite the fact I can't sing"). Her work has appeared in *Dick for a Day*, *It's Only Rock-n-Roll* and *A Gathering of the Tribes*. She is a 1997-1998 Van Lier Fellow.

Blow

You say: I need to see trees
Your eyes cracked pothole pavement
smoke emitting through nostrils once shaped fresh oysters
Face a crater in my hands.
When we were ten
clouds sailed through our stories past midnight
and the trees broke through dawn like flowers
Flower
You a flower
A kilo in autumn
Keeping you awake through predawn hours
Those heavy lids propped open like iron doors
models swinging past celebrities that NY rats lifestyle
Rats keep your hours
Rat, I call you
You say, Rat
You're a rat in NY
Living off sunshine like cocaine
haze what sun you see at 6 in the morning and again at 5 pm
is an eclipse
the purple under your eyes
You're an eclipse
shadowing my heart
the caffeine in coffee can't chase your thoughts
like blow you swirl pleas in dairy clouds
whispering before the light
sets. set. sunset
You say: I need to see the sunset before I die
the setting sun on leaves reaching
root in the sky
But sunset never seemed so far away
When flying miles on asphalt at dawn
your mumblings not even making sense to the taxi
driver because you lack the language of direction

north south east west are points on a map
your thoughts a broken headlight on the West Side Highway
you ribbon through traffic like the blood and dust
in your veins
You say: My mother planted trees before she died
her hands reaching vegetable in the earth
My heart, you said, my heart went with her
and every whisper of every breeze speaks her name.

If I took you down to Central Park
the lanes, the trees it wouldn't been enough
I'd have to bury your body as corn in the earth
box of solid pine to anchor
iron to rust your hair
you long to see the ground from within
to grow root seeking water like blind men
beneath the dirt
stains
sniffs
powder
your body
leaves
my fingers.

Gold in Pocket

"One hundred percent Chinese!"
My grandfather always prefaced at introductions
Hand on my head, despite the mute Chinese tongue lame with English
classmates too ready to slur their words and eyes when the teacher wasn't looking.
"One hundred percent Chinese!"
was not what he'd call my cousins
Biracial with blond-haired, blue-eyed mothers to wipe their Connecticut mouths free
of any ethnic dust that could possibly touch them from the city.
Cousins who taunted *Chinese! Chinese!*

and could pass for white until the name got in the way
Wong! which sounded too much like *wrong!*
and they paled even lighter than their skin would allow.
When grandpa spoke he didn't need a translator
but my cousins didn't have the ear to make it through the fierce underbrush
of Toi San wa interceding like rising watercolor Guangzhou mountains
and so smiled Protestantly, patting the Good Book for solace
hoping he'd find Jesus before it was too late.
"One hundred percent Chinese!"
wasn't even what he was, a special kind of Asian American
speaking a dialect only the old-timers understand
sieged between the layers of Chinatown and Queens
Smiling as deftly at the brush of a customer's tip,
as his children moving to the suburbs
sons unable to distinguish his mutterings from the noise of Canal St.
to the roll of his joints as he makes his way home at 12:30 in the morning
the change rattling like fool's gold in his pocket.

Daycare

In the first year mama went to work teaching amid
the concrete blocks and weeded lots of Bushwick
counting the tiny heads and rhyming the alphabet,
taking care of other people's children when
she wanted to be takin' care of her own.
By 6 months there were itinerant sitters
Solitary black mothers rocking a Chinese baby by the
daylight of their windows
humming soft song and God's savings
over the heavy bass of trucks along the boulevard,
taking care of other people's children when
they wanted to be takin' care of their own.
At two there was Tita and her granddaughter
me and LaWanda the same age
hair black but different

turned up noses and fingers candy sticky
running past Tita's wheelchair
to the second floor
grabbing the railing and giggling
we'd taunt the long, long arm
of Tita's wooden rod
missing us,
rapping the stair.
At four name pinned to collar
and nursery rhymed
White methodist-run daycare center in the heart of Jamaica, Queens
Jesus was a dead guy who lived long ago
beyond the patchwork storefronts
and slouching couches hanging like broken
fingers on slanting porches off Sutphin Boulevard
we dreamed through boarded windows
eyes lowered fingers folded under the blue-eyed gaze of the minister.

The first time I heard a Southern voice
speak my name it was a question
from the new missionary young and pretty,
"Are you little Ms. Chin? I've heard about you, Ms. Chin.
I hear you're good with pencil and paper, scissors and glue, Ms. Chin.
Can you draw this, Ms. Chin?"

I couldn't render the sketch but drew the inference as did
the other children and for the first time I had no friends.

There were other misfits
The girl who ate dirt
eastern-bloc accent at angles lying incongruous her pretty mouth
The boy who bled rivers his blanketed matted hair
The cleaning woman pailing water picking dirt between the strands asking,
Do you like red? Because Chinese like red and do you like red?
And, why not?

That day we were under the trees watching the
falling pods pile like feathers
The girl who ate dirt stuck a Pinocchio nose on my face
In her hand an open seed her father said we ate.
Eat, she said, as I swallowed.

Now if I ate some dirt, I knew
A tree might someday grow in my stomach.

Diane Mehta

The essential is to excite the spectators. If that means playing Hamlet on a flying trapeze or in an aquarium, you do it.
- Orson Welles

Biography

Diane Mehta was born in Germany and grew up in Bombay and New York. Recent publications include *Callaloo*, *Gulf Coast*, and *Contours of the Heart: South Asians Map North America*. She has come to the realization that she can never leave New York because it's the only place in America she can get fresh-squeezed sugarcane juice.

Open Space

Blue far overhead, handles jerk haunches in unison.
A couple's dialogue magnifies crowded quiet,
Red coat shifts, seated sleepers sleep off Unisom
Two stops more. To capacity. Speed of light
Shaking through tunnels, shirts crisp, ties
Clipped, on the express. Tunnels we might
Get intimate in. Techno, a Walkman turned up high,
Deaf, quiet corpses seesaw like frozen meat
Between timeless and time clock. It's 9 a.m.,
Doors slide open, Bally shoes clip-clop from the belly.
A second chance or coming? Let them
Stampede stairs to sea level, concrete daily
Footfalls to elevators' skyscraping reach. Metropolis.
What you wanted, in your working years, bliss?

Roses

The act of finding is more interesting than the thing found
so I went to Brooklyn's Botanical Gardens,
having no interest in roses.

The underground, engineered people
had the transparent blue glazes of glass vases.
One man's shoes were caked with mud.
He seemed to understand that he did not belong on the subway.
Nothing rushed by the train's black windows
but the Atlantic was there, cascading with the craft
of Coney Island rides children eventually outgrow.
All was silent in the car, and the rocking of the cars
rocked the passengers almost to sleep.

Over their heads, jerking in unison to the left
and then to the right, the grainy independent film
of each of their lives passed slowly into thoughts of wild
varied roses, wild yellow and ivory and crimson roses
in their perfect, packed aisles, waiting for the gardener's
generosity or scissors, labeled with historical names
on white placards two inches high.

The perimeter gate seemed as if it were guarding
the genetics of April. Inside the greenhouses
steam-white incubators, barrack after barrack
of life sustainers unusual to Brooklyn,
cultivating an entire population of blossoms.
Like me, my grandmother didn't care about roses.
Never disappointed, she loved the wet shade's geometry,
which she compared to buildings on Eastern Parkway.

Stagefright

Winter raises curbsides in the north.
     The sound of water runs
upstairs, providing background, like a myth
     journeying across
pages of shelves: majorities of years
     unused, unread, untouched
under the paragraphs of love. And tears
     not wept—marriage is the giving
up of free verse: its bacchanal of type
     around the page
like sloppy specimens under a microscope.
     At the boathouse we agreed
perfect marriages included lovers
     on leap years, in an office,
and cycled home as rain fell in commas.
     We repeat the phrase

I love you while we plan affairs together.
    Love becomes a theater:
planned applause and needing the director
    more than we expected.
Wanting the performance, we memorized lines
    like those on self-addressed
envelopes. An actor feigns emotions
    without expectations
of sadness. Wanting to be utterly
    unfree
onstage; the spotlights, words and memory
    of someone else's life.
In dreams someone was filming us on stairs
    at City Hall. You turned
back over like an engine when the air's
    freezing, divining
words from explanations, a chapter
    from a verse. I paused
while commas fell around you, unsure.

Jimin Han

Exploring the words means plunging down
not skimming across
or watching whitecaps however lovely.
Not balking at fear either:
the walls are filled with sounds.
            - Kimiko Hahn, *Revolutions*

Biography

Jimin Han holds an MFA from Sarah Lawrence College. She was born in Seoul and moved to New York in 1970. A finalist for the Charles Johnson Award in fiction for 1998 and an associate editor of *Global City Review*, she is currently at work on a novel.

Deliveries

He made it permanent by scratching the words into her mailbox: FUCK YOU. All the people who had ever hated her, children from the playground to people on the street, all jeered. She was center stage. Everyone in her building had already seen that she was the object of hate. Did they wonder what she had done to deserve it or did they smugly assume they knew she had it coming to her? Her with her flat face and slanted eyes? She went numb.

She stood there with her key in her hand. FUCK. FUCK YOU. Who would be so determined to send her that message? She inserted the key slowly, still engrossed in the words. The broken tip of a pen forced into the smooth golden metal surface. A small sharp knife. She focused reluctantly on the contents of the mailbox: bills and advertisements. It was Monday and she hadn't checked the mail on Saturday, so the box was full. She pulled them out slowly, and closed and locked the door all the while sounding out the words in her mouth, tasting FUCK.

"Shit," her boyfriend Eddie said on the phone that night. "Are you sure that's what it said? Jinny? You there?"

"Yeah. Couldn't miss it." She wished he had never left New York to take that job in Boston. They had first met in the airport six months ago, she on her way in and he on his way out. "Maybe it was someone in my building," she said, and mentally checked off those she knew. Raoul Jacques and Marie, the Haitian newlywed multimedia artists in 3C who left their TV on all night; old Italian Josie Della who rescued injured pigeons and looked at Jinny suspiciously; Mr. Swanson the white librarian who stood too close to her in the elevator and rode all the way up to her floor even though he lived on the second; the Sanchez family in 2F; the Smith-Joneses in 1B with the half-dozen pug dogs.

"Don't worry about it. Probably just random," he yawned. "Let's talk about it when I get there next weekend, okay?"

She pictured him lying there in his suit and tie, on the bed. Too tired to change. He was probably rubbing his eyes. "Did you just get home?" she asked.

"Yeah, ten minutes ago. Maybe it was someone who doesn't live there. Delivery people, your mailman, kids just messing around."

"I don't know." The hand holding the phone to her ear swelled, in waves.

"Jinny, listen, don't worry. Got me? How was your day otherwise?" He sounded as if he were on the edge of sleep.

"Okay. Long day, huh?"

"Yup," he paused. "A long day. . . . .Hey, what's the matter?"

"It's just there, you know. On my mailbox." She tried not to think about her hand.

"The super will replace it."

"I just—I mean, someone slashed a racial slur on my mailbox and you aren't upset?" Racial? There wasn't anything about Koreans or Asians in those two words: FUCK YOU. Why did she think this was racial?

"Why do you think it was racial?"

She pulled her blanket closer. "Isn't it?" She pinched her hand tentatively. It continued to expand.

"Not necessarily. Okay. I forget that you grew up in a small town. New York takes getting used to."

"Eddie, there was racism in Brookside. I had my share of kids calling me names when I was growing up."

"I'll bet you did. But it's different in the city."

True enough.

"Jin? I miss you."

She took a deep breath. He was right. She switched hands and made a fist with the one that had grown.

"I miss you too. I'm really tired, Eddie. I'll call you tomorrow?"

He yawned again. "Okay, Jin, goodnight."

She hung up the phone and waited for her hand to return to normal. In Brookside people weren't so blunt about their feelings. "Chink" and "Jap" became distant and hazy taunts from her childhood, like an ordeal that didn't have any value in being remembered. She became a young woman and from then on dealt with grown-ups. An adult white person in Brookside, New York, did not scream obscenities to a quiet Asian person. It was not polite. Regardless of what you thought of her; you could only inquire as to her origin and perhaps mention which city you visited in the armed forces or on vacation.

No one abided by such rules in the city. Over fifteen incidents in these past few months. She could remember them all. The African American caramel nut vendor who shouted after her, "Chink, go home," on deserted Lexington Avenue on an early Saturday morning to the white homeless Vietnam veteran who sat on his couch of plastic bags near her apartment building on Nineteenth Street and Second Avenue and knitted long orange yarn furiously with copper needles, screaming, "Stinkin' Gook! You, I'm talking to you, you took my job!" when she skitted by.

And the men in business suits were just as bad. Pushing her out of their way during a rainstorm, accosting her in the grocery store, like that man last week. Grabbing her arm, no less. "*Konnichi wa?*" She had ignored it the first time she heard it.

Then again. "*Konnichi wa*? No? Not Japanese? How about *shea shea*?"

She turned. A white man in a gray pinstripe suit and gold-rimmed glasses beamed at her. "No? Oh, I got it." He slapped his forehead. "Korean, right? Listen to this: *Ahnyounghahsehyo?* Not bad, huh?"

She shook her head. He touched her arm. "I was right, wasn't I?" She longed to say, "Look at yourself? How would you like it if someone grabbed your wife's arm, your mother's arm? Tested her knowledge of Swedish, German, whatever?"

"Not bad," she said, and turned her attention to the cashier. Calm down, Jinny.

He poked her shoulder. "You know, I work on a law journal and I wonder if you could give me your opinion on the politics over there?"

Think, think, what could she say to get rid of him politely. But she never could think of the right thing. So began the bubble. That's what she used to imagine when people asked her in Brookside: How big and protective her bubble body was. Only now the bubble began whenever it wanted.

"Politics in Korea?" she said.

"Yes. What do you think?"

Jinny handed the cashier her discount card, watched the card slide over the electronic eye. Red, red, then green. The register blipped.

"My family left Korea when I was really young," she explained. She felt her bubble body inflate.

He leaned back. "I think you should know what's what over there all the same, if you pardon my opinion."

Sheesh. Jinny's heart was pounding. This guy was not going away. Even with that. Even with her selling her family history when he hadn't said anything about his. A little more and her bubble feet would leave the ground and she would float. And still he wouldn't go away. "I'm in a hurry," she said, but she couldn't get enough volume into her voice to make it sound like a reprimand or a brush-off.

"Just trying to be friendly," he shrugged. The cashier nodded sympathetically at him. Someone in the back of the line said, "Amen."

Jinny barely squeezed her body through the aisle and out the automatic doors. She walked as quickly as she could, hoping the air would escape.

The next morning the Sanchez boys, ages twelve and thirteen, rode the elevator down with her. Manny said, "Hi, Jinny," and Mikey said, "Hi, Ching Chong," and giggled before his brother punched him in the arm. "Stop being a jerk," Manny said.

"I'm not. She knows I'm fooling," Mikey protested.

She smiled and rolled her eyes to ease the tension, but her knees sagged a little. When they reached the lobby, she said, "Hope it doesn't rain," and held up her closed umbrella. Summer vacation had just begun for them. "Yeah, right," Manny said. "Bye."

She glanced at her mailbox after they left. It looked the same. She swallowed the lump in her throat and headed for the basement to drop off her garbage bag. Ever since she had moved to the city, she felt assaulted by noise and colors and movement, so fast, so abundant, she could hardly contain it all in her head. Just to get through the day, she knew she drifted about in a protective haze. But here it was now, next to the row of plastic bins, she saw the crushed pizza box from the weekend. And suddenly the mailbox made sense.

The memory of the man came back to her. Sure, she had ordered pizza on Friday because Eddie was driving in and she had gotten home late from work. At eight o'clock he had buzzed. She had hit the button to release the front door, then opened her apartment door to wait for the elevator to retrieve him. He had seemed pleasant enough at first. A young white man with prematurely gray hair and white apron over his white baking suit. But as he approached, she felt uneasy. His eyes were creeping from her shoeless stockinged feet to the top of her five-foot frame. He took his time, saying hello, setting his red thermal bag on the floor, unzipping it and handing her the hot cardboard box leisurely.

He told her the total was $12.50. All she had was twenty, which in the past had been fine. That night it wasn't. All he had were a couple of dollar bills and fifty cents. He shrugged at her.

"I could run back and get you change," he sneered. Strong word? No, he sneered. It was the only word for the way he lounged there in her doorway, holding on to one tip of her twenty while she held on to the other. He was willing to take it as though she would give him the fattest tip of his life. Or maybe not. Maybe other Asian customers didn't know English or felt threatened enough to get rid of him with that twenty as quickly as possible. She looked back at the pizza settled on her table. It wasn't feasible to let him carry that pizza all the way back to the restaurant and she was afraid he would sabotage it somehow because she wouldn't let him take her twenty right now the way he wanted her to so he could pocket the entire change. She pictured the pepperoni substituted with rat meat or worse, he would take a rat and put it right in the box to surprise her. She had heard stories. Her arm tingled.

"Look, you know where I work," he said.

"Why don't you get the change and I'll wait here," she answered, tugging at the bill.

"I can't do that. Give me back the pie then, and we'll do it the hard way." He snapped his gum and looked at her steadily, narrowing his eyes.

She felt stupid. Still, she plunged ahead. Holding her arm steady.

"I don't mean to suggest I don't trust you, it's just that I've heard about people who don't get their change back so I'm just trying to come up with another solution."

That sounded good. Fair and proper and logical. Defensive, too.

"Whatever you want, honey." He tapped the top of the door frame with a Bic pen. She let go of the money.

"All right, go ahead, go," she answered. And felt defeated.

After he left, she worried. She worried for the next thirty minutes—after Eddie arrived and ate a piece of pizza and urged her to eat. He was starved, he said. Just seeing his face and folding herself into his arms took her mind off her skin expanding.

She had to mention that the delivery man was coming back. He'd wonder about it when the buzzer rang. She worried that he'd ask her if she had let the delivery man take the twenty or if she had sent him away empty-handed. He didn't even ask for details. He seemed to assume that she would never let anyone leave with her money. She was relieved.

When the buzzer sounded again, she answered it and then waited. He saw her in the hallway and smirked as he handed her the change.

"All there?"

"Thanks a lot," she said, doing her best to appear calm and friendly as she held out two dollars to him as a tip. As much as it killed her.

Slowly, he reached for the bills, watching her reaction. Inwardly, she cringed, then as he turned and headed for the elevator she shut the door and listened. After a long pause, the elevator began its descent. She waited another minute before bolting the door and chaining it. She didn't want him to hear all that dead-bolting while he stood in the hallway. He might think it was to protect her from him. Defensive again. So why should she care what he thought? You don't just trust anybody. Especially a stranger who delivers food. Do you?

Race. She walked to her subway stop slowly. Neither she nor Eddie had noticed the mailbox all weekend. Did that white-haired white man go maliciously for his pocket knife or pen and deface her mailbox once he reached the lobby? Did he know she lived alone? Maybe it was nonchalantly done; maybe he was a compulsive defacer of property. It didn't make FUCK YOU any less shocking. She buttoned her jacket to give her hands something to do.

The next day Jinny's friend Sunnah agreed that the pizza man had done it. "Probably. People here are nuts. Stark raving," she said over lunch. "Yesterday, someone pushed me into the middle of the street. Almost got hit by a cab."

Jinny looked at her in shock. "Are you okay?"

"Fine, luckily. So weird. I should have been on the lookout. I usually am. I was thinking about my deadline, you know. Just trying to get back to the office when I feel this hand on my back and wham—my feet are trying to get back under me and I'm in the street. Happened so fast."

"Did you see who did it?"

"Nope."

"Sheesh. That's awful." It was a marvel. Sunnah was the toughest, meanest-looking Asian woman Jinny knew. The expression that came over her face when she stepped outside made you wince if you thought you were friends and didn't know better.

"Do you think it's because we're Asian?" Jinny ventured.

"I don't know. Maybe. Then again, maybe someone thought I brushed past them or maybe they just had a bad day and felt like it, or maybe, and I like to chalk it up to this: they're just crazy. And they'd do it to anybody who lets them."

Did she let him do it to her? She let it sink in. "I guess so."

"Plus, it's not only about being Asian. Sometimes it's other Asians."

This was news. Or was it? Something familiar flapped in the corner of her memory.

"What do you mean?"

"You know, like when I go cover a story in Chinatown." Sunnah shuffled her deck of napkins. "Sometimes I don't feel safe. Like last year when I was covering the Hirohito story and there were protests in Chinatown. Just because of what that damn emperor did to the Chinese I thought they'd mob me as part of their protest because they thought I was Japanese."

Jinny nodded, but she didn't see how people made those distinctions. She couldn't tell until she heard the last name. "I get it in restaurants all the time," Sunnah continued. "In Japanese restaurants they're nice to me until they learn I can't speak any Japanese. In Chinese restaurants I get the cold shoulder."

"Really, in every restaurant?"

Sunnah nodded.

Jinny shook her head. "I don't see it."

"Anyway, the thing to do is figure out how to deal with it. I think it's important to deal with shit right on the spot."

"Yeah, I guess so. Sunnah, have you ever seen that homeless guy on my street?" she asked.

"On Second Avenue?"

"Yeah."

"The homeless vet who knits?"

"That's him."

Sunnah waved a hand, dismissing him. "He's pathetic. Plus he's too fat to be homeless."

"But did he ever say anything to you?"

"He says stuff to everybody, but if you mean that gook shit, I told him to fuck off. I'd like to see him try that shit on some big Asian dude. Bet he wouldn't dare." She laughed.

"Oh, sheesh." She laughed with her, picturing it.

Sunnah laughed even harder. "Shit, Jinny. I've been meaning to tell you this. It's either 'Jeez' as in 'Jesus' or 'shit,' not 'sheesh'. What's 'sheesh'? Say it. Try 'shit'!"

Did it matter? Did saying shit protect you? Jinny rolled her eyes.

"You have INNOCENCE emblazoned on your head, girl." Sunnah continued to laugh.

She thought about Sunnah's words on the way home. Innocence, shit, not sheesh, New York, not Brookside, crazy. Just crazy. She remembered something else too. Maybe Sunnah was right. Maybe there was someone else who wanted to send her a message.

On Sunday, she had opened her door abruptly when a menu had slid underneath. An extremely thin Asian man with a tuft of black hair, wearing a short-sleeved brown shirt and gray trousers, crouched at the foot of her door. The lines in his face as he looked up, startled, made him as old as her father. Usually, she felt connected to Asians in the city, giving them directions or watching them ruffle their children's hair with a recollection of her own parents. But at that moment, she felt frightened.

"I wish—" she began.

He narrowed his eyes and scowled at her as he stood up. He left the menu on the ground. She pointed to it and began again, "I wish you wouldn't do that. You see, I've got enough Chinese food menus already and I really wish you wouldn't."

He brushed off his pants and fanned the pink menus in his hand. "You Japanese? You want to order?" he said.

"No. No more menus," she repeated. "I know it's your job, but please, don't leave your menus here." But not loud or firm enough to change his mind. He ignored her and moved on to her neighbor's door. She followed him down the hall, saying she would call the police, and then felt abruptly foolish. He looked at her with disdain. She flinched. You are nothing. She returned to her apartment and closed the door.

She woke up with dread on Wednesday morning. She'd have to call her landlord and explain about the mailbox. He'd take out the cost of replacing the door from her security deposit. She had also overslept, which made her angry at herself for no reason she could fathom. At the elevator she scolded herself for not taking the stairs as the elevator ascended all the way from the ground floor. She was late, didn't she get it? Hurry. But then the elevator was there and there was a part of her that protested. Delivery goons and kids and homeless vets and what was wrong with 'sheesh'? Everything she did was wrong. She didn't belong here. She wanted to go back to Brookside.

She stepped in and punched 1. Hurrying wouldn't make a difference. Why should she hurry? What difference did ten minutes make? They didn't pay her enough at the magazine. They took advantage of her like everyone else. Would they fire her?

She looked up at the lights. She looked again. JAP. JAP—as in Japanese? On either side of the numbers for the floors, someone had scratched: JAP. It was happening. JAP, for her, hate and racial slur for her. Had it been there yesterday when she rode down with the kids? Why hadn't she noticed it when she got back last night? What did it mean? She stomped her feet and flexed her hands.

The elevator door opened abruptly. Instead of stepping into the foyer she stood there, astonished. The Chinese man from the restaurant stood in front of her. His eyes met hers. "You, Jap."

She blinked hard. "What have I ever done to you?" she asked, but he had vanished. She thought about running upstairs and crawling into bed. I could go home, she thought. I could quit my pitiful job and run back home where they didn't write obscenities on you as they did in the city. Where people hid their racism beneath polite smiles and inquiries. Where they didn't touch your arm, or deface your property, or claim you took their jobs. At least not yet in her town. She stomped again.

"Hi, Jinny," Manny said, running down the stairs. He flashed such a beautiful smile. She hoped he didn't notice her watery eyes.

"Hey, Manny. Did you see a man standing here just a minute ago?" She felt silly, but it was worth a try.

"Nope."

"No one ran down the stairs ahead of you?"

"Nope. Are you okay?" He was throwing his glove lightly up into the air and smiling gently. Wait until he grows up and breaks a few hundred hearts.

"More baseball today, huh?" She rubbed her palms together. No air. She would squeeze the bubbles out.

"Yep. Got a game. You should come watch sometime. On the Lawn in the park."

"Thanks, sometime I will." And she meant it. A game of baseball seemed blissfully safe, with rules and umpires, and practice. Don't be a baby, Jin. Don't cry. Go to work. When he held the door for her, she followed him outside.

The sun shone so brightly they raised their hands to shield their eyes. Seventy-five degrees. Low humidity. Perfect. At the traffic light on Park Avenue, a white fruit vendor offered them plums and smiled even when they refused.

It was when Manny raised a hand good-bye as the light changed and stepped off the curb that she saw the shaft of sunlight on aluminum ten yards beyond him. Then its origin: a cyclist shot out between two yellow cabs, plowing straight for the boy. Didn't matter what the red light said. Her heart stopped, then flushed blood into her face.

"Watch out," she shouted, reaching to pull him out of the path even though he was beyond her grasp. But his head turned at the sound of her voice and he lurched backward. The messenger swerved, twisted his masked face and hissed, "Fucking get out of the way, little shit."

In that instant, Jinny wanted to say: Manny, Don't listen. But she didn't get the chance. He was already back in the street, shrugging a shoulder back in step, hardly skipping a beat; continuing on his way, waving her back to the curb. He stopped in the middle to casually raise his middle finger at the cyclist's hunched form retreating down the avenue. That was all.

Once on the opposite curb, he gave her the "okay" sign, then hitched his pants up and strolled into the crowd. She had to shake her head. The flush ran corkscrewing down her arms.

A black limousine stopped beyond the crosswalk. How dare these people on bikes and in cars think they owned the road like this? How dare they hurtle at some ungodly speed and nearly hit a little kid; Manny was just a kid. And then to turn around and throw curses at him that way. It was fucked; she could hear what Sunnah might say.

She glared at the limo. It was fucked that this limousine driver could sit smack in the middle of people trying to get to work and expect everyone to walk around him, like a stone, a huge, fat stone in the middle of her river, Manny's river, anyone just trying to get across the fucking street. She sucked air through her teeth and let it out in a rush. Pound out those bubbles, Jin. Get out.

She couldn't let assholes get away with this. This was it. End of the line. No more. She had almost cleared the taillight of the car when she reached out her hand and beat on the trunk twice.

"Fucking cunt!"

Jinny stopped short. What the fuck was that? Cunt? That was disgusting. Cunt? She stared at the limo driver, a white guy with Ray-Bans on the tip of his nose getting a look at her with his eyes over the top of his sunglasses.

Let him look. Take a good look. "Fuckin' dick!" she shouted. Blood rushed to her chest and fell into a dead pit there. She waited. Nothing happened. He didn't open his door, jump out and pummel her. She didn't expand. Her heart let the blood in. She breathed.

He turned the wheel and rolled along beside her, heading south on Park Avenue, the congestion caused by other cars preventing him from going any faster. "Jap bitch!" he slung.

Heat ran into her belly, down through her legs. Bubbles popped open. She felt a surge of energy. Looked him dead in the eye. Oh yeah? It wasn't hard throwing things back at people. She strode along, screamed, "Oh yeah? You're an asshole!"

He smirked, leaned over, "Com'ere and suck on this—"

Fucking asshole, smug and so sure of himself. His arm out the window. "Sure, mother-fucker!" she said. And then her legs were carrying her directly toward him and she was spitting through his open window.

In the next instant she was off, quickly walking through the crowd. Behind her a stream of obscenities. She laughed out loud. The heat was gone and she felt like she did when she was a child hitting her running stride on the last straightaway toward home. She was ready. Let him come. Let them all come.

Yumi Heo

Yumi Heo, born and raised in Korea, now lives in White Plains, N.Y. She has written and illustrated picture books including *One Afternoon, The Green Frogs* and *Father's Rubber Shoes*. In *The Rabbit Judgement* written by Suzanna Crowder Han and Illustrated by Heo, a popular Korean folktale about justice and morality is retold. A man walking through the forest hears cries for help coming from deep within a pit into which a tiger has fallen. Although the man fears the tiger will eat him, the animal's pleas are so pitiful that he rescues him. Once out of the pit the ungrateful tiger declares he will eat the man after all. A small but clever rabbit saves the man from his terrible fate.

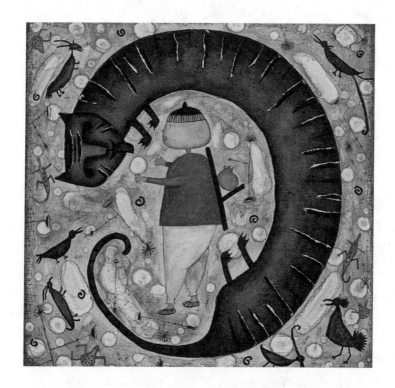

Edward Lin

I hate the slick Asian magazines that suck up to the model minority stereotype: rich, successful people who only want fashion and sex. This story is from the realm of the tired, poor and huddled masses yearning to breathe free.

Biography

Edward Lin was born in Howard Beach, Queens, and was educated in various disciplines at Columbia. He edits business news for a living and has been published in *The Asian Pacific American Journal*. He is a member of Peeling the Banana, a New York-based performance group.

The Last Picture Show in Chinatown

For years, I walked by the the Music Palace's ticket window, mummified in cellophane with the sign saying INCLUDES ENGLISH SUBTITLES.

There were a number of things that kept me away from the last movie theater in Chinatown.

I was afraid of how scummy it had to be inside. You know how raunchy restaurant bathrooms are, and they're subject to health inspections.

There were sleazy posters on the six glass panes of the front doors of the theater, covering the upper bodies of the people in the lobby. Gratuitous tits-and-ass shots that sometimes weren't even in the movie. The looks in the women's eyes were more like "Geet ovah 'ere!" than "Come hither." Those pictures and the view of men's legs in ugly polyester trousers crossed or pacing in the lobby made the Music Palace look like a complex of beat-off booths.

There was also the stigma of going in to see a movie alone, because you wouldn't want to go there with friends and God forbid certainly not with a date. It looked as classy as hanging out in a subway stop.

The first time I went into the theater, it was with my girlfriend at the time, around the fall of 1995. We had pretty much done twice everything there was to do in the city, and a lull had set in on us earlier that day. Not much talking over lunch at the Vietnamese place and the food was sitting in my stomach like an old smear of toothpaste stuck on the side of the sink. It was one of those days when all you really want is to go home and doze, but you stay out because of some warped sense of obligation to the other person.

We went up the Bowery, passing by the Music Palace, about two blocks away from the D train stop at Grand.

The north side of the theater has an old mural on it. You can see gamblers, Chinese immigrants, Africans being brought to the United States as slaves and a big dragon that encircles the entire work. The mural had been defaced a bit by kids tagging the wall but you still get the general picture. We were standing there looking at it when something seized me. I pulled her arm and swung open the door to the theater. The glass was battle-scarred with tape scraps from years of weekly poster changes.

It cost six dollars each to get in, and they showed two features continuously. Two movies for six bucks, how bad could it be? That week, the posters looked more like goofy comedies than smut.

The ticket agent was a very short man, not quite a midget, who I had seen around Chinatown in a fake policeman's outfit, complete with toy billy club, TV-dinner tin badge and a blue cap that was probably stamped with IRREGULAR on the inside. He looked about forty years old and had scraggly black hair poking out of his hat. The guy should have been charged with parodying a cop rather than impersonating one. He walked around Chinatown on a beat marked out with imaginary dashes, getting calls over his walkie-talkie from some twisted precinct in his mind. I never knew what he really did until that day. After he took our tickets, his hands shot back to the butt of his club.

The lobby floor was covered with peel-off instant adhesive kitchen tile squares, now scuffed and cracked and broken. Where pieces were missing, I could see the original ceramic tile. I gave only a cursory look at the sparse snack stand, since we had some pastries from my favorite bakery on Mott and some herbal tea drink boxes. We went upstairs to the balcony and plopped into two sets of springs.

I can't remember the title of the movie we saw, but it was completely funny. This woman and her father conspire to kill this rich guy but then the rich guy gets hit on the head and forgets who he is before they can do him in. A few years later, the woman and her father run into the former rich guy, who now begs in the street, still mentally impaired. The rich guy's family had taken over his fortune and booted him out.

The woman and her father take pity on the former rich guy and clean him up. Later, they find that he's eligible for a sizable inheritance, but he has to go through a game show setup to prove he's mentally capable of claiming it. The recurring motif is that the former rich guy's name was Ford, but everyone now calls him Fool. If you ever see this movie, you'll realize that there is no shorter way to summarize it. We thought it was a riot.

I nuzzled her ear and we smooched a little bit. We didn't stay for the second movie. A few months later, we broke up. That event was not related to the movie or the theater.

I started going to the Music Palace alone after that. At first, I sat upstairs because the bathroom was closer and in the back. I moved downstairs because I grew uncomfortable with the way the whole structure shook slightly when heavier men, including me, trudged through the aisles.

The only problem with the lower level was the location of the bathroom. You have to practically walk in front of the movie screen to get there. I couldn't shake the feeling of embarrassment when the light played on my face on my way to the john. There's a certain amount of anonymity you expect in New York City. You don't want to be seen by people, least of all other men, in the Music Palace.

The men's room on the balcony was small and strictly pedestrian but the one on the lower level was as haunted as that Amityville house. You expected to hear this voice growl, "Get out!"

The urinals are the oldest I've ever seen. They start at eye level and run all the way to the floor, tall, enigmatic monoliths to piss in. They looked big enough to bury a large dog in. Akitas or something. There were chunks of soap in the drain because the water from the flush thins out and can't take away the smell. And I've never had the courage to look inside one of the toilet stalls.

There's this ride at Disneyland where you're going through a haunted house and at one point you face this mirror, seeing ghostly apparitions on either side of you. That's what washing up in the Music Palace's bathroom is like. The flickering fluorescent lights give the old men around you a sickly blue-green pallor. You look into the mirror at the sink and see these tired, discolored faces looking vacantly back.

The best thing to do is keep your head down, piss, run cold water over your hands and get the hell out, wiping your fingers on your jeans before you rejoin the corps of lost men in the dark.

About 99 percent of the people who came to the theater were men. There were two types of these men. Most were in their forties to fifties but there were also groups of teenagers in packs of three. The men and boys all smoked like hell. The older men sat alone. In a theater with a capacity for about fourhundred but audiences of about thirty, they could have a whole row to themselves. Their heads looked like lopsided grave markers in the moonlight. The only sound from them was a light crunching when they cracked watermelon seeds or nuts.

The teenagers were usually quiet until their beepers went off and they made calls on their cellular phones. It didn't matter to me since I read subtitles and don't understand a lick of spoken Cantonese—movie dialogue or talking shit into a cell phone.

I was particularly aware of body language, though—with the recent loss of my love connection, it was magnified beyond exaggeration.

Couples in the movie didn't just hold hands—they melded. They didn't just kiss—they breathed life into each other's souls. They didn't just have sex—they tore down the ceiling.

The first time my new girlfriend and I went to the Music Palace, the first movie was some sappy love thing. She leaned over and whispered to me that she was going to stay at her place that night, which meant, "You're sleeping by yourself."

Then the second movie was this off-the-wall psycho sex killer flick. It was nuts! This fiend who looked like a heavy metal singer dragged retarded young women upstairs by the ankles so their heads banged on each step of the stairway until he reached the rooftop, where he raped them and broke their necks. There was a constant stream of blood flowing to the bottom of the screen. My girlfriend held my hand tighter and tighter. I was so freaked out, my feet were back-pedaling on the sticky floor, trying to get away. We stayed together that night.

We were a couple for a year and went to the Music Palace about a dozen times. The double features we saw were almost always comedies packaged with thrillers. One of the coming attractions was *Six Devil Women*. Tough-looking cookies in short skirts brandishing machetes. We said we were going to see it and then our timing was off and we missed it. Our relationship was running on its last reel. I ended up seeing it by myself a few months later.

These days, I go there alone, again. I cultivate my solitude, sitting in my own row, putting my knees up and cracking the bones in my neck.

Sometimes I worry that I'll end up like one of the ghouls in the men's room, my face trapped forever in the metal frame of the mirror.

Then they'll show a totally amusing movie, and I forget myself and laugh.

Luis Cabalquinto

When I first came to the U.S. in '68, there were two exciting cities between which I could choose as the place for me to settle in. Thirty years later, I'm still congratulating myself for picking New York City.

Biography

Luis Cabalquinto retired early from his job at Pfizer International to devote more of his time to writing poetry and fiction. His literary work has appeared in numerous publications, including *The American Poetry Review, Prairie Schooner* and *International Quarterly.* Aside from English, he writes in two Philippine languages, Tagalog and Bicolano. He resides in New York City but spends part of each year in his birthplace, Magarao, in the Philippines, managing an orchid garden and a rice farm—as well as writing.

Alignment

It happened again this afternoon
While watching a Wertmuller movie
In the East Village
This alignment that comes
Like a magnet's work on iron filings
When most things of the mind
As well as of the body are turned
Toward the one direction
Where all must come from
And where all must one day begin
Again: it comes unsummoned, a shift
Now familiar, a quick
Turning over of an event.
It comes as a small wind in Central Park,
The noontime hammering heard in a Philippine village.
It is an afternoon walk on a rain-wet street in Agra,
Neon lights seen from a hotel at midnight in Tokyo.
It came once from the bend of a woman's body in Rome,
From a late flamenco show in Barcelona.
Also it came on the Monterey road
Riding the Greyhound from San Francisco—
And, again, in the odd light of an old man's eye
Photographed in New Mexico.
When it happens a strong grip takes over
In the body: the head becomes light.
The hairs stand on end, the pores open
And currents run down to the palms and feet:
Aware at this moment of a new knowledge
That makes the old truths untrue.
Still, each time this happens,
The clarity lasts only seconds:
Before full possession can take place
Something changes the air, reworks the body:
The mind is dislodged, recalled
To an accustomed disorder.

The Body-on-Ice Meditations

1

Let's begin by saying that this snow-clad Saturday
can be seen in all its fine guises before it slowly
melts into something unsettling and different,
when the body takes the mind out and tosses it
to these new troughs of resonance, until something
changes into something you remember watching over
and over on public television or reading, like the
white-robed rampage of mourners in a foreign city.

2

For only the second time this winter it snowed thickly,
white flakes serenely falling, like the feral remains
of discontinued leopard fights in the sky, a Saturday
night celestial special from entities neatly passing off
as gods. But of course you have your new earth smarts.
It takes more than just shreddings of an astral origin
to get you suckered in, to be drafted like the others
into a foreign legion of undocumented ice bearers.

3

To stretch some more the snowbound metaphor:
instead of black, everything this morning wears
a shroud of ceramic white, like costly ivory combs
or Spanish mantillas for the beautiful or young,
as your mother said she wore more than once
for Saturday night *rigodons* at the town plaza,
before the tall Americans arrived, when soon after
everybody started humming "White Christmas,"
putting up false pine trees in their polished *salas*
all hung up with tinfoil and stretched cotton balls
to come close to snow and cold frosted windows.

4

Or maybe it will be more accurate to relate
that the snowbound Saturday view before us
brings back the immaculate Sisters of Charity nuns
at our First Communion, shepherding their white-
vested charges, meek and milling into the vast
maw of the great Naga Cathedral with its heavy
double doors, dark bat-festooned ceilings and felt-
upholstered pews. But now we are the old and
sin-seasoned parishioners who approach, still
in awe, at great personal risk of final redemption.

Satori: June 8, 1996

I let the hours go
Until it is too late
To make it to the writers' Village
      beer party I've been invited to.

Instead, I amble down to the oval park,
      kick my shoes off,
And watch the three tall fountains
      under the trees.

All around me the pigeons do
      their business.
I'm taken by their comic loops. I listen
      to their funny noises
As they hunt for thrown bread scraps.

Small, bird-smart and swift,
The brown sparrows dart down
      from the oaks, filching the food
      bits from right under the doves' beaks,

Then fly back to the branches to feed
            at their leisure.

On the broad grassy lawn, the black
            and gray squirrels
Paw the ground to get to the nuts
            they missed in the long winter
            because of record drifts of snow—
Oak nuts they gathered and buried in the fall.

The blue jays, oddly mute for a change,
Perch, pondering, on the black-painted
            wrought-iron fences,
As if amused by the raucous children's
Games in the crowded playground.

The adults stroll about, their strides slowed
Down by the cool darkening afternoon.
In this rare oasis of a park in
            the middle of Manhattan
There's hardly anything to remind us
            of the city.

Our bodies are stopped, thoughts
            green and rural—
As when the voice takes hold of me:

        "Simplicity,
        Serenity,
            Harmony. These are now
Given to you. Use them
To dismantle your life."

Henry Chang

Biography

Henry Chang has been published in *Yellow Pearl*, *Bridge* and most recently in *On a Bed of Rice*. He lives in New York City.

Running Dogs

The rain came down in thick sheets, rattled the stairwell windows as Jack climbed with leaden legs the five flights of tenement squalor.

Pa lived here his forty-nine years of Chinatown life. A dead dog, the Chinese numbers meant, forty-nine. Say gow.

Time and again Jack had asked Pa to move. Uptown. Crosstown. Queens, maybe. A decent apartment they could rent somewhere, where the winter freeze didn't sneak in through the windows, where the wet dank misery of changing seasons didn't settle on the bedcovers. Where vermin didn't feast on the kitchen table, in the toilet, under the pillow.

Pa wouldn't hear of it, got mad each time Jack brought it up. Where would he get his Chinese vegetables? His Chinese newspapers? Where would he find his old cronies to gossip with, keep track of who died, who lost at the track? All the important things.

They trapped themselves, the old bachelors, wrapping themselves in their fierce Chineseness, finding pride in their disdain for American ways. Jack's ways. Father and son at cross-cultural odds, their lives a clash.

The keys were old and tarnished, the metal edges worn smooth and rounded from a hundred thousand turns. The lock itself was older than the keys, older than the grime in the hallway.

Jack twisted the key and heard the bolt open smoothly, effortlessly. He pushed open the creaking door and stepped inside Pa's world, his own past.

Nothing had changed. He wondered why he even thought things might have. Under the dim lifeless circle of fluorescent light spreading along the torn gray ceiling, everything looked the same.

He stared at the scuffed and dented linoleum floor, slipped out a silver flask and took a deep swallow. The black knapsack swung down to the floor.

He crossed the stillness of the room to Pa's bed, pulled plastic packets of photographs from the bedside table, saw they were thick with dust except for where fingerprints had touched down more recently and crushed across clear lines in search of memories.

How soon at the end do we grope for our past?

When he opened the albums, the fingerprints led him to streaked and faded black and white photographs of himself as a child, then pictures of Ma, sometime in the 1940s, her hair shiny and combed back away from eyebrows perfectly curved and sharp as razors, her mouth of slightly opened and dark lips smiling out teeth framed in gold. She couldn't have been more than nineteen, an arranged bride, with almond eyes showing small lights of hope, resignation.

And then there was the picture of himself with Pa, taken in the Tofu King, it had to be a decade ago, by the front counter with the dao foo and the flat sheets of white noodle.

Jack was never the filial son, but he struggled to maintain the truncated sense of family he had with Pa, who, in the few hours he was home from the laundry or the restaurant, was full of criticism or complaint, the smell of whiskey on his words.

Other times, around holidays, Pa was more melancholy, but managed a smile and brought home gifts for his son, the jook sing, the American-born, the empty piece of bamboo.

Jack flipped the cellophane pages, came across yellowed prints of Pa in the laundry, with Grandpa, who went back to China, beside him.

He took another swallow, then the slide of fingers through dust came to a curled print of himself, in the poolroom, in between Tat Louie and Wing Lee, all mugging for the shot.

Now, sitting on the crumpled bed of his father, Jack was unable to find the peace of mind he needed. It wasn't the neon lights from the Lee Luck restaurant sign that intruded colors into the darkened room. It wasn't the clawing sound of rat feet scratching for entry somewhere along the baseboards, near the radiators. And it wasn't the smells of lop cheung and hom yee leached into the walls, becoming one with the cracked and peeling green paint after thirty years now making time stand still.

Somewhere down the stairs across the hall, he could hear the vague singsong of Chinese opera and, closer, the ratatat action of Hong Kong videotapes.

Decades of Chinese smells and sounds hung so thick he could almost touch them, settling on him this feeling of his father's presence. It wasn't him in the bed after all. It was his father's presence mixed with the spirit of his father's son—himself—enveloped by the ghosts of his father's bachelor apartment, ghosts of his young man pasts.

Jack felt the thirst grabbing in his throat and emptied the flask. Pulling the pictures from the packet, he slipped them inside his vest pocket and tossed the rest into the empty Seagram's carton on the floor.

When his head hit the pillow the memories came flooding back to him, then the alcohol reached his brain and rolled him back a decade and four.

It was a nightmare.

The three of them, Tat, Wing and himself, are racing across rooftops, leaping the spaces between buildings. Tat is throwing stones at windows as they run, three teenagers shrieking juvenile laughter, trailing curses from inside the tenement apartments.

They are clambering down a fire escape, dropping to a courtyard below.

Wing is shouting, "Race! Last one out sucks lop cheung!"

They are sprinting through a back alley, jumping cinderblock partitions, dashing for a connecting tunnel. The other end of the tunnel leads out to a side street, and they never see the gang of Wah Yings until Wing crashes headlong into the leader.

He cuffs Wing with a backhand punch, snatches a gold chain off his neck. Wing lunges for the chain and the nasty boys break out with knives. They're flipping the chain from one to another, taunting Wing. Tat steps sideways, launches a side kick into the leader's groin, and suddenly everybody's screaming, cursing.

The Ying leader swings his switchblade around, turns up a short punch that blunts Wing's desperate charge. Wing lurches back, then charges again, his eyes white now.

There is a crashing black and white across Jack's forehead, gash blood running into his eye, as he watches Wing dropped by a chopping right hand, the color of wine suddenly spreading across his white T-shirt. Tat is screaming, and the Yings are beating the shit out of him.

Then everything is black, filled with the wails of family overcome with grief. Racks of flowers fail to brighten the room cloaked in the choke of incense and death.

Wing is lying in the casket and mourners are bowing, bowing, bowing and burning death money. Tat is speechless and Jack watches him flee the funeral parlor as Wing's mother explodes with grief.

It was the sound of gunfire that awoke him, screaming and shooting in the connecting back alley that led out to Mott Street. In the dark of Pa's apartment he could not tell what time it was, only that it was still black out. More gunshots and screaming. He groped for his Colt Special, found it and crept out onto the stairwell landing.

From the hallway window he could see shadows and figures darting through the alleyway. He slapped out the hallway bulb with the gun barrel, crouched to observe the action below. But in another instant it was quiet again. When he climbed down the fire escape into the alleyway, they were all gone, only a few spent shell casings on the ground and the burnt smell of gunpowder in the dark air. No bodies, and too dark to see if there was any bloodshed. He tried to shake the grogginess from his head, his adrenaline rush subsiding now, just a ferric taste in his mouth.

Back in Pa's apartment he sat upright on the bed and closed his eyes. The sleep didn't return and he reached for the flask and tilted it, but it barely wet his lips. He picked up the gourd, shook it, refilled the flask with mao tai. Then he found the keys to his Fury and went back out into the deadness of night.

Erna Hernandez

Biography

Erna Hernandez is a Barnard graduate perpetually in search of time to write creatively.
Born and raised in New York, going "home" to the Philippines as often as possible, she has
been published in Columbia University's *Asian Journal* and is part of Arkipelago, a progressive New York-based Filipino cultural organization.

Tsismis

Have you eaten yet?

No, I just arrived.

The food smells delicious—I wonder if it's any good . . .

Where is she, Nita's daughter?

Doon, see she's talking to her Lola.

Smile.

Oh . . . Lola Cruz, Lola Cruz, *kamusta na ho?*

I'm surprised she invited so many people just to see her granddaughter.

Ang sarap!

Aaah, the food's okay.

You know what I'm thinking, though . . .

Uh-huh . . . why is she here?

Yeah, *ba't siya na'n dito sa Pilipinas?*

Don't Amerikanos have school 'til May?

I think so, *na*-kick out *ba siya?* I thought she was a scholar?

That's what they say . . . Did she break the law?

Maybe she's hiding out here? Did she have to leave the States?

I can't believe her parents would let her come by herself. She's only nineteen! How long is she staying?

And why was she in a hospital?

Ewan, God only knows!

Is she pregnant? Did she get an abortion?

Nag-attempt suicide *kaya siya?*

Did someone try to kill her?

Look at her. My god, she's gained so much weight! *Ang taba!* When was she last here?

Siguro she was only fifteen when she last came here.

What is that? Lipstick?!

It's Sunday *pa naman.* Thick and red, too! *'Ka hiya!*

What's that in her hair? Did she dye it?

It looks like blue streaks.

Yaaaaks! *'Ka diri!*

How inappropriate *naman.*

I wonder what her Lola is thinking.

How could she talk to her with a straight face?

When did she arrive?

I think she arrived last Thursday. From L.A. ba?.

New York.

You know how crazy those New Yorkers can get. I know these things—I've seen *Die Hard 3*! It must have been *mga itim*.

Believe me, I know—I saw *Menace II Society* and *Boyz N the Hood*.

Wasn't that in L.A.?

Oh, but they're all the same. That's why the crime rate is so high in New York. They're all criminals. You know how crazy those Amerikanos are, especially *mga itim*.

They're all crazy—trying to kill people for no reason at all. I've seen it on *NYPD Blue* every Tuesday. 'Day, I have Sky Cable Manila.

At least here, it's for the money.

Look at her . . .

Why is she wearing all black?

It's so hot!

She should be wearing lighter colors.

Better yet, brighter colors. God, don't these people have aircon?

Why the dark colors?

Is she in mourning? That's IT isn't it? She must have had an abortion!

I don't think so . . .

No? Then WHAT? Why is she here in March?

Ewan . . . oh, but New York City? That's where all the rapists and psychopaths are.

Ay naku! Was she raped?

Why are they keeping it secret? I wouldn't tell anyone. How can we help her if I . . . uh, we don't know why she's here.

So smart, *sayang naman,* such an intelligent girl with her life wasting away, stopping her schooling.

Sayang ang studies *niya.* Is she going back to school?

Did she quit? She's too wild, *naman eh.*

Just like her mother. I bet that Nita lets her daughter stay out late. That's where the trouble begins, you know.

Did she have problems with her boyfriend? Did he rape her? Did he get her pregnant?

Itim siguro. You know all those black people, they're all drug addicts. They'll do anything when they're high.

I'm telling you, that girl is too wild. Maybe she was drunk and something happened.

Addict *ba?* Are they trying to keep her away from drugs?

With those streaks in her hair . . .

Those dark clothes . . .

And the dark red lipstick . . .

And big earrings . . .

She must be on drugs. *Susmariyosep,* she's not even trying to fit in. Why does she try to bring attention to herself?

Just like her mother. Hmmmph!

Did she fight with her mother?

You know that Nita Cruz. She was trouble *noong bata pa siya.* Too many friends when she was younger. That's why she never finished school.

I thought she stopped because she had to get a job . . .

Even if she was working, it was probably the barkada, you know—"friends"—that caused her to quit. You know that Cruz blood.

All the women in that family are too strong-willed and stubborn. That girl probably inherited it.

We should pray for her, you know. That's what I will do. I will pray a novena for her tonight and light a candle for Santo Niño.

The shame her parents must be feeling. *Ay naku!* An only child, too.

We should pray for Nita and Ramon for all the hell they must be going through.

You know, I heard Ramon had an affair.

Really, is that true?

I don't know for sure, but I heard Ligaya making gossip about Ramon and another woman.

Ligaya is such a gossip, such a tsismosa!

Yeah, she'll talk about anything. She won't care if its true or not. If it's *intriga,* she'll tell anyone.

Let's pray for her, too.

Oh, you know what I heard? Nita's daughter ran away.

You mean, Nita did not know her daughter left until she arrived here *sa Pilipinas?*

Well, you know their neighbors, the Ponces?

Uh-huh?

Yeah well, they heard a lot of loud crying and yelling last night. I think it was Nita's daughter screaming over the phone. Anyway, that's what Mrs. Ponce's maid told me today. If anyone asks, you didn't hear it from me. I don't want people thinking I'm *tsismosa,* not like Ligaya.

You know what I think *really* happened? I think Nita threw her out of their house in the States because her daughter was too hard-headed.

Wouldn't listen to her own mother?

Can you believe it? I'm so lucky my kids are so respectful. They always listen. Never talk back.

How is your daughter?

Oh . . . Sunshine is in her third year already. She's . . .

Was that her second helping?

I think so . . . Amerikanos sure do eat a lot.

But she should really control herself. She's getting so big.

Ang taba!

Oooh, she just looked over here.

Smile.

Ang taba!

Did everyone get to eat already?

Is there enough for everyone?

I hope she didn't finish all the food.

Wasn't the *pancit* too salty?

The chicken, too.

And she just keeps eating . . .

They should really tell her to diet.

Why don't you?

Oh, I would never say that to her face. It's not my place. *Hindi ako pamilya.*

So what is it? Why is she here—now?

And how is she going to feed herself?

That Nita better be sending money, the way that girl eats!

Nita is always bragging about having so much money.

You talked to her?

No, but she is always sending those expensive Stateside clothes.

If Nita really had money, she'd send her daughter to Europe, not here!

That Nita is such a fake. She knows living is cheaper here.

Yeah, that's why she's here and not in Europe.

Is it so expensive sa States that she has to send her daughter here?

Her mother is too cheap to raise her own daughter.

Is that why she's here?

Yeah, but why was she in the hospital?

Ssshhh . . . I think she is bringing us some soft drinks.

Smile.

She's so big!

Oh hi! *Kamusta na iha?* How is your mother?

You're so big *na!*

Purvi Shah

Like millions of other New Yorkers, I spend too much of my time on the city's public transportation system.

Biography

Purvi Shah was born in Ahmadabad, India. She first experienced the gritty New York City streets during frequent family visits to an aunt in Jersey City. After swearing never to live in such bedlam, she dove headfirst into the Big Apple in 1994. Her work has been published in *Descant*, *Weber Studies* and the anthology *Contours of the Heart: South Asians Map North America*. At the University of Michigan, she won the 1994 Virginia Voss Poetry Writing Award.

Made in India, Immigrant Song #3
(a Note from a New York City Streetwalker)

The New York streets swell with feet;
multihued tracks glide over the flat steel
disks which offer entry into the city's interior
lairs. The writing seeps through our soles
though few fathom the signature, "Made
in India." These alien

metal coins, transported
like my birth, mask
a labyrinth of tunnels
in a city where origin
and destination are confused.
Sometimes I wear the stamp
on myself; sometimes I feel
the wear of a surrounding world erase
the fine etchings. Here the imprint
of India is a traveler's
mutation: the body's chamber is made
hole, the skin not smooth, circular,
but cloaking a bumpy network
of channels, spirit mobile, expanding.

Wanting Spring, a Vista from the Office Cubicle

Noise is what inhabits us when we are silent to our thoughts. Here, shut in from the world,
windows faced away, we await signs, the spring of air, the residue of scent. On the streets, girls
carry plums, hard and black. When night thaws and we are free to the dusky roads, we stroll to
a city stand, sneak a bite of sweetness, hold chunks pressed to our cheeks until pits could melt in
our mouths.

Synapse Maps

Subways buzz through New York City, tremors
to my nerves. Here I feel the real
sting, the fruit of thick Massachusetts
woods sucking my skin's juice. Clothes

melt to my pores and humidity
is a conversation that slinks
through my limbs.

Flashes of electronic Georgia: sweat,
sorrow and sixteen years of separation
pulse back.

Tomie Arai

Tomie Arai was born in New York and currently makes her residence there. Using photographs from family albums and public archives, she creates silkscreen images that blend familial and social history into a personal narrative.

Rene J. Navarro

Biography

Rene J. Navarro was born in Bamban, Tarlac, Philippines, in 1940 and lived in Brooklyn in the seventies just across from the drug detox center on Albany Avenue. He is now a wanderer, acupuncturist, herbalist and teacher (Taoist meditation, *qi gong*, massage, sexology and internal alchemy; Yang Family Tai Chi Chuan; Shaolin Temple boxing; and Arnis de Mano). Navarro is the editor of the Taoist alchemical text "Greatest Kan and Li" (*Water and Fire*, #63 and 64, I Ching) and *Chi Nei Tsang Internal Organ Chi Massage* by Mantak Chia. He is featured in *Masters of Arnis, Kali and Escrima* by Edgar Sulite and *Martial Artists as Healers* by Mark Wiley (forthcoming).

A Clearing in the Sky

(Erwinna, Bucks County, Pennsylvania)

Although the sky
is still dark and the May
clouds threaten another
downpour, the rain
has briefly stopped
for the outdoor
wedding
to begin, and I watch
my son Albert
in his transparent
piña barong Pilipino
waiting by the altar of fresh cut
branches and dogwood trees
while his Laura all radiance
and hope marches on her father's
arm down the aisle of grass
to the music
of the brass band and the cackling
of the peacocks and guinea hens
in the barn,
and I see him,
6 years, in Prospect Park
running and turning
back and laughing,
black hair flying,
bright eyes
blazing with the morning
as he pulls the string
of the red kite, its long white
tail trailing, as it ascended
like a Zhu Bei Hong horse,
trembling against the wind,
the greening

trees and meadows
spinning
around him, the tenements
and the city
traffic dissolving
in the spring sun,
as his stallion cantered, sniffed
the grass and air,
floated and glowed
in the Stillness,
a tracery
of Light,
eternal, pulsing
in the clear blue
space
that opens
between
heaven
and earth.

Company

Early morning in Brooklyn:
My children, Al and Norman,
6 and 9, and Lolit, my wife, are still
asleep. I take the elevator
down to the lobby
and go out into the dark,
carrying my rattan
sticks for my martial practice at 5
in the park. Unseasonably warm
in late October. Nobody
around, only a couple
of joggers in the oval.
A mist paints

a gray efflorescence
over the handball and tennis
courts where I stand facing
a graffitied wall to do a thousand
strikes of *sinawali*, a hundred
abecederos with
my right hand,
a hundred with my left,
chanting my Pilipino mantras
agos, *kumpas* and *indayog*
ng katawan, thinking
of the images that these words
evoke—a river flowing,
a syncopated beat
and a cobra ready
to strike—and I repeat
the routine 2 or 3 times more
in silence before the sun
comes up, until I break
into a sweat, feel
an exquisite
ache shooting
through my arms,
legs and chest, and I come
back from a tropical island,
where I had as my guide
and company
the warrior
Lapu-Lapu, who slew
Ferdinand Magellan, April
1521.

      —For Norman F. Navarro, M.D.

At Marble Collegiate Church with Marla and Donald

I was listening
to the Very Reverend
Norman Vincent Peale
as he spoke
about the power
of faith as small
as a mustard
seed, but I couldn't sit
still, I kept
sneaking a look
at Marla,
itching to
play with her,
touch the tips
of her fingers,
lick them,
see her breasts,
her navel
under that silk,
but Donald
was watching
by her side,
a sharp-eyed
dog guarding
his trophy,
as we sat
in a balcony
pew along
with others,
and so my restless Taoist
spirit
fled to the
rafters and the
stained glass

windows while
my meridians
and vortices
were flashing
lights and colors,
eddies and trajectories
of energy
in the dark, oozing
like the aurora
borealis, and
the preaching voice
was gone,
I was on my own,
my shell of a body
was left
on the seat
clutching
a purple hymnal,
while I flew
off into space
with the
8 immortals.

Marli Higa

The world of the book is a total world and in a total world we fall
in love.

                                  - Jeanette Winterson

Biography

Marli Higa is a writer of fiction and the editor of *Dialogue*, a magazine for Asian American
artists. She is currently working on a novel, *Earth of the Heart*.

The Craft of Fiction

When I was fifteen and an ungovernable little hellion at the Hawaii School for Gorillas, I decided enough was enough and hitchhiked across the country to live with my lover in a sun-drenched, book-piled loft on the edge of Manhattan, with old wine crates and abandoned motorcycles for furniture and a plastic Elvis that rotated and sang "Love Me Tender" to the one-eyed gray cat that slept on a lumpy blue-and-white-striped cotton-ticking mattress with the sheets torn off and tacked up to billow out white and free through the giant windows that overlooked the Hudson River, the river just like the one George Washington threw a silver dollar across on some bright winter's day a long time ago to launch a whole new nation of wildness and possibilities that was free from the taxes and totems and traditions of centuries of suffocating history, with liberty and justice for all and we hold these truths to be self-evident so let freedom ring.

Actually that is not true. What I mean is, I went to the Hawaii School for Girls and fulfilled many kinds of requirements, so I could go to the University of Hawaii and fulfill many more. Below the stack of diaries in my closet there is a box labeled "rubber noses" that is full of evidence of this—report cards, clippings, class pictures, snapshots of various boys and me in *pikake leis* and complementary prom drag. But that is the dead weight of history, and this is about how I threw my rubber noses across an ocean, a continent, the Hudson River one bright winter's day a long time ago and launched a whole new life of wildness and possibilities that was free from the ideals and expectations and anxiety of my younger years, with sufficient income and a room of one's own and in fiction we are born again.

It was a difficult passage. Eventually I got an apartment share on the Lower East Side and a job inhaling dust at a rare books shop, but there were many lessons I had to learn first, and most of these came through hard experience. For example, the timetables at bus stops are best ignored, unless you actually want to know how late the bus is. Those kids panhandling on St. Mark's Place go to the Hamptons with their parents in the summer. Everyone has a therapist and this is perfectly normal. And I had been in New York six months before I learned not to put much faith in any variety of health muffin that is shrink-wrapped and bigger than one's head.

Despite such lessons, though, New York seemed to me a place of excellent beginnings, and loaded with symbolism. On the crisp paper bags into which they slipped my Yankee Doodles was the optimistic life begins at store 24! And standing on every corner in the Village were men wearing bright orange sandwich boards that read mini-storage can change your life! They were so organized I began to wonder if mini-storage was actually a cult. More than once I was given reading material by religious groups that stated almost the same thing: THE CHURCH

OF TODAY AND TOMORROW CAN CHANGE YOUR LIFE! I suppose it was my perpetual air of wonderment and my islander looks that made me seem ripe for conversion. I certainly didn't mind being accosted, because the cultists were usually self-confident, friendly women with whom I had several minutes of intriguing conversation before they invited me to a prayer meeting in Central Park. I began to feel depressed, though, when I realized that cultists were the only women who did sidle up to me at park benches and fruit stands with stirring questions and fervent promises to change my life.

I had been clerking in the rare books shop for several months when I began to notice a woman who worked in the bookshop right around the corner from mine. Hers was a specialty bookseller whose specialization I could never quite figure out; there was a wall of health and spirituality books, a butcher block table of theology books, a cherrywood display case of ethnic and gender studies books, and fifteen shelves of foreign-language books. Once a week during my lunch break, rising like a spirit from among the musty, dust-quilted rare books, I floated around the corner toward the scarlet awning of the glass-fronted shop to check out the new titles and to see if the bookshop girl was working. Soon I began to associate the smell of newly printed pages, the sound of squeaky floorboards and the feel of polished wood with her. Too awestruck to approach her, I buried myself alive in the stacks—studying every book jacket, running my fingers across the smooth, straight spines, turning my selections over and over in my mind.

I suppose I was not very good at talking to women in whom I was interested. I had never had any practice growing up, and the resulting feeling of isolation had turned me into a hesitant and somewhat oblique conversationalist. I also had a tendency to fill in the blanks when information was not immediately available. When I first got to New York and worked part-time in a very large publishing company, a cute girl whom I thought read unsolicited manuscripts and perhaps wrote poetry at night turned out to be a corporate lawyer named Regina Brockton Broder with a husband, three kids in boarding school and a brownstone in Brooklyn Heights. In other words, I browsed for long periods of time in that specialty bookshop, and lingered over books I couldn't afford to buy.

One day, when I had been there for the better part of an hour and it was July and sweltering and the books seemed to be trembling in their own compressed heat, the bookshop girl came over to do inventory in twentieth-century fiction. She was wearing jeans and a red t-shirt with the sleeves and collar cut out, and at the top of her spine, right where her spiky blond hair became soft and downy, there was the thin blue line of a delicate tattoo—a woman symbol interlocked with another woman symbol. At that moment my internal churnings suddenly dissolved into a clean blank page, and I heard myself asking her something about an author, and something I already knew about Moments of Being. She mentioned a book of criticism and I told her I worked at the bookshop around the corner, and she said she'd been there, and we talked about women and fiction, and fictional women, and before I knew what was happening, I had asked her out.

There was a new little restaurant on Seventh Avenue and Bank called The Study whose distinguishing feature was its unusual menu. I hadn't eaten there yet, but according to their ad in the paper, all of the dishes were inspired by classic works of fiction, "From *Beowulf* to *Beloved*," and the interior was in the style of a Victorian library. The wines were French, the desserts were Italian and the waiters were probably former English majors. I thought this would make for a memorable first date—a reminder of how our paths had crossed in the bookshop, and a salutary gesture toward the romantic power of fiction. I made reservations for the very next Saturday, and spent the rest of that week in a daze at work.

So Saturday came, and the first thing I noticed as we settled into our table was that the soft, romantic lighting reflected sickly yellow off the shelves and gave everyone the appearance of liver damage. The music was a distant baroque and the waiters moved so slowly, and to such little effect, that the entire room seemed suspended in amber. My date looked dramatic if somewhat forbidding in a beautiful black ribbed blouse that covered her from neck to wrists. I was wearing an orange silk sleeveless and it occurred to me that in this yellowing light I must look like something very high in beta carotene. I was glancing surreptitiously at my arms when suddenly she set down the menu and snorted.

"Get this—'*Inferno*: A fiery blend of Italian herbs and pastas that guide you through culinary levels of excruciating beauty.' Excruciating beauty." She snorted again and pushed her fingers through her spiky blond hair. "Christ. You'd think they'd at least give you an idea what it tastes like, if they're going to write such bad copy."

I was a little taken aback by her tone. It was not the tone of someone enchanted by the evening. "It is unfathomable, and yet tempting," I suggested, hoping she would see it in a different light. I myself had chosen *Wuthering Heights*, a passionate blend of wild English moor lamb and vegetables with a gypsy rogue seasoning.

We ordered our meals, fidgeted with the silverware and exchanged news about our bookshops, and when the salads finally arrived, we poked at those. As she sat there spearing cherry tomatoes and describing her most recent run-in with the bouncer at the Clit Club, it began to dawn on me that not everyone would find this atmosphere romantic. I had chosen the place because I thought we could establish a relaxed and friendly rapport by making little jokes about the menu, such as entrees that never became popular—*Lord of the Flies, Death in Venice, Things Fall Apart*. Then we would get into a deep and revealing conversation about our favorite books, discussing scenes we had loved, characters we had lived through, lines we would like to have said. After several attempts to steer the conversation in this direction, however, it became apparent to me that she was not interested in such talk. To my dismay she had a very recent ex. To my dismay she had been in many relationships, each one more wrenching and memorable than the previous one. The pasta dangled carelessly from her fork as she talked about the girlfriend she'd met at a Brooklyn Women's Martial Arts class and the year in college she'd experimented with S&M. I drank very small sips of water and tried not to look orange and said very little about my own history, drowned as I was in hers.

Presently the evening came to an end and we were standing outside the restaurant, the meal heavy in my stomach and the midsummer night air an unbearable suffocation. She indicated that she needed to take the PATH train home to Jersey, so I walked her down Seventh Avenue to the Christopher Street station.

"I'm glad we got together," she said. "We should definitely keep in touch."

"Yeah," I said.

"Well—you know where I work."

Then she disappeared down the curving concrete stairwell, a narrow figure in ribbed black and blond, a slip of a shade to be zipped away to the other side of the Hudson.

I never went back to her bookshop after that. I missed the polished gleam of the hardwood bookcases, and it was difficult giving up the weekly dalliance among the promising new stacks of unopened paperbacks. But I realized that over the years I had acquired many books I hadn't examined very closely, and it was probably a good time to reevaluate my own collection before attempting to acquire any more new titles. As it turned out, then, I didn't happen to see the bookshop girl again, but I knew I'd eventually run into her at some political demonstration, or some meeting, or some bar or party or nightclub.

I never did see her at any of those, but where did I end up remaking her acquaintance? At a used books table on the street. On a balmy Sunday several months later, at the southwest corner of Washington Square Park, I saw her standing over a card table of paperback books—one hand moving across the worn paper spines, the other massaging the back of her neck. I picked up *Our Dead Behind Us* and said hello; she looked up through a soft blonde fringe and smiled, and soon we began to talk again, about books this time, about our bookshops, about what we had been doing since the last time we met—not much, she said; a lot of thinking, I said; and when I saw *One Hundred Years of Solitude* in her hand and that she had no money, I bought it for her with the last of my paycheck money from the rare book shop, that book she was holding and three books I saw with 'rose' in the title: *The Name of the Rose*, *A Red Rose for Love* and *The Day the Sun Never Rose*—I would buy you a dozen, I told her, if there were a dozen here to buy.

But what actually happened is this: I never saw her at a meeting or in her bookshop, or at a used books table on the street. I got a better job at a different bookshop and I went out more, and met more people, and I spent an inordinate amount of time glancing around every time I walked into a club or went to a party, hoping that the woman in the corner with the short blond hair and the black ribbed blouse, standing in the light of half-shadow, was not her.

Jean Fong Kwok

Language and culture change our perception of reality and, thereby, the actual reality we live in. To Mrs. Chen, the mugger with the pale blue eyes is a demon. Who are we to say that he is not?

Biography

Jean Fong Kwok was born in Hong Kong and raised in New York City. She holds a BA in English and American Literature from Harvard University and an MFA in Creative Writing from Columbia University. Her stories and poetry have appeared in *Story* and *Prairie Schooner*, and she has cowritten an original feature screenplay, "Tempting Fate," which is being produced by Eureka Pictures. At present, she teaches English at Leiden University in The Netherlands and is working on a novel.

Disguises

On the night Mrs. Chen got lost, she was wearing a golden amulet of the goddess Kuan Yin underneath her clothes, for protection. She took the subway home from the factory in Chinatown. Sitting on the long seat with her feet lightly grazing the floor, she felt the weight of sleep drag her head forward, her permed curls sinking toward the small neat hands cupped politely in her lap. As the half-empty subway car lurched through the tunnel, its movement sporadically flung her head upward. She caught herself from sleep in those moments, looking about her, alarmed, only to have exhaustion fall over her again like a blanket. The swaying of the subway threw her back and forth against the hard seat, the thin fabric of her flowered pants brushed against the shopping bag full of sewing.

One . . . two . . . she had to take the subway fourteen stops to get home. The conductor's voice in English was a river of sound in her ear, noise following noise like the falling of water over rocks. Three . . . four . . .

Mrs. Chen lifted her heavy head. Five . . . six . . . the door opened and her factory supervisor strode out of the elevator with her polyester skirt flicking about her legs, stepping quickly and fastidiously, as though the clumps of fabric dust on the sewing room floor dirtied her high-heeled shoes. As she walked, she waved one wide hand in front of her mouth to clear away the dust in the air—the other gripped a wadded piece of clothing. The supervisor came into the work area only when there was a problem; otherwise, she stayed in the air-conditioned offices upstairs. Mrs. Chen could feel the supervisor's presence passing through the rows of silent women bent over their Singer sewing machines; no one dared look up, their needles racing, piercing the fabric.

The supervisor threaded her way through the pack of women, bright in her silver-toned suit; its light gray material stretched across her fat stomach like the skin of a snake. She stopped next to Mrs. Chen and with fingers thick with rings of jade, snapped open the garment she had been holding—a skirt. Mrs. Chen, knowing it was not her place to meet the supervisor's eyes, cautiously raised her gaze to the round collar of her shirt, while everyone about her seemed to busy themselves with their work.

"Your seams are crooked," the supervisor announced, wrenching her mouth around the crisp Cantonese words. "This is not acceptable." She always attempted to speak Cantonese, one of the so-called "sophisticated" dialects, although her accent was painfully rural. She told everyone that she had been born in Hong Kong, where the cleanest Cantonese is spoken, but, Mrs. Chen thought, her peasant roots shone clearly through her words.

Mrs. Chen stood up.

"I am so sorry," she said, her pronunciation flawless. She knew the supervisor resented her for the breeding that meant so little in this country. She could see the skirt was one she had labored over at night, sewing between the soft breaths of her sleeping family.

"May I see it?" she asked, taking a step closer.

The supervisor held it away from her. "If this ever happens again, just one more time, you will no longer be allowed to take work home," she said. "Please remember, Mrs. Chen, you are very new to this country—we have had much trouble with recent arrivals—and my uncle is doing you a great favor to allow you to take home extra sewing, and indeed to work here at all. I do not like to see ungrateful employees. You will, of course, not be paid for that entire bundle."

Then, before Mrs. Chen could reach for the skirt, the supervisor took one corner of it in her teeth and the other in her hands, and tore it down the seams, in half. She tossed the pieces onto Mrs. Chen's table as she turned on her heel and stalked from the room.

Mrs. Chen sank onto her seat, spreading her fingers to shield her hot face. What crime have I committed, in which past life, to deserve these evil winds of fate that blow at my back, she wondered. She realized that everyone was watching her out of the corners of their eyes, pretending they had noticed nothing. No one said anything to her. The subway doors closed and her head nodded forward.

The last station sped behind her. The overhead light went out, and the fluorescent flashes from the subway tunnel gleamed in the darkness behind her eyelids, pane after pane like frames of a movie.

Mrs. Chen, then just a girl named Lai Fong, was in China again. She was wearing green silk, preparing with her mother the ceremony for the seven goddesses who protected virginal maidens; it was the last time she would do this, because she was soon to be married. She bent to kneel on the cushion before the goddesses at the altar. Her mother, already kneeling, stopped her with a touch on her arm. Slowly, her mother gazed up at her, and her small rounded features, so much like Lai Fong's, were filled with grief and tenderness.

"My only daughter," she said, "before you pray with me this final time, you must remember this: it is said, one who is human must kneel only before the gods." She paused, and then said fiercely, "Never before anyone else."

The screech of the subway rang in her ears, startling her. Mrs. Chen brushed her forehead three times, to clear away painful memories. She touched the amulet of Kuan Yin hanging from the gold chain around her neck; its shape underneath her blouse reassured her. Everyone knew that pure gold protected you from evil, but even more important, the monks at Shaolin Temple had "opened it to the light," so that the goddess could truly live in it, as though it were her temple. The amulet was the only part of her mother Mrs. Chen had been able to take with her when she left China.

More people filled the subway car than she had remembered. Two well-dressed black women across from her chatted, and as one laughed, the long yellow feather on her hat wiggled. A homeless man wearing a cardboard sign with English writing on it had wrapped himself around a pole near Mrs. Chen.

He gingerly peeled his hands from the pole, as if it caused him pain to do so, and holding out his left palm, began to make his way through the car. His rancid smell, like sour milk, reached her before he did, and she tried not to breathe too deeply. Spittle clung to the sides of his mouth, suspended in droplets in his rough beard, but his lips were full and red, as though they alone had not lost their hold on life. When he stood in front of her, she studied his dirty face, and she was not afraid. It is said, she thought, that we must all be beggars for one life, and we only hope that that life has already past.

She opened her change purse and pressed a quarter into his palm. She had none to spare but in this world, she mused, the times when you are able to give are so few that when you can, you must; the gods always view compassion kindly.

"Haf nice day," Mrs. Chen said, smiling. This was one of the few English phrases she had managed to learn.

The homeless man closed his fingers around the coin, his stare not leaving her smile as though it surprised him more than the quarter. He turned to the two women sitting across from her. They had stopped talking to watch Mrs. Chen. Now, they also took out their purses and gave him some change. As the homeless man went on his way, Mrs. Chen nodded to the women and they smiled back before resuming their conversation.

Mrs. Chen settled into her seat and closed her eyes. The subway car clattered; it was as though she and the women and the homeless man were all in a carriage together, riding to the same place. But where were they going? We are the Monkey King, the monk and their two companions, seeking enlightenment on a road filled with demons and goddesses in disguise, she thought, and the voice of the English-speaking conductor sounded like her father's voice in China when he would tell her stories that she was too tired to understand. Then it seemed to her that the homeless man had put his head on her shoulder and they were resting together, sleeping, with the women across the way looking on.

Suddenly, she sat up. What stop was this? This must be number fourteen! This should be the right one but why did everything seem so unfamiliar? Where should she get off? The black women were gone; there was no sign of the homeless man. Mrs. Chen grabbed her shopping bag and hurried out of the train just before the doors closed, hoping this was indeed her station. Mr. Chen always scolded her for being overly imaginative. But as she stood on the platform, with the rush of the subway wind at her back, she realized that she had never seen this place before.

She watched the few passengers make their way to the stairs. Then, from behind her, she heard the sound of footsteps. She panicked and fled for the exit, the shopping bag bumping against her legs. She had been mugged only a few weeks ago; she was the last one leaving the subway platform and a teenager in a leather jacket had blocked her way. He pulled out a long knife and held it in front of his body, half-hidden by the folds of his coat. His eyes horrified her. They were pale blue, blue as she'd seen only in the eyes of those blinded by cataracts in China, yet this man was able to see, as if he were some sort of demon. Without a word, he gestured with his knife. She gave him her purse; he took it and ran.

Mrs. Chen reached the token booth, passed it, and raced up onto the street. She stood outside the subway station, gulping in the cool night air, holding on to the stair rail. She looked around. No one had followed her. A desolate avenue lined with streetlamps stretched before her, the concrete buildings smothered in graffiti, interrupted by long alleys. In the distance, a dark figure walked down the block, only to quickly disappear around a corner. A skeleton of a car, windshield broken, stripped of all four wheels, loomed next to the subway entrance. She did not recognize anything.

This was a terrible place. She took the amulet out of her blouse and clutched it. A low wind whistled through the avenue, setting stray pieces of litter skittering across the concrete. She went back to the token booth.

She was relieved to see the clerk, a heavy man with a gray goatee, through the murky glass; he was an official, he could help her. She went around to the front of the booth and rapped on the glass with her knuckles.

"Hello? Hello?" she said.

He was talking on the phone, and when he saw her, he shifted so that his back was to her. She tapped on the booth more insistently. He waved for her to wait. She searched through her purse to find the piece of paper with her street address on it. Her son had written it out for her, just in case she got lost.

"Hello, hello," she said, her voice growing shriller.

Hunching over the phone, the clerk ignored her.

"HELLO!" she screamed.

He turned around. Mrs. Chen quickly pushed the crumpled paper toward him. He studied it, and said some words to her in English.

"No," she said, "no understand."

He repeated what he'd said, only louder. She shook her head. The man ran his fingers across the top of his puffy hair, then pointed at the receiver he was holding, like she was keeping him from something. She pressed her ear as close to the glass as she could. She tried to understand something, anything, of what he said, but it was just babble to her.

"Dank you," she said, "Bye bye." The man shrugged and returned to his phone conversation.

She slowly climbed to the street. Please, Kuan Yin, let me get home to my child and husband, she prayed. There was a pay telephone on the corner. She walked to it as fast as she could, put down her bag, fumbled for a quarter and dialed her home number. Her husband answered on the first ring.

"Big Brother Chen?" she said. She never called him by his first name because that would be disrespectful, even though they had been married more than ten years.

"Where have you been?" he asked angrily.

"I don't know—I'm lost." She leaned against the side of the phone booth and began to sob.

"How could you be so stupid?" he yelled, as he always did when he was afraid. "Your son is here, waiting for his dinner—why don't you ever pay attention to where you're going? Where are you?"

"I don't know."

"You have to stop that crying," Mr. Chen said. His voice grew quieter. "Listen, don't be afraid. We have to find out where you are and then we will come get you. Let me put Sonny on the line."

She wiped her eyes on her sleeve and tried to pulled herself together. Her child must not know how upset she was.

His voice seemed much higher over the phone. "Mommy, where are you?"

"You have to help Mommy," she said. Sonny was only nine years old but he was as smart as the boys a grade ahead of him. He was learning English so rapidly. She described her surroundings but he did not recognize them.

"I know," Sonny said. "Can you spell the name of the street by you? Can you see the street sign?"

She found it but the word was very long. She had never been that good with the English alphabet.

"M . . . I . . . no, E . . . and then A . . . no, R . . ." she began. In the middle of her spelling, she had to put another coin in the telephone. Finally, she came up with something that Sonny thought could be the name of a street.

"But I don't know where it is," he said.

"Do you have any maps?" she asked.

"Yeah," he said. "Let me check in my geography book. That has maps."

She could hear him getting off the chair and running to his books. He was gone for a few minutes. Mrs. Chen looked at her amulet, glinting brightly against her dark blouse. She brought the golden goddess to her face and laid it against her cheek.

She heard shuffling, then Sonny came back on the phone.

"Mommy?" he said. "I can't find it. It's not in my book. I'm sorry." He started to sniffle. "When are you going to come home, Mommy?" he asked.

"Shhh . . . don't cry," she said, trying to sound calm. She could hear Mr. Chen cursing in the background. "Mommy will be fine. I will walk around and maybe I will recognize something. Just tell your father that I will call soon."

She hung up before she had to speak with Mr. Chen again. It would be more frightening to talk to her husband; he was just as helpless as she, and he would not be as easily comforted as Sonny. Her quarters were almost gone and she did not want to waste another. Perhaps she shouldn't have given one to the homeless man, she thought. What was kindness in this world? She rested her head against the telephone for a moment. I invite the goddess Kuan Yin, she said under her breath, from the Shaolin Temple in the hills of Canton, to come to me now; so soon as I . . .

She felt a hand close to her ear reach for the amulet, as though it were trying to take it before she could finish her prayer. Mrs. Chen screamed and ducked at the same time. Grasping the shopping bag, she swung it in a circle, felt it hit, heard the sides rip. She hugged the bag and fled toward the subway station, hampered by its bulk. Someone or something seemed to race away in the opposite direction. So soon as I call her, she gasped, running, so soon will she appear . . . .

As Mrs. Chen rushed to the steps, she caught a glimpse of features that looked Chinese. She skidded to a stop.

"Mister! Mister!" she shouted.

The young man turned, surprised. "Yes?" He was Chinese. He must be a student, with his thick glasses and a green book bag slung over his narrow shoulder.

Mrs. Chen almost cried from relief. "I am lost," she said, breathing hard, "and someone just tried to take my necklace."

"My Cantonese is very bad," he said in Mandarin.

"We are both Chinese," Mrs. Chen said, part in Mandarin and part in Cantonese. "Please help me."

She explained the situation to him, her voice breaking—how she was lost and almost robbed, how she couldn't follow the token booth clerk, how her son and husband couldn't help her—using as much Mandarin as she remembered and filling in the rest with Cantonese. She put her bag on the ground and took out the piece of paper with her address on it. The young man listened and nodded; he seemed to understand her story. He took the slip of paper and the two of them went into the subway station. As they approached the token booth, the clerk recognized Mrs. Chen, rolling his eyes.

The young man spoke to the clerk in English and showed him her address. Then he said to Mrs. Chen, "The train you were on must have been rerouted. They probably announced the change but you did not understand. What you must do now is take the train over here for two stops and then switch . . ."

But Mrs. Chen was frantic. She clutched his arm, shaking her head. He stopped speaking and looked at her fingers buried in his jacket. "I will go with you," he said.

Mrs. Chen sighed and then offered to pay for his token, but he put one in the slot as he waved her hand away. When they got on the subway, the young man took out a book and began to study, peering at her only occasionally to check that she was all right. She was too exhausted to even try to make conversation. Kuan Yin, thank you for your aid . . . . The student escorted her the entire way to her own station. Mrs. Chen asked him to come to her house, so she could at least give him something to eat to repay his kindness, but when she passed through the gate, he did not follow.

She turned back to him. "Thank you," she said.

The young man grinned and bowed, his schoolbag slipping off his shoulder. She bowed in response but by the time she straightened, he was gone.

When Mrs. Chen got home, Sonny threw himself at her and cried, while Mr. Chen roughly patted her on the arm. They were quiet as she told them how the young man had helped her, how he must have been sent by the gods. Mrs. Chen lit incense at the altar in their kitchen to formally give thanks and noticed there were extra incense stubs in the holder—Mr. Chen had also prayed for her.

"We were afraid for you," he said. "We thought we might have lost you."

Later that night, she had to stay awake to do her work. She bent to sew the pieces of the torn skirt together, joining again the severed parts with thread.

Meena Alexander

Manhattan, island of rich density broken by fissures of light, your stones cry out to me, and the cells of my body respond. I landed here in 1979 and this is how space comes to me. This is my America. The borders I cross in dreams mark the lines of passage through your numbered streets. I play hopscotch through your city blocks, lift up my skirts, leap to the brink of the river.

Biography

Meena Alexander was born in Allahabad, India. She is the author of the memoir *Fault Lines,* the novels *Nampally Road* and *Manhattan Music* and the poetry volumes *Stone Roots, House of a Thousand Doors, River and Bridge* and *The Shock of Arrival: Reflections on Postcolonial Experience.* A recipient of awards from the Altrusa International Foundation and the National Endowment for the Humanities, Alexander is a professor of English at the Graduate Center and Hunter College, CUNY.

Unquiet Borders

The unquiet borders of poetry: I muse on Mirabai, poet mystic of the *bhakti* movement in India, she who left home and princely husband and roved across the thresholds, borders. Leaving the confines of domesticity her saris are worn; her hair matted, lacking the oil that Indian women prize. Her feet were dry, chapped.

And she roved, she sang of Krishna continually, that perpetual absence, her beloved.

Was Mira's body covered with dirt, like that of Akkamahadevi, another great woman poet, such that she might have been said to wear a skin of dirt?

And what of menstrual blood? How did she wash it off? Or did it mix in with the mud?

I ask all this quite deliberately, here, now at the tail end of this century, on this North American continent and I ask, what would it mean if Mirabai were alive, here, now in America? How would she write? What sense would our complex, multifarious world make to her?

I will try and answer by pretending I can see into her soul. We poets do that a lot and falling short stand dismayed at our own shortfalls. Still . . . first her body. She let her body show. It was warm in Rajasthan in most seasons. Her skin was brown. It was not enough crouched in the hot alleyway to sing of Krishna—I am your knife, you my noose—sing of palaces that did not offer food for the soul, dirt shacks, soiled thresholds.

She crossed a border, never to return. I imagine her, here, now. But what do they make of her, a brown skinned woman in tattered oriental clothing at the edge of Broadway in Manhattan. Or by the railroad tracks, in New Brunswick? Is she hunched on the sidewalk? Is she rooting in the garbage for food?

Then again we might find Mira like many other Asian immigrant women working in a sweat shop in the lower east side, her rhythms of poetry beaten to the tracking needle, silks spinning out of her skin, English syllables edgy, forced, brajbhasha flowering only in dreams.

The hidden language that flowers only in dreams torn from the body.

Frantz Fanon, who Mirabai did not need to read—in his work women are so much cast aside—in a crucial section of *Black Skins, White Masks* imagines people crying out, "Look, a negro!" So she might find the fingers pointing—"Look, a brown woman!" The shame, the torment, the turning, beseeching others. Stumbling, falling, the body splintering into a thousand shards. The body split open.

"I burst apart" Fanon writes. "Now the fragments have been put together again by another self."* What is this other self? What might this putting together of a racialized body mean? A body not male, but female, haunted by its femaleness, earth it cannot shed. Will Krishna put her back together again? Or is this the secret of her genius, the impossible sense that Krishna who lies in wait for her, under the waters of sleep will not stitch her back again, piece together the broken bits?

So who will put together a body torn by border crossings, skin marked by barbed wires, bandages hastily knotted, the body of a pariah woman?

Why do I conceive of the female poet like this? Perhaps because I think that she needs to slip her flesh in order to sing, yet it is only by being drawn back into a larger, more spiritual body, the mouths of many others, the hands that labor in the sweat shops, on the street corners, in the market places and yes, in the academies, that she can write.

A few points to conclude this reverie. Our world is filled with unquiet borders. It would be a terrible error—too grave to be borne—to think that our capacity for words can lose us our bodies. Bodies banned, beaten, jailed, twisted in childbirth, bodies that are the sites of pleasure, of ecstasy. Female bodies that can babble, break into prophetic speech, rant.

Any aesthetic implications I hear someone ask. None except what I have called elsewhere "a back against the wall aesthetic."** The woman poet that faces the borders her body must cross, racial, sexual borders, is forced to invent a form that springs out without canonical support, a rough and ready thing, its order crude, its necessity beyond the purchase of self-invention. There is something in this species of play, the body in pain or pleasure, crying out for a sense that a multicultural, multicultural feminism might learn from.

And I try to learn from Mirabai, from her nakedness. The most delicate play of words is what we aspire to in the face of terrors that confront us. The beloved perpetually lost, the body fragmented, its bits and pieces spelling out a map that a new Fanon, female now and a poet, might make, crossing unquiet borders.

* Frantz Fanon, *Black Skin, White Masks* (New York: Grove Press, 1967)
** "Skin with Fire Inside: Indian Women Writers" in Meena Alexander, *The Shock of Arrival: Reflections on Postcolonial Experience* (Boston: Southend Press, 1996), p. 170

Indian April

(in memory of Allen Ginsberg)

I

Allen Ginsberg, on a spring day you stopped
naked in a doorway in Rajasthan.
You were preparing to wash, someone took a snapshot:
I see your left hand bent back,
cigarette in your mouth,
the metal basin set at your ankles,
heat shimmering at the edges of your skin
in Indian air, in water.

Rinsed clean you squatted
at the threshold again,
struck a *bhajan* on a tin can,
watched Mira approach,
her hair a black mass,
so taut it could knock over a lamppost,
skin on her fists raw
from rubbing against chipped honeypots.

In the middle distance,
like a common bridegroom
Lord Krishna rides a painted swing.

You ponder this, not sure
if an overdose of poetry
might crash a princess.

Later in the alleyway you noted
a zither leapt from a blind baul's fist.
William Blake's death mask,
plaster cast with the insignia of miracles.

In a burning ghat
the sensorium's ruin:
a man's spine and head poked with a stick
so bone might crisp into ash,
vapors spilt into terrible light
where the Ganga pours.

II

I was born at the Ganga's edge,
my mother wrapped me in a bleached sari,
laid me in stiff reeds, in hard water.

I tried to keep my nostrils above mud,
learnt how to use my limbs, how to float.
This earth is filled with black water,
small islands with bristling vines afford us some hold.

Tired out with your journals you watch
Mira crouch by the rough stones of the alley.
Her feet are bare, they hurt her.
So much flight for a poet, so much persistence.

Allen Ginsberg, where are you now?

Engine of flesh, hot sunflower of Mathura,
Teach us to glide into life.

Teach us when not to flee,
when to rejoice, when to weep.

Teach us to clear our throats.

III

Kaddish, Kaddish, I hear you cry
in the field of Central Park.

He brought me into his tent
and his banner over me was love.

I learn from you that the tabernacles of grace
are lodged in the prickly pear,
the tents of heaven torn by sharp vines,
running blackberry,
iron from the hummingbird's claw.

He brought me into his tent
and his banner over me was love.

Yet now he turns his face from me.
Krishna, you are my noose, I your knife.

And who shall draw apart
from the misericordia of attachment?

IV

Holy the cord of death, the sensual palaces
of our feasting and excrement.
Holy, the water of the Ganga, Hudson, Nile,
Pamba, Mississippi, Mahanadi.

Holy the lake in Central Park, bruised eye of earth,
mirror of heaven.

Where you leap beard first
this April morning, resolute, impenitent,
not minding the pointed reeds, spent syringes,
pale, uncoiled condoms.

You understand the kingdom of the quotidian,
groundhogs in heat, the arrhythmia of desire.

I see you young again,
teeth stained with betel and *bhang*,
nostrils tense with the smoke of Manhattan,
ankles taut in a yogic asana, prickly with desire.

You who sang America are flush now with death,
your poems—bits of your spine and skull—
ablaze in black water drawing you on.

Allen Ginsberg, your flesh is indigo.
The color of Krishna's face, Mira's bitter grace.
Into hard water you leap, drawing me on.
I hear you call: "Govinda, aaou, aaou!"

Reggie Cabico

Biography

Reggie Cabico was a recipient of a 1997 New York Foundation for the Arts Fellowship in Poetry. His work appears in numerous anthologies, including *Aloud: Voices from the Nuyorican Poets Cafe*, *Political Voices* and *Returning a Borrowed Tongue: Filipino American Poetry*. He was the winner of the 1993 New York Poetry Slam, a Road Poet on Lollapalooza and the opening act of MTV's Free Your Mind Spoken Word Tour. He is the editor of *Poetry Nation: An Anthology of North American Spoken Word & Written Poetry* (Vehicule Press, 1998). He teaches at The Writer's Voice.

Benny's Burritos

I finish my glass of water and a non-English-speaking busboy quickly refills my glass and runs away. There's nothing in the personals and I contemplate eating the uncovered red and green hot sauces on the table. I'm by the door and a draft comes in. Drizzle beats the windows. I want my vegetable-of-the-day plate with black beans. Where is my waiter?

And then it happens.

"Do you mind if I sit here with you? There are no tables for one and I really don't feel like sitting at the bar." (Here is divine intervention at play)

"Are you all right?" he clinically says to me.

The man's black hair is dripping wet, as if he's come from the ocean naked in a shell like Aphrodite. But this is no goddess. This is a Roman god.

I stare at him like seeing a black and white 70-millimetered Sal Mineo for the first time. He shakes his brown beaten-leather airplane jacket like a graceful matador in the ring.

The black hair and rich blue eyes are the fatalistic combination of pain and a tortured past.

"I have severe gas," he struggles to say, collapsing on the chair in front of me.

"What did you say?" I fall five floors into reality.

"Well, it's work. The whole 9-to-5 thing, the city, the people, the pressure. Do you know that I cursed an old woman at the Mid-Manhattan branch of the library? Have you ever done that at a library?"

No, but I cursed out mothers and their children when I played Mowgli from *The Jungle Book* for Disney.

"Well, I was standing in the periodical line and the sweetest woman straight from Norman Rockwell . . . I mean you just knew that she could bake an apple pie . . . Well she got in front of and acted like she belonged there and I don't care how old you are—you *don't* get in front of me—and then she plays this help-I've-fallen-and-this-guy's-an-asshole-routine and then their fat guards come in and their cocaine Cujo drug dogs start sniffing my crotch."

Lucky dog. He is definitely gay. I sense this from the gaydar detector deep within my loins.

We breathe simultaneously. Our gaze does not leave each other's eyes. He smiles and displays teeth as white as a package of Johnson & Johnson dental floss.

"I'm Wayne." He extends his pitcher's arm to me.

"I'm Reg."

Our hands lock forever.

"And I'm Robert, your waiter . . ."

We release our hands on the table, losing equilibrium. Maybe looking for a menu.

"Together or separate?" says Robert like a time bomb. "I mean the check."

We keep our eyes on the menu.

"I'll be right back in a minute," says Robert.

He was never seen again.

I am ready to marry him on the spot, live on Long Island, adopt children and work as an accountant—but we decide it is too late. He is leaving for a law conference in Los Angeles.

It's a little after midnight and I come to my slum hole of an apartment, dazed from some tropical liqueur. I play Barbra Streisand's *For the Record* compilation and sing "Happy Days Are Here Again."

Wrapping the pile of ragged comforters around me, I turn the halogen off and fall sound asleep to Whitney Houston and Dolly Parton singing, "I Will Always Love You," repeatedly throughout the night.

From *The Shortest Distance*

My geometry teacher, Mrs. Watchko, handing me my first D (after that I called her Mrs. Warlock), told me, "The shortest distance between two points is a straight line, don't forget it." Back then, I was only interested in the drama club and knew that I could portray anything but straight.

I'm teaching a poetry class for seventh graders. Their first assignment is to write a list poem with their wishes: killing Courtney Love and transferring her soul to Miss Piggy, to have X-ray vision and live next door to Sonic Youth. Everyone wants free Knicks tickets. When they ask me how to write a poem, I tell them that there are no rules, anything goes.

Other poets ask if it's like teaching in *Dangerous Minds*—the junior version. I say, "No, it's more like *Dead Man Walking* because you've got a short time to leave a lasting impact. Poetry that will be the difference between survival and death."

For example, I'm teaching them the Nikki Giovanni kidnap poem—the one that goes: "lyric you in lilacs/ode you with my love songs." I ask them what *ode* means and Julio says, "Like if you give money then I ode you it back."

Julio asks me what I wish for and I say, "I wish I were a Disney cartoon voice, that I could time travel and were a bit taller."

Worn out from a university tour, I called Guillermo from O'Hare Airport not expecting him to answer at seven a.m. EST. "Bad news, Koka is in the hospital. It doesn't sound good. They think it's AIDS but they're not sure. I remember she lost weight, but . . ."

Guillermo and I had been dating for six months and even though Koka was Guillermo's college friend from Buenos Aires, she took the place of his older sister delivering an ancient oracle, whose approval I sought. It seems absurd, but while she was in New York, I wanted to impress her with Thai dishes I never cooked and spontaneous witticisms that fell flat by the time Guillermo made the Spanish translations.

Her photo is above the computer. She's wearing dark glasses and leaning against a lamppost on Bleecker Street. She took the first picture of Guillermo and me by Battery Park. And I believe that I received her blessings before she left. Over the year, she sent postcards with her illustrations and a quote from the Bible's Apocalypse.

In Williamsburg, spring seems impossible. Frost covers our windows, while on the other side of the East River stores like Saks display gigantic calla lilies and bumblebees. Headless mannequins sport the season's latest collections. In their hollow palms rest jars of homespun honey.

This evening, Guillermo received the call that Koka had died. Her body was cremated to avoid infectious contamination.

Tomorrow, he'll take the day off. I imagine he'll go through her letters again, laying her pictures and postcards in chronological order on the living room floor, in search of an explanation:

a thumb print
subtext
writing analysis
a ring

Sometimes the shortest distance between two points comes in an inexplicable cycle that has nothing to do with Jesus Christ or karma.

It's 10:30 p.m. and a halo of calm surrounds Guillermo.

Maybe he wants to tell me that he's tired of eating white tuna and garlic and fears he might lose me by breaking the pattern that we've set or maybe he really liked the meal and wants to curl in a heavy sleep.

Next week, I'll find myself in Heidelberg, reading the same poems by mechanical rote and Barbara, a flower child, will teach my class. Maybe she will ease my queasiness of flying across the Atlantic.

Perhaps she'll give me suggestions of things to do besides praying the rosary. As a girl, she'll narrow her eyes to locate the auras of people crossing the terminal—if they are not visible then she'll know that's the end of their future.

The last assignment is to write portrait poems of family members and pets, using photographs. The older the better. Explain to the class the artist's valuable tool: sense memory. Not the kind used to list the names of dead presidents and rap songs or phone numbers, but the one, when with their eyes closed and arms stretched outward, they can invoke from the air what was lost in childhood—the shortest distance between themselves and the paper.

Spring Poem That Was Supposed to Be a Sestina

Living with another poet
can make you crazy

like the waiting list to use the computer

or the way he sneaks up behind you
to check
what's on
the screen

You're tempted to steal
each other's metaphors

like the loose change hidden
in his crumpled trousers

Take the dove
on our fire escape, who we've named Rita

and her babies: Paz, Bishop, Ai & Neruda

He wants Rita for an upcoming elegy
and I want them all for a spring sestina

You understand how difficult it is
to develop an allegory

with little money—

but we still drive in each other
a hard bargain

Ken Chu

"Boys Will Be Girls" addresses queer presence in ethnic communities, our position in the sexual hierarchy and social bias toward its marginalized members. It places the concern of Asian and Pacific Island gay and lesbian youths in the public arena. A large number of young people attempt suicide because they have nowhere to turn to address questions about their sexual identities. These are challenging issues for second- and third-generation Asian American youths with very little support from families with gay and lesbian children. Installed at eye level, a bathroom wall mirror hurls "GOOK FAG CHINK FAIRY" in its reflection. On a glass shelf below the mirror is a pile of bubble gum embedded with single-edged razor blades.

Marianne Villanueva

In the early 1980s, I worked as an executive secretary at the accounting firm of Ernst & Whitney. It was an education in many ways. I
discovered that a master's degree in East Asian Studies was worthless
in the American job market. Then I realized that all I really wanted
to do was write.

Biography

Marianne Villanueva was born and brought up in Manila. She has master's degrees in East
Asian Studies and Creative Writing from Stanford University. Her book *Ginseng and Other
Tales from Manila* was a finalist for the Manila Critics' Circle National Book Award in 1992.
Her stories have been widely anthologized. Villanueva has just completed a second collec-
tion of short fiction, *Bad Thing*, and contributes regularly to the *San Francisco Chronicle Book
Review*.

Personal History

I

Accidents

She landed in Flushing by a series of accidents. She was in graduate school in California, studying for a master's degree in English. The month before she was to graduate, she found out that her parents didn't want her to go back to Manila.

She began to remember snatches of conversation from her various phone calls. She remembered her parents saying that they were worried there might be an imminent military coup. These worries seemed to have cropped up suddenly, without warning. Was her father's business all right, she wanted to know. He was president of a large credit corporation. No, was the reply. Many people had defaulted on their loans.

Dreams

She had planned to become a teacher, back in the Philippines. It seemed she had always wanted to do this. But she had no idea what to do with herself, with her masters degree, now that she had to change her plans.

She found herself thinking more and more of New York City.

Her mother had lived there as a young girl while attending music classes at Juilliard.

Teresa was full of her mother's stories of the museums and the recital halls. She knew Carnegie Hall and Radio City Music Hall, if only from her dreams. And so she packed her things and went to New York.

Big

And the city was big—just as she had always imagined it would be. Walking down the avenues, the intermittent and powerful rumble of subway cars rushing past below her sometimes caused her to feel light-headed with happiness. She found that, in New York, everything matched perfectly with her expectations: the busy, grimy streets, with their constantly steaming manholes; the sour-faced people; the looming buildings. She was thrilled by both the squalor and the grandeur of it.

Every day she took the 7 train from Flushing to Grand Central Station, and from there took the IRT Lexington line up to Fifty-third, to her office at the top floor of the Citicorp Building. She was twenty-one. Everything seemed to be an adventure. She was an executive secretary at an accounting firm.

Her Apartment

The accounting firm paid her $13,000 a year. She could not afford an apartment in Manhattan. After asking around among various friends and acquaintances, she was told about a Filipina who lived all by herself in the basement of a house in Flushing. This Filipina's last name was Ocampo. Teresa had known some Ocampos, back in Manila. One, Mario, was a good friend of her father's. She might have been thinking of Mario when she eagerly accepted the woman's offer to split her apartment's $200-a-month rent.

She was still thinking in terms of relationships back home. She was still not really at home in America.

Winter

When the weather turned cold, she worried. She didn't think she would be able to make it to work. Already, it took her an hour and a half: the half-hour walk to the Flushing station, and then two changes of trains taking her a full hour before she got off at her stop on Fifty-third and Lex.

Because it was cold and had begun to snow, she spent fifty dollars for a pair of winter boots. The boots had smooth undersoles and would not keep her from slipping on the slushy sidewalks. She asked the salesman to cut the synthetic material underneath, to give her a better grip. This he did, scoring the soles with long diagonal slashes he made with an X-Acto knife.

When she first felt the frigid wind blowing down the avenues, she felt as though she were being stabbed by a thousand needles. She called home; her mother was not much help.

"Take vitamins," her mother said. Her mother suggested a brand, Theragran-M. "They will give you more energy."

Cristina

Her roommate, Cristina, was studying for a business degree, taking night classes. She slept in most mornings and Teresa got up by herself in the early dark and made herself coffee in the cold kitchen. Then she set off for work, always glancing regretfully at Cristina's gold car as she passed it, parked in the driveway.

When Teresa arrived home from work, late in the evening, Cristina would still be in the apartment, talking on the phone. She could talk for hours. She stopped only when she heard Teresa moving about in the kitchen. Then she dashed out the door, her keys jangling, shouting, "I'm late for class! I'm late!"

When she returned from her night classes, she would be on the phone again until past midnight. She would keep the phone cradled to her ear while she got into bed, and continue talking, curled up under her blanket.

The First Strange Thing

It was while Teresa was living in Flushing, Queens, that the first strange thing happened.

It happened in the winter: her first winter of dark and cold. She remembered sliding on slippery sidewalks in her thin-soled boots, hanging on to bushes to keep from falling when the wind blew. She was bundled up in layers of clothes and wore a heavy coat. A woolen hat was pulled down all the way over her head, half covering her eyes. The subways stank. There were more people crowded into the cars. Everyday Teresa was crushed by the presence of so many bodies, pressing up against her. Her spirits sank lower and lower.

One day she heard from a friend in California that a Filipina had been murdered. This fact, with its awful finality, struck her full in the face and filled her with fear as she walked home alone in the dark and silent evenings. Now Teresa was always afraid in the city, even though at first she had loved it so much. Who hadn't heard of the nun who'd been raped in a church on the Upper West Side, forty-six crosses carved into her body afterward with a nail file. Lurid stories like this were with her always, screaming out from the tabloids lined up in racks on the sidewalks. But this murder in California was different. California was safe, or at least she had come to associate it in her mind with safety. Now that this had happened, she felt that she had no net beneath her at all. Anything could happen, anywhere.

Park Merced

Teresa came to learn about the murder in this way: Ben, a friend in San Francisco, used to visit two Filipinas who lived in a high-rise apartment building by a lake. The lake was Lake Merced, and the building was known as Park Merced. Everyone knew this lake. Her friends and she used to pass it on weekends, going up the Great Highway to San Francisco. They'd often wondered what it would be like to fish in it, since they always saw one or two people— never more than one or two, for some reason—in boats with fishing poles.

Cristina said that the murdered girl was related to her—a cousin, Cristina said. It always surprised Teresa that Cristina seemed to know every Filipino that Teresa mentioned by name, whether that person resided in Manila, San Francisco, or New York. She used to say, "Oh, I know so-and-so; she ran away from home when she was eighteen." And Teresa would fall silent, feeling she had relinquished all right to talk about the person at all.

Cristina theorized that Ben liked her cousin. Her cousin's name was Mia. Though Ben never said he was courting this girl, that is what it apparently seemed like to Cristina. Teresa said nothing.

The News

So—it was winter, the darkness pressed in on the tall buildings, weighing her down, and there were reports coming from California of these visits. They were also having very bad weather over there: lots of winter storms and rain. News broadcasts showed the Golden Gate Bridge swaying, all its cables creaking alarmingly, rain washing over the span.

One night, Teresa came home from work and Cristina was lying in her bed, sobbing. She came out to greet Teresa, her eyes swollen, but in answer to all Teresa's questions, she only shook her head. Ben called a short while later and told Teresa the news. The murder was very recent—only yesterday.

His voice, as he spoke, was detached, even clinical. He communicated the bare facts, and that was all. After they hung up she remained sitting on her bed, looking out the tiny basement window. She saw it had begun to snow.

Tea

The apartment was cold. After a few minutes Teresa roused herself to make some tea. Cristina came out of her room and joined her at the kitchen table.

"She was raped," Cristina said.

A kind of anger filled Teresa then, but she gave no sign. She continued to look down at her tea. The hot steam blanketed her face with a delicious smell of jasmine. Her fingers curled around the rim, as though trying to hold in the fragrance.

Without further prompting, Cristina began to describe how her cousin and the roommate had just come back from a party. Teresa found herself listening with reluctance.

The girls found the parking lot was full. Mia had to use the bathroom, so she asked her roommate to drop her off at the building. The roommate, Cristina said, was careful: she watched until Mia had entered the building before driving off. But when she went up to the apartment, Mia wasn't there. She looked around, all over, and then she began to get a bad feeling. She called the building security guard. They searched the building. They found her in the basement.

Now and then as she talked, Cristina stopped and took heaving gulps of air. She held a balled-up handkerchief to her nose. Teresa looked at her. It seemed that everything—the hard winter, the trash on the sidewalks, her own rising fear—conspired to stop up her mouth. Strange emotions were growing inside her and taking root somewhere around her heart. If she let them, they would rise up, like water over a dam, and overwhelm her. But unlike Cristina, she could not cry. She could only offer Cristina tea and then more tea. After a while, she made an excuse that she was tired. She went to her room and closed the door.

Teresa Imagines

Months later, someone was arrested. A very large man, Cristina said. She kept repeating how large he was.

"He was mildly retarded," she said. "He hung around the apartment buildings."

She imagined him in dirty white overalls—workmen's clothes. Why? She did not know. She imagined him having a small, misshapen head and a large body. She imagined the moment when Cristina's cousin got into the elevator. Would the man have been there already, or would he have entered after her? The basement was a cold, dark place, with pipes crisscrossing the ceiling. The cement floor would have been cold. There would have been a kind of stillness, afterward.

All winter, these images stayed with her.

Shortly after news of the murder reached her, she remembered walking home at night down a deserted street, when someone—a man—shouted very loudly behind her: Teresa! She knew he meant it in a friendly way. No one would call out to her that way if they wanted to hurt her. But she was frightened and didn't turn around. She held her breath and kept walking. Actually, she knew the man. Another Filipino, who lived a few blocks away, on her street. She recognized him after glancing, briefly, behind her. But Teresa didn't know anything about him. He wore a strange knit hat, almost obscuring his entire face. She didn't know where he worked and she knew only that they took the same train every morning, into Manhattan. Teresa kept walking and didn't stop until she'd reached the house where she lived, her heart pounding. It seemed the sound of her name, shouted out in the frigid night air, echoed in her ears all the way home.

Move

Eventually, she made plans to return to California. She wanted to move out of the basement apartment, and she never wanted to see Cristina again.

II

Memory lies. In the years after she moved to California, her brief time in New York began to assume unusual weight and significance. She began to think of it as a happy period in her life, a time when she was daring and bold, when she was a young woman capable of getting her first job in the big city, of finding her own apartment.

All reminiscence is a kind of fiction, we have to remind ourselves.

When Teresa was older, married, and had become a woman with a house, a dog and a young son, she saw a girl killed.

The girl was young. She wore denim cutoff shirts and white sneakers. On her back was a green knapsack. She had an abundance of curly black hair. Teresa remembered everything about her very clearly.

Claudio

The car that hit her was a blue BMW convertible, shiny and clean. The driver bore a striking resemblance to her next door neighbor, Claudio de Benedetti, who was from Italy. Sometimes Teresa saw Claudio puttering around in his backyard, and sometimes they would meet over the fence and exchange pleasantries. One year he helped Teresa and Ben trim their walnut tree. In exchange she gave him a bowl of giant strawberries.

The Driver

Teresa didn't speak to the driver. They only stood together over the girl's body, while he felt for a pulse. Pressing two fingers calmly to the side of her throat, he looked up at Teresa. Teresa looked down at him without saying a word.

They waited together for the ambulance. Someone—a man with red hair who had been engaged in construction work nearby—said he would call the police. He ran into one of the nearby houses, but though Teresa waited and watched, she never saw him come out again. A woman who happened to be passing by came up to the driver and flung a blanket around his shoulders. Afterward, he sank to the ground and wept.

Girl

Teresa had seen the girl flung up in the air. In the air, the body looked stiff and awkward and didn't seem quite real. Then she landed on the windshield of the car and Teresa heard a loud crack. The crack was what told Teresa what had happened. After that, Teresa wrung her hands and wailed, "No, no, no."

There was a dog, too—a Scottish terrier that the girl had in her arms, as she crossed the street. The dog was in the air as well. At first Teresa didn't know what it was. She thought it was a wig. She thought it was very curious, that a girl so young should be wearing a wig. Later she saw the dog on the ground. It was whimpering and trying to move its legs.

Work

Teresa didn't speak to anyone while she was waiting for the police to take her statement. At that time she'd been working full-time as a program administrator in Stanford University. Her office was in the basement of a large building.

Sneak

That day, the day of the accident, she'd decided to sneak out of her office early and surprise her son. She thought she would treat him to a pizza. She hadn't told her boss she was leaving because—this was a highly unusual arrangement—he had his office in another building and hated to walk over to where Teresa was. So there were many times—whole weeks—when she never saw him. In her annual evaluations, he would write that they were in frequent email contact, which was true. Teresa supposed she could have left early every day if she had wanted to, but she was afraid to let herself do that, because she knew she would get worse and worse. She knew that if she let herself, she would simply stop coming to the office at all. This one day only, she told herself. For this one day, she had screwed up all her courage.

Teresa was impatient because each minute that the digital clock in her car moved forward, she felt that she was missing precious time, time she could be spending with her son, in the Round Table pizza parlor on El Camino. She could already imagine them sitting there, with his favorite pizza between them, talking about his day.

Police

Afterward, she was disappointed that the police didn't ask her very many questions.
They asked her about the location of her car.
"The girl flew"" she offered.
"Hmmm . . ." the officer said. "Can I see your driver's license?"

Ambulance

An ambulance pulled up behind her. Men got out, and Teresa watched as they cut off the girl's clothes. The paramedics pressed an oxygen mask to the girl's face.

People were watching. A Filipina nanny with two blond children in tow sidled up to her. "What happened here?" she asked Teresa. She looked curious; perhaps she wanted to gossip.

"A girl has been killed," Teresa said.
She saw the nanny pushing her charges forward for a closer look.

Aftermath

Because Teresa had to drive that way every day to pick up her son from school, it was impossible for her to avoid thinking about the accident.

Images would recur at odd moments, usually during the night. She began to take Benadryl, cough syrup, bottles of Nyquil. In bed she tossed and turned and cried out, once hitting Ben with such force that there was a bruise on his cheek in the morning.

Workmen

Things were happening at the intersection. Workmen were there one day, painting two parallel lines in yellow paint across the street. Then one day Teresa saw two police cars, one parked along the curb, the other parked in the exact position her car had been in when the accident occurred. The policemen were walking around, talking. Teresa passed them quickly, without turning her head.

Other Men

Once she saw a man in a dark suit, pacing the sidewalk near the intersection. He walked up and down, up and down, his hands clasped behind his back, his head lowered, giving the impression he was deep in thought.

And once there was a young man who came every day for about two weeks. He had dark, curly hair, like the girl who was killed. He would pace, looking at the ground, and then suddenly squat on his haunches, squinting at the street, at the passing cars.

But gradually, she stopped seeing so many strangers pacing about the sidewalk. There was nothing, even, in any of the papers, not even the small city paper that was delivered free to all their homes in the afternoons.

Her nights became peaceful again.

Veins

All this took a long time, a very long time. So that before Teresa knew it, winter had come and gone. The trees in their pocket-size backyard had come into leaf. Suddenly her son had added two inches to his height and his body looked long and bony, though there was a kind of wiry strength in his arms when he pushed her away from him at odd moments, moments when she would try and put her arms around him. At work, things were not going so well. Her boss had decided that their center would host a large national conference on American cultural identity. Teresa thought it was impossible for her, the lone staff member, to handle all the correspondence and at the same time keep the office running smoothly. But she said nothing. She watched the veins on the backs of her hands deepen and take root, spreading across her fingers.

III

Memory

Why did the accident, the seeing of the girl killed, remind her of the dark and cold of her winter in New York?

When she was alone in her bedroom, lying down and looking at the patterns thrown on the walls by the window shades, she felt as though it was winter again. She tried to reimagine her time in New York as a happy time, but could not. Instead, she remembered the fear.

One day she decided to walk out of her job. Just like that, without giving any notice. There was a leak in the basement of the building where she worked, and the carpets were soaked. Her boss was very upset. Without saying anything, Teresa gathered her things together and left a note saying that she was not coming back.

Ben was upset when he found her at home, lying on the bed. When she told him the news.

These events seemed a long time ago.

Mojácar

For a while after leaving her job, she was in Spain. A friend who had moved there urged Teresa to come and visit her. Her friend lived in a large house in a small village. The village was called Mojácar. The village, on the southeastern coast was dry, rocky, with white-washed Moorish houses. One night, Teresa walked uphill, up winding narrow streets, and ended up facing a house. There was music coming from it, and through one of the open windows she could see a huge oil painting on one of the walls. She thought it looked like an image of a woman with horns.

Afterward, on the way back to her friend's house, Teresa stopped at the bottom of the hill, where there was an old Moorish fountain. Old women clothed in black were drawing jugs of water. Teresa sat on a stone bench and listened to their whispery voices, dry like the sound of crackling paper. She worked the edges of her skirt between her fingers until the sun went down.

Pebble

Somehow, things had all come right. One day Teresa told her friend, "I am going home." "No, stay with me a while longer," the friend said. She knew Teresa was not happy with Ben.

"No, I'm going," Teresa said. She had a pebble in her right fist. She'd found it on the terrace that morning, and something about it reminded her of the granite rocks her son liked to collect on his hiking trips. I am going home, Teresa repeated.

To prove it to herself, that very day Teresa took the bus down to the Playa, to the big travel agency in the Parque Commercial. There was a large woman sitting behind the desk. Surrounded by a wreath of cigarette smoke, she smiled at Teresa and said, *Dígame.* Reaching into her bag for her credit card, Teresa had a flash of knowledge: All my time in Spain, she thought, was meant for just this moment. The woman's hand on her arm seemed weighty and significant. *"Dígame,"* the woman repeated.

Eileen Tabios

"Time is merciless; it ravages us all. (Jasper) Johns' paintings may seem to hint at this unrelievable sorrow, but they never succumb to it."

> — John Yau

Biography

Eileen Tabios was born in the Philippines, grew up in Los Angeles and first moved to New York City to attend Barnard College. Editor of *The Asian Pacific American Journal*, her poetry, fiction and essays appear in numerous publications internationally as well as in cyberspace. Her books include a poetry collection, *Beyond Life Sentences*; a collection of poetry, essays and interviews, *Black Lightning: Poetry-in-Progress* and, as editor, *Doveglion: Selected Works of Jose Garcia Villa*.

Blue Richard

The first time I lay beneath him on his bed, I thought gray paint stained the hollows beneath his eyes. As if I could lick away the shadows, I couldn't help myself from darting out a tongue. But he swiftly captured it with his lips and I drowned. From the far distance of the streets, the sounds of raucous horns and vendors yelling in Chinese only served to make me grasp him tighter. Once I opened my eyes toward a window and noticed the fall of dusk surrounding a red neon sign flickering.

He took me to Africa. Drums sounded in the distance, far behind the rain that fell outside our tent and served to enhance the warmth of its interior. Or perhaps I only thought it would be appropriate to have invisible men beating on taught animal skins to provide an arbitrary rhythm for my uncontrolled heaving as he lay before me, willingly pinned beneath my thighs while his hands held my swollen breasts to his suckling lips.

The first time he noticed me, another woman was leaving his lips. He was tall, so she had to reach up to his darkly tanned face, allowing her also to press her breasts against the white camellia painted across his chest. It was winter in Manhattan but he wore a short-sleeved Hawaiian shirt.

He caught me staring when he lifted a Bass Ale and used the movement to wipe off the pink stains from his lips. I quickly looked away, but not before he managed to lift an eyebrow at me from across the crowded room of the gallery. Beyond the window, a streetlamp flickered through the mist. I heard rain end.

Later, he had my back against the wall. He said he liked my paintings that were hanging in the group show. He was the gallery's most important artist. I shook my hair forward to cover my eyes. I peered at him and mumbled, *Thanks. Not like your paintings, of course.*

I meant it as a compliment. He pretended to misunderstand and said something about the individual vision unique to each artist. But what I recall most clearly was the graze of his fingers against my cheek as he drew away the curtain of hair that hid my eyes. His fingers were tipped by calluses whose roughness on my skin I wished would never end. Later, he would say he noticed me part my lips at his touch and he had to force himself to walk away.

He called me after we met at the gallery. I looked at the hour as I heard his voice. *Five a.m.?* I asked. *I wanted to wake you,* he replied. Then he told me to go back to sleep and dream of him. I dreamt of him using a knife to slice away at the tight rubber pants encasing a redhead whose hair matched the stains on his lips. She also wore black bikinis that fell as he flicked a blade. She wanted to lift a cashmere sweater to show her breasts but he said it wasn't necessary. When I woke, my cheeks and thighs were wet.

He insisted on feeding me dinner that weekend, but I met him unexpectedly on the street the day after I dreamed of him. I was looking at a painting through a window. The artist failed, his voice rippled my hair. *How?* I asked as he turned me around to face him. *Because in painting a woman dropping an orange, the artist painted the orange in midair,* he said before placing his lips on my cheek, then lingering for a while as I stood, immobilized. *A fall is always complete*, he added as his lips touched the corner of mine. Snow began to fall as he walked away.

The sake was cold in entering. *Heating it hides imperfections*, he said as he refilled my tiny cup. I raised my cup once more to avoid his eyes, even as I felt my first sip begin to simmer within. The clear liquid revealed a series of blue concentric circles on the bottom of the cup. I tasted tart green apples as I took a second sip. I noticed a vein throbbing in his wrist. I could feel his gaze on my lips and wondered what he looked like when he smiled.

Afterward, he took me to a party in a neighborhood I didn't recognize. The party was in a brownstone and its revelers spilled forth onto the sidewalk. He was greeted with happy cries as soon as we turned into the street. We walked toward the brownstone. The other houses on the block were dark, with no signs of life. Light sparkling through all of its many windows, the brownstone glimmered like a solitaire nestled in black velvet. I felt his friends' glances like little stabs. He introduced me to no one. He merely circled an arm around me and spoke over my head to the others. They kept coming up to him as if they couldn't help themselves. I found it easier to cling to him and bury my face beneath his chin. The others kept stabbing at me.

He left me once, shortly after midnight. He drew back and breathed against my closed eyes. *Look at me*, he whispered. After I obeyed, he said he had to talk to someone in another room. I'll be right back, he promised. He returned after two hours. I was in the corner of the room where he left me. He saw my eyes grab him as soon as he looked through the doorway. He took his time walking to where I sat trembling on a chair, where I had been ignored or stabbed by the others. One woman in the first hour of his absence hissed, *He'll leave you, too*, as she pretended to place an empty glass by the table next to my chair. In the second hour, a man tried to engage my breasts in conversation until I bluntly said, *Go away.*

I wouldn't look at him when he finally stood in front of me. I watched his hands slowly lift to reach for me. He drew me up and returned me to the comfort of burying my face beneath his chin. *I wanted you to know what it is like without me*, he whispered as he tightened his arms. I could feel his heart beating erratically. I refused to look at him, even when he said, *I'll never lie to you again.* I refused to look at him until he added, *I missed you, too.*

No, I said the next day, and the day after. No, I repeated again when he called the following week. Then a new month began and I marked it by having dinner with another man. Afterward, we went to listen to jazz at several clubs. I was drunk by the time I also rejected him and left the cab that returned him to where he came from. For a moment, I stood there watching the cab's orange headlights recede. I thought, *He would have been kind.* I noticed a slight mist turn its way onto my street. When I turned toward my door, he was waiting for me.

I walked up the stoop and tried to ignore him. But my hands shook as I tried to insert my keys. His voice was soft as he took them from my hand and opened the door. *I'm glad you turned him down.* He followed me into the foyer. I made another effort, stopped and said, *I can manage from here.* He lifted his hand and palmed my cheek, then began rubbing his thumb against my lips. *No, you can't.* I fainted into his arms. When I woke, I was in my bed, naked. It was morning and he was nowhere in sight. I had flung off the bedsheets and the sun was warm as it streamed through the window, melting the ice on its panes.

I rose and walked toward the full-length mirror behind my bedroom door. I saw blood-shot eyes drop to the rest of my body. I noted one breast was still slightly smaller than the other, the bones of my ribcage still protruded, my waist still expanded into my hips, dark strands still curled into one another between my thighs and the birthmark shaped like a tear still stained my left thigh. I also noticed my nipples were puckered as if they were small fists, tightly clenched. I reached for a note stuck in the side of the mirror. He had written, *I love the teardrop on your thigh.*

He rarely smiled with his lips. I had to look into his eyes. It took me a while to discover this because I fought him for a long, long time before I first drowned in his arms. The second time was in the bedroom of a stranger hosting a party. The sounds of cocktail chatter and a string quartet permeated through the closed door. I slowly unbuttoned the high neck of a silk dress and let it fall. At his request, I had worn nothing underneath. I walked to where he sat on the bed watching me intently. I sat on his lap and hid my face in the nape of his neck while he stroked my breasts. Then he picked me up and laid me on the bed. *Open your eyes*, he whispered. *Keep them open*, he added as he parted my thighs. *Keep them open*, he whispered again as I began to undulate against his fingers. *There*, he said. *There.*

But I did fight for a long time. *No*, I said when he called the afternoon after he left me a love letter to face when I sought my reflection. *No*, I said again the following day. A few days later, I saw him across the street from my door, leaning against a car and an unlit cigarette between his lips. He had seen me first and watched my steps falter when I noticed him. He continued to watch me walk toward my door, open it and step in. He didn't try to stop me.

I visited the gallery during the last day of the group show that featured two of my paintings. I stood behind a column trying to listen to the comments of an elderly couple who had paused in front of my paintings. My dealer had whispered they were fairly well-known art collectors. I saw him enter the gallery and divert their attention. *Sweetheart*, the wife called out and he walked over to join them. He gave no sign of noticing me, though he must have seen me. *What do you think of this painting?* she asked, touching his sleeve familiarly. *A lot of promise, but not quite there*, he said after giving my painting five seconds. *Dear, that's what I told you*, the man told his wife. *Let's talk about you. Do you have any new pieces?* I heard them make an appointment for dinner before I walked away and out the door.

I paused in front of a red light and felt my heart beating quickly, desperately. *You could join us for dinner*, he said. I wasn't surprised that he had followed me. I turned around and looked into his eyes. He was smiling. *Come, let me buy you a black dress*, he said, taking my hand. My rage died and I felt separated from my body, as if I was curious to see what I would do next. He paused before we entered a small, expensive boutique and raised both my hands. He started rubbing them as he observed, *Your hands are cold.*

Monsieur, the designer and shopkeeper greeted him familiarly. *It's nice to see you again*, she said as they traded kisses on both cheeks. I refused to utter a word even when he introduced us. Her smile didn't slip as she asked him, *A black dress?* She turned toward a rack and confidently chose five outfits. Four were minidresses while one had a long skirt with a thigh-high slit. *Mademoiselle, after you?* she said, drawing aside a curtain to a dressing room. He asked to see me in each outfit, smiling each time and ignoring my ankle-high workboots. Afterward, he said, *I'll take them all.*

It's the first time Monsieur has bought more than one outfit at a time, she whispered to me as she packaged the dresses. I replied brusquely, I don't care. She smiled serenely and said, *I don't believe you.* When I opened the boxes later that day, I discovered she had included sheer black stockings and a different bottle of perfume with each outfit.

I chose a dress at random and wore it to *Chanterelle* that evening. By each table, huge mounds of lilies bloomed, their scent weighting the air. I had insisted that I would meet them at the restaurant. Don't forget or pretend to forget, he whispered after raising my chin with one hand and brushing aside my hair with the other. I kept my eyes closed and said, *I never break my promises.* He responded, *Neither do I.* I opened my eyes when I felt he wanted to kiss me. But he didn't, only rubbed his thumb once more over my lips.

The art patrons were pleased to meet the young painter who, he had said, showed immense promise. They also had bought one of my paintings after I had fled from the gallery. *We agreed it would be a nice way to encourage a promising artist*, the man said. *But I genuinely love your painting*, his wife quickly added. I spoke only to her after that, carefully ignoring both men. Afterward, he said, *I'll take you home.*

I let him in but before we could take off our coats demanded, *How dare you!* He merely smiled and took off his coat and flung it on the sofa. *Let me*, he said, turning me around and taking off my coat, which he threw over his. Then he picked me up and carried me into the bedroom. *No*, I said. *I know*, he replied, and laid me gently on the bed. Then he sat beside me and began to watch me. After a few moments, I closed my eyes and whispered, *Please.*

The third time I drowned, it was my birthday and he had reserved a suite at the Plaza Hotel. The fire blazed. We sat opposite each other on armchairs enased in gold and red brocade. As he sipped cognac, his eyes never left me. *Thank you*, I said about the emerald pendant dangling on a gold chain. I'd like to see you wearing nothing else. My fingers fumbled as

I put it around my neck. Without looking at him, *I began to take off my pearl earrings*, my silver watch and my jade ring. Then I looked at him as I stood. Slowly, I stepped out of my shoes and rolled down my stockings. His face remained impassive even when I stepped out of the damp fragment of lace that had sought to cover my flesh. Then I drew the dress over my head. I stepped back into my high heels before walking toward him. *You're right*, he said as he dribbled the remaining drops of cognac on my breasts. *The emerald and your legs in high heels*. Then he licked my breasts as I arched my back, my fingers lost in his hair.

After he took me home from dinner at Chanterelle, I had whispered, *Please*. I opened my eyes. No, he said. *Not yet*. Then he leaned over and kissed my forehead. I grabbed his arms as he started to withdraw. *Please*. Easily, he freed himself then held my hands still against the bed. Still, I raised myself and tried to kiss him. He kept his lips still as I pressed them with mine. *Please. Don't you want me?* I pleaded. Without a word, he withdrew. After I heard the front door close, I wept before dropping off into a fitful sleep. When the phone rang the next morning, I knew the hour was five a.m. He told me to dream more dreams and go to his studio in Chinatown that evening.

As I walked into his studio, I saw myself as he sees me. The paint was still wet. I just finished it, he said. *Until last night, I couldn't finish it*. Most of the color was in my eyes, enlarged off scale and with red cracks across their surfaces. The rest of the painting was in shades of white and thin, black lines. Despite the bloodshot eyes, the figure posed in a relaxed, almost serene manner. *Why last night?* I asked, firmly keeping my eyes on the painting. Look at me, he said. When I met his eyes, he said, *Because you knew to beg*.

The first time I lay beneath him on his bed, I thought gray paint stained the hollows beneath his eyes. As if I could lick away the shadows, I couldn't help myself from darting out a tongue. But he swiftly captured it with his lips and I drowned. From the far distance of the streets, the sounds of raucous horns and vendors yelling in Chinese only served to make me grasp him tighter. Once I opened my eyes toward a window and noticed the fall of dusk surrounding a red neon sign flickering.

Others must have wanted you, I said after the first time, my face buried beneath his chin, his hands slowly rubbing my back. *No one showed as much promise*, he said. I raised my head and looked into his eyes. He was smiling. *Promise at what?* He quickly flipped me on my back and started nuzzling my neck before continuing to my breasts while his fingers teased my thighs. *Promise at what?* I gasped insistently even as my hips pressed toward his fingers. But he would-n't say and I soon stopped asking, trying instead to breathe.

The last time I drowned, we were surrounded by Africa. Drums sounded in the distance, far behind the rain that fell outside our tent and served to enhance the warmth of its interior. Or perhaps I only thought it would be appropriate to have invisible men beating on taught animal skins to provide an arbitrary rhythm for my uncontrolled heaving as he lay before me, willingly pinned beneath my thighs while his hands held my swollen breasts to his suckling lips. Thrice, I gasped, *Richard.*

The next day, he left early for a safari while I stayed behind to finish a series of paintings for an upcoming show. The next time I saw him, he was barely breathing. The guides had shot the lion, but that was no consolation. *Please*, I begged. But he died in my arms. Before he closed his eyes, he smiled one last time.

In New York, my show opened to rave reviews and was quickly sold out. You certainly lived up to your promise, the art collectors said after they bought two more of my paintings. I finished another glass of wine before asking, *Did Richard ever mention what he first saw in my early works?* She smiled and patted my arm gently. *Oh yes, dear. Richard said you would have the courage to fall completely. Fall completely—didn't he have such a way with words?* Her husband nodded and said, *These paintings, for instance, you can walk into their center forever. In your early paintings, you hadn't yet figured out, as a critic once said, how to punch that hole in the canvas.*

I forced myself to smile, then accepted their congratulations once more before excusing myself. I walked into the gallery owner's office and shut the door behind me. The painting I had withdrawn from the show was still poised on a chair. I walked toward the canvas with its heavily-layered brush strokes featuring a vortex that spun into a center of a dark blue circle. In each curve on the top half of the painting, I saw his eyebrow raised at me. In each curve on the bottom half of the painting, I saw his smile. I followed the curves in *Blue Richard* until they led me to the center where I drowned so that I could feel his arms lift me up to breathe.

My Staten Island Ferry Poem

"To be taken up higher and higher by uneven stone stairs and to stand there with your heart beating outside the gate of the near world. To gather laurel and marble for the white architecture of your destiny.

And to be as you were born, the center of the world."

- Odysseus Elytis

You tell me the lights remind you of Tuscany, the fires in homes dotting the hillsides. I am looking at these same stars and see dying men in white shirts toiling past midnight in the sky-scrapers of Manhattan. Beneath our feet, the Hudson is gentle for once, like the cheek of a woman's face in repose. Are you looking at me as I tilt my face elsewhere to hide the yearning in my gaze? A cloud lifts and the pale moon is unclothed. Then its silver shadow ripples across the water, loosening languid drops of mercury. Translucent pearls warm my skin. I hear flint struck on the other side of our earth: gasp with delight as its heat burns white against my eyes. I often amuse you with my fantasies of other men you know better than I do. These are the poets in Manila who feel I am only five years old—they tape all my watercolors against their windows so that the sun's rays enter their homes as rainbows. And you? You merely keep loos-ening the generous ball of twine from which I soar: a kite in flight, dangling, but which you never let fall. I might be a dragon, a raven, a butterfly or Glinda riding her broom. Or I might be a salvaged piece of pockmarked paper, its edges glued around sticks to approximate some shape of geometry. Always, you never enforce gravity, though we know it is a temptation you ignore.

Later, our friend Curtis will cackle about this all-night ride on the Staten Island Ferry. "Boy, you'd think you all were in high school or something!" he will tease. I remember when I was that young. I had more hair and it fell to the back of my knees. I wore platform shoes with seven-inch heels. Dittos was *the* brand of jeans—I wore them in saffron shades of orange to befit the California sunshine. I had a waist (oh, those 24 inches!) that my low-slung Dittos and abbreviated blouses revealed. An ocean away, in a city I know today as Manila, you were chasing Rimbaud and smoking. We would have hated each other back then. It is no longer back then.

The stairs are uneven and I cannot see where they halt their rise. I climb, pause for air by inhaling whole whirlwinds, then climb once more. Still, the stone ledges do not reveal their climax—is it a "happily ever after" or a cruel joke's punch line? I climb and climb until the rush of water is turbulent in my ears. It is like what I am hearing with you tonight on the

Staten Island Ferry. The river is lyrical with its minute swells. The clouds are so far away. The moon is replete. And all I hear as the fires burn in Tuscany straight ahead is the rush of memories yet to be birthed. The dock approaches. I peer through the darkness and latch on to another breeze to soar. Straight ahead is a sunlit day, the press of the sky against the horizon as careful as you. Consequently, the horizon is invisible, masking where journeys are thought to end.

Grey, Surreptitiously

Sometimes I am not tired. And I begin to pace the perimeter of Manhattan. I am always drawn to the East River, how the water is consistently grey and this sensibility mists over the entire East Side: it swathes the total territory in a wool suit. And it makes me recall interchangeable cities in Eastern Europe where the only spots of color are offered by tiny pastries silently waiting behind glass. Afterward, I finish with memories of museum exhibits salvaging dusty armors from the crusades of a different century.

I am surprised that I linger in this part of the city, that the river's surface loses its drabness to enfold me like cashmere. Unexpectedly, patchouli and cinnabar begin to linger in the air though I see no one dodging my careful steps. I feel the birth of pearls in tropical ocean beds tended by boys burned by the sun. Then I feel one pearl's inexplicable caress in the hollow between my breasts.

A woman rounds a bend and sees me. I pause by a white birch tree stripped by winter of its leaves. She smiles as she approaches. I wish to feel my fingers loosening her jeweled combs. Already, I can feel her hair curl shyly against my fingers like the breaking of surreptitious surf. No words would be spoken, but a window from an anonymous building would open to loosen the faint tinkling of piano notes. They would be plucked from the highest scale.

My fingers would turn blue in the cold. They would freeze in their fraught pose, laid against a stranger's scented cheek while her hair would continue to flutter in a faint breeze. And her lashes would trap a beginning snow. And her life-generating breaths would occur through parted lips. And her eyes, too, would be the deadening of a river: translucent and grey.

Lisa Yun

Biography

Lisa Yun is a professor at SUNY Binghamton. She was born in Queens, baptized at
Chinatown's Transfiguration Church on Mott Street, and now lives in Brooklyn and
Binghamton. Her family came from Toisan, China, and settled in Manhattan's Chinatown,
including her grandmother, who recently became a U..S. citizen at the age of ninety-four.
Her work has appeared in *The Paterson Literary Review*, *The Seattle Review*, *The Georgetown
Review*, *The Hawaii Pacific Review*, *LIPS* and *Illya's Honey*, among others, and is included in a
forthcoming anthology from Viking Penguin.

Saturday in Chinatown

Every Saturday
I visit my grandmother.
Like thousands of the faithful
after college, employed
"erudite"

guilty
frustrated
by the silence
of their ancestors
no speaky English.

I climb
steep stairs
of a narrow
building
beige paint
peeling
ceiling
slung low
steps kneeling
to the next
American-made
grandchild.

I smile
as she peers up carefully
from the crack in the door.

Every Saturday I visit my grandmother.
She makes me soup.

I slurp carelessly
while she sits
alone

dark
on a small wooden stool.
Quiet
eyes blinking
hands folded
feet unbound.

She had a man, across the ocean,
but now her face is
silent
far away.

"Grandma," I say softly.
She stares into space
and I leave her be.

Sewing by the Piece

Eight years have passed
and I still wear him, his 24-karat ring,
still wear him and his smell
      my husband in gray trousers and white shirt
      pungent smell of garlic, scallion, soy chicken, *chow fun*
the kitchen deep in his collar
deep in his skin, under the square jaw, under the muscular arms, even between his thighs, deep
in his sex, I could
smell it still
the unspoken smell of early bitterness and yearning
the sweat of Joes in the back, wasted youth,
straining against the two p.m. to two a.m. shift, the busload of tourists,
      "vegetarian fried rice" and tea with sugar
two quarters on the table
         the disappearance of brothers known as
         Uncle One, Two and Three
      clacking knives and woks, clacking knives and woks

a long long journey from the sea to
the back door

Eight years and we are still together
his thick hair
deep black eyebrows arched in wonder
            or pain, oh yes, anything was possible
he said, let me hold you
his fine legs wrapped around me
village boy holding on to this sinking raft
jumping on the last boat to somewhere
            skin to skin, we are alive
we lick lips, salt wounds, and pull at skin
but in the day
our voices fall short, crippled wrens
we lose direction

In a fourth-story walk-up
the cracks in the almond plaster wall
gape wide open
our neighbors fight and their baby screams
I sew by the piece and the hum of the machine
            chesh, chesh, kik, kik
not far from the paper shuffle of the
INS, IRS, or the shuffle of the Wall Street banker
            maybe a woman who looks like me
            with an MBA and the amnesia of sewing machines
                chesh, chesh, kik, kik
my little girl recognizes the daily routine
it gives her comfort to have me home
I look over and tell her to sing
            our neighbor comes across to use the bathroom
            he becomes a captured audience
                chesh, chesh, kik, kik

When my husband comes home
he brings rice and chicken, we spread out the plates and pour tea. I rub my tummy, our second

baby is due in two months

the neighbors are quiet now, and my girl is asleep with

my old art books

           classical bird and flower painting

she likes to cut and paste the birds together, families,

their wings overlap

sharing the air, giving mouth-to-mouth resuscitation

Vincent Young

Of all the shit that I have seen, heard, felt and tasted, only those
famous last lines from Jim Carroll's *Basketball Diaries* have made me
physically break down and cry myself to sleep. They go something like
this: "I can see the Cloisters with its million in medieval art out
the bedroom window. I got to go in and puke. I just want to be pure
. . ."

Biography

Vincent Young was conceived in a filthy tenement in Brooklyn, born in a sterile ward at
Columbus Hospital in Manhattan, raised in Queens, and has spent his tender adolescent
years roaming the Lower East Side. His work has been published in *American Writing*,
Excursus and *Wallpaper*. He is currently procrastinating on a "novel" based on the stories of
love and survival he's heard hanging out here and there.

Dit Da Jow

The bottle broke on the back of his neck.

Its jagged mouth nicked his jaw in a shallow path that ran from right below his ear to the corner of his lip. He stumbled, reaching out to place a hand firmly over her mouth, to whip her head into the wall of the narrow hallway between the front door and the living room. He could hear her choking, trying to force the spittle back down her throat. He could hear his boots crackling and thundering on the wooden floorboards as he staggered to the bathroom.

Sometimes love isn't what's in the picture books.

Sometimes love is just what it is.

She laid her head on his shoulder as he rubbed an odd-smelling ointment he called *Dit Da Jow* on the throb at the back of her head. She churned the bottle in front of her gently, watching the faint transparent film on the surface of the bongwater murk that clung and oozed off the glass. It was a dingy brown liquid, thin and tainted with a metallic, alcoholic scent. His grandmother made it herself. She had sent it to him a long time ago in a shoebox wrapped in brown paper and bandaged with postal tape. The bottle was tiny, a Mott's Apple Juice bottle with a scrap of looseleaf paper taped over the big green letters. An uncertain *d* and cursive *it* where the "t" is for "daaih" (Big) and one stroke short of meaning "sky." The liquid inside it was slowly being lapped up by their growing assortment of bruises. Although he had hoped that he wouldn't, he would have to ask for more.

As he massaged the ointment into her scalp in slow, measured circles, she clenched her teeth and let out short, heavy breaths. It tingled, goose-pimpling her arms, when he reached the fringes of the bump on her skull. She pictured the network of veins in her head lighting up like a nighttime panoramic of a stop-motion city. Seconds later, she bit her bottom lip and fought the nausea that rose when he circled his way to the peak of her swollen flesh.

Her body unfolded. The sour odor of his grandmother's *Dit Da Jow* enveloped the room. He carried her to bed and tucked her in, kissing her good night and brushing the hair from her eyes. He left the bedroom door slightly ajar behind him as he turned out the lights, pulled a chair up by the window, and looked out into the night. Beer and cigarette in hand, he imagined what it might look like if the building directly across the way were not blocking his view of the horizon. He imagined it being expansive, stretching from where he sat to way beyond, where the streetlights and cars shrank into pinheads. A gentle breeze, faintly perfumed with barbecue charcoal and fresh-cut grass, traced a phantom finger softly down the thin sliver of flesh that the broken bottle had penciled onto his face.

Time swept by him in the dark. When he reentered the bedroom, she had totally disheveled the neat wrapping he left her in. She had kicked away the sheets and lay with his pillow tightly clutched under her arms. He checked the alarm clock and slipped into bed, folding the sheets this way and that until they were snugly tucked in together, then slipped one hand into the cool niche under her pillow. He put the other around her waist and pulled her close, until the curve of her ass fit into the jigsaw space of his genitals.

"I love you," he started to say, but she turned, placing two fingers to his lips as she kissed him gently on the cheek.

In the dark, he remembered other nights when she would trace his grandmother's words with her pinky. "Dit . . . Da . . . Jow," she would say flatly. The writing was unsteady, with thin lines that seemed to shoot up at points and speed down at others. Wispy lines like a stray hair on a pillow. So different from the kind of handwriting she saw every day but rarely paid attention to.

"No. Not like that. *Dit* . . ." he would say, lifting a pointed finger into the air to stress the higher tone of the latter half of the word.

She would get it right just once, losing the correct intonation in a quick sputter of, "dit, dit, dit, *dit*, dit . . ." She would do the same with "da" and "jow," before her spine would give way and she would wrap herself around him and fall asleep.

"*Dit* . . . *Da* . . . *Jow*," he would say once more, letting his tongue taste every syllable of the lost language.

Dit. As in to fall, or to stumble. Or maybe even as in the summer, when new winds whip thick clouds into thin wafer-thin wisps.

Da. To hit. Like you have to sometimes when the person who loves you just doesn't understand.

And *Jow*. As fast and as far as you can, until you build enough momentum to rise up and catch the stars and bring them down to light your way down here.

Bad Eulogy for a Dead Junkie Depicted in a Movie about Junkies

A hot sun
comes,
gaseous
ball of goo,
tearing
through
the clouds
like some junkie
through a sack of Sani-Flush,
and it hurts me
to see you
this way,
sitting in
your own
shit and
blood,
stinking
of hope,
with
your eyes
bugged
out from
staring
too long,
wondering
where the
shadows
went,
when
you know
damn well
that it's
high noon

and the
shadows
are
right
under
your
feet!

Counter to a Knife Attack to the Head

Years:

How does the Buddha meditate
when he's too cold?

The ancient made
the severe climate:

> There was no heat,
> you wore maybe one blanket
> and you wore the same
> winter and summer,
> which meant that you were hot,
> when you were cold,

Shiver!—What's the matter?

Seems at first glance
it says the opposite:

> "Heat kills!" But
> it's not the heat and cold
> themselves that kill—

It's the ideas about them:

Where were you last night?
I tried calling.

Sodom-You-Sodom-Me

in another time in another me
in another boy-meets-girl
another boy-loses-girl
in another world
sleep spare me from
another alternate reality
another Romeo suicide
another teenaged trauma
sweet melodrama
pretty pretty flowers
that devour
late April showers
thundering and lighting
another weekend
diminished in another room
that sometimes is too small
but most times too big
for another cigarette
another cup of coffee
another shot of
whatever you've got
in another time
in another me
save mediocrity
for a Sodom-you
and a Sodom-me

The Tale of Iwas

I am *Iwas*, captain of a craft, cruising
the galactic infrascape of memories, hushed spaces,
a TV pilot built on your flesh and fantasy-stuffs of a sitcom,
a soap opera melodrama, the voice of warm molasses oozing
over loudspeakers, under the thump and slam of an electronic pulse.
What is it that you want me to say? Who is it that you want me to be?
Do I still buy you tangy hearts come Valentine's Day? Sweet "Forget-me-
nots?" The heart has four chambers, four walls offering four "breakthroughs,"
each time looking back and saying, "I'll never make that same mistake again...
I'll never play that fool again . . . I'll never—never (what?)—again . . ."
Lost. Lost in infrascape. Hushed memory space.

I am Iwas, long before I was
a charcoal sketch penciled onto mornings,
struggling with my jeans, on the edge of our bed,
with the light slipping in from behind closed blinds,
a mass of hair and bony elbows that prick you in your sleep,
an alarm clock that wakes you with still two hours of night
to be undone, an unnerving silence, a pregnant pause,
a fumbling apology, the many regrets that I'm afraid
you already know—but shhh! I never said a word.

I am Iwas and I was born of a need to connect,
for a vision of the future, a sense of continuance,
the hidden and the inevitable, the probable and the impossible,
the sensual and nonsensical, for a name, a sense of duty, of filial piety,
the natural order of things, the survival of a species, a grand scheme
of things, destiny, progeny, family, a mommy, a daddy, siblings, purpose
and what just seemed like the right thing to do at the time.

I am Iwas and I was growing up in a womb at the time,
living in a fleshy sepulcher, a murky catacomb of meat and muscle,
red room, blood-rich, the dirges a tragic fetus sputters, wasted
on a mother's postdigested muck, ancient Chinese brews and Life Savers
candies, saved for social occasions and snapshots in a green felt album,
evidence of existence, of being, of loss, of a dream of a big city, filled
with neon lights and taxicabs, rainy nights, jazz clubs and cocaine.

I am Iwas and I was living out some notable words,
stretching out some quotable feats, when the stars came out
and pimpled the night, a billion little whiteheads on a time-told
complexion, a light breeze singed my skin, an uncharted dimension,
a subcosmic divination for a pinprick of a life, a magic trick and then some.

Ik-Joong Kang

Ik-Joong Kang is a Korean-born artist who lives in New York City. His job entailed a two-hour commute by subway, so in order to keep painting he began to work on three-inch-square canvases that he could make anywhere. His paintings are inspired by his experience of sudden immersion in urban America.

Walter K. Lew

Biography

Walter K. Lew was raised in Baltimore and now resides in Los Angeles. He has lived and written in New York at various times since 1977. His publications include *Excerpts from* Δ *IKTE DIKTH: for DICTEE* (1982), a critical collage on the work of Theresa Hak Kyung Cha, and *Premonitions*, an anthology of new Asian North American poetry, and he is preparing the selected works of the Korean modernist Yi Sang. He has received grants and fellowships from the New York State Council on the Arts, the National Endowment for the Arts, the Association for Asian Studies and the Korean Culture and Arts Foundation. His television documentaries and news stories on Korea have been broadcast internationally and his multimedia "movieteller" performances have been staged for Asian CineVision, the Asian American Renaissance and the 1990 Los Angeles Festival.

Brine

1

My woman's blood
Is of dark and salt.
She has a clay, red mouth

Which I mouth, but it will not
Sing or seal.

2

When I eat her blood
I return down a smooth dune
From the hills, and enter

A raspberry path: My mouth and fingers
stained ripe.

3

Grass, mist and sand
My woman's blood
Is of loam and rain.

With sleek wings she combs
My bloated sides.

Whispers,
And the ear is a conch.

Our heads shake
And hair is a grove,

The baywind luffing
Black shocks of
Reed and laver.

4

Morning blooms on the stained linen.
Sea mist on her hairs
Curls round my fingers

On that short, fine lawn
Wet crystals bead. In her
Thick wound, rubies smear
Like fish eggs.

5

When she is not here all week
I walk around this same town
And all the storefronts seem hushed
And flimsy, as if my eyes, salt-crystalled,
Could only dwell in her
Dense light. Dark city!

Four days I wore her deep ink
Down my waist and
Along my thighs, like a jewelled
Girdle.

6

I wait at the station,
My mouth, organs
Like a flock of mussels, shut up
To sun
And hands

Until their green wave revives.

1973

An Apartment in the City

Her new flat
West Village
"Good part of the country"
What I always

Wanted: 1200, A/C,
High walls.
                    Stockings of her apt. mate—
Would like you,
      likes Korean food.
"Fucks like a bunny." (Ray)
      Ray!   "Kicked me in the disco,
                    didn't say a thing, then
                    she hit me again
                    in front of the Coke machine.
      Shit . . . what you do then?
                    Didn't do a thing. Bitch
                    went up to the room. Hey,
                    Where else could she go?"

Goes to the couch
To turn A/C on—jesus, her hair, shoulders, and
back of knee. Miles' *E.S.P.*
on a good Sansui. "Iris." Iris
Herbie's perfect chords—   Herbie
                              Don't play like that
                              Anymore!
Doesn't matter. For her
It's a mood. 1200!
What I made the last two months, sometimes hustling
A kid, me.
But she
Honest
Money,

Father a good doctor.

Little spark plug,

Jumped up and crooned

With B.B. "The Thrill is Gone!" who

Teased him with a mike

And told him sit the hell down.

"Good doctor."

Up at Sinai,

Jew help a Jew.

Buys "the poor kid's painting." In spare time,

Keeps up on Tel Aviv poets

Unlike Mr. Kim, who thinks literature went out with

Yangban and Confucius.　　　Doesn't know his characters

　　　　　　　　　But crazy about Jeejush

　　　　　　　　　Reads Yohan again & again

　　　　　　　　　While running a fruit stand

　　　　　　　　　with wife and kids up on

　　　　　　　　　Amsterdam.　80 hrs/wk 6 years. Just bought

　　　　　　　　　a Cape Cod in Mt. Vernon.

　　　　　　　　　Son's an accountant, daughter plays

　　　　　　　　　the violin: Dartmouth, Juilliard.

　　　　　　　　　Wife got shot

　　　　　　　　　tending the shop at 3 in the morning.

　　　　　　　　　Why the fuck was she alone?

　　　　　　　　　That's not the point.

　　　　　　　　　Kkamdung-i did it.

　　　　　　　　　That's not the point.　Then,

　　　　　　　　　Stupid cousin blew away

　　　　　　　　　Nigger cunt next Sunday.

　　　　　　　　　Dancer. Friend cries out

　　　　　　　　　She just went in for a box of tampons, man!

　　　　　　　　　Koreans crazy

　　　　　　　　　Run half of Harlem.

　　　　　　　　　Walk around the warehouses

　　　　　　　　　like wolves. Stink. Blood

　　　　　　　　　in their eyes. Chinks and Niggers

(Aint *Chinese*, you asshole!)
Killing each other over
What? Of course don't have no time for your
stupid lit'chwer. Why can't you
speak Korean? Go back
to med school . . .

She broils a few big sea scallops
With lemon up for me.
Real coffee table books on a coffee table.
Rug you wouldn't mind getting buried in.
We go out to the balcony: "There,

And there!" she laughs
Pointing at windows
Where people are making love or taking their clothes off.
But I look at the pianos
Pianos. I say, *Look, I can't pretend*
anymore . . . And all I can think of is
you, Oh

My people.
I place my hands like octaves
    into
The humid breeze, and feel
Pathetically
Its sadness.
The record stops
And "Mood"'s
Last perfect chord goes out
Like a sigh, a star, like a burning prayer
Over the cooling, scarred rooftops.

1977

Fay Chiang

After growing up in the back room of a laundry in Queens, I entered
Hunter College of the City University of New York in 1969 and was
catapulted into a frenzy of meeting people from all walks of life.
It was there that I began the life-long process of defining who I was.
Marches, demonstrations, leafleting, sit-ins, organizing, learning,
educating, questioning, challenging, accepting, losing . . . and most
of all growing in awareness, making different life choices and forging
my place in this society.

Biography

Fay Chiang has been living and writing in New York City for the past three decades. She is
a founding member of the Basement Workshop, a seminal, Chinatown-based multiarts non-
profit organization, and the author of two volumes of poetry, *In the City of Contradictions* and
Miwa' Song. Her work has appeared in numerous anthologies, most recently *Girls*, *Voci Dal
Silenzio*, and *Changer L'Amerique.* Chiang is working on her third collection of poetry,
Chinatown, and lives in the East Village with her daughter, Xian.

Journal Entry, October 26, 1975
Basement 199

getting the electricity hooked up in the loft has been one experience; it all started by calling chino who told me to get bimbo who hooked me up with angelo who took days to reach and days to get up to the loft.

went down to 6th street the other night where bimbo was working with rabbit, chino, louie and else, mixing cement to put cinderblocks into the building windows Teatro was in the process of buying from the city, fireproofing it from vandals. back and forth I walked from 6th street to the stoop on 3rd street where angelo was waiting for the babysitter to come and watch his two kids. finally by 2:30 a.m., bimbo came instead to 199 to test out the electrical lines by flashlight, promising to come back the next day with charlie, his licensed electrician friend to design new electrical lines.

when we were in the loft, I said: bimbo, it scares me, this space and I told him what other people had been telling me, that the space was too big, that I needed people, not space. it was people that moved.

bimbo said: it's all in the Dream. you've got to keep the Dream, honest and pure and that if that was the focus, then it would work. that it was going to take sacrifices and a lot of hard work. if you weren't afraid of work, then you had nothing to fear and there will be people who will tell you you are crazy and all kinds of ugly things for all kinds of reasons, but if you feel that it's time, then you put everything into the Dream, there's no holding back. he said: fay, look here you can start some small industry to pay the rent or have parties. that's it, we'll come help you raise the rent money. what is $800?! many things will happen.

then I asked him how he had come to be a poet. he said he had gone to CCNY, got his M.A. working under a fellowship, with 11 years at the Transit Authority at night and making 20,000, raising a family. But it was time to put all that aside and to work on his dream for Teatro. he had heard about jorge brandon, a sign painter who kept a storefront on pike street and read poetry in the streets, this old man. the two challenged each other to a duel and tried to outread the other on 6th street while people threw things at them from windows above to try to shut them up and they went on for hours till finally it was a draw.

jorge started training bimbo by sitting in a bathtub through months of summer while bimbo was working on his and margie's apartment. talking about writing, about a vision of theater for the people, all through the summer he talked and bimbo wrote. then jorge officially name bimbo a poet and they got a storefront on 6th street. el coco que habla. a prophet, a poet. el teatro ambulante.

bimbo said he came to a decision to quit his job, the security. he sat down with his family ad his older daughters said, yeah, daddy, we're behind you. so he says, you know, fay, it comes to 14c an hour, but we have to do it. we have to give it a try. go for broke. and if we make mistakes, at least we would have tried, learned from it.

walking back to 6th street with bimbo, carrying a pailful of tools for chino and the work on the building, I told bimbo I felt much better having talked with him, and he said, you know the way, "they" had it, we were never meant to meet and here we are!

on 6th street at 4 in the morning, people from teatro ambulante, charas, 4th street were frying salted fish pancakes on cinderblocks, warming hands, bodies from the flames, continuing the work.

I left walking down first avenue heading back to the loft, thinking and thinking about the Dream of Basement Workshop: an asian american cultural center with music, dance, pictures, the words to be written, oral histories and stories to be told and made by little children, youth old people, men and women my parents age. working, learning, and laughing with all kinds of people from many parts of the city, the country, the world in this part of the universe, this life-time. there are too many people too broken down to have dreams and risking dreams and visions, yet if we do not have visions, then what is the use of all this.

we must feed the Dream.

Images

image 1: Jesus Light My Fire

Friday after the fundraiser event we were walking the three of us down second avenue to buy some ice cream on St. Marks Place and this old woman in raggedy coat and kerchief tied round her face with graying wisps of hair (it was a cool night, but spring enough to go walking) followed us pleading for us to sing to her, to play the guitar to her, to speak to her. we walked a little faster. she walked a little faster and said as we approached the bodega on the corner:

> I say, see that man in the corner sitting with his hands folded to his chest (indeed, he was wearing a purple shirt and had a mustache and terribly disinterested look on his face, he was sitting). Well, that louse wouldn't give a starving grandmother or a starving nun, which I am, and I let you know, I am an artist, but I do not want to go on with this, but he wouldn't give me a dollar's credit and you know what I'm gonna do, I'm gonna go up to his window and stick my nose at his face and give it to him, the bastard. (which she did, which I thought was terrific and told her so. We quickly developed a great rapport, the other two had quickened their paces)

I'm an artist nun, dear. And you know that lesbian bar on Bleecker. (I think so, murmuring politely. My friend who lives three doors away has mentioned it to me.) Well, do you know that rock song, it was on the radio a few years ago . . . Come on Baby Light My fire? Do you know that I went into that bar and sag: Come On Jesus Light My Fire? which the both of us thought was hilarious: starving nun on a dollar's credit singing Jesus Light My Fire in a lesbian bar. We parted.

image 2: Let It Be Known

april 1970. antiwar scene, washington, d.c.

> bring the boys home. a naked man dances in the reflecting pool with a red, white and blue ribbon bow on his penis. a circus carnival atmosphere pervades. a contingent. marches here and another there through the monuments and graves, the promenades of our country's vitals: socialists vs. trots, vs. commies vs . . .

new york city 1970, 1971. uniform policemen astride horses stomping impatiently in the

> winter wind cutting through the demonstration at the red cross lights while helicopters circled overhead beating mothlike wings; then the riot squad charged. fifth avenue, bryant park, wall street, columbia duffy square, 125th street and lenox avenue. they came hurling down the street with the fucking bricks flying at us, and this one burly construction worker started beating the shit out of this kid next to me, and I started running and crying and the roar of the crowd and screams . . . they ran into trinity church beating wounded people.

campuses across the country. 1969 to 1972. ethnic studies. we are asians in america with a heritage and culture, a history past, present and future to be proud of and we demand the following unnegotiable demands, that ethnic studies is our right.

chinatown, new york city. 1969. in chinatown, the median income was 2,400 dollars for a family of four, and tell me what can you really buy for a family of four at less than 40 dollars a week, in america.

the question: I saw this picture of a woman crying over the plastic shrouded remains of her husband in *Life* magazine. a vietnamese peasant woman shading her face with her hat and the saliva and tears falling off her face. though from photographs of black and white we do not smell, do not taste, do not touch, do not hear the pain and grief. in america, we have become complacent and dull and numb and do not feel or hear or touch or see or smell our own pain and grief, alienation and hate. end the war. where is it?

so where does one go from here? down highway one in california there is a road of radiant sunshine bursting with oceans and green growing turf and a mellow way with waves, rock and seagulls at dawn.

other images recede: sounds and images of hurt, lost dreams and people living on a thin string line between realities which will never come true to life, simply because of the economics of this capitalistic country.

last night there was a gentle wind on the roof as I watched the wind blow the clouds across the moon face and I felt very tenderly the mortality of it all. above there on the roof and treetops upon the street noise, people doing their business, in the houses and apartments with bright lights blinking in the distance; a constant stream of airplanes leaving for all parts of the globe and

there are nights I cannot sleep and rise agitated, to ponder in wearied brainfever, the things that each of us must do and responsibility we have in making the changes necessary for social revolution. each time there is a personal struggle there is a narrowing of choices in cutting away those things superfluous, artificial.

in this lifetime, we should see the world and its people, travel continents and america, our own country and taste the ways of the people not from books and television which perpetuates the filth of mind mad t.v. syndicates and soap ads brilloing in peoria someone's backyard american apple pie, madison avenue slick.

destroy stereotypes we have been fed about one another of the different minorities: indians ain't tonto and neither were the blacks steppin' fetchit or the asians bread from charlie chan and the chicanos weren't half baked little people cookies in god's oven. and all them blue eyed devils are not one and the same. even now the hills of appalachia hold the poor white children of debtors from the days of colonial america. class is not easily erasable.

on the highway one never has to stop for long except to fill up on gas and take a leak once in a while and stop for something to drink, and go to the mardi gras in louisiana when it's festival time, or dig on the oranges in florida or the deserts in the southwest of the frozen earth in fairbanks, alaska, something like that.

I will do this; skies with eyes thirsting for answers.

For Those Who Run Away from the Movement

I   mahjong and dice on the tables upstairs
        the noise confusion of trucks and cars and calls and
            children and cats and dogs and
                traffic stream of people
                    traffic upstream downstream
        and children and women and men and
            people and people locked in the safety
                feeling trapped
                    in crumbling tenements
        slipping/sliding down the
                    mountain of gold
    —it's too close—
eddie died yesterday
        another street kid shot his fucking brains out
        and eddie's in heaven upstream east river
did you know
        mrs. tong jumped off her building
            looking for peace six stories above mott
and hey, old louey
        just passed away in his sleep
        the fool—sleeping with the gas pipes on, again

did you hear about lee?

      that he couldn't take his henpecking wife and

      screaming babies and rotten kids and his waiter

      job and promises that couldn't be bought with

      pennies

          that he split before his head did?

II   shipping line boston, massachusetts december 1956

          from boston to new york city

            I saw a sunrise on empty streets

         filled with old buildings and dark fire escapes

         overspilling with people running

             to make a dime in the factories and restaurants

                trying to beat time

             people into making a living

             and making some American Dream

                        come true.

and I ran too

    in restaurants

      aged 10 standing on milk cartons washing dishes

folding papers for the China Times

      stringing beads for the old lady

          and trying to be good

          and trying to be bad

    worrying about my brothers and sisters

        being beat in the school yard by some other ethnic

        and being tough when I wanted to run

          being smartass when I wanted to cry

            trying to be big when I was really small—

all the time

    walking on the poverty line

      all the time

        feeling the deprivation and lacking of things

            the wishing and the wanting:

american t.v. sold shirley temples and g.i. joes

    to little alices and jerrys and run spot run

      in the suburbias of white picket fences

and automobiles
and american society sold cheap labor and self hatred
to little chins and wongs and run-dog-run
in the ghettos of black barbed wire
and dead-end streets

III   understand:
I studied asians in america
I demonstrated against the war in indochina
and shouted *chilai, kaiho, makibaka*
don't forget
all the nights we wrote newsletters and flyers
the times we leafleted and petitioned
for community issues
street permits for street fairs
I struggled to learn to say and to believe
right on
people's struggle and all power
to the people
I can sympathize
but
when I hear a bathroom flush in the middle of the night
I'm a five-year-old kid listening to funny sounds
in a dark hallway in a rickety tenement
while I take a pee
when some kid tells me about her folks hassling
and I see my mom screaming at my dad for
gambling again and me and my brothers and sisters
are crying for candy
when I read a psycho-sociological essay on the
problems of adolescence
and wonder back when I didn't ever feel old
you have to realize
though I sympathize
my mind's fatigued and my spirits worn out
and I'm plain worn out from running
the learning, the experiences, and acrobatics

of making changes in the society
   and going through changes and changing
sometimes,
   not knowing what next—

I want to be mobile and hitching cross country
   through europe and africa
    the great escape
  before the blue collar job
    where I'm living at least on the poverty level
I want a piece of the golden mountain
 a piece of the big apple pie-in-the-sky
so please,
  don't tell me it's all a lie

IV Me
   can't get away
    can't run away from the movement
you can't get away too far
    from the people's struggle
   you can never forget

  sister, brother
  take a rest and
  come on back

Ameena Meer

Biography

Ameena Meer's journalism has appeared in *Actuel*, *Interview*, *Details*, *Frieze*, *Harper's Bazaar*, *Allure*, *Paper* and *The Times of India*. Her more creative work has been anthologized in *The Portable Lower East Side* and has appeared on men's underwear boxes, among other places. She divides her time among London, Mexico and New York City and has two daughters.

The Frog's Girlfriend

I got to the swimming pool and I realized I had forgotten my towel. It was too late to go home and come back again so I decided to swim anyway. Hope there were enough paper towels in the bathroom. Or just drip dry. Throw my clothes on while I was still wet and zip up my down jacket and run all the way home and dry off there in the comfort of my own bathroom.

As I walked to the showers I noticed a net bag of swimming gear hanging on the hook, a plump white towel seductively peeking through the bag. If I grabbed it, would the woman come out of the shower fast enough to tell who took it? One white towel looks like another. Would I be able to act nonchalant and politely concerned when she came rushing past? Would I be able to say, What is that woman so upset about? Perhaps she wouldn't even notice it was gone, until she came back to her locker and realized she didn't have it.

A second later, the water went off and I was saved from myself by a wet arm reaching through the plastic curtain.

The sun is rising earlier these days and now shines through the windows in wide sparkling swatches, making pools of light in the water. My last few laps, I swim breaststroke and I love the instant I swim into the sunlight. For a few seconds, it is as clear and bright under the water as it is above. As my goggled eyes rise and sink beneath the surface of the water, I feel like I am swimming through liquid sunlight. I had a rough time last night. My sleeping was fitful. I slept in stops and starts. Somehow, I kept running my hands over my body and not recognizing it as my own. In the past few months since I had begun to subjected it to a regular swimming routine, it had remained unchanged. Now, it has suddenly responded, as if overnight. The muscles are firm and my limbs feel sinewy. In my dreams, I kept saying, "Who's that?"

The answer was, "It's the Frog's girlfriend."

And then I'd say, "Oh, of course it is."

It was also a strange night because Vivek had just come back from his show in Minneapolis and we'd had a horrible argument about our finances. One that seemed to have, as its only resolution, a harrowing end no matter which of us won. I stormed off to bed. I tossed and turned. Took a painkiller enhanced with a sleep aid. I had just put a new mattress pad on the bed in the hopes of making it more comfortable, but it just seemed to make it all slippery and squidgy.

My feet were hot. I opened the window.

The room grew icy. The baby cried. I got up to cover her and then pulled the big down comforter over myself.

Then I felt I was suffocating beneath its feathery bulk. I pushed it off. I got up. Vivek was still not in bed. I returned to my strange dreams. I awoke. I was hot. I was cold. And so it went on.

The next thing I knew, it was six-forty-five and the baby was saying, "Mama? Mama?" from her crib.

After I swam, I pulled a huge handful of paper towels from the towel dispenser and hung them precariously on the edge of the shower stall. I rubbed myself down with the brown paper. The dry, acrid smell of the towels permeated my skin, stronger than the perfumes in my soap and shampoo. It brought back memories of school and the smell of the bathrooms first thing on Monday mornings before they were overwhelmed with a week's worth of stale smoke and bodies. On the other hand, it worked. I was dry enough to put my clothes on.

I took the girls to a party yesterday. The house of a friend—or friends, I'm not sure—whose son is one of my daughter's friends. The husband—who I thought was my friend—has been having an affair for some time. The wife—who is now acting like my friend—just found out and cannot stop talking about it. They are in the process of splitting up. The whole thing seems strangely improbable. They've been married for almost two decades. They've got gorgeous children. A funky, comfortable loft. The wife is slim, beautiful, vivacious. She makes torrid, sexy paintings. She's a great cook. And she's an Italian contessa. What more could you ask for?

The husband is a gawky American, with a wide-lipped smile that almost splits his head in half. He has a cartoonishly fuzzy shock of hair and round glasses that make his eyes vague and imprecise. He is sweet, with a tough, street smart way of talking, but no ladies' man, by any means. He's what a photographer friend of mine would call a mensch. A nice guy. But it's always the ones you least expect. I feel incredibly uncomfortable around them now. Especially as the wife becomes more vocal. I suppose we couples are all huddled together in a weak wobbly little boat and anyone who jumps overboard, or even considers it, makes us all realize how shaky our stable domestic lives really are. Occasionally, some smart aleck thinks he can survive as well in the water as he can on land and he dives overboard voluntarily, dragging his mate along with him. And even though we all respect his courage and envy his freedom, we look away. We wait. We huddle closer together. Because, most of the time, it doesn't take long. Soon, they are both flailing and gasping for air.

They are drowning. And as they go down, those of us still in the boat start rowing as fast as we can in the other direction.

The frightening part is that some of them don't go down. Some of them get stronger. Some of them learn to swim. They are few and far between. And as much as we ignored them while they struggled, we welcome them when they jump—breathless and exhilarated—back on board.

I mean, here we are, several months into couple's counselling, and a two-week break from seeing our shrink makes everything fall apart. All that aside from the fact that we had an arranged marriage and the failure rate of those is 1 in 100,000. Good odds. Except that .01 percent of them live in New York City and try to be artists.

I never met my friend's affair. Or I have and I don't remember. ("Oh, you'd remember," says another friend.) I think I met her at a time when I was gender specific. When I was a hungry young writer stalking her first break and her meal ticket. When you're hunting men, the women you meet are just scenery. Foliage.

My friend has just moved in with his girlfriend. His three children are staying with their mother. She says, "I would be out every night. I'm going to be out every night this week. If I didn't have the kids, well, I wouldn't be at home. What am I going to do? Stay home with the kids?" She clasps her very shapely décolleté. "It's so weird. I was never the domestic one."

As I got dressed I thought about having an affair. I wonder if I could have an affair. If I should have an affair. Occasionally, someone flirts with me and the thought sends a buzz to my brain, giving me a brief high. Something new. Something unpredictable. The games. The banter. The anticipation. Will we kiss today? The electric hum in your skin when you first begin to touch. It's magical. You're floating. You're breathing underwater.

Would the feverish intensity of an affair lend a new perspective to my marriage? Would it make it more rich and variegated by contrast?

In a few seconds, my lightheadedness turns to lead belly. An affair quickly looks like the frying pan to the fire. It's only a matter of time before you get embroiled in a whole new relationship. Then you're stuck again. Suddenly, your fascinating conversations change from the scintillation of your emotions to good old-fashioned logistics. The excitement's over. You're back to square one and your only choice is to move on to the next one. Or return to the prosaic. And the stray hairs around the bathroom sink. An already wet towel when you get out of the shower. So you might as well stay put.

Now, of course, there are all the questions of fatal social diseases. And, that oldest of worries, the unplanned pregnancy. If the affair was truly absorbing, it was inevitable the birth control would fail at your most fertile moment. The frenzy of passion would burst condoms and shake loose diaphragms. The delirious hunger would overpower simple spermicides. Then, in the exhausted glow of contentment, you'd be too spent to minister to the situation. You'd both abandon yourselves to the tangled sheets, the carpet, the disheveled sofa cushions. And the sperm—like tadpoles on amphetamines—would race to their mark. Then what? Would I have an abortion? Could I do it after twice seeing the result of that instant? Twice riding out that ballooning. Twice learning the unbelievable bliss of loving a child. Difficult thought. Would I risk a child of uncertain parentage? And would I uproot my entire family and overturn my home? After living out the fantasy in my imagination, I always think it isn't worth the effort.

My hair was still dripping when I put on my coat. The strangest thing about my dream was that I never saw the frog. Strange, if you know my history with frogs, toads and other similar reptiles. I am absolutely terrified of them. In fact, it's beyond terror. It's a phobia. If I even see a picture of a frog or a toad in a book, I am terrorized with endless nightmares that leave me screaming and drenched in sweat. But here I was having a dream about a frog's girlfriend and he is invisible.

When I think of what a big part frogs played in my relationship with my husband, I wonder how we stayed together. Why just the association of him with the huge slimy creatures didn't revulse me from the start.

When we first met, in India, I had made up my mind that there was no way I was going to have an arranged marriage. Actually, I wasn't going to get married at all. Ever. I'd decided that on my last trip there in the chaos of a big family wedding. Now it was me making the rounds. This was my first extended trip "home" as my parents called it, wistfully, (and my brother and I, sarcastically), since I was twelve.

We arrived in India in early spring, while the damp East Coast winter still stuck like an icy crust of gray slush in our memories. I had graduated from college the year before with a B.A. in English Literature (magna cum laude) and my parents had temporarily funded a low-budget apartment in New York as a prize for my hard work. In return, I produced a résumé full of brief jobs at doomed literary magazines and a handful of published poems. But I had gained street smarts and a head full of radical feminist and political ideas. My tough new airs aside, my parents were setting up a marriage for me.

Let me tell you why the idea seemed so bizarre. I had spent my childhood as a spotless urchin roaming the well-kept streets of uppermiddle-class Westchester. My father had been too involved in one business venture after another to have the time to take us to school, let alone cart us all back and forth to India. My mother was all wrapped up in the social programs that women of her station patronized, like preserving historical landmarks or improving local playgrounds. She didn't pay much attention to our religious or cultural education. So my brother and I were pleasantly neglected. Our day-to-day care was in the sturdy hands of a cheerful Eastern European housekeeper and our social identities were the same as those of our friends.

In fact, my first trip to India took place at the age of six, for a two-week crash course in religion and extended family. My grandmother took her little American grandchildren to the temple to introduce us to the deities. When I was told that I had to offer a prayer to the gods in order to receive some prasad, I shook my head. "I want to go to McDonald's."

My aunt interjected, "Darling, we don't have McDonald's in India because Hindus don't eat beef."

I said, "Well, I'm not Hindu, I'm Jewish." The priest looked at my grandmother, tears welling up in his eyes in pity. My poor grandmother clasped her breast in horror. She did not take my hand when we walked home. I don't remember much else of her. By our second trip, another fortnight sojourn six years later, she was long gone. With her only son gone to America, she had slowly faded away along with her photograph on our mantelpiece. Just like that old photograph, no one had really noticed until it was too late. Until it was yellow-spotted, curled and cracked. Until there was nothing left to see. My father returned only to scatter her ashes on the warm waters of the Indian Ocean.

In any case, my incipient wedding brought out my Jewish roots more strongly. An arranged marriage. I was about to be a participant in a cultural antique that had outlived its value. A cliché. An anachronism. I was educated, independent, self-possessed. Enough of this nonsense. This was something out of the Style section of the Times. One of those stories that would make me protest, "Oh, come on, that's just the result of the lack of education, that's what happens in a poor country. But it doesn't happen to people like us." I'd blame the ethnocentric press for fanning the flames of Orientalism.

Even complaining about it seemed boring and predictable. Indian girl has arranged marriage against her will. Yawn. Ho-hum. This was a classic struggle in a number of primitive cultures. But I had no interest in being more than an anthropologist. I made up my mind to have a holiday and then get myself back to the civilized world—where girls sat around waiting for the phone to ring, my mother reminded me. And hope that their boyfriends will marry them when they're tired of using them, she added.

I convinced myself that if I dug in my heels for a few weeks, my parents would give up and head back to reality. I didn't run off to the American Embassy to seek asylum or beg them to give me shelter—that sounded as pathetic and melodramatic as a Hollywood script. I humored my family. I dressed up in saris. I met a couple of "boys"—as they were called—bankers and accountants who'd gone to college abroad and miraculously come back with American accents twangier than my own. Vivek wasn't even in the running then. But a couple of months went past, it was summer. Indian summer. The real thing. The shimmering heat brutalized the ancient air conditioners. The sun seared your eyes and broiled your skin the minute you stepped out of the shade. It left me with blinding headaches and raw, sunburned lips. The holiday was wearing thin. I wondered how much more time my dad could afford to take off work.

They stayed put. The heat grew still more intense as the summer ended and my brother got on a plane to go back to college. I waved good-bye enviously from the airport. My father started to do his work with fax machines, but looked more and more harried. This endeavor was becoming expensive. Yet it all carried on, in the name of my marriage. Given the circumstances, my father still managed to get some mergers and acquisitions started. My mother enjoyed the opportunity to do some socializing and shopping—the best part of the wedding fantasy. For them, my continued obstinacy wasn't a complete disaster. For me, the worst was yet to come. Because, as summer ended, the monsoon began.

In the beginning, it seemed soothing. A cool rain after a scorching summer. The ubiquitous dust turned to sweet-smelling earth. The plants grew profuse and glossy. And then came the deluge.

Not the rain. The frogs. They were everywhere. When I got up in the morning, one popped out from behind the sweating porcelain of the toilet. I screamed and jumped into the shower. But when I turned on the water, hundreds of tiny frogs came spurting out of the drain, skidding across the tiles, their wet bodies sticking to my bare feet. Their tiny heartbeats pulsed through their stomachs against my skin. I howled. I had awoken into my worst nightmare.

Neon flashes of panic exploded through my brain. Terror screamed like a siren in my ears. Blind and deaf, I ran outside, my muscles convulsing as my synapses detonated. Vivek, the son of the next-door neighbor, heard my shrieks from the other side of the garden and came to see what was wrong. Hysterical, I did a frenzied St. Vitus dance around the wet grass, sobbing and shrieking. Brown toads appeared everywhere I stepped, their soft limbs squashing underneath my toes. My screams turned into unintelligible gasps as the fear pulled a tight noose around my throat.

Vivek rushed to me, threw me over his shoulder and carried me back into my aunt's house. I collapsed where I fell—a shuddering heap on the sofa. He sat for a few minutes to watch my lips turn from blue to pink again as I started breathing. When I calmed down, he got up to leave. Grateful, my parents insisted he join us at breakfast. That gave them a chance to grill him.

Fortunately for Vivek, they quickly realized why my aunt hadn't included him in her eligibles list. While he had studied in America, he didn't plan on going back to the first world. "It's so uncivilized," he said. "No one has the time to enjoy life."

Worse. He hadn't done accounting, law, business, computers or even engineering. Or anything remotely useful. He'd been studying art at the Rhode Island School of Design. After he finished, he came home—along with his Indian clothes and accent—and began to paint.

With Vivek safely out of the picture as a possible husband, we were free to become friends. One particularly trying afternoon (that also seemed remarkably dry and free of amphibious life), I held my breath, closed my eyes and dashed through the garden to the studio behind his parents' house. His parents were very well-off, indulgent industrialists, and they had outfitted him well. He had a huge whitewashed studio, a surfeit of imported oil paints, a slick stereo system and stacks of canvases awaiting his mark. Strangely enough, it was in his studio that Vivek's foreign side came out. His huge paintings were all portraits of a sort. Larger-than-life visions of a chaotic moment in an Indian train station, or a sleepy camel driver resting in the shade of his animal. It was in these paintings—and in the rarefied atmosphere of foreign paint fumes and imported brushes—that Vivek became the outsider. The first time I came into his studio, I felt faint. Partly because of the oil paint, but mostly because the sheer size and power of his images shocked me. They were huge and confrontational—throwing you in the midst of a fight between two wrestlers in a low-rent circus so you had to duck the next blow. Or shoving a beggar's dirty palm blownup a hundred times right in your face, making his shrill demand impossible to avoid. They were a vision of India that most Indians go to great lengths to avoid.

I spent a couple of hours there, complaining about the absurdity of outdated Indian social graces. How could he possibly live here, after his time in Rhode Island? "Oh, you'll get to like it, too," he smiled. "No one comes here who doesn't fall in love. It just takes some people longer than others. But then again, the longer you take to fall in love, the longer it lasts."

"Good start for an arranged marriage then—you've got five minutes to fall in love."

"Don't let anyone hear you, that's heresy!" He put on a heavy-duty accent, "Arranged Marriage is not Love Marriage. You're not meant to fall in love when you meet the boy. Actually, most ladies are finding they are falling in love after first issue only."

"Issue?"

"You know, a kid."

"Kids! Who thought of kids?"

"Well, that's either here nor there. The point is, you—one—is meant to fall in love slowly. It can take years. If you—if it's done properly." He started cleaning his brushes. His jeans were covered with paint, but they were, I noticed, Indian-made Benetton instead of Levis. He was surprisingly big-boned for an Indian man. The jeans ended at his shins. On his feet, he wore a battered pair of kohlapuris—Jesus sandals made out of camel skin. His fashion sense was questionable, but he was attractive.

"Can't you help me convince my parents to forget about this?" Vivek painted a thick white stripe of paint across the lawn to his studio—the frog's girlfriend with the idea that the shiny paint and the toads, or at least make them more visible and avoidable. And on clear days, it worked. So whenever the sun shot a bright ray through the clouds, I went to visit his studio. When the charade seemed too real, that was where I went to be myself.

My parents did not discourage our friendship. They hoped he would introduce me to his better-placed friends. In Vivek's defense, I have to say he tried his best. He introduced me to accountants, brokers, doctors and economists.

But I blew every single meeting. Or the frogs did. Because somehow, every time, a frog would flop in like a water balloon hitting the floor. Vivek would scoop up the sloppy creature, its limbs flapping haplessly against his hands. But even as he tossed the frog into the grass, I was possessed. The sight repulsed me to the extent that I could do nothing but run shuddering back into the car. All his friends thought I was an insanely neurotic American. The only one who seemed more tolerant—the economist—gave me a wet smile the minute we were alone together and then whispered that there must be some Freudian symbolism in my phobia. His fingers were ice-cold on my arm and the alcohol made his eyes glassy and unblinking. I slipped out of his grip. He later told Vivek I had come on to him.   Vivek took my side and didn't leave us alone together again.

As the monsoon wrung the last drops of water from the air, my parents looked like they were finally beginning to give up hope. I was so relieved that I actually started to enjoy India. One afternoon, my mother said to me, "Well, if you want to spend the rest of your life alone, so be it."

My father said, "You know, we'll be very unhappy if you don't choose to share your life with someone of your caste and background. But we are thinking about going home."

I ran to Vivek's studio. I was so thrilled I hugged him. "Vivek! I'm leaving! I'm going back home!" I didn't even care about the paint smearing the last of my favorite V-neck Gap T-shirts. No problem. I could buy more when I got back.

"Lucky girl," he said, not sounding as enthusiastic as he might. "You've got your wish." Then he went back to staring at his painting. The singer on the CD player was going on about some woman's mysterious ways. I was pleased to think that I was not mysterious. No silly games for me. I was straightforward and I knew what I wanted.   And I did not want to get married. Nor did I want to have children. Ever.

Vivek was putting the finishing touches on a painting of an old temple in a trickle of monsoon sunlight. The rainy skies had turned the sandstone a rosy pink, marbled with blue.

"What a beautiful place."

"Do you want to see it? There's a son-et-lumière show there tonight and I'm going with a bunch of friends—maybe your parents will find someone they like in the group—and it might be your last chance to learn some Indian history firsthand."

"I'd love to go." My parents agreed. It was a last ditch effort. So, at sunset, I sat with everyone else on wicker chairs, drinking Campa-cola, watching the monuments melt like marsh-mallows into the sky. As the daylight disappeared, the little lights came on, illuminating the temples. However, they also illuminated the lawn around us. Silhouetted in the light, the ground began to come alive. Hundreds of tiny bumps began to move. Soon the earth below my chair was a sea of writhing shapes. Toads!

My skin crawled. It was all I could do to swallow my scream and jump onto the chair. In my frightened squirming, my feet went straight through the woven seat. I climbed onto the chair next to me. But after a few minutes, the caning on that one gave way as well. I moved to the next. Within twenty minutes, I'd gone through ten or twenty chairs and I couldn't control myself any longer. "Vivek," I hyperventilated through a wave of adrenaline, "you have to get me out of here!"

Vivek looked back and saw me on the chair, clinging frantically to its scrawny skeleton. "What's going on?" he whispered.

"Help! Toads!"

To his credit, he again leaped to my protection, and carried me piggyback to the car. "It's almost your last night," he said, reassuringly. "Let's go and wait in the restaurant for everyone else." The rest of his friends joined us later—a good number of seriously eligible types among them—but I had a great time anyway, because, for once, the pressure was off.

The next morning, I woke up late and found a tea tray near my bed, a crisp fall sunbeam filling my room. The bathroom was dry and quiet and the anticipation of finally returning home made me so happy I dressed and bathed singing.

When I came out, I found the household all a-twitter. They'd gotten a last-minute proposal for me at breakfast. The servants and cousins had all been dispatched to make final inquiries into the character of the boy. However, the inquiries were only details because the boy's mother had gone to school with my aunt. In fact, our family had known his father's family for generations so it was already a done deal. They were practically planning the wedding.

"Aren't you required to get my consent?" I asked through the tiny space left in my throat as the lump filled it. I blinked hard to control the tears. I tried to stay tough. I could ride this one out, too.

"Not anymore, you're too fussy," said my mother. "We've had enough. You've met the boy. Vivek said you seemed to get along well, so that's that."

My aunt was doing the arrangements with the old priest and the temple, making sure they had an auspicious day and the horoscopes checked out all right. She started explaining to me what I would be required to do at the ceremony. About the same time, Vivek popped in to see what all the commotion was about. My aunt was telling me what the priest would say, in Sanskrit, and I was protesting that 1) I wasn't marrying anyone and 2) I didn't speak Sanskrit, and neither did she as far as I knew. She said, "All Hindu ceremonies are conducted in Sanskrit, you silly Angrez-ki-bacchi!"

"I'm not Hindu! I'm Jewish!"

Poor Vivek looked completely taken aback. "You're Jewish?"

"That's enough!" my mother growled.

I was trying to figure out where the nearest American Embassy was when I heard that Vivek's father had sent the proposal. My first thought was, did he have a brother? When I realized who the intended was, I was truly incensed. How dare he try to trick me that way! I ran to my room and started throwing stuff in my bag. "I can't trust anyone!" I shouted. I grabbed my passport.

My mother rushed into the room and tried to calm me down. She got my brother on the phone and got him to talk some sense into me too. My father convinced me that Vivek had been equally uncertain about it all, but that the parents had come to an agreement between them. "You're not a very easy girl, you know," my father said. I could hear the relief in his voice that he'd finally got a bite.

My mother said, "The beauty of an arranged marriage is that you have the excitement of discovering another person . . ."

And on the phone, my brother added, "Listen, you can always get divorced." Even with that, I can't remember how they managed to get me to agree. But no one tied me up or drugged me or threatened to beat me to a pulp. I remembered that I'd once thought Vivek was quite good-looking. So I did it of my own free will. I had an arranged marriage because I chose to. I faced my new life filled with the multicolored bubbles of hopefulness that are probably common to most brides. But sometimes I wonder if my being in India hadn't managed to trigger that Asian sense of filial duty that had been lying dormant in me until then. Because the next thing I knew, I was in a scarlet sari and we were joined together around a herb-scented fire.

I didn't give up everything, though. I did some tough bargaining on my side. Despite Vivek's adamant refusal to leave his homeland, I got back to New York. We ended up spending our first year together in the slums of New York's Lower East Side. We were in a fifth-floor walk-up. It was a railroad tenement with peeling, dirty wallpaper and a clawfooted bathtub in the middle of the kitchen. Vivek made a little studio on one end and I set up my desk and papers on the other and we slept in the middle on a futon that we folded into a sofa during the day. And all around us was the detritus of an Indian wedding: three ornate silver tea sets, hand-embroidered tablecloths, Wedgewood china and Waterford crystal glasses, antique shawls, heaps of silk saris, necklaces and earrings so bejeweled they looked fake and enough art to insulate a castle.

Even stranger perhaps was that it was on my return to New York that I met real Indians. For the first time. Not the kind who live in Connecticut and dress up in saris for national holidays like halloween costumes. The Indians I met on the Lower East Side were the kind of Indians Americans expect. The kind I'd never have talked to. Busboys who spoke English in the same sort of broken phrases I used when I tried Hindi. Newsstand owners who'd spent their entire lives in dusty villages in the Punjab, only to find themselves on the corner of Essex and Rivington in another tin shack wallpapered with magazine pictures from a world they kept waiting to see. Taxi drivers who just knew their next fare would be Madonna or Sharon Stone.

Suddenly, I was a new wife fresh off the boat and full of promise. I was an icon, even in my jeans and leather jacket. I must have lost some street edge as well, because every minute, someone would stop me to ask if I was from India. And if I was, did I know how they could find a bride as well? Or could I tell them how to navigate that complicated visa process? Even if I couldn't, maybe I needed a magazine, a glass of water, a taxi ride. No, no, sister, please. Free of charge. I wasn't sure where I was in the hierarchy anymore, so did I accept or refuse? Vivek was lucky in that his contacts from Rhode Island all remembered him fondly and he had a made a certain name for himself. He got a teaching gig and managed to ride the wave of multiculturalism to a decent living. I carried on with the poetry for a while. But I couldn't stand asking Vivek for money, so eventually I broke down and started doing articles for women's magazines. Unless a taxi driver took a liking to us, we were still walking more often than riding the subway. I found our life very hip and romantic. We were beats. We were starving for our art. We were the only upper-class Indian couple this side of Houston Street.

Nevertheless, it took only one visit from Vivek's parents and my first bout of morning sickness (in my case, it tended to set in as I was boiling the pasta for dinner) to get us moved uptown with the rest of our community. They bought us a little row house on East Thirty-eighth Street. Our first daughter was born there. Despite our prime real estate, we were still very short of cash. I often pushed Chaiti in her cheap, rickety stroller past all the crisp bankers and businessmen I might have married. Their lives—their families' lives—must have been so easy. I had slowed down, at the end of my pregnancy, on the work, but our expenses just kept increasing. My only hope was that Vivek's parents might spring for her education when the time came. If they reconciled themselves to their only son having a daughter.

Not surprisingly, Vivek's parents were disappointed with her gender, having just bought a palace for their little prince of a first grandson. But, being modern and open-minded, they overcame it. They decided they could just wait for the second child.

When, at the five-month ultrasound, the watery amphibian in my uterus turned out to be another female, Vivek's parents broke down. They implied I might have an abortion. I had one girl. Why not try again? Wait for a son. This was the twentieth century, one could make choices. I was amazed. Could they really still be in the dark ages? I was even more surprised when I complained to Vivek. He did not disagree with them. He never even opened his mouth—all that Indian respect-for-parents stuff. He held the telephone receiver and listened, for as long as those squeaky phone voices scraped his eardrums.

When he put the phone down, he told me patiently that there was a reason for everything. A reason for all of those old rules and ideas. That everything was based on a real foundation. That those older than us have the wisdom of the years behind them and their good advice might be beyond our own comprehension.

I'd hoped my own parents were more enlightened. But when I called them, the passing years seemed to have made them backslide even further. They said, "It's up to you, darling. Just remember that a good Hindu wife should take her husband's views seriously."

I'm not a good Hindu wife, I thought. The marriage was one thing, but this was too much. I put my foot down and said I'd just pack up both my girls and leave. Where to, I had no idea, but I had to take a stand. I was not having an abortion. Even if my parents wouldn't take me back. I imagined myself a single mother, waitressing in an Indian restaurant in Queens. Would my newsstand-owner friends take me in? Definitely not. I would be a wife who had failed in my duties. Irresponsible, unlucky and disobedient. They'd be the first to send me packing. Though, to be honest, I wasn't sure I wanted another girl either.

Vivek confessed, in a weak moment. He admitted that he'd hoped for a girl. In fact, that's what he'd wished for when he'd blown out his birthday candles the week before. He also told me that he'd back me up, no matter what path I chose. Of course, his parents adored their new granddaughter the minute they saw her. On the other hand, they do keep hinting about the next one.

So there you are. Or here we are. Two kids later. Five years later. Still trying to figure out how to make ends meet. Still wondering how couples manage to stay together. Is it effort? Or inertia? Though, I have to say, the arranged-marriage part does have its advantages. There's a lot less guesswork. A lot more you can take for granted. Even if everything else falls apart, we'll always have a whole culture—and a number of relations—in common. It does work. After you sort out the kinks.

That's what I was thinking when I walked in from the swimming pool. I opened the door and a blast of Hindi movie music crashed into me like a gale-force wind. The house was turned inside out as usual, as it is whenever Vivek is alone with the kids, and we can no longer afford a cleaner. Toys, books, half-eaten waffles and spilled tippee cups of juice were strewn decoratively around the living room carpet (one of Vivek's family heirlooms—it's about five hundred years old). The VCR was playing Hindi movies on autopilot. "Mama!" shouted the baby.

The frogs in the city are all contained. They are inside glass walls so everyone can see them, but they can't get out. Occasionally, I dream that a frog is trapped somewhere in my bedclothes and I awake in a cold sweat, kicking and screaming in the tangled sheets. Sometimes I dream that they've all been set free, exploded out of the zoos and science projects, and the wet streets teem with their gleaming bodies as they wriggle and squirm over one another trying to reach me. Only Vivek's sleepy voice through the darkness brings me back to our bedroom.

There's an aquarium in my daughter's preschool class with an index card taped to it. In block letters, in that ubiquitous black marker, it says, "FROGS." When I drop her off at school, I'm always really careful not to look in that direction. I never say anything about it, but I look at her coat buttons or her lunch box to distract us. Then I hurry out the door to the swimming pool to get my half-mile in before it closes for the afternoon.

Vivek gives me a kiss. "How was your swim?"

"It saves my life," I say.

Adrienne Su

In New York City, all the world's foods are native.

Biography

Adrienne Su was born in Atlanta. She lived in New York City for five years and once competed on New York's national poetry-slam team. She is the author of a book of poems, *Middle Kingdom*, and has essays in *Saveur* and *Girls: An Anthology*.

Sacred Foods of Brooklyn

One of my Italian cookbooks contains a warning that goes something like this: *Never throw away bread, no matter how stale, no matter how small a piece. Turn it into bread crumbs, bake it in a bread pudding, mix it into a stuffing, do whatever you like—but* never *throw it away. Bread is a sacred food, every crumb of which should be treated with respect. Bad things will happen if it is wasted.*

Predictably, the warning makes me feel guilty, if not a bit worried. I've already got a big plastic bag of homemade bread crumbs in the freezer, so when we get down to those rock-hard baguette-ends or stale last slices of sandwich bread, I, uh, throw them away.

I don't do it without a pang of conscience. I know I should have found a use for the ends or at least stuck them in the freezer for a future bread-crumb-making session, but the freezer is jam-packed, my dog, Tayto, is clamoring for a walk, and I'm cooking Chinese food tonight, so my mind is on another sacred food: rice.

I may not have learned the Chinese language from my parents, but I did learn something about respect for rice, which is a serious matter. There is probably not a Chinese person on this planet who wasn't required at least once in childhood to show a clean rice bowl at the end of a meal. The disasters that were said to befall the boy who left one grain in his bowl included starvation and, worse, marriage to a pock-faced woman. The only circumstance in which it is appropriate to leave some rice behind is when you are a guest at a banquet, where meats and vegetables may constitute 90 percent of the meal and a little bowl of rice is served at the end, to settle the stomach. To eat a lot of rice at a banquet is to insult the cook, to show that you find the food so unpalatable that you must satisfy your hunger with rice.

I find such banquets hard to take. I'm attached to eating lots of rice with Chinese food, and I can eat more of it at a meal than my non-Chinese friends—even men twice my size—can. I'm also very particular about having plain, boiled, white rice at a Chinese meal. Fried rice, served as a base in many Chinese restaurants in America, interferes with the taste of the food eaten with it and is best consumed on its own. How can you know what the long beans with hot chilies taste like if you're eating them on top of rice flavored with egg, scallions, carrots, bamboo shoots, soy sauce, oil, and garlic? Plain, boiled rice is like a clear sky against which to view a landscape, or a quiet room in which to hear a song. I miss it even during a splendid Chinese feast, and I'm always happy to get home, where I don't have to be self-conscious about my appetite for rice.

When I'm cooking, I love rice no less. I don't consider my kitchen complete without a twenty-five-pound sack of jasmine rice parked under the butcher block. A brand called Family Elephant from Thailand is my choice for Chinese and Southeast Asian cooking, as it's fragrant but not overpowering, it's easy and quick to cook, and it sticks together just enough that even the unini-tiated can eat it with chopsticks. I like having other varieties of rice around, too: Arborio for risotto or rice pudding; wild rice for game birds; basmati for Indian cooking; short-grain brown for almost anything. Rice is also the perfect pantry staple, as it keeps for up to ten years. And I've never met anyone who doesn't like rice. It's comforting to children and adults alike, even to animals: the vet recommends chicken and rice for our dog when she isn't well.

Rice, to me, is so basic, so egalitarian in its availability and appeal, so fundamental to human well-being that I can't understand why, in a land of plenty, anyone should be stingy with it. For instance, I do not understand Asian restaurants that serve each person a tiny bowl of rice, then charge extra for each additional bowl—perhaps even charge for the first bowl, too. This is like charging extra for bread in a French or Italian restaurant. I'd rather pay more for the entrée than pay in increments for the rice. While the entrée might be plentiful, the penurious doling out of rice to accompany it takes the comfort out of the meal. It's a reminder that you're not in somebody's home but in somebody's business, where everything you eat is recorded against revenues.

Rice is so many things to me that when an Italian cookbook writer discusses the sanctity of bread, I know exactly what she's talking about. Working my way through her recipes, I start to understand her culinary universe. It takes only one bite for me to learn to love a plain bowl of spaghetti with oil, garlic, minced anchovies and bread crumbs. When I walk through my Italian neighborhood in Brooklyn, I admire the loaves of bread stacked in bakery windows and wonder what's happening tonight in the kitchen of the stout, elderly woman whose every step is a distinct labor but who has expertly selected a quantity of ripe plum tomatoes, smooth baby eggplant and a loaf of seeded semolina. Over many months, I try to learn how to make my own bread—not because I'm dissatisfied with the bakery bread but because knowing how to make bread strikes me as crucial to understanding Italian food. Gradually, I learn to tell the temperature of water for proofing yeast, and my hands get a feel for how much flour to add, what a "smooth and elastic" dough feels like, and how hard to punch it down after it's risen. I start to understand why there is so much lore surrounding bread, not only in Italy but across Western Europe. French cookbooks, for instance, don't bother to include recipes for bread; the authors assume that you either know how to make it or buy your daily bread from a neighborhood bakery. When French and Italian recipe writers call for bread crumbs, they assume you have leftover bread for making crumbs. Sometimes they append a warning, for total novices, that it is heresy to purchase bread crumbs at the supermarket, as those airtight canisters of seasoned crumbs with an expiration date sometime in the middle of next year simply are not food. The quality of the bread served in European-style restaurants is generally taken as an indication of the quality of the food to come, and it's carefully evaluated by reviewers.

There is nothing new about bread's fundamental importance in the West. In England during the Middle Ages, a baker who cheated his customers by selling loaves below the standard weight would be dragged through the city streets, to be punished at will by angry mobs. The fall of the Roman Empire seems to be partially attributable to the need to import grain, as lands were increasingly devoted to more profitable crops, such as olives, for export. And perhaps most significantly, the

Judeo-Christian symbol of pure sustenance—that is, of life itself—is bread.

Alerted to these things, I look at each night's dinner table with a fresh eye. And while there's room in my heart, I start to wonder if there's room in my narrow urban kitchen for more than one sacred food. There's barely enough counter space to make a tuna-salad sandwich, and storage is so limited that staples long ago spilled over into the dining room and living room. For someone who switches cuisines every day or two, it is simply not practical, at least in this environment, to treat every ingredient with religious respect. There's bound to be a leftover heel of bread when my mood shifts from French to Thai, and I very well might (shhh!) throw away the heel so I can start slicing *galangal* and chilies in an uncluttered kitchen. So, now that I understand the sanctity of bread, do I have the energy to put it into practice?

I try. I dry out leftovers in the oven, whir them in the food processor, and use them to stuff artichokes and coat chicken pieces for baking. I make tapenade, crostini, hummus, aioli. I eat more sandwiches than I actually want when the bread is at its prime, and what's left becomes French toast or bread pudding with rum. Eating the latter at midnight, I have to admit that bread is vital, as are its buddies in comfort, butter, eggs, milk and sugar. They are my friends. The world is not such a bad place.

But meanwhile, my husband, whose eating patterns are dependent on my cooking moods, is getting a little restless. He appreciates being fed; he, too, loves jasmine rice; he accepts the frustration of eating stuffed artichokes; and there is one neighborhood bakery whose bread practically sends him back to his European boyhood—but he's beginning to feel, cumulatively, that something is missing. He won't say so, because who'd be fool enough to complain to someone who cooks elaborately for you every night, but he's been away from home for nearly a decade, and all the restaurants in Manhattan can't bring back the beloved foods of his childhood. As we dig into a platter of fried calamari—rolled in fine bread crumbs, of course—I finally realize that although he's enjoying his dinner, he's a little bit homesick. I should have thought of this long ago. Even our dog is named after his favorite imported snack. My man is a born-and-bred Dubliner, and he's hungry for the sacred food of his mother's kitchen: the potato.

Jessica Hagedorn and Kimiko Hahn

Biographies

Jessica Hagedorn's first novel, *Dogeaters*, was nominated for a National Book Award in 1990 and was voted the best book of the year by the Before Columbus Foundation. A well-known performance artist, poet and playwright, and formerly a commentator on "Crossroads," a syndicated weekly magazine on National Public Radio, she is also the author of *Danger and Beauty: Poetry and Prose,* as well as the editor of *Charlie Chan Is Dead: An Anthology of Contemporary Asian American Fiction.* Her new novel, *Gangster of Love,* was nominated for the Irish Times International Fiction Prize. She lives in New York City.

Kimiko Hahn was born outside New York City in 1955 to two artists, the late Maude Miyako Hamai from Hawaii and Walter Hahn from Wisconsin. Her previous books include the poetry collections *Air Pocket*, *Earshot* and *We Stand Our Ground* (with Susan Sherman and Gale Jackson). She has received fellowships from the National Endowment for the Arts and the New York Foundation for the Arts. In 1995, she was granted the Theodore Roethke Poetry Award for *Earshot. The Unbearable Heart* won the Before Columbus Foundation's American Book Award in 1996. A professor of poetry writing and literature at Queens College/CUNY, Hahn lives in Brooklyn with her husband, Ted Hannan, and their daughters, Miyako Tess and Reiko Lily.

Fuel

(Outtakes from "Eavesdropping;
A Conversation with Jessica Hagedorn and Kimiko Hahn"
Saturday, April 25, 1998, Cornelia Street Cafe)

Transcribed and arranged by Rahna Reiko Rizzuto, *The NuyorAsian Anthology* associate editor.

It's in the basement. When you walk into the Cornelia Street Cafe, the first person you see is Jessica Hagedorn, one of the most recognizable contemporary writers, sitting at the bar with a young Filipino man. Kimiko Hahn approaches and Bino A. Realuyo, moderator for the evening, warns her with a wave; the two women are not to speak to each other until they are on stage. The center aisle in the stuffy space becomes standing room only. The three slowly make their way through to a table with three microphones, one of which will not stay erect.

Billed as a conversation about motherhood, literary voyeurism, New York City yellow cabs as metaphor, the millennium, Divadom and more, "Eavesdropping" will never get to the topic of taxis. New York, which is intended to be the star of the program, will prove to be insidious, showing itself as much in the writers' appearances as in their conversation. Shoulder-length earrings. Crushed velvet and combat boots. Stereotypes exist because they are often true, and there is more black fabric on the stage than in the state of Hawaii. The longest hair belongs to the freshly shorn man.

My cat is very demanding

Hagedorn: Even in a really progressive household or relationship, the demands of children often end up with the mother figure. Even though my partner is there for our two girls, they generally come running to me. There are days when I am so frustrated: I'm trying to write, I'm trying to figure out how I'm going to get to my kids' school at three o'clock, get on the road, make some money and figure out who's cooking tonight. And I think, Does Robert Stone have to do this? And then some days I think, I need a wife. I need a wife.

      The flip side for me is, having children has raised the stakes. I have less time for bullshit. When I write, I really think about how much it matters for me. What the moral stake is of fiction and of whatever it is that I'm writing about. It becomes a real life-and-death thing. And I think in that way its been really good.

Hahn: I've always completely compartmentalized my time. Now's the time to write; now's the time to shop; now's the time to do this and that. People always say to me, "Oh, you're so disciplined," but, for me, writing is not something I have to discipline myself to do. Everything else I do is about discipline: buying food, making the food, picking up the children. Writing is what I try to do as much as possible. I mean, I write when I'm on vacation; that's part of what I love to do. And I don't bullshit around. I don't sit around and think, Oh, I don't know what I want to write about, because either you write or you're not going to write that day, and that's it. I write on the subway; I find other moments because I have that pressure. Which was true before a family but especially so now.

Realuyo: I guess I shouldn't complain, then. I live with a cat. She's demanding. But really, writing is such an ego trip for most people. It's something you do for yourself. And when you share your life with someone, much less sharing it with children, you are breaking your ego down and extending yourself. They are stealing your time, and you are stealing time from your children.

Hahn: Jessica and I are both lucky that we don't have nine-to-five jobs. If we did, the picture would be very different, and our husbands have helped us construct a situation where that's possible. Not to change the subject, but a lot of times people think that strong women don't need anything, because we're naturally strong, and I think that's just the opposite. Strong women need a lot of fuel, just like anybody else. Maybe even more so. And that fuel comes from husbands, sometimes children (although I wouldn't really count on a child for that fuel), from colleagues and friends. It's tough for my husband to be married to me sometimes because, in order to be a strong woman and produce work, I need a lot coming in.

Hagedorn: We're both with people who are artists. So I don't know what it would be like to be with someone who doesn't understand what that selfishness is about. That energy and absorption with your work. Sometimes it is really tough, because I do get very selfish. But you have to be to get the work done.

One of my daughters wants to be a dog walker

Hahn: My children see that I love what I do. They come to readings and see other people who are madly in love with what they do, and that's really catchy. As for whether they will become writers, they're very particular to detail, and that's a writer's eye. They'll get under the skin of things; look under the surface of stuff, which children do anyway. But the important thing is that they have something they love equally, and that they're re proud of it, too.

Hagedorn: I think my girls have the ability to be writers, but I'm not sure they're going to do it, because having me around they also see the worst of it: My horrible frame of mind when I have writer's block for days or weeks—I'm really miserable and they see that torment. Both girls have a lot of artistic talent, but I don't know which way it's going to go for them, and I've stopped trying to see myself in them. If they turn out to be writers, wonderful! I'm interested in them having passion for what they do. They have it all there: love of language, the detailed eye, facility. They have vision. But I don't know, they could end up at McDonald's.

Realuyo: And you don't care? You'll write about it.

Hahn: One of my daughters wants to be a dog walker. In Prospect Park.

Realuyo: We have dog walkers in Chelsea, too. They dress up along with their dogs.

You could lose your mind

Hagedorn: The thing about New York is, we have access to everybody's stuff here. Great stuff that helps you when you are feeling down. You feel alone and you think, Bino's in Chelsea with his cat; he wants to strangle the cat because she's too demanding.

Realuyo: Cat eaters?

Hagedorn: Right. And you realize that you are not so isolated, really. Everyone's struggling in the same way.

Hahn: At one point, we wanted to move out of Manhattan because we needed more space. We were looking in the suburbs, and the last place we looked at—we drove out in our little car—we didn't even get out of the car, we drove right back. I grew up in the suburbs and it was way too scary. The suburbs are nice when you have really little children, but by the time they're older they don't want to be sitting in their backyard with nothing to do, or to be driven over there or over here. And I certainly wasn't going to do that.

When my children were really little, I would put them in a stroller and take them to the park. "Go play. Go play". I'd go sit with all the nannies or mothers or fathers and have my morning cup of coffee and chat, chat, chat. I'd get to talk to people. Then I'd put the girls back in the stroller and take them home. It was a way for me to not be isolated. Especially in the winter, with little babies. Even just going to the park keeps you from losing your mind.

You can have only so much tiramisù

Hahn: I write in coffee shops. I say, "Good-bye, everyone. Clean your rooms!" and I go and write or read for a couple of hours. You know, with a bottomless cup of coffee. People take care of me there. It's great.

Realuyo: I love doing that. It's my favorite activity. I have a really nice one in the Village. I'm not telling you which one. It's very quaint. Very old. I sit by the window; you can see me if you are walking around the Village at midnight. One time I brought my laptop, and they said no. They have a very antiquated philosophy. You can bring your notebook, but not a laptop. I have to tell the owner of the place that I finished my novel there.

Hahn: Is it on the second floor?

Realuyo: No. That one is very expensive. They time you there. It's a beautiful place, but I can only eat so much tiramisù.

I read all kinds of shit

Hagedorn: I love to read everything. I read all kinds of shit: total trash to high-falutin' stuff. It's exercise to me. It opens my brain cells; it teaches me how people see things, how different artists see things. I read things I don't like. I make myself do that. I don't see influence as necessarily negative. There are certain writers that are very exciting to me; they thrill me in the way they approach a story. I'm not a schooled writer—I didn't go to college or writing programs, so everything I've done I have taught myself through just reading other people's work, so for me it's like school always, but in a joyful way.

The first time I ever read Manuel Puig (in translation), it blew my fucking mind! An entire novel that was a conversation between two men, in a jail cell, without any description about who these guys were. That was wonderful to me, just to see how he made it work, how I got to know who these two men were. It was very funny and marvelous. That helped me write Dogeaters because it freed me up, because I realized I can't write those conventional one-two-three novels, so why am I trying? It bores me to fucking tears. Just like it bores Kimiko to write short stories. I can't do them. I admire them. I'll read Moby Dick; I'll read all those novels they require you to read in school. And I get them. They're very satisfying. They'll lead you down a path and come around in a circle—beginning, middle and end—but I don't think that way. I used to beat myself up: why am I so bored every time I try to write these conventional narratives? Then you start to read other people and think, Well, I don't have to because look at this. This is brilliant.

Hahn: It gives you permission.

Hagedorn: So it's cool to me to keep embracing what's out there and not being afraid of it. And not all of it's good; there's a lot of junk out there. But I trust that we all have our own tastes and can see what's good and what isn't for our own styles. I want to keep growing as a writer. I don't want to get stuck in some stagnant pool and be predictable. That's the struggle I'm having now with this third novel: how to make it fun for me and exciting in the same way that Dogeaters was.

Trusting the dark

Hagedorn: I don't like to show my work until I'm pretty far down the road. I feel like, if you get too much feedback too early, it gets ridiculous. Even people I trust, adore as writers. Everyone has their own opinion—they'll say, "It's you, it's not you"—and who needs that too early on? Once I have a draft that's completed or close to the end, when at least I have most of the baby there, then I might show it to one or two people, but I really don't want it jinxed. I have a friend who talks about what she's writing about. I don't know how she has the energy to do it. It's almost like she's thinking out loud with me and I wonder, by the time she gets back to the page, if it's become deadened. There's a certain unconscious magic that's at work when you're writing, whatever you're writing, that's a very delicate thing. When you're in it, you know it. But you don't know what it is. It's fueling you, but you cannot talk about it. I really think that once you talk too much about it, you fuck it up. It's like trusting the dark. If you talk about it.

Hahn: You lose the unconscious element.

Hagedorn: And that unconscious is really vital to me. It's like not knowing what the book's about. If you know too much, you just kill it.

Hahn: I really go for the raw material. When I teach, I tell my students—I may be the only person who tells them not to think. Just sit down, get to the raw material, and look at it later. Don't bother thinking.

It's almost like living in a tunnel

Hagedorn: The hardest thing to me about fiction is the sustaining of it. Even if it goes around the bend and changes, and I do believe in breaking those forms and going wherever your gut tells you to go. Right now I'm working on my third novel and it's the toughest thing because it's my first draft, so I'm writing in the dark and I feel really blind. I know the story I want to tell but I don't know how to tell it—whose voice it's going to be told in. Maybe a million voices; maybe only two; maybe only one. My main thing is to just keep writing and surrounding myself with all the materials I need to keep inspiring me. There are certain things, certain films I've been looking at over and over again because it's important to this particular story. And there are certain books that I'm reading over and over again as research and that's all I look at. I don't read fiction when I'm writing a novel; I stay away from other people's work. It's like playing, but in a very controlled environment. The movies I go see all have something to do, in some subtle way or some not-so-subtle way, with the work.

Confronting the demons

Hahn: There's a lot of sex in my poems and fooling around and stuff. I have a daughter who is twelve, and she says, Well, I hope in your next book you don't have any inappropriate material, and I say, Of course I do, or who would want to buy it, dear? But there is some stuff that I'm worried about, so I usually write about it differently, take a different form or shape. Maybe it's veiled, or in third person instead of first person. Or in the voice of Bluebeard; I'll find different ways to write about it. But my main rule is, if I don't want to write about it, then that's what I need to write about.

Hagedorn: That's what writing is about: confronting the demons or angels. For me, it's not about the obvious taboos. There isn't any one thing I can throw out at you and say, That's what I'm worried about. It's the oddest stuff that you end up confronting day-to-day as you write. It's more a certain honesty that I want to keep up with instead of a subject I'm avoiding. I think it's whether I'm being honest or not when I write.

Hahn: I've been really lucky in that regard. My husband, so far, has been very open and supportive about whatever I write about. And my parents are both artists, so they would never criticize me. My children, we'll see. I'm probably a little bit more worried about that than anything else. But on the other hand, I absolutely agree with Jessica. It's a matter of getting to a true experience. I mean, not true as in factual but true as in what's in your body. *Who am I to speak for this prostitute?*

Hagedorn: I love history. It's a wonderful source. Recent history, long ago history—it's like this wonderful game to read. Sometimes, I don't even know why I'm looking into something and suddenly the mystery becomes deeper. The book I'm working on now has a lot of that in it. Very ancient history from Magellan's expeditions to Apocalypse Now! I really want to mix all that up.

Hahn: When I was reading Orientalism to prepare for a class, I came on a bit on how Flaubert constructed this whole vision of the Orient based on his several experiences with a particular Egyptian courtesan. I became so outraged by that that I started reading all of Flaubert's letters and diaries from that time, which—lucky for me—were in one volume. So I actually did research and then I started writing from the voice of Kudra Khan, the prostitute Flaubert had visited. It's called "The Hemisphere." What I had to do was to say, Hey, who am I to speak for this prostitute? I've never been a prostitute, I'm middle-class, I'm fairly comfortable. Who am I to speak for her? I could either stop or I could include my questions and experiences in the piece. It was a way to be true to my historical connection, saying, "This woman was made into a symbol of the Orient as I am made into a symbol of the Orient at times when guys ask me, Hey didn't I meet you in Saigon? I see that relationship; I see my relationship to Flaubert and other guys like Flaubert. But I also have to see where I don't have a relationship and understand that. And it's fun; it's so much fun. And it is fuel.

Hagedorn: History is fuel for me as well, but always with that personal stamp because I feel the answer to Kimiko's question, Who am I to be taking on the voice of this prostitute or Magellan or whoever? is that you're a writer; that's what you're supposed to be doing. But the fun of it, and the interesting part, is that you are going to personalize it, and you're going to put some of yourself in there, because otherwise what is the point?

This is where it gets really cuckoo

Realuyo: In an article I was reading in Publishers Weekly, the author said that, had he been a woman, he would have published his book. I'll be honest with you—while I was doing this anthology, most of the submissions were from women. There are a lot of women writing out there who are being published. If there are men, they're usually gay. Why that's happening, I don't know. I was really concerned, though, when I was looking at the list of acceptances.

Hagedorn: It's the age-old Frank Chin question. It's also the age-old Ishmael Reed question about African American writers. I know that, when I was editing the anthology Charlie Chan Is Dead, I had more submissions by women writers, and maybe there are more women writing, but I think it's more complicated. There's probably a grain of truth in what both Frank and Ishmael perceive about how this industry marks its people and what they see as threatening or nonthreatening. At the same time, every time they talk about the great novelists or the great writers, they're always a bunch of men, so I guess it balances out. We get published and nobody pays attention. And the big shit goes to the big guys.

Realuyo: Last year, Time magazine ran a little article about three Asian American women who had books coming out at the same time. I thought it was fascinating.

Hagedorn: You know, this is where it gets really cuckoo. I think you have to be aware of the marketplace but at the same time not get consumed by it. It's like the Millennium depression that everyone is predicting or like reading the newspaper every day—you'd really want to kill yourself. On some level you can look at that and you can say, Okay, the three women, but then, should I start whining and weeping because Chang-rae Lee is on the cover of New York magazine? It gets so petty, and we're all like crabs in a barrel pulling each other down. If Chang-rae Lee is on the cover, fabulous, because you know we're going to go out of fashion and we all have to support each other and enough of this fucking backbiting. It's so small-minded. It's tiresome and if there's two thousand queer writers out there, great. Everyone get published! Because that's really the fight—to be heard.

Weird, alarmist stuff

Hagedorn: What's this crap about the twenty-first century? I think it's false. I think it's just this thing that everyone goes around saying: it's the end of the cycle. They put it out there: the Millennium, the Millennium. We're all going to get depressed because we're supposed to. But really it's false, like weird, alarmist stuff.

Hahn: Now, turning forty, that's nasty.

Hagedorn: Let's not go there.

Hahn: It was nasty for me. Actually, with respect to writing, Asian American and other minority writers, writers of color, are often considered "emerging" writers forever. So I don't really think of myself as being over the hill; I just think of myself as someone who's had many years of experience.

Hagedorn: I'm almost fifty years old, so, in your terms, I'm probably close to death now. But I do think about it all the time, not just because of my age but because, in the last fifteen years, I've seen too many people go around me. My parents recently died and that was a big blow to me, because I feel like my family is disappearing. I could die . . . I always think I'm going to die. I am absolutely death-conscious. I have a headache now and I think, Oh my God! But when you say you don't have children to carry on, are you talking about them as a continuation of self? Because I don't know what they're going to do.

Realuyo: I guess in a sense it's a continuation of self. I think writing is a continuation of self.

Hagedorn: I do, too. I think that's realer, in a weird way, than children, because on some level I have no more control over them. I had my children, but they are going to go. I mean, my parents had no control over me at a certain point and probably wish I had never written a book. For me, the only thing I can hang on to is my work because that is totally mine. Even having children doesn't mean that they are totally yours. I guess that's what I'm trying to say.

Realuyo: Morbid, morbid stuff.

Hagedorn: I don't think it's morbid. I think it's wonderful.

Realuyo: Death is wonderful?

Hagedorn: Death is okay, its something else. I mean, it's real.

Li-Lan

Li-Lan establishes in her work a language system centered on the metaphor of correspondence. She often paints blank envelopes, postcards, postage stamps, cancellation marks and other postage markings, which she uses as a means of correspondence to her viewer. Her meticulous images are improvisations on, not copies of, the postcards and stamps that friends sent to her from many countries around the world, such as Malaysia, Denmark and Egypt. The images are impressionistic and always interpretive. In the end, her airy and light-filled compositions, and the rich textural nuances of the surfaces, are quite far removed from the source material.

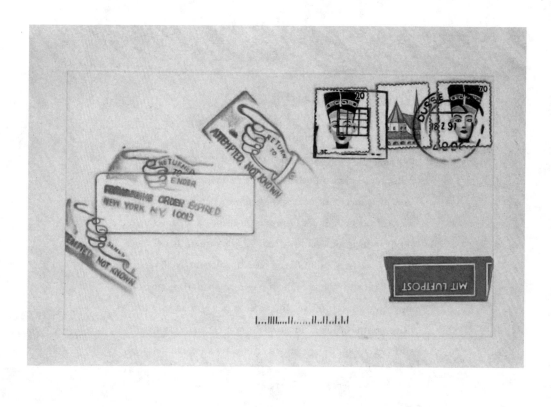

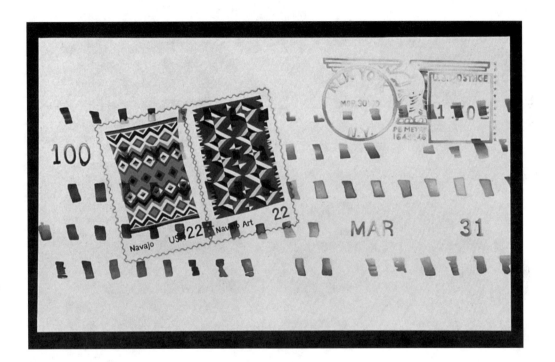

Rahna Reiko Rizzuto

Biography

The NuyorAsian Anthology associate editor, Rahna Reiko Rizzuto, was born and raised in Hawaii, and was recently horrified to discover she has lived in New York longer than anywhere else. She is the author and editor of numerous articles and publications, including four young adult mysteries under a pseudonym. Her work has appeared in *The Asian Pacific American Journal* and the *Salon* magazine anthology *Mothers Who Think* (Villard, May 1999). Her first novel, *Why She Left Us*, will be published in September 1999 by HarperFlamingo.

How to Give Birth

Home Stretch

1. Discover the true purpose of Barnes and Noble. This chain of clean bathrooms must have been planned by a pregnant woman. They are spaced less than a New York mile apart (about fifteen blocks), which is the maximum distance you will be able to travel before your baby-to-be starts playing soccer with your bladder, and not one is protected by an increasing thicket of FOR CUSTOMERS ONLY signs. Feel truly blessed if this pregnancy trail actually takes you somewhere you want to go, for it will keep you out of the subways and away from the temptation to continue your tired tally of who will not give you a seat. Face it: you may be a genius at quickly assessing your fellow passengers; you may even get a kick out of sticking the apex of your forty-five-inch abdomen into their air spaces; but when every compassionate person has been accounted for—four black men and two women; one Hispanic man and one boy; and one white woman—you will still get fewer than ten seats, and yes, an older but not quite old white man in a suit will actually nudge you out of the way to grab a seat that's being vacated directly in front of you. This very short list does not mean you are so dainty that people are not sure you are actually pregnant. After all, on your walks to and from Barnes and Noble, at least three times as many people will weigh in on the gender question. Every man will assure you that you are having a boy; six in ten women will guess a girl; and the rest of the women will ask if you know. (If you don't, they'll tell you it's a girl because you are carrying low, or high, or wide, or forward.) If you are still interested in statistics, half of these people will be wrong, beginning with the woman who seemed to be so in tune with the vibrations of the universe that she guessed you were having a girl before your mother-in-law could tell that you were pregnant. When you meet this woman, start considering names for a boy.

2. Speaking of in-laws, do not invite your family to be in town for the birth. Even if they live in Guam and you live in New York, which makes it difficult for obvious reasons to call and say, "Hey, I had my first contraction, why don't you hop a plane at meet me at Beth Israel Hospital in eight hours?" Whatever you do, never invite them to come early, as this will guarantee you an additional two weeks of pregnancy in the middle of the summer with family members (five, six, seven—they will keep multiplying for a while but don't worry; if you hold off long enough, they will begin to leave) staring at you. They will be wondering why you don't bother to put on a shirt anymore and whether you truly believe you look good in spandex shorts and a sports bra (especially when you laugh and your belly button pops in and out), and they will be toying with the idea of suggesting that you request a cesarean section so that the baby is born before they, too, have to get on the plane. The danger of this scenario is that it leads to castor oil—a lumpy

addition to your very large glass of morning orange juice at best (keep a towel handy to wipe your lips clean between gulps), and a totally inefficient way to induce labor. Castor oil is, however, quite good at giving you a taste of what it's like to be doubled over with diarrhea and cold sweats, wishing someone would slap a diaper on you and tuck you into bed. Even if you are lucky enough to have a diaper big enough for a 170-pound woman (next to your stockpile of newborn diapers, which, by the way, your baby will outgrow before they are half gone, so split a package with a friend), every member of your family will still be waiting outside your bedroom door when you emerge.

Labor

1. Before you leave for the hospital, take the tennis balls out of your overnight bag. No one is going to roll them on your lower back for pain relief. Ten minutes after you have been admitted, you aren't even going to remember the short, shallow breathing you were taught to use during childbirth classes because you are being induced tonight. Instead, your evening will include: a very uncomfortable pelvic examination with your hips elevated on an upside-down bedpan; a sonogram to check the baby's position and to give your father, who drove you here, his first look at his grandson if he can rise above the sight of your pubic hair (he can do that and more—when your nipples are so cracked and bloody from trying to breast-feed your new baby that you are again wandering around your house half-naked, he will even be able to pat your bare back as he passes on his way to the refrigerator); some prostaglandin gel, which will be applied to your cervix, ostensively to "ripen" it but effectively to start contractions that are painful enough that you won't be able to sleep (nor will your husband, but that's because he is lying on an orange Naugahyde recliner), but which will subside by sunrise; and a fetal monitor, which will broadcast your contractions and your baby's heartbeat for the nurses, and which requires that you buzz for a nurse to remove the monitor every time you have to pee (every fifteen blocks, remember?). Do not make the mistake of unhooking the monitor yourself. When your biorhythms flatline, the nurse assigned to your room will panic, and, once she has determined that you are alive, she will decide that you really need an enema. This is the moment when you get to experience firsthand how impossible it is for a woman who is forty-two weeks pregnant to roll off a bed, jump four feet to the floor, and make it to the toilet in ten seconds or less with her gown closed. Rest assured that, even if you send your husband out of the room (and, as it turns out, out of the hospital for an Egg McMuffin that you are not allowed to eat), the nurse will stay in the room to make sure your digestive tract is completely clear.

2. Beg for painkillers before it's too late. Now that your doctor has had a good night's sleep, she will arrive to administer the Pitocin to start labor, saline to keep you hydrated and between ten and fifteen other intravenous fluids. Do not let her walk out of the room with a cheery

"Why don't you wait a bit before you get an epidural so you'll know what the contractions feel like." She will not return when the tsunami-size waves of pain begin to hit you in the side of the head. When you ask for the anesthesiologist, he will not appear either. Instead, you will be informed that he is in the operating room with one of the twelve women who will have cesarean sections that evening, and that he'll stop by when the operation is over. You might get the impression, at this point, that you have no control over this hierarchy of decision-making. You would be wrong. In fact, if you thrash and scream when your water breaks and it feels like your molars were just extracted through your ears, both your doctor and the anesthesiologist will appear very quickly. This is an important lesson to learn about your hospital stay—one you will have to remember several times before you go home. Begin screaming before your contractions are two minutes apart so that the anesthesiologist has more than thirty seconds to position you properly (bent over with your back "curled like a cat," holding your husband's hands and shriek- ing into your doctor's face) so that he can stick his foot-long needle into a pocket of spinal fluid between your vertebrae. The shorter this window of opportunity is, the greater the chances are that he will miss, and—especially if he misses more than once—that he will dispense the most excruciating pain you have felt since entering the hospital, not to mention a tender spot in your back that will stay with you until your child is a year old.

3. Remember that labor, even on Pitocin, is very long. Drugged, IVed, catheterized and moni- tored as you are, now would be a good time to get some sleep. This might be possible if you do not have large friends. The larger they are, the more likely it is that the nursing staff will let them walk unimpeded past the gauntlet of NO VISITORS signs in the Labor and Delivery Ward. If your friends are taller than six feet (and especially if they are six foot ten), the nurse may even point out the room where you have been secluded for more than twenty-four hours and where you are now eight centimeters dilated. These friends will be childless, or they wouldn't be there. They will not understand that you are not the slightest bit interested in meaningful conversation and why you—who have been known to lead skinny-dipping parties on Miami Beach—don't find it particularly funny to watch them stretch surgical gloves over their heads. If you have a young, open-minded doctor, you are in real trouble because she will not insist that these visitors leave—they will chat and no one, including your husband (who, your friends will insist for years, looked as if he desperately wanted them there), will acquiesce to your demands that they get out. Possibly because you might not be moving your mouth. All you can cling to is the fact that eight centimeters will eventually become ten, at which point your doctor will tell you to call your parents and let them know that you are about to begin pushing (don't forget to mention that there is no need for them to drive the wrong way down one-way streets—your labor is nowhere near over), and will finally shoo your friends away to give you a little privacy.

4. Ask for your vomit tray now. Since the brown-stew chicken you ate before you left home

twenty-eight hours ago was very effectively washed out of your system by the vengeful nurse, and given all the drugs that are still being pumped into you, it's understandable that you will feel a little queasy. In fact, it's such a common response that there is a stack of vomit trays nearby. However, no one will mention them to you until you actually throw up. The good thing about vomiting, though, is that holding your tray gives your husband something to do. Sure, he and his Egg McMuffin have been there the entire time, on little or no sleep, sifting through the tapes you brought for songs that will keep you from going mad and maybe even singing them, but let's face it—this is not his element. Your doctor is busy looking for your baby's head; her new partner (who started today—sixteen days after your child was supposed to be born) is holding your legs back, which is just as well since you can't feel them let alone move them; and neither you nor your husband can tell when you should be pushing, but thanks to medical technology your contractions and your baby's heartbeat are being broadcast wardwide on a television screen, so the doctors, at least, know when you should push. You do, on the count of ten. Then you push some more. You throw up, then pause, but mostly you want to sleep. At least you can tell something is happening because you can watch your contractions rise on the monitor while the baby's heart rate falls.

5. Understand that the baby's heart rate is not supposed to be falling. Your child is in distress—no emergency yet, but not a situation your doctor wants to prolong. You are asked to change positions. Now you are on your knees, arms draped over the back of the raised bed, pushing "out your behind" on your doctor's count. Your husband is standing directly in front of you, which gives him a bird's eye view of the doctors, residents, interns, nurses and (with your luck) workfare trainees who rush in, alerted by the monitor which might as well be televised throughout New York City, and then back out with the excuse that they are "just checking the tape" when they realize that there are already twelve people in the room. You won't notice them. If you do, you won't remember or care that you are naked. You have a repeating ten count in your head and you are holding on to that because your epidural is wearing off. Your doctor will decide to try a forceps delivery, which requires her to cut a larger opening than nature has provided you with, so the anesthesiologist will reappear. You look into his face as the drugs take effect and love him. Then you turn over on the bed so the doctor can make the incision and the baby's heart rate plummets. Your bed begins to move.

Delivery

1. Don't even try to follow what's happening. All the extra doctors in the room will now be lined up on either side of your bed to push you down the hall to the operating room. The words, "We have to do a c-section, we can't play around with this anymore," have already been

spoken, but you will begin to hear them only now. They were uttered after you lowered yourself, after someone yelled, "Get her back on her knees," which there was no way you could have helped with since you are so numb you can't move. Even twelve doctors haven't been able to flip your 170 inert pounds, so they have rolled you onto your side with your legs sticking off the bed. Your husband is frantically trying to put surgical bootees over his shoes, but, even though they were thrown at him within the last ten seconds, he has already lost one. He can't find it, even on the floor where the bed used to be before it began gathering speed. You feel like you should be on television, except that, if you were, your legs would be tucked nicely under you instead of banging into every piece of medical equipment you pass on your trip down the hall. Before you can adjust them, you are in the operating room being lifted off the bed on some kind of board. The doctor is telling you to turn your head when you throw up, and directing your one-booteed husband to tuck his hair under the surgical cap, so you know he is there and you can ask him nicely to make sure you don't choke on your own puke like Jimmy Hendrix. Let him hold your hand. The doctor will ask if he wants to watch his son being born, and even though he always said he didn't—that he would faint and take all the operating room equipment down with him—he will stand and watch the gray back of a not-so-small person being lifted out of your uterus.

2. Check the time. After thirty hours in the hospital, the birth itself took five minutes and already you are asking yourself why you didn't demand a c-section upon arrival. You can already feel the nausea receding. There is a baby crying somewhere and your husband asks permission to leave your side and go to the incubator to look at it. Asks your permission. So sweet. The doctor is sewing you up, and you believe that the worst is over—which it is if you remember to scream loudly and continuously for morphine the minute you wake up in the recovery room, especially when the nurse on duty tells you you'll have to wait because she's busy. But you don't know this yet, and you don't care because your husband has just carried your son into view. The child's head is pointed from being stuck in the birth canal for two hours; it completely fills the knit cap he is wearing. Say his name. He will look at you. His eyes will be blue-black and cloudy, and you will think he can't possibly see you, but he will turn his head toward yours. Later, you will have a picture of this moment: his body curled near your face, both of you with closed eyes, and there will be no sign of the stalactite of vomit you were sure was hanging out of your mouth, or the tracks of tears. But for now, when you croak his name, he will hear it. His spindly gray fingers will reach out and touch your face.

3. Pass out. And when you wake, write your experience down so you can remind yourself that you swore never, ever to get pregnant again—at least not for another thirteen months.

Marie G. Lee

St. Mark's? I love it for its Indian food, tattoo parlors and great
bookstore - some of my favorite things, and all in one place.

Biography

Marie G. Lee was born and raised in Hibbing, Minnesota. Her novels include *Finding My
Voice*, which won the 1993 Friends of American Writers Award, *If It Hadn't Been for Yoon
Jun, Saying Goodbye* and *Necessary Roughness*. Lee's work has also appeared in *The New York
Times, The American Voice, The Kenyon Review* and *The Asian Pacific American Journal*, as well as
several anthologies, including *New Worlds of Literature, Making More Waves: Writings by and
About Asian American Women* and *Direct Address*. She is a founding member and former presi-
dent of the Asian American Writers' Workshop.

St. Mark's Place at Night

But that's just the thing. The break was clean; it had to happen. I needed to get back to Minnesota. He was going to stay in Korea. I wouldn't see him again, and the course of my life would bend around this fact.

So it's not supposed to happen, him tracking me down. He was upsetting the balance, breaking one of the few cardinal rules my life depended on for structure. Whatever I was going to do next was going to be wrong.

This is what I was thinking:

If a wound is only superficially healed, it has to be reopened so it can heal from the inside. That happened to our cat when she got a scratch on her head when she ran into the bushes to escape dogs. Even though her wound looked okay, our vet made us keep picking the scab, where we found amazing amounts of pus and dead-looking stuff that would need to be cleaned out so we could sprinkle in the medicine. We had to tie up the cat's paws in cloth bandages so she wouldn't kill us while we did this. I don't think psychic scars are any different.

A week later, my adoptive parents drove me to the airport. I insisted on paying for the ticket myself, making a show of counting out the cash—a collection of bills and coins culled from my waitressing tips—at the ticket counter. But just as I was about to board, my mother leaned forward and gave me a hug, enveloping me in some new Elizabeth Arden perfume, and my father slipped something in my hand—I thought it was a note—but halfway down the jetway I realized it was a new hundred-dollar bill. I should have known: they wouldn't feel like parents unless they could give me a little "something."

The plane ride to New York was three hours. Not like staying on a plane for sixteen hours to get to Korea. The New York airport was surprisingly dirty and dingy; there were sad-looking travelers huddling everywhere.

I trudged to the security checkpoint, scanning the faces lined up at the cordon. Chauffeurs had signs for their customers: Ibrahim, Swartz, Vallee. A group of short women started to chatter excitedly in Spanish when another short woman came out. In front of me, the Indian man in Western clothes and a lady in a sari strolled past the crowd and disappeared down an escalator.

I felt abandoned again. Was he late? Had he forgotten? No problem. I would break the hundred-dollar bill, buy a bag of chips, and wait for the next plane back to Minnesota.

"Sarah."

I looked at the person standing in front of me.

"You cut your hair," I said. He had gone from having glossy raven hair to being bald.

He shrugged and took my bag. He was Doug, yet he wasn't Doug. I was staring at him in a way that was strange to me. If he was picking me up at Kimp'o Airport, pushing his way to the taxi line, swearing at the drivers in Korean, I would be taking his hand and following, as if the whole process were entirely natural.

"This is so weird," I found myself saying. "I don't know anything about you, what you do in New York."

"I play in a rock band," he said. "Well, and during the day I work for a law firm."

We sounded like we were on a first date.

We took a bus and two subways. Doug apologized for not being able to afford a cab. But I liked taking the bus and subway. New York is so gloriously crowded in a way Minneapolis isn't and could never be. Those icy Swedes and Norwegians would never stand for it. I thrilled at the sight of the bus, like the prow of a boat, gently nosing into the sea of people jaywalking and double-parked cars. It looked like there was a parade going on, or some kind of holiday. But no, it was just another day.

"This is Queens," said Doug. "We're in Jackson Heights. My mom and I used to live in Flushing, which is also in Queens. You'll see that, too."

I settled happily against the window of the dingy city bus. Everyone in Queens looked so brown. I loved the names of the stores and restaurants we were passing: Anojitos de Colombia, Happy Supermarket, Polish Bakery.

"Look," I said, pointing. "A sign in Korean." Of course, after all that school, I could no longer read. The characters once again receded into total mystery.

"That's a billiard hall," Doug explained. "There are a lot of Koreans here. Just wait until you see Flushing." He said it like he had an unopened Christmas package waiting. I was beginning to think that maybe this trip was a good decision after all.

Of course, as I do, I began to wonder. What if my mother somehow emigrated to the United States and ended up in Queens? What if I might pass her on the bus, stare straight into her face and then keep going?

"Where is your mother?" I asked. "I thought she was still here.:"

Doug blinked. "She's living in Colorado now with her new husband. Another army guy. She has a thing for uniforms, I guess."

I didn't know if he was joking, if he expected a laugh. I let a tiny puff of breath, not a vocalized chuckle, but just an airy heh into the air. I don't know why I was suddenly in such a good mood.

Doug's apartment had the bathroom in the kitchen. Well, the tub was in the kitchen, squatting defiantly in the middle of everything. There was a big board on top of it that made a counter, on top of which was a mineral water bottle filled with a few stems of fresh flowers. In the room, where there was no boundary between the kitchen and the rest of it, there were a few beanbag chairs and a futon neatly folded into a couch.

"Wow," I said. "New York apartments are small."

"This is how it is if you're not rich and you want to live alone," Doug said, gently setting down my bag.

"I see," I said, surveying. Even though the walls were dingy and the tiles on the floor cracked with age, everything that could be cleaned was clean: the sink was spotless, there wasn't a speck of dust on the floor, a single gracefully leafy plant sat on the windowsill enjoying the small shaft of light that made its way between the buildings.

Doug laid his hand on my shoulder. Then I realized the potential pitfalls of this trip. What if he wanted to make love? I could hardly say no, him being such a gracious host and all. But, like usual, before I came, I hadn't even sorted out my feelings about him, about everything. I could almost hear my mother yelling at me: "Sarah, that's the problem with you. You always just act, you never think." That's me.

Doug's hand felt warm. My shoulder felt warm. The body has its own kind of memory.

"Are you hungry? We can go out for dinner."

I hadn't eaten all day. "I'm starving," I said.

We walked to a block that was just Indian restaurants. They were all in these narrow storefronts that looked challenging toward anyone moderately wide of girth. Rose of India. Vindaloo. Calcutta. India Palace. Ghandi. Sonar Gaon.

"Pick one," Doug said, gesturing expansively. "They're all the same."

In the Rose of India, the menus were laminated plastic that had been burned and crinkled and bore the traces of stubborn yellow stains. The food was good. I was realizing that I hadn't had any kind of spicy food since Korea. In our family, black pepper is as spicy as you can get. I ordered my dish—spinach and chickpeas—mild, but I kept tasting some of Doug's lamb dish that he had ordered to be fiery hot.

When the check came, I pulled out some money, and noticed Doug staring at me. We had eaten $15.93 worth of food. In my hand was a hundred dollars.

"I'll treat, you're the guest," he said levelly. He gently whisked away the grease-stained slip of paper, leaving me standing with the bill sticking out absurdly from my hand.

At the corner deli, Doug bought beer, and we took it to the roof of his building. The breeze flapped some laundry hanging next door. There were stars and a moon, too, which I realized I had quickly forgotten about, being on the ground with so many buildings pushed so tightly together.

I took a sip of my beer. It was cold, sparkly, exactly perfect for the moment. I was thinking of the leaden August in Korea, where the humidity would press on us like a thick synthetic-fiber blanket, where Doug and I would lie like slugs in a cheap hotel room bed, listening to the pouring rain that offered no respite from the heat. And I remember the too-flowery alkali smell of Korean soap, the defiant stink of kimchi on Doug's breath.

And I remember being happy in just the way I was at this very minute.

"Why did you try to find me?" I asked.

Doug took a puff of his cigarette. His alabaster face in profile was like another moon in the dark sky.

"It's not that I'm mad or anything," I added. "But I guess I thought it was so melodramatic and romantic to part like that after the summer. I didn't think I'd see you again."

He shrugged. A cloud of smoke caught the breeze and then moved in a big apparition, like a mist. "I was thinking about you. I'm always wondering if you're going to find your lost family. And that makes me wonder if I'm going to find mine."

I understood. Doug's mother and father had divorced a few years after they had come to the States. It would have happened eventually; his father beat his mother when he wasn't too tired or drunk. His father took in a new girlfriend while his mother cleaned toilets for minimum wage, still not speaking any English. His father had started in on beating him, too, and Doug knew this would be time to go—his mother wouldn't stand for that. Her capacity to endure pain was infinite, having grown up dirt-poor in a family of five daughters and a father who drank too much. Her working at the army base wasn't so bad in comparison, it was the first time she actually got to sleep on a bed (well, a cot) rather than laying her head on a dirt floor.

And the United States, with the flush, not squat, toilets that she would soon be cleaning with her own hands, well, that was paradise.

But she wouldn't let her husband hurt Doug. She always did everything for her son.

One day he dislocated Doug's arm in a fit of beating, and she and Doug had to take a taxi to the hospital, and they told the doctor he'd fallen off the monkey bars. The doctor said little, then had a huge male nurse hold Doug down while another snapped his arm back into place. Then they went back home, and acted as if nothing had happened.

She came home one day to find the house empty, of everything except Doug. No forwarding address, nothing. His father was gone.

Possibly it was too much for Doug to ask that his mother provide him with a family life, in that she already had so many things on her mind. She had had to work two, three jobs to keep him in shoes for the winter. Why they didn't move to somewhere less expensive, less cruel than New York had probably never occurred to her. His mother had started the race three steps behind, and it was all she could do to try to catch up, never mind, go forward. He had never forgiven her for that.

"I tried to not think about you, too, but I couldn't," Doug said. "We're like different sides of the same coin. I'm always searching for that family I was supposed to have—the one in the house with the yard, the dog and the money tree—and you're the one who grew up with all that, but you're looking, too."

He took another sip of beer, pushed the hair he no longer had out of his eyes.

"No one else could possibly even begin to understand," he said.

I was actually getting a little drunk, and then I had to pee. We went back into Doug's little apartment, where he unfolded the futon. He smoothed some new sheets into it and motioned that it was mine. As soon as I was horizontal, I realized how tired I was from the day. I heard him brushing his teeth in the bathroom, and I moved over to make room for him.

When I woke up, light from the next building illuminated the single plant on the windowsill and continued on to spread a ghostly glow on the floor. I realized I was sprawled all over the bed. Where was Doug?

He was on the floor next to the bed, crunched uncomfortably atop a Korean quilt, but he was sleeping. He looked like an angel, a child when he slept. He had one hand curled under his chin. He didn't have a pillow. There was only one in the house, it seemed—the one I was sleeping on.

I gently worked the pillow under his head. He gave off a little groan, but didn't wake up. His hand stayed under his chin.

He is somebody's son, I was thinking. Just as I am somebody's daughter.

I folded my arms under me and went back to sleep. In the morning, the pillow was back under my head. I wondered how much of everything I had dreamed.

Andrea Louie

"Everything is miraculous. It is a miracle that one does not melt in
one's bath."

> - Pablo Picasso

Biography

Andrea Louie was born in Ithaca, New York, and grew up in Ohio. She is a freelance writer
and editor in Williamsburg, Brooklyn, and is the author of a novel, *Moon Cakes*.

Prank

Little Italy, New York City

Last evening, I had my first bad New York City experience. It was bound to happen. Your number comes up in this town from time to time; you can be careful all you want, but your number comes up.

I am heading down the sidewalk on Second Avenue. Three boys on bicycles are yelling as they careen through the throngs of people. There is a cocky timbre to their voices, a street-smart, bad-ass attitude that marks them as somehow more than neighborhood punks: These are kids who know no limits. They are not from the genteel veneer of the Upper East Side but from the mythic Elsewhere, full of rage and sperm and blind ego.

So I hear these boys from afar; they are coming, weaving across the street, wheeling onto the sidewalk. They are too close. I know it. But I edge over by the building anyway, as close as I can. The first one goes by; his arm is stuck out, playing that game where he lifts his hand a second before he passes a pedestrian. (Where I come from in rural Ohio, kids played this game leaning from car windows, sometimes wielding baseball bats and smashing mailboxes.)

The second goes by. Lift, down. They are screaming at one another.

I hear the third bicycle approaching, the tires buzzing on the sidewalk. I hold my breath, but my luck's run out: He hits me on the back of the head, slap whap. I lurch forward from the blow, which stuns more than hurts, but I am winded; my mouth is agape, my eyes bulging from the force.

"Fuckin' Chineeeeeese!" one of them screams at me.

I catch my balance.

A man who has been walking toward me turns around and shouts after the boys, "What the fuck do you think you're doing?" I want to thank him for saying something, but cannot. I want to sob, but simply stare, openmouthed and mute.

They are gone. Everyone keeps walking.

I stagger home, in a roundabout way, just in case. Maybe someone is watching. Once inside my door, I weep in exhaustion and humiliation. Damn damn damn that it is these boys—these children—who have pushed me over the edge. A stupid punk prank they've no doubt forgotten already. Three black boys who think they will live forever, three boys of color who levy a racial slur at a woman of color. Thank God they were not carrying pipes, I think. Nothing was stolen, I am fine, no one was hurt.

I am not consoled.

My Sunday evening turns sour and dark. At home, I drink herbal iced tea and cry in jags, feeling the spot at the back of my head that stings from pain and strange shame that I have crumbled so easily. For years, I have not reacted to things people have said in passing. I did not flinch when, as a child, I would walk down a northeast Ohio street and have other children cry out to me in sing-song voices, "Ching chong ching chong!" I continued on with my parents when, in the early seventies, a man yelled out his car window, "Fucking Vietnamese!" and my father said, under his breath, that we were not Vietnamese.

I have exhausted my stoicism.

Today, I feel a need to be away from the Upper East Side, the neighborhood that has betrayed me with its veil of yuppie-family safety. I worry that I'm overreacting, but I feel fragile and torn. It is as though, when those boys hurtled past me on the sidewalk, they snatched something from me like a purse, adding to their own spoils of immortality. I long for comfort, so I gather myself and come to Chinatown.

Unconsciously, like one who is led in sleep, I take the 6 train down the length of Manhattan and am disgorged at Canal Street. For a moment, I am amused that, as if on cue, all the Asians in the car stand up and get off. Sprinkled among us are young artist types, who no doubt must be going to Pearl Paint, the least-expensive art-supply store in the city. The horde of us clot in the narrow stairwell. We wait, shuffling out into the light.

I emerge on the sidewalk and immediately regret leaving my apartment. There are too many people. I always forget this about Chinatown, how every day the sidewalks are crammed with the Middle Easterners selling beef on skewers, black Muslims hawking incense, South Asians peddling fruit, African American and Hong Kong men dealing fake Rolexes and mainland Chinese men selling thin New York City T-shirts. The street is teeming. Tiny, tiny old Chinese ladies walk together, linked arm in arm, carrying red plastic shopping bags bursting with green, leafy vegetables and enormous oranges. City Hall office women in cheap blue suits saunter down from tall office buildings for their lunch. A knot of bewildered tourists tries not to cling to one another in terror. A young Chinese woman squats near me on the sidewalk; in front of her is a small see-through aquarium with a hot pink lid. Inside are maybe ten little turtles, a half-dollar in diameter, climbing over one another in a furious attempt to escape.

I blink, overwhelmed by all these sights. I stare at the nearby McDonald's storefront, which suddenly seems too brightly colored. I want to go home, but I resist the urge to rush back down into the subway station. Instead, I start walking as calmly as possible, keeping my fear between clenched fists. I head east on Canal Street. I look around, but everything frightens me. The glass storefronts steam; lynched on metal hooks are soy sauce ducks and chickens, complete with perfectly marinated heads. I press on, but the smell of the open fish markets makes me sick; I hurry past to avoid looking at the slick corpses displayed on crushed ice, but it's too late. Out of the corner of my eye, I still see them—thick-bellied, steel gray fish gazing with vacant eyes; blue-red crabs clawing their way out of bushel baskets; enormous cross-sections of fish, as big around as coffee pots, bleeding into red ice. I squint, swallow my nausea.

Finally, I approach Mott and Elizabeth streets and try to breathe more evenly. The atmosphere is less dire here, the colors less threatening. There are clusters of vegetable stands, with the produce carefully arranged. There are a hundred subtle shades of green (tong choi, napa cabbage, bok choi, long beans, watercress, broccoli, scallions, cilantro); there is the pretty purple of the long, thin Asian eggplant and the reds of plums, strawberries and apples.

I stand there, distraught.

I do not know what I want. Most of this food requires cooking, and I cannot think. Green peppers? Choi sum? Garlic? Do I have to buy meat, then? Tofu? What about just a pear? Finally, I buy two pounds of green beans for a dollar and am drained by this exercise; I have to get out of here.

Normally, I am energized by this Chinatown scene. It is so different from where I come from in the Midwest, with its harmless landscape of evenly mowed lawns and identical shopping centers. Instead, Lower Manhattan invigorates; I love the sights of garish red-and-gold signs and the harsh sounds of urban life. Vendors will speak to me in Cantonese, and I will answer, yes, thank you; no one will mock my speech, even if I speak in perfect Dan Rather English. All this is a feeling of kinship, of blending in, luxuries that I never experienced before. I will drift through the aisles of supermarkets, looking at all the strange, dried foods that you cannot find in mainstream stores—hundred types of desiccated fungi, seaweed, fish, herbs, roots, twigs, bark and beef. I will love the smells of noodles fried in sidewalk stalls; I will become lightheaded from the thick, powdery scent of yellow funeral incense. The streets will be dirty and approaching squalid, but I will still find them lovely, somehow. The unchanging chaos will be reassuring. There will be the ginseng and Tiger Balm vendor; there will be the woman selling socks out of a cardboard box fashioned into a cart. There will be the fashionable Hong Kong girls with their whiny-sounding speech. I will feel oddly at home.

Yet today, I cannot bear it. I am gun-shy, every sudden sound making me flinch. I cannot stand the crush of people around me; I fled to the city to become invisible, and now I feel marked, branded and soiled. The incessant ringing from displays of plastic alarm clocks makes me want to club someone to death with a nearby umbrella. I dart across Canal Street and slip into Luna, a dark patisserie in Little Italy where the tabletops are cool and made of marble. I am relieved. When the server comes, I order hot chamomile tea and a scone with golden raisins. I eat hungrily. The bland food soothes me, and my heart quiets.

I am exhausted.

Chang-rae Lee

Biography

Chang-rae Lee garnered quick acclaim for his first novel, *Native Speaker*. He is a professor of creative writing at the University of Oregon in Eugene, where he is at work on a memoir.

From *Native Speaker*

I thought it would be the two of us, like that, forever.

But one day my father called from one of his vegetable stores in the Bronx and said he was going to JFK and would be late coming home. I didn't think much of it. He often went to the airport, to the international terminal, to pick up a friend or a parcel from Korea. After my mother's death he had a steady flow of old friends visiting us, hardly any relatives, and it was my responsibility to make up the bed in the guest room and prepare a tray of sliced fruit and corn tea or liquor for their arrival.

My mother had always done this for guests; although I was a boy, I was the only child and there was no one else to peel the oranges and apples and set out nuts and spicy crackers and glasses of beer or a bottle of Johnnie Walker for my father and his friends. They used to sit on the carpeted floor around the lacquered Korean table with their legs crossed and laugh deeply and utterly together as if they had been holding themselves in for a long time, and I'd greedily pick at the snacks from the perch of my father's sturdy lap, pinching my throat in just such a way that I might rumble and shake, too. My mother would smile and talk to them, but she sat on a chair just outside the circle of men and politely covered her mouth whenever one of them made her laugh or offered compliments on her still-fresh beauty and youth.

The night my father phoned I went to the cabinet where he kept the whiskey and nuts and took out a bottle for their arrival. An ashtray, of course, because the men always smoked. The men—it was always only men—were mostly friends of his from college now come to the States on matters of business. Import-export. They seemed exotic to me then. They wore shiny, textured gray-blue suits and wide ties and sported long sideburns and slightly too large brown-tinted polarizing glasses. It was 1971. They dragged into the house huge square plastic suitcases on wheels, stuffed full of samples of their wares, knock-off perfumes and colognes, gaudy women's handkerchiefs, plastic AM radios cast in the shape of footballs and automobiles, leatherette handbags, purses, belts, tinny watches and cuff links, half-crushed boxes of Oriental rice crackers and leathery sheets of dried squid, and bags upon bags of sickly-sweet sucking candy whose transparent wrappers were edible and dissolved on the tongue.

In the foyer these men had to struggle to pull off the tight black shoes from their swollen feet, and the sour, ammoniac smell of sweat-sopped wool and cheap leather reached me where I stood overlooking them from the raised living room of our split-level house, that nose-stinging smell of sixteen hours of sleepless cramped flight from Seoul to Anchorage to New York shot so full of their ranks, hopeful of good commerce here in America.

My father opened the door at ten o'clock, hauling into the house two huge, battered suitcases. I had just set out a tray of fruits and rice cakes to go along with the liquor on the low table in the living room and went down to help him. He waved me off and nodded toward the driveway.

"Go help," he said, immediately bearing the suitcases upstairs.

I walked outside. A dim figure of a woman stood unmoving in the darkness next to my father's Chevrolet. It was late winter, still cold and miserable, and she was bundled up in a long woolen coat that nearly reached the ground. Beside her were two small bags and a cardboard box messily bound with twine. When I got closer to her she lifted both bags and so I picked up the box; it was very heavy, full of glass jars and tins of pickled vegetables and meats. I realized she had transported homemade food thousands of miles, all the way from Korea, and the stench of overripe kimchee shot up through the cardboard flaps and I nearly dropped the whole thing.

The woman mumbled something in an unusual accent about my not knowing what kimchee was, but I didn't answer. I thought she was a very distant relative. She didn't look at all like us, nothing like my mother, whose broad, serene face was the smoothest mask. This woman, I could see, had deep pockmarks stippling her high, fleshy cheeks, like the scarring from a mistreated bout of chicken pox or smallpox, and she stood much shorter than I first thought, barely five feet in her heeled shoes. Her ankles and wrists were as thick as posts. She waited for me to turn and start for the house before she followed several steps behind me. I was surprised that my father wasn't waiting in the doorway, to greet her or hold the door, and as I walked up the carpeted steps leading to the kitchen I saw that the food and drink I had prepared had been cleared away.

"Please come this way," he said to her stiffly in Korean, appearing from the hallway to the bedrooms. "Please come this way."

He ushered her into the guest room and shut the door behind them. After a few minutes he came back out and sat down in the kitchen with me. He hadn't changed out of his work clothes, and his shirt and the knees and cuffs of his pants were stained with the slick juice of spoiled vegetables. I was eating apple quarters off the tray. My father picked one, bit into it, and then put it back. This was a habit of his, perhaps because he worked with fruits and vegetables all day, randomly sampling them for freshness and flavor.

He started speaking, but in English. Sometimes, when he wanted to hide or not outright lie, he chose to speak in English. He used to break into it when he argued with my mother, and it drove her crazy when he did and she would just plead, "No, no!" as though he had suddenly introduced a switchblade into a clean fistfight. Once, when he was having some money problems with a store, he started berating her with some awful stream of nonsensical street talk, shouting "my hot mama shit ass tight cock sucka," and "slant-eye spic-and-span motha-fucka" (he had picked it up, no doubt, from his customers). I broke into their argument and started yelling at him, making sure I was speaking in complete sentences about his cowardice and unfairness, shooting back at him his own medicine, until he slammed both palms on the table and demanded, "You shut up! You shut up!"

I kept at him anyway, using the biggest words I knew, whether they made sense or not, school words like "socioeconomic" and "intangible," anything I could lift from my dizzy burning thoughts and hurl against him, until my mother, who'd been perfectly quiet the whole time, whacked me hard across the back of the head and shouted in Korean, *Who do you think you are?*

Fair fight or not, she wasn't going to let me dress down my father, not with language, not with anything.

"Hen-ry," he now said, accenting as always the second syllable, "you know, it's difficult now. Your mommy dead and nobody at home. You too young for that. This nice lady, she come for you. Take care home, food. Nice dinner. Clean house. Better that way."

I didn't answer him.

"I better tell you before, I know, but I know you don't like. So what I do? I go to store in morning and come home late, nine o'clock, ten. No good, no good. Nice lady, she fix that. And soon we move to nice neighborhood, over near Fern Pond, big house and yard. Very nice place."

"Fern Pond? I don't want to move! And I don't want to move there, all the rich kids live there."

"Ha!" he laughed. "You rich kid now, your daddy rich rich man. Big house, big tree, now even we got houselady. Nice big yard for you. I pay all cash."

"What? You bought a house already?"

"Price very low for big house. Fix-her-upper. You thank me someday . . ."

"I won't. I won't move. No way."

Byong-ho, he said firmly. His voice was already changing. He was shifting into Korean, getting his throat ready. Then he spoke to us as he rose to leave. *Let's not hear one more thing about it. The woman will come with us to the new house and take care of you. This is what I have decided. Our talk is past usefulness. There will be no other way.*

In this new house, the woman lived in the two small rooms behind the kitchen pantry. I decided early on that I would never venture in there or try to befriend her. Her manner unnerved me. She never laughed. She spoke only when it mattered, when a thing needed to be done, or requested, or acknowledged. Otherwise the sole sounds I heard from her were the sucking noises she would make through the spaces between her teeth after meals and in the mornings. Once I heard her humming a pretty melody in her room, some Korean folk song, but as I walked toward her doorway to hear it better she stopped immediately, and I never heard it again.

She kept a clean and orderly house. Because she was the one who really moved us from the old house, she organized and ran the new one in a manner that suited her. In the old Korean tradition, my presence in the kitchen was unwelcome unless I was actually eating, or passing through the room. I understood that her two rooms, the tiny bathroom adjoining them, and the kitchen and pantry, constituted the sphere of her influence, and she was quick to deflect any interest on my part to look into the cabinets or closets. If she were present, I was to ask her for something I wanted, even if it was in the refrigerator, and then she would get it for me. She became annoyed if I lingered too long, and I quickly learned to remove myself immediately after any eating or drinking. Only when a friend of mine was over, after school or sports, would she mysteriously recede from the kitchen. My tall, talkative white friends made her nervous. Then she would wait noiselessly in her back room until we had gone.

She smelled strongly of fried fish and sesame oil and garlic. Though I didn't like it, my friends called her "Aunt Scallion," and made faces behind her back.

Sometimes I though she was some kind of zombie. When she wasn't cleaning or cooking or folding clothes she was barely present; she never whistled or hummed or made any noise, and it seemed to me as if she only partly possessed her own body, and preferred it that way. When she sat in the living room or outside on the patio she never read or listened to music. She didn't have a hobby, as far as I could see. She never exercised. She sometimes watched the soap operas on television (I found this out when I stayed home sick from school), but she always turned them off after a few minutes.

She never called her family in Korea, and they never called her. I imagined that something deeply horrible had happened to her when she was young, some nameless pain, something brutal, that a malicious man had taught her fear and sadness and she had had to leave her life and family because of it.

Years later, when the three of us came on Memorial Day for the summer-long stay with my father, he had the houselady prepare the apartment above the garage for us. Whenever we first opened its door at the top of the creaky narrow stairs we smelled the fresh veneers of pine oil and bleach and lemon balm. The pine floors were shimmering and dangerously slick. Mitt would dash past us to the king-sized mattress in the center of the open space and tumble on the neatly sheeted bed. The bed was my parents' old one; my father bought himself a twin the first year we moved into the new house. The rest of the stuff in the apartment had come with the property: there was an old leather sofa; a chest of drawers; a metal office desk; my first stereo, the all-in-one kind, still working; and someone's nod to a kitchen, thrown together next to the bathroom in the far corner, featuring a dorm-style refrigerator, a half-sized two-burner stove, and the single cabinet above it.

Mitt and Lelia loved the place. Lelia especially liked the tiny secret room that was tucked behind a false panel in the closet. The room, barely six by eight, featured a single-paned window in the shape of a face that swung out to a discreet view of my father's exquisitely land-scaped garden of cut stones and flowers. She wrote back in that room during the summer, slipping in at sunrise before I left for Purchase, and was able to complete a handful of workable poems by the time we departed on Labor Day, when she had to go back to teaching.

Mitt liked the room, too, for its pitched ceiling that he could almost reach if he tippy-toed, and I could see he felt himself bigger in there as he stamped about in my father's musty cordovans like some thundering giant, sweeping at the air, though he only ventured in during the late afternoons when enough light could angle inside and warmly lamp every crag and corner nook. He got locked in once for a few hours, the panel becoming stuck somehow, and we heard his wails all the way from the kitchen in the big house.

"Spooky," Mitt pronounced that night, fearful and unashamed as he lay between us in our bed, clutching his mother's thigh.

Mitt slept with us those summers until my father bought him his own canvas army cot. That's what the boy wanted. He liked the camouflaging pattern of the thick fabric and some-times tipped the thing on its side and shot rubbertipped arrows at me and Lelia from behind its cover. We had to shoot them back before he would agree to go to bed.

When he was an infant we waited until he was asleep and then delicately placed him atop our two pillows, which we arranged on the floor next to the bed. We lay still a few min-utes until we could hear his breathing deepen and become rhythmic. That's when we made love. It was warm up there in the summer and we didn't have to strip or do anything sudden. We moved as mutely and as deftly as we could bear, muffling ourselves in one another's hair and neck so as not to wake him, but then, too, of course, so we could hear the sound of his sleeping, his breathing, ours, that strange conspiring. Afterward, we lay quietly again, to make certain of his slumber, and then lifted him back between our hips into the bed, so heavy and alive with our mixed scent.

"Hey," Lelia whispered to me one night that first summer, "the woman, in the house, what do you think she does at night?"

"I don't know," I said, stroking her arm, Mitt's.

"I mean, does she have any friends or relatives?"

I didn't know.

She then said, "There's no one else besides your father?"

"I don't think she has anyone here. They're all in Korea."

"Has she ever gone back to visit?"

"I don't think so," I said. "I think she sends them money instead."

"God," Lelia answered. "How awful." She brushed back the damp downy hair from Mitt's forehead. "She must be so lonely."

"Does she seem lonely?" I asked.

She thought about it for a moment. "I guess not. She doesn't seem like she's anything. I keep looking for something, but even when she's with your father there's nothing in her face. She's been here since you were young, right?"

I nodded.

"You think they're friends?" she asked.

"I doubt it."

"Lovers?"

I had to answer, "Maybe."

"So what's her name?" Lelia asked after a moment.

"I don't know."

"What?"

I told her that I didn't know. That I had never known.

"What's that you called her, then?" she said. "I thought that was her name. Your father calls her that, too."

"It's not her name," I told her. "It's not her name. It's just a form of address."

It was the truth. Lelia had great trouble accepting this stunning ignorance of mine. That summer, when it seemed she was thinking about it, she would stare in wonderment at me as if I had a gaping hole blown through my head. I couldn't blame her. Americans live on a first-name basis. She didn't understand that there weren't moments in our language—the rigorous, regimental one of family and servants—when the woman's name could have naturally come out. Or why it wasn't important. At breakfast and lunch and dinner my father and I called her "Ahjuhma," literally *aunt*, but more akin to "ma'am," the customary address to an unrelated woman. But in our context the title bore much less deference. I never heard my father speak her name in all the years she was with us.

But then he never even called my mother by her name, nor did she ever in my presence speak his. She was always and only "spouse" or "wife" or "Mother"; he was "husband" or "Father" or "Henry's father." And to this day, when someone asks what my parents' names were, I have to pause for a moment, I have to rehear them not from the memory of my own voice, my own calling to them, but through the staticky voices of their old friends phoning from the other end of the world.

"I can't believe this," Lelia cried, her long Scottish face all screwed up in the moonlight. "You've known her since you were a kid! She practically raised you."

"I don't know who raised me," I said to her.

"Well, she must have had something to do with it!" She nearly woke up Mitt.

She whispered, "What do you think cooking and cleaning and ironing is? That's what she does all day, if you haven't noticed. Your father depends so much on her. I'm sure you did, too, when you were young."

"Of course I did," I answered. "But what do you want, what do you want me to say?"

"There's nothing you *have* to say. I just wonder, that's all. This woman has given twenty years of her life to you and your father and it seems like she could be anyone to you. It doesn't seem to matter who she is. Right? If your father switched her now with someone else, probably nothing would be different."

She paused. She brought up her knees so they were even with her hips. She pulled Mitt to her chest.

"Careful," I said. "You'll wake him."

"It scares me," she said. "I just think about you and me. What I am . . ."

"Don't be crazy," I said.

"I am not being crazy," she replied carefully. Mitt started to whimper. I slung my arm over her belly. She didn't move. This was the way, the very slow way, that our conversations were spoiling.

"I'll ask my father tomorrow, " I stupidly said.

Lelia didn't say anything to that. After a while she turned away, Mitt still tight against her belly.

"Sweetie . . ."

I whispered to her. I craned and licked the soft hair above her neck. She didn't budge. "Let's not make this something huge."

"My *God*," she whispered.

For the next few days, Lelia was edgy. She wouldn't say much to me. She wandered around the large wooded yard with Mitt strapped tightly in her chest sling. Close to her. She wasn't writing, as far as I can tell. And she generally stayed away from the house; she couldn't bear to watch the woman do anything. Finally, Lelia decided to talk to her; I would have to interpret. We walked over to the house and found her dusting in the living room. But when the woman saw us purposefully approaching her, she quickly crept away so that we had to follow her into the dining room and then to the kitchen until she finally disappeared into her back rooms. I stopped us at the threshold. I called in and said that my wife wanted to speak with her. No answer. "Ahjuhma," I then called to the silence, "Ahjuhma!"

Finally her voice shot back, *There's nothing for your American wife and me to talk about. Will you please leave the kitchen. It is very dirty and needs cleaning.*

Despite how Ahjuhma felt about the three of us, our unusual little family, Lelia made several more futile attempts before she gave up. The woman didn't seem to accept Mitt, she seemed to sour when she looked into his round, only half-Korean eyes, and to the reddish highlights in his hair.

One afternoon Lelia cornered the woman in the laundry room and tried to communicate with her while helping her fold a pile of clothes fresh out of the dryer. But each time Lelia picked up a shirt or a pair of shorts the woman gently tugged it away and quickly folded it herself. I walked by then and saw them standing side by side in the narrow steamy room, Lelia guarding her heap and grittily working as fast as she could, the woman steadily keeping pace with her, not a word or a glance between them. Lelia told me later that the woman actually began nudging her in the side with the fleshy mound of her low-set shoulder, grunting and pushing her out of the room with short steps; Lelia began hockey-checking back with her elbows, trying to hold her position, when by accident she caught her hard on the ear and the woman let out a loud shrill whine that sent them both scampering from the room. Lelia ran out to where I was working in the garage, tears streaming from her eyes; we hurried back to the house, only to find the woman back in the laundry room, carefully refolding the dry laundry. She backed away when she saw Lelia and cried madly in Korean, *You cat! You nasty American cat!*

I scolded her then, telling her she couldn't speak to my wife that way if she wanted to keep living in our house. The woman bit her lip; she bent her head and bowed severely before me in a way that perhaps no one could anymore and then trundled out of the room between us. I suddenly felt as if I'd committed a great wrong.

Lelia shouted, "What did she say? What did you say? What the hell just happened?"

But I didn't answer her immediately and she cursed "Goddamnit!" under her breath and ran out the back door toward the apartment. I went after her but she wouldn't slow down. When I reached the side stairs to the apartment I heard the door slam hard above. I climbed the stairs and opened the door and saw she wasn't there. Then I realized that she'd already slipped into the secret room behind the closet.

She was sitting at my old child's desk below the face-shaped window, her head down in her folded arms. When I touched her shoulder she began shuddering, sobbing deeply into the bend of her elbow, and when I tried to coax her out she shook me off and dug in deeper. So I embraced her huddled figure, and she let me do that, and after a while she turned out of herself and began crying into my belly, where I felt the wetness blotting the front of my shirt.

"Come on," I said softly, stroking her hair. "Try to take it easy. I'm sorry. I don't know what to say about her. She's always been a mystery to me."

She soon calmed down and stopped crying. Lelia cried easily, but back then in our early days I didn't know and each time she wept I feared the worst, that it meant something catastrophic was happening between us, an irreversible damage. What I should have feared was the damage unseen, what she wouldn't end up crying over or even speaking about in our last good year.

"She's not a mystery to me, Henry," she now answered, her whole face looking as though it had been stung. With her eyes swollen like that and her high cheekbones, she looked almost Asian, like a certain kind of Russian. She wiped her eyes with her sleeve. She looked out the little window.

"I know who she is."

"Who?" I said, wanting to know.

"She's an abandoned girl. But all grown up."

During high school I used to wander out to the garage from the house to read or just get away after one of the countless arguments I had with my father. Our talk back then was in fact one long and grave contention, an incessant quarrel, though to hear it now would be to recognize the usual forms of homely rancor and still homelier devotion, involving all the dire subjects of adolescence—my imperfect studies, my unworthy friends, the driving of his car, smoking and drinking, the whatever and whatever. One of our worst nights of talk was after he suggested that the girl I was taking to the eighth-grade Spring Dance didn't—or couldn't—find me attractive.

"What you think she like?" he asked, or more accurately said, shaking his head to tell me I was a fool. We had been watching the late news in his study.

"She likes *me*," I told him defiantly. "Why is that so hard for you to take?"

He laughed at me "You think she like your funny face? Funny eyes? You think she dream you at night?"

"I really don't know, Dad," I answered. "She's not even my girlfriend or anything. I don't know why you bother so much."

"Bother?" he said. "*Bother?*"

"Nothing, Dad, nothing."

"Your mother say exact same," he decreed.

"Just forget it."

"No, no, *you* forget it," he shot back, his voice rising. "You don't know nothing! This American girl, she nobody for you. She don't know nothing about you. You Korean man. So so different. Also, she know we live in expensive area."

"So what!" I gasped.

"You real dummy, Henry. Don't you know? You just free dance ticket. She just using you." Just then the housekeeper shuffled by us into her rooms on the other side of the pantry.

"I guess that's right," I said. "I should have seen that. You know it all. I guess I still have much to learn from you about dealing with women."

"What you say!" he exploded. "What you say!" He slammed his palm on the side lamp table, almost breaking the plate of smoked glass. I started to leave but he grabbed me hard by the neck as if to shake me and I flung my arm back and knocked off his grip. We were turned on each other, suddenly ready to go, and I could tell he was as astonished as I to be glaring this way at his only blood. He took a step back, afraid of what might have happened. Then he threw up his hands and just muttered, "Stupid."

A few weeks later I stumbled home from the garage apartment late one night, drunk on some gin filched from a friend's parents' liquor cabinet. My father appeared downstairs at the door and I promptly vomited at his feet on the newly refinished floors. He didn't say anything and just helped me to my room. When I struggled down to the landing the next morning the mess was gone. I still felt nauseous. I went to the kitchen and he was sitting there with his tea, smoking and reading the Korean-language newspaper. I sat across from him.

"Did she clean it up?" I asked, looking about for the woman. He looked at me like I was crazy. He put down the paper and rose and disappeared into the pantry. He returned with a bottle of bourbon and glasses and he carefully poured two generous jiggers of it. It was nine o'clock on Sunday morning. He took one for himself and then slid the other under me.

"*Mah-shuh!*" he said firmly. *Drink!* I could see he was serious. "*Mah-shuh!*"

He sat there, waiting. I lifted the stinking glass to my lips and could only let a little of the alcohol seep onto my tongue before I leaped to the sink and dry-heaved uncontrollably. And as I turned with tears in my eyes and the spittle hanging from my mouth I saw my father grimace before he threw back his share all at once. He shuddered, and then recovered himself and brought the glasses to the sink. He was never much of a drinker. *Clean all this up well so she doesn't see it*, he said hoarsely in Korean. *Then help her with the windows.* He gently patted my back and then left the house and drove off to one of his stores in the city.

The woman, her head forward and bent, suddenly padded out from her back rooms in thickly socked feet and stood waiting for me, silent.

I knew the job, and I did it quickly for her. My father and I used to do a similar task together when I was very young. This was before my mother died, in our first, modest house. Early in the morning on the first full warm day of the year he carried down from the attic the bug screens sandwiched in his brief, powerful arms and lined them up in a row against the side of the house. He had me stand back a few yards with the sprayer and wait for him to finish scrubbing the metal mesh with an old shoe brush and car soap. He squatted the way my grandmother did (she visited us once in America before she died), balancing on his flat feet with his armpits locked over his knees and his forearms working between them in front, the position so strangely apelike to me even then that I tried at night in my bedroom to mimic him, to see if the posture came naturally to us Parks, to us Koreans. It didn't.

When my father finished he rose and stretched his back in several directions and then moved to the side. He stood there straight as if at attention and then commanded me with a raised hand to fire away. "*In-jeh!*" he yelled. *Now!*

I had to pull with both hands on the trigger, and I almost lost hold of the nozzle from the backforce of the water and sprayed wildly at whatever I could hit. He yelled at me to stop after a few seconds so he could inspect our work; he did this so that he could make a big deal of bending over in front of me, trying to coax his small boy to shoot his behind. When I finally figured it out I shot him; he wheeled about with his face all red storm and theater and shook his fists at me with comic menace. He skulked back to a safe position with his unsuspecting eyes fixed on me and commanded that I fire again. He shouted for me to stop and he went again and bent over the screens; again I shot him, this time hitting him square on the rump and back, and he yelled louder, his cheeks and jaw wrenched maudlin with rage. I threw down the hose and sprinted for the back door but he caught me from behind and swung me up in what seemed one motion and plunked me down hard on his soaked shoulders. My mother stuck her head out the second-floor kitchen window just then and said to him, *You be careful with that bad boy.*

My father grunted back in that low way of his, the vibrato from his neck tickling my thighs, his voice all raw meat and stones, and my mother just answered him, *Come up right now and eat some lunch.* He marched around the side of the house with me hanging from his back by my ankles and then bounded up the front stairs, inside, and up to the kitchen table, where she had set out bowls of noodles in broth with half-moon slices of pink and white fish cake and minced scallions. And as we sat down, my mother cracked two eggs into my father's bowl, one into mine, and then took her seat between us at the table before her spartan plate of last night's rice and kimchee and cold mackerel (she only ate leftovers at lunch), and then we shut our eyes and clasped our hands, my mother always holding mine extra tight, and I could taste on my face the rich steam of soup and the call of my hungry father offering up his most patient prayers to his God.

None of us even dreamed that she would be dead six years later from a cancer in her liver. She never even drank or smoked. I have trouble remembering the details of her illness because she and my father kept it from me until they couldn't hide it any longer. She was buried in a Korean ceremony two days afterward, and for me it was more a disappearance than a death. During her illness they said her regular outings on Saturday mornings were to go to "meetings" with her old school friends who were living down in the city. They said her constant weariness and tears were from her concern over my mediocre studies. They said, so calmly, that the rotten pumpkin color of her face and neck and the patchiness of her once rich hair were due to a skin condition that would get worse before it became better. They finally said, with hard pride, that she was afflicted with a "Korean fever" that no doctor in America was able to cure.

A few months after her death I would come home from school and smell the fishy salty broth of those same noodles. There was the woman, Ahjuhma, stirring a beaten egg into the pot with long chopsticks; she was wearing the yellow-piped white apron that my mother had once sewn and prettily embroidered with daisies. I ran straight up the stairs to my room on the second floor of the new house, and Ahjuhma called after me in her dialect, "Come, there is enough for you." I slammed the door as hard as I could. After a half hour there was a knock and I yelled back in English, "Leave me alone!" I opened the door hours later when I heard my father come in, and the bowl of soup was at my feet, sitting cold and misplaced.

After that we didn't bother much with each other.

I still remember certain things about the woman: she wore white rubber Korean slippers that were shaped exactly like miniature canoes. She had bad teeth that plagued her. My father sent her to the dentist, who fitted her with gold crowns. Afterward, she seemed to yawn for people, as if to show them off. She balled up her hair and held it with a wooden chopstick. She prepared fish and soup every night; meat or pork every other; at least four kinds of *namool*, prepared vegetables, and then always something fried.

She carefully dusted the photographs of my mother the first thing every morning, and then vacuumed the entire house.

For years I had no idea what she did on her day off; she'd go walking somewhere, maybe the two miles into town though I couldn't imagine what she did there because she never learned three words of English. Finally, one dull summer before I left for college, a friend and I secretly followed her. We trailed her on the road into the center of the town, into the village of Ardsley. She went into Rocky's Corner newsstand and bought a glossy teen magazine and a red Popsicle. She flipped throughout the pages, obviously looking only at the pictures. She ate the Popsicle like it was a hot dog, in three large bites.

"She's a total alien," my friend said. "She's completely bizarre."

She got up and peered into some store windows, talked to no one, and then she started on the long walk back to our house.

She didn't drive. I don't know if she didn't wish to or whether my father prohibited it. He would take her shopping once a week, first to the grocery and then maybe to the drugstore, if she needed something for herself. Once in a while he would take her to the mall and buy her some clothes or shoes. I think out of respect and ignorance she let him pick them out. Normally around the house she simply wore sweatpants and old blouses. I saw her dressed up only once, the day I graduated from high school. She put on an iridescent dress with nubbly flecks in the material, which somehow matched her silvery heels. She looked like a huge trout. My father had horrible taste.

Once, when I was back from college over spring break, I heard steps in the night on the back stairwell, up and then down. The next night I heard them coming up again and I stepped out into the hall. I caught the woman about to turn the knob of my father's door. She had a cup of tea in her hands. Her hair was down and she wore a white cotton shift and in the weak glow of the hallway night-light her skin looked almost smooth. I was surprised by the pretty shape of her face.

"Your papa is thirsty," she whispered in Korean, "go back to sleep."

The next day I went out to the garage, up to the nook behind the closet, to read some old novels. I had a bunch of them there from high school. I picked one to read over again and then crawled out through the closet to turn on the stereo; when I got back in I stood up for a moment and I saw them outside through the tiny oval window.

They were working together in the garden, loosening and turning over the packed soil of the beds. They must have thought I was off with friends, not because they did anything, or even spoke to one another, but because they were simply together and seemed to want it that way. In the house nothing between them had been any different. I watched them as they moved in tandem on their knees up and down the rows, passing a small hand shovel and a three-fingered claw between them. When they were finished my father stood up and stretched his back in his familiar way and then motioned to her to do the same.

She got up from her knees and turned her torso after him in slow circles, her hands on her hips. Like that, I thought she suddenly looked like someone else, like someone standing for real before her own life. They laughed lightly at something. For a few weeks I feared that my father might marry her, but nothing happened between them that way, then or ever.

The woman died sometime before my father did, of complications from pneumonia. It took all of us by surprise. He wasn't too well himself after his first mild stroke, and Lelia and I, despite our discord, were mutually grateful that the woman had been taking good care of him. At the time, this was something we could talk about without getting ourselves deeper into our troubles of what we were for one another, who we were, and we even took turns going up there on weekends to drive the woman to the grocery store and to the mall. We talked best when either she or I called from the big house, from the kitchen phone, my father and his housekeeper sitting quietly together somewhere in the house.

After his rehabilitation, my father didn't need us shuttling back and forth anymore. That's when she died. Apparently, she didn't bother telling him that she was feeling sick. One night she was carrying a tray of food to his bed when she collapsed on the back stairwell. Against her wishes my father took her to the hospital but somehow it was too late and she died four days later. When he called me up he sounded weary and spent. I told him I would go up there; he said no, no, everything was fine.

I drove up anyway and when I opened the door to the house he was sitting alone in the kitchen, the kettle on the stove madly whistling away. He was fast asleep; after the stroke he sometimes nodded off in the middle of things. I woke him, and when he saw me he patted my cheek.

"Good boy," he muttered.

I made him change his clothes and then fixed us a dinner of fried rice from some left-overs. Maybe the kind of food she would make. As I was cleaning up after we ate, I asked whether he had buried her, and if he did, where.

"No, no," he said, waving his hands. "Not that."

The woman had begged him not to. She didn't want to be buried here in America.

Her last wish, he said, was to be burned. He did that for her. I imagined him there in the hospital room, leaning stiffly over her face, above her wracked lips, to listen to her speak. I wondered if she could ever say what he had meant to her. Or say his true name. Or request that he speak hers. Perhaps he did then, with sorrow and love.

I didn't ask him of these things. I knew already that he was there when she died. I knew he had suffered in his own unspeakable and shadowy way. I knew, by his custom, that he had her body moved to a local mortuary to be washed and then cremated, and that he had mailed the ashes back to Korea in a solid gold coffer etched with classical Chinese characters.

Our gift to her grieving blood.

Josephine Foo

There is no such thing as the wild belief style. The question of structure is an urgent one beginning from the first lines, these very lines, for this is the literal mountain.

Biography

Josephine Foo was born and raised in Malaysia and was, for a time, an undocumented resident of New York City. Her prose and poetry are anthologized in *The Best American Essays 1995*, *Dog Stories* and *Premonitions* and found in her book, *ENDOU: poetry, prose, and a little beagle story*. She won the Eve of St. Agnes Poetry Prize in 1995. She is a public defender in Philadelphia.

From *The Destination of Pears*

I feel I can continue into memory and distort a place in which I take my daily walk. Memory is a subjective position, after all. Bad memory damages places. Strangers may reclaim them, invest in them a mythmaker's talent for making history for that which is mute, isolated from origins. *My life has been nomadic.* I am ashamed of movement, I am proud of the agency of my own feet taking me from one lived-in space, a momentary settling, and then the need to belong to a place that means for me not memory, not the familiar, somewhere else.

There is a landscape, maybe a bittersweet part-dream part-place, the lived-in landscape set into story and then made into the outside scene. *The spaces I've known have been terrifying. My life has been nomadic.* These are the temporal maps—a progression of my life in land's sensual forms, the history unknown and then the turning against its weird affective power. Nourishment can be found inherent in that world. The world extends and exposes its inner construction.

I will try to do the work of spaces. Each is a struggle without the naming, only a distinction from the American place which is, on this walk, further than the eye can see. Space after space enfolds where shapes of unknown places begin. From the beginning the results of my choices and my value system alone give me a sense of belonging.

A child is standing in front of a large yard, newly seeded. Once, on the same piece of land, before the child's arrival and before the picture was taken, there had been wooden shrines leveled with a bulldozer some five years before. Women out of frame remark on some cherished feature of land. The picture shows fair weather. The image can be reproduced to give the illusion of place, which is not New York City.

The Treasures of a City

Sometimes I pull up a chair, a piece of chalk in my hand. On a table the level of a chair, I mark a country in mental rule. This shows and qualifies an actual one in the world where sparseness of life and lack of life are in a killing. My country is formed and approached, and how quickly the new replaces. It is a defiant act of walking from immediate fulfillment, peace and quiet, toward promise of quiet differently framed. The chalk becomes more heartfelt that even the dwindling daylight. It is dusk. The last light (as I've known it) catches the top of the outside wall and then smears it with ashes in a layer massive, mountainlike at this hour, one stroke. The rugged chalk lines confine what isn't in front of me, making these hands an unbounded valley. Night comes to it for the first time, and I respond for the first time at this level of skill.

Pleasures of a City

Smokestacks, roof lines, electric wires. The sun is fully up and I see the varied thickness of these lines and the old shoe factory being gutted out. Soon, the pigeons will roost on a genuine "line" and a thin blue line will form between the unbounded and the framed. It seems all about setting the scene, but the focus today is on finding a latitude higher than oblivion, which is the country of power. This direction means admitting a diversity I do not feel. Much the same dialogue as the getting higher, speaking of the pieces that have entered the sweep of the brush, yet look at them—the city is part of brushstrokes, of fires, insinuates itself into the soul however far you run away from power. That is why dreams have moments of quiet, to exert their will, to make changes linked to this one purpose that has the most meaning to those with mountain in their hands.

Nina Kuo

Nina Kuo has been addressing gender stereotypes in her work, particularly those conventions of femininity prevalent in Chinatown. Kuo parodies the stereotypical image of Asian women as exotic and delicate, reproduced over and over on calendars, in advertisements and on a wide array of products. The artist strategically overlays these pictures with excessive images of food, jewelry and phallic objects in order to underscore their psychosexual content and reveal the way in which Chinese gender stereotypes have been largely appropriated from Hollywood.

Sung Rno

The city is both inspiration and obstacle; it questions you with the gruffness of a thrown elbow, tries your patience like a cup outstretched for change; but sometimes the weirdness and noise, the smell, the whanging (Ashberry's term) intersect so that yes, you do hear something underneath, a baseline, a tune that lingers in your senses.

Biography

Sung Rno came to New York after growing up in Cincinnati and receiving a BA from Harvard and an MFA from Brown. His work appears in the anthologies *Premonitions* and *But Still, Like Air, I Rise.*

THE NUYORASIAN ANTHOLOGY

October Blue

Outside the leaves start to smell each other. We are only shades
        of blue. Blue morning. Blue restaurants with tables that scratch at our elbows.
It seems like fall, but when you think it is, it's winter.

Sleeping next to the highway, the roar of cars becomes its own kind of dream.
        In the morning, the jackhammer pounds and pounds
thinking I will finally get the point, get the point.

All day I think of green. A tree with a shade cooler than ice,
        cooler than wrists; a field greener than grass, greener than itself,
me lying in the middle of it, letting the wind swallow me whole.

In the evening there's the highway again. When it rains the pavement
        shines with the headlights of the oncoming cars. The moon could be blue too
but, no, it is more the usual shade of white, streaked with fumes.

Woolworth's

At last, finally, we see the frontier that lies ahead
        for what it is, the air calling itself to us
here, now, thereafter—a descending order of angels,

storebought coupons pasted to the greased combs
        of our heads. In the back of your mouth caramel
sticks to your teeth, settles into a permanence, cold,

it feels metallic, altarlike, and the music from the electric carousel
        drowns your ears in cotton candy. This being
your Sunday dream come true, what you've been saving for

all week long, quarters stuck to palms, nickels chained
        to fingers, humming the grease song of hot dogs
as they spin and spin above your outstretched bun.

Now you maybe don't want to ride anymore.
        You maybe don't want the cheap plastic jewelry,
the key chain that sings "Blue Moon"
        as you open the door to your dark apartment.

Icon

Maybe it should not have been said. This way.
This particular way. But that's the truth of the matter.
Nothing you say can change this. Not your hand
brushing my face, not a fall day. A fall day like any other

when the sky is a stained glass window, the sky is a church
we walk into on a noisy Friday afternoon. Outside,
cars and tourists, daylight garish on the glass buildings.
Inside, a silence of stone, large as it is small,

the murmur of quiet prayer, and a man who sits staring upward,
his entire world stuffed into a plastic bag, his face ignoring his own smell.
The lips on the woman next to me move to some secret music all her own,
while a tourist sweeps a camcorder across the walls, hoping to save

the stained figures rising to meet their truth in air,
hoping to imbue electrons with faith and desire.
I wonder when we should leave, and what we'll say about it afterward.
A woman walks down the aisles, her heels echoing like gunshots.

How would it be to sleep here—waiting out the night, without rushing
onward to the next spiritual moment, the next—to wait—to see—
the light as it burns through the glass and brushes our faces,
light colored with skin, fire, the sky above.

Mei Ng

Biography

Mei Ng is the author of *Eating Chinese Food Naked.* She lives and works in Brooklyn. She frequently does public readings in New York and is at work on her second novel.

From Eating Chinese Food Naked

After she hung up the phone, her boxy apartment felt too quiet. From down the hall, she heard a neighbor opening her door. Ruby jumped up and grabbed the half-filled garbage bag from the kitchenette and walked casually down the hall as if she just happened to be on her way to the trash chute. She had never lived in a building with a trash chute before. In fact, she had just found out about taking the trash out by opening a slot in a wall as if you were mailing a letter but instead you tossed in a bag of garbage and walked away without worrying about turning bags inside out or about dogs getting into your trash and littering the front of your store so you'd get a ticket. What would they think of next?

Her neighbor made a sound of impatience as she locked her door. Ruby waited for her to look up, but the woman turned and walked briskly toward the elevator. The sign by the trash chute warned against incinerating paint cans, oil-soaked rags and camphor balls. Ruby stopped to consider the contents of her garbage bag before sending it down the chute. Then she went back into her apartment. She had only wanted to say hello.

A walk, she would go for a walk. Her clothes lay scattered around the room and piled up in the closet. She still hadn't done laundry. She pulled on a pair of jeans and a T-shirt that was an awkward length. Her clothes didn't actually show dirt and they didn't exactly smell, but there was a grubbiness about them, as if they'd picked up the smells from everywhere she'd been—smoke, sex, old food.

As she was lacing up her boots and wondering when she'd start feeling at home in her apartment, the phone rang. She jumped for it. It was Miranda. Ruby hadn't seen her all summer. Miranda was having a last-minute party, would Ruby like to come? "You saved my life," Ruby told her. If Miranda hadn't called, there was a good chance Ruby would've ended up in some crowded bar.

Ruby stood in the deli, trying to decide between beer and flowers. At school, Miranda had coached Ruby on how to use a tampon. She had also advised her to get rid of her pastel clothes and her beige pumps. Ruby had been glad for her friend's help. Drinking was important but so was ambience, she thought, as she decided to get both the beer and the flowers. She hoped it would be a dark party with dancing and not a bright party with talking and bad music, like the last one she had gone to.

When she got there, Miranda berated her for disappearing all summer, then kissed her on both cheeks. Ruby handed her the gladiolus, which were just starting to open, and the six-pack. Miranda gave her another kiss and ordered her to get her butt over to the kitchen and get herself a drink. She sure looked like she could use one, her friend said affectionately.

Ruby headed for the kitchen. In the living room, a few people were trying to dance.

Ruby stood in the doorway and watched. She felt grateful suddenly that later she wouldn't have to stand on the corner trying to find a cab that would go to Queens.

Hazel was standing in the kitchen. She was drinking a beer and just starting to feel that being single wasn't so bad after all. Girls were a distraction she didn't need at the moment. Then Ruby came into the kitchen and Hazel changed her mind. Hazel had a weakness for beautiful women in frumpy clothes. They both stood absolutely still and their eyes went wide, as if they were in shock. They looked away at the same time.

Hazel wasn't pretty like the girls Ruby usually lusted after. She was tough. Ruby never wanted to kiss a smoker before. Hazel drank her beer as if she were in a big hurry. Then she lit another cigarette before she had finished her first one. Ruby realized that Hazel was even more nervous than she was. That made her relax just enough to walk over to her without tripping.

They said hello and then they just looked at each other. "You need another drink?" Ruby asked her finally. Hazel squeezed close to the counter so Ruby could open the refrigerator. Ruby took out two bottles. She had to concentrate to get them open. "So, what do you do?" Ruby asked her and then kicked herself for asking such a dumb question.

"You ever look at toy boxes? Like on the side, it might say 'Collect All Ten Action Figures.' That's me. That's what I do."

"You love your job, I can tell," Ruby said.

"God. I keep saying I'll get my portfolio together one of these days. You know how many people are looking for illustration work in this city?"

"A lot?"

"About six." They laughed. Ruby couldn't tell if Hazel was just being friendly. She wasn't. "What about you?" Hazel said.

"I'm a temp." Ruby wanted to tell her about cooking school but was afraid she'd blurt out that she was dying to cook for her, that she was seized with a sudden desire to shop at open markets for her, to buy only the most beautiful string beans and patty-pan squash and red bliss potatoes and herbs from Amish farmers. She also wanted to run out and buy some phyllo dough and wrap up something fancy in it and bake the whole thing until it was golden brown. "I might go to cooking school," Ruby said. "Maybe you'll come for dinner some night. I'll cook." She told herself not to be so forward. At least she didn't say she wanted to kiss Hazel, which was what she was really thinking. Hazel's lips looked round and soft, not like the thin line Ruby was used to kissing.

Ruby watched her hand reach out and touch Hazel's sleeve. Right after that, Hazel reached out and touched the front of Ruby's hair where it was white. "Where'd you get that from? Your high-powered temp job? Or heartbreak?" Hazel asked.

Ruby stood very still and when Hazel took her hand away, Ruby wanted to say, "Do that again. Touch me again." She watched Hazel smoke. "Heartbreak. I went away to school. Left my mom," Ruby said suddenly.

"Oh, honey," said Hazel. Their joking tone was gone now. People came into the kitchen for beer.

Hazel and Ruby talked and looked at each other. It seemed an agreement that they would leave together at the end of the evening, although no one said anything about it. But Ruby couldn't believe it and then she started wondering whether there was an agreement after all and suddenly she felt foolish. She told Hazel she had to say hello to someone and then she fled.

Outside, she walked a few blocks and then she stopped. It was too late to go back. Hazel would think that Ruby was stupid, running out and then running back, as if she couldn't make up her mind. When Hazel touched her hair, Ruby had almost kissed her. But instead Ruby had squeezed her hand. God, who knew that touching someone's hand could make her so wet.

It was too much for her, so she had to run out. Maybe Hazel was just a flirt. Maybe Ruby had imagined the whole thing. But if she hadn't, they would've left together and caught a cab. Maybe they would've kissed in the backseat.

Then she thought about Nick. Although she had just met Hazel and might never see her again, suddenly it seemed wrong that she was with Nick. He seemed too tall or maybe too pale. Too easy somehow.

But at least she wasn't scared of him. At the party she hadn't thought about him, but now she wanted to see him. He would be sleeping, his long white body curled around the pillow she slept on when she stayed over. How soft and white he was when he was sleeping. Like a worm. Somehow, thinking of him as a worm endeared him to her. He might be a worm, but at least he was her sweet white worm.

When they were fucking he wasn't a worm, though. He was a man in bed and she liked that. She walked faster. Hazel's face would have been soft next to hers. Ruby remembered one night she had complained about Nick's bristles and he had gotten out of bed and shaved.

Then she was turning the key slowly in the lock, stepping carefully over the creaky boards. She climbed into bed next to him. His back was warm. She curled behind him and he turned to her as if he had been expecting her, and pushed his face into her breasts.

"Where you been all my life?" he said. She missed Hazel and kicked herself for leaving. He started kissing her neck, her long, curving neck that was now an asset, but back in junior high they had called her Pipe Neck and she couldn't get a date.

In her ear he told her all the things he wanted to do to her. That got her going and she pressed her legs together so he could push them apart. He held her down and touched her, slipped a finger in her mouth.

But she was angry now and with one shove she got on top of him and kneeled at his head and lowered herself just out of reach. He said please. When she was close to coming, she put her hands against the wall and moved around on his mouth. The blankets slipped to the floor. Then she slid down and put him inside her. She started moving like she would fuck away any regret she had.

He looked up at her face, which seemed intent, but on what, he didn't know, and his uncertainty made him start to lose it. She kept going, touched his nipples matter-of-factly to make him hard again, but there was something he didn't like about her tonight. With her hand she put him back in her. He came too soon, but she didn't let that stop her, she just hurried herself and came again.

It was past midnight. She sat naked in the warm room. The food was on its way. She had just ordered from Hunan Delight. It was her job: she did a better Chinese accent. Nick and she both agreed the food was better when she ordered. From the bathroom, she heard water running in the sink, then Nick slurping and swishing water around his mouth, and it sounded just like her father gargling at the table after dinner to loosen bits of food stuck in his teeth. Ruby reached into his closet for the dark silk robe he had found for her at Goodwill. She put it on. It cost only a dollar but made her feel rich and slutty at the same time. Her mother had never seen the robe; if she had she would worry that Ruby might catch diseases from other people's clothes. But once she stopped worrying, she'd be impressed: only one dollar. You can't even buy half a chicken for that.

Ruby pulled the blanket over her head so she didn't have to listen to Nick's gargling. Hey Nick, it's Ruby, not Adrian. I like the taste. Adrian was his last girlfriend. She wouldn't kiss him until he rinsed the taste of pussy from his mouth.

He came back to bed. His hands were wet and cold. The doorbell rang and she watched him step into his crumpled boxer shorts and pull on his paisley robe. She laid the bedspread on the floor, picnic-style, and set out plates and bowls. Nick came back as she was setting the kettle on the stove. He shed the robe and the boxers and unpacked the familiar tins. The smell of greasy gringo food mixed with the smell of sex.

For the first time, the sight of his soft penis didn't seem to fit with the tins of dumplings, noodles, rice. It had just been in her mouth, but suddenly she didn't want it so near her food. It seemed too exposed, as it did when she stood behind him, holding his dick over the toilet, assisting. She wanted him to put his boxers back on. Not hungry, she sat with her legs folded under her and picked at her beef lo mein.

"Eat. You ordered all this food. Aren't you hungry?" He offered her an egg roll. Grease fell on her robe when she bit into it, leaving a dark circle. It would never come out unless she got up and did something about it right away. On any other day, she would have jumped up and soaked it in soapy water.

"Nick?" She wanted to say something about going to the party and the woman she kept thinking about.

"Yeah?" He barely looked up.

"The broccoli done enough for you?" she said. He took a piece, crunched it a few times, then swallowed it down. Her robe kept falling open and she wished she had a sash to keep it closed.

"I can eat it," he said.

"I went to a party tonight. At Miranda's."

"You should've told me. I would've gone." He didn't really seem mad.

"I just went. At the last minute."

Nick picked up a piece of duck with his fingers. "So how was it?"

"Oh, same old thing. Everyone was drunk, lots of people making out."

"Really?" He had stopped eating and she could see the interest in his eyes. He loved to watch.

"Did you meet anyone?" He looked down at the food.

"I talked to a few people."

"Who? Who'd you talk to?" He was eating again, so she knew he wasn't worried.

She told him about seeing the old crowd, but she was thinking about Hazel.

"Michael was there? Did he chat you up? He always had a crush on you." He kept putting duck in his mouth. She was talking and not eating. He was eating all the good meaty bits and leaving the bony parts for her. This made her quiet, and she felt sad suddenly that she loved a man who took the good bits for himself. She had been taught to give the good bits to the other person and that the other person would give her the good bits, and in this way, they would take care of each other. She watched the duck disappearing into his mouth. She refused to scrabble around in the dish for the last good bits.

"You kiss anyone?" He stopped eating and waited for her answer. He knew how those parties got sometimes.

"Here. Want a dumpling?" She put one on his plate.

"Did you?"

"In the kitchen." She was about to say she was just joking, that she had wanted to but hadn't.

"Goddamn it, Ruby," he said quietly. He wiped his fingers and now he was mad. "What's he got? A bigger dick? How many dicks do you fucking need?"

"Don't yell at me." Then she sat stony and still. The fatty parts of the duck were turning white. Maybe she could sneak a dumpling while he ranted. She was hungry again. Knowing that Nick could go on, she grabbed him by his shoulders and shook him. He didn't fight her but let his head flop around like a rag doll. That made her remember that she loved him. "Sweetheart. Stop now. I love you," she said. He had gone far away and she pummeled his shoulders, trying to get to him. She longed to slap his face but knew he wouldn't let her. She punched his arm until he winced and grabbed her wrists.

"Stop hitting me. What? You love me or something?"

"Yeah. I love you."

"You love me," he said, serious. She loved him but wondered whether she ought to leave him anyway. She thought of the way he ate his noodles, the excess falling to the plate. That was no reason.

"The dumplings are greasy today," he said finally, pushing at the food as if it were to blame. She sat down next to him. He got up and started clearing the dishes.

He stopped at the door. Without turning around, he said in a low voice, "How come I'm not enough?" She wanted to go to him, but her legs felt stuck to the floor.

"It's not you. I don't know. I met a girl. Her name's Hazel." Making up the kiss had started as a joke, but now it was too late. She would probably never even see Hazel again. When she thought about Hazel she felt afraid, as she had been afraid in the sixth grade when she would sleep over at Mary Ann's house. Ruby wore one of Mary Ann's nightgowns that seemed softer than her own and then she would brush her friend's hair. Then they would get under the covers and practice kissing. They became good at it and Ruby became afraid that she would like practicing better than the real thing, so one night when Mary Ann turned to her and said, "Want to practice?" Ruby answered, "No, thanks," as if beautiful Mary Ann in her long flowered gown had just offered her a hot chocolate or a peanut-butter cookie. Ruby stayed up that night and watched Mary Ann's eyes moving back and forth under her lids.

"Hazel? She's a girl?" Nick had a funny look on his face.

"Yeah, she's a girl."

"Why didn't you say so?"

"I just did."

"I thought you meant another guy."

"Why are you so happy all of a sudden?"

"Oh, I don't know. It's different."

As they had been talking, Ruby had gotten angrier and angrier and now she thought of putting all her clothes back on and going home. Nick opened his arms. "Come here," he said. She went ahead and fit her head carefully against his chest.

"No more fighting," he said.

"Okay." She was tired of talking and still a little drunk.

They were quiet for a few minutes and she was starting to fall asleep when he said, "You know, it's funny how people say, 'Oh, isn't she beautiful when she's angry?'" Something in his tone made her stiffen and draw her arms closer to her chest.

He went on. "How can they mean that? They're just saying that. Just before, when you were standing there in your robe, not holding me, not even looking at me—you know it drives me crazy when you do that, when you go so far away—I was thinking, Who is that ugly Chinese woman standing in my room? But now here you are and you're beautiful. I don't even notice your Chineseness. You're just Ruby who I love." His voice was tender and awed.

His arm draped around her back suddenly felt unbearably heavy. And hairy. She had never noticed it before. Her arms fell away from his body and she got up to brush her teeth. It was incomprehensible to her that he could sleep without brushing his.

In the bathroom, she thought about Mrs. Strain. Behind her wide straight back, the third-grade class had called her Mrs. Strain the Pain on the Brain. That made them crack up laughing. Mondays meant spelling homework and Fridays meant quizzes. On Monday evenings, Ruby sat at the ironing table and she'd ask her father for a pencil even though she had plenty of pencils in her schoolbag. It made him happy when she asked him for one. He made a big show of choosing the nicest one, a tall one with a good eraser. He sharpened it, inspected the tip and blew the dust away until it was just right.

One night she wrote her homework with special care, recalling penmanship lessons, made sure her swoops and dives stayed within the lines. The spelling words were getting longer and she was writing bigger. They didn't fit five across. She wrote three across and then two on the next line.

The next day she stood in line and looked at Mrs. Strain's hand, brown as her wooden desk and decked out in big silver rings, fingers tapering to dark polished nails. She drew big red checks on other kids' homework. Some kids had done five across. They must have written small. Another kid had done five down. Ruby put her notebook on Mrs. Strain's desk and waited for her check mark.

Mrs. Strain looked at Ruby's notebook as if she couldn't understand it. What was the big deal? Ruby wondered. Three across on one line and then two on the next. Mrs. Strain pointed at the notebook and wrinkled her nose as if she smelled some food she didn't like. "What is this? Some kind of crazy Chinese crossword puzzle? I don't have all day to figure this out." Ruby reached out to take her notebook away from her teacher's eyes. Mrs. Strain slapped her hand and wrote a big red X across the page. Ruby took her notebook, holding it close to her chest so she wouldn't drop it. She went back to her desk.

She put the notebook back in her schoolbag and saw that the hole in her bag had gotten a little bigger. Her mother could sew that for her. Ruby kept her head down as if she were looking for something way in the back of her desk, something that wasn't there anymore. They were all waiting and she kept her face in her desk so they couldn't see her. I will not cry, she told herself, I will not.

Maybe if she looked hard enough for that thing at the back of her desk, she would find it. Maybe it was back there behind the pencil case and the broken eraser. She had liked Mrs. Strain.

At lunch when the other kids pulled up the corners of their eyes and chanted. "Ching Chong, Ching Chong," she did not cry. She did not cry as she walked home, dragging her schoolbag on the sidewalk. She did not cry at dinner when her mother asked her how was school today or even when she said fine and then shut her mouth real quick.

She cried in Nick's bathroom. She wanted to tell him why her face was twisted shut. Her angry face, her ugly Chinese face. Not you too, Nick, she said to him in her head, not when I trusted you with my face, trusted you not to slap it and twist it out of shape.

She dressed quietly.

Sunaina Maira

Charles, Jane, Bank, Cornelia, Hudson, Grove, Greenwich Ave.,
Greenwich St. Concrete, spring, steam, miniskirt. Bollywood Jam,
Mere Angne Mein, Dil Hai Pyar (A Case of Bass!), Mere Khwabon Mein
(Frog Mix), Sexuality (2 xcentric), Make Way for the Indian.

Biography

Sunaina Maira was born in New Delhi, India, and moved to the United States at the age of seventeen. She is coeditor of the anthology *Contours of the Heart: South Asians Map North America,* which received the American Book Award in 1997. Her fiction has appeared in the *Journal of the Asian American Renaissance, India Currents* and *The Asian Pacific American Journal.* The most exciting things she has done in New York City are to help found Youth Solidarity Summer, a progressive summer program for South Asian youth, and to learn how to do club-bhangra.

Liquid Seasons

There is rain, and then there is rain. I hate freezing drizzle on winter sidewalks, slippery slabs made resolute by snowstorms endured. I've never really liked March showers either, but at least they drench the skin with the titillation of sprouting green. And then there are the monsoons, the rain-bearing winds I've heard of from my mother that assault the earth for months, seeping into the parched cracks of hungry earth, flowing through city streets in muddy brown rivers, beating down on roofs for days and days and days. A deluge would be depressing, but at least it would suffuse the air with sound; I wanted the sky to pour forth rhythm and thunder and liquid beats that give way to pauses of damp quiet. Boston swathed me in historic peals and powdery snow but it was always white noise. I wanted to hear traffic running through the night outside my window. So I moved to New York, two weeks after I graduated from college, with my futon four crates of records and two jars of my mother's homemade lime pickle.

When I stepped out into the languorous heat of the Manhattan summer and felt the heavy, humid air, it occurred to me that perhaps I was just another drop in the steady stream of eager young musicians and wannabe deejays that passed through this city in frustrated obscurity. I had been here for only three months, but already I was beginning to wonder if my decision to move here to get into the Indian music scene had arisen less from career ambition than from a fit of postcollege confusion. My parents had, in their odd way, been surprisingly calm when I announced I was moving to the big city. They were far too preoccupied with the potential family scandal they feared would erupt when my sister turned thirty and remained blissfully unmarried. So my plans to go into the music industry seemed, by comparison, an innocuous obsession that would surely pass. I wondered if it had ever occurred to my parents that this was how they had always talked about my sister's lifestyle after she had come out—a passing bout of waywardness that would subside with the help of time, and vigilant protection from the corrupting influences of America, where depravation and debauchery curdled the rivers of milk and honey. Luckily for me, they didn't know much about Manhattan, let alone the West Village, so they were quite charmed by the leaf-shrouded streetlamps and cobbled sidewalks in the area where I worked. I walked to the music store in a metropolitan daze, grooving to my favorite trance dub. My tiny studio in the crumbling walk-up seemed a spacious haven, the walls receding with the spreading relief of a guilt-free room.

When the humid air began to waft in from the sea, however, the city became unbearable. Traces left by dogs on the sidewalks floated up in putrid vapors, the steam of warmed concrete mixing with garbage and exhaust. At night, I slept between two fans pointing at the bed but still the mattress clung to my back like a slab of soggy vinyl. At the store, the other deejays became crabby. I was morose, not having been able to get a single gig at any of the Indian parties that were springing up all over the city. This irony was brought home to me one day when I was sitting on a stool behind the cash register and DJ Sunshine walked in. I knew her instantly. Red baseball cap worn backward, large eyes etched in black kohl againt her sun-burned skin, and jeans so wide they made her tiny frame practically disappear. I scrambled off my stool, hitting my knee against the counter and knocking several records off the table.

DJ Sunshine didn't even blink. I fumblingly collected myself and the records and stared at her, groping for the right, career-sealing introduction.

"Hi," I said. "I'm Tahira."

"Yeah? I'm Sunny. I was wondering, do you have my CD in here?"

Somehow it hadn't ever occurred to the store owner, DJ Karma Cool, to ask me to rec-ommend music that we should stock. I shook my head dumbly, my vision of spinning bhangra at the Banana Club on Friday night disappearing into a kohl-black void.

"Well, I guess I'll be movin'." DJ Sunshine grabbed her backpack and strode out the door, taking the last ray of my remixed, gold-shot fantasies with her.

"Sunny, Sunshine, wait! I love your music, I hear you on the radio every Friday, I just moved and . . . can I talk . . ." But the sticker-studded backpack was just another shaky blob in the shimmering afternoon haze.

That was the same day I first met Isabel Alvarez. I had gone up to Karma Cool's apartment, which was just above the store, to get his cellular phone for him. When I turned his key in the lock, a woman's voice spiraled out from behind the door, *"Quien es?"* I was completely taken aback. Karma Cool had never said his girlfriend spoke Spanish.

"It's just me . . . it's Tahira from downstairs . . . I work in the store. Karma wants me to get his phone." I waited.

The door swung open. It took me a few seconds to get used to the dimness of the apartment, the black rug and black shades absorbing the little light there was inside. Isabel was standing near the entrance to the tiny kitchen, leaning on a blue-handled mop. Her hair must have been silver, because it gleamed softly, and there was something about the quiet, poised way in which she stood that made the mop handle look like an elegant lamppost.

"I'm sorry if I scared you." She seemed to have guessed that I didn't understand Spanish. Maybe she slippped into her mother tongue when she was alarmed, like my grand-mother used to do with her alarmed *"Tauba, tauba!"* I was pretty taken aback myself. I had no idea that Karma hired a maid to clean his compact apartment. Lazy bourgeois pig, I thought, enjoying a sense of moral superiority over my boss.

"Hi, I'm Tahira."

Isabel took off a plastic glove and wiped her forehead with the back of her hand. Something about her face, the way her hair was parted in the middle and pulled back in a bun, seemed familiar. It suddenly struck me that she was wearing something startlingly like a salwar *kameez*, the pink *pallav* tied efficiently around her waist, like Nani did when she used to go for her morning walks in the summer—there I was thinking of my grandmother again. I was about to say something when Isabel switched on the kitchen light. The folds of her fuschia skirt rippled as she bent down to squeeze the mop. I felt oddly disappointed, and then a bit sad. I hadn't really thought about Nani since she passed away last year, and it was strange to have these flashbacks now. It must be the heat, I thought, and the strange thin light inside.

"Want some tea?" Isabel asked. The familiarity of her tone washed over me, making me feel cozy and despondent at the same time.

"Sure, I'll get it. What the hell, I mean, so what, I don't have to rush down to work. Karma's probably still getting his frappucino."

Isabel laughed, and I began giggling too. We sat in the living room, Isabel sinking into the big black leather armchair, nervously at first, and then calmly swinging her legs up onto the leather footstool with a sigh. I giggled again.

Isabel arched an eyebrow over the steaming mug. "What do you do?"

"I, er . . ." I looked into the glass coffee table and saw a small pale face, large raccoon eyes glowering at me. "I don't know what I want to do. I guess I moved to New York because I thought I'd get into the music world, you know. Indian remixes, that kind of thing."

"Are you Punjabi?"

I almost spilled my chamomile tea on the white rug. Jesus, how could she tell where my family was from originally?

Seeing my answer, Isabel said, "I know because my grandfather was Punjabi too. He came to California . . . oh, way back when, he was a farmer in the Imperial Valley. He grew peaches, then he moved into grapes in Fresno."

I put down my mug and stared at Isabel, barely there muslin *dupattas* fluttering in the windows. I had heard about those North Indian men who traveled by ship, often boarding in Calcutta or other outposts of the British empire such as Hong Kong, where they were stationed as soldiers or police officers. They came to Canada, and then to California, working on railroads, farms and lumber mills.

Isabel went on placidly, "Then he married my *abuela,* she was Mexican. She left him, but came back a few years later. They kept fighting. My mother, Maria Singh, she married a Mexican. Grandfather was the one who walked out that time. Got drunk and almost fell down in the irrigation ditch, I heard." Isabel laughed, her teeth white against her golden-brown skin. "He wanted his daughter to marry a rich Hindu farmer."

"Hindu?" My mother had told me Singh was a Sikh name. I remembered because she said it meant "lion," brave warrior from the Punjab.

"Oh, that's just what all the children called them. 'Hindu,' 'Hinda.' They were part Mexican, my mother and her friends, and they were very close to their Mexican mothers and godmothers. My mother was Catholic, and she knew my grandmother would stand up for her when she married Ramón Alvarez."

My mind was swirling, intoxicated by this unheard-of genealogy, a lineage bottled and kept away in an old cellar no one had bothered to tell me about. "There were other Mexican-Punjabi Mexicans?" Picking peaches together in the California sun, dreaming of rivers back home, of sisters and aunts fanning themselves on the verandah. I felt that twinge of missing someone again. Only now it was mixed with excitement. The summer was long, but there had been summers before this, drier, and longer.

"Oh yes, honey." Isabel got up and patted her bun. "We ate tortillas, you know, except we ate them like chapatis, with our hands." Isabel must have seen my eyes growing wide, because she continued, "We did the bhangra, too, except instead of . . ."

"Bhangra? You mean, Punjabi folk dance . . . like mixed with Mexican music or . . . ?" I could barely stop the beats from pounding in my head.

Isabel suddenly threw her head back and laughed, a very bubbly, tinkly laugh for a woman of her composure. I wasn't sure why she was so delighted. She turned to look at me, smiling, "Ay, *chica,* you love stories, I can tell." She rubbed her eyes, trying to wipe the amusement away. "Of course, we didn't eat chapatis, maybe some of the others did, but I never did any bhangra dance. My mother wanted me to be a good little Catholic girl—I wore frocks and took communion."

The fluttering white *dupatta* became a frilly confirmation dress, starched and white against brown skin. My daydreams were apparently transparent, that shimmering rope I wanted to tie between the continents my family had traveled, only Isabel had been skipping rope since she was a little girl, many, many years more than I had.

I saw her almost every other day after that first meeting. Karma Cool seemed to have become increasingly absentminded and was perturbed to find that when he thought his phone was downstairs, it was actually upstairs, and when his shades were meant to be in the apartment, they were suddenly missing and took ages to find. Isabel and I made iced tea, and sank into the leather sofa and painted our toenails vixen red—I introduced her to Wine with Everything, with a clear topcoat. She smuggled in sangria one day and we talked about our fathers and the sound a door makes when it slams behind you in an empty room on a long, rainy night. I showed Isabel how to use a butterfly-clip to hoist her hair above the dampness of her neck. She braided my coarse waves, gently pulling tendrils over my ears and firmly tying them at my nape, her fingers brushing my shoulders with the lightness of certainty.

I thought at first that perhaps she had really become just another grandmother, or the mother I would have wanted to have, who knew what it was like to be brown in a schoolyard of white, yet who spoke in something other than English, who thought at a tangent to the straight line I had been taught in school. Was it so simple? I don't think so. And I don't think she wanted a daughter either. She told me once that she had never married because she didn't want to raise children in another home where someone was always leaving. Isabel never talked about why her own mother left Ramón Alvarez, but she said that she was very young at the time—she remembered only that her mother woke her up very early one morning and said that she didn't have to go to school that day, they were going to take the train all the way to San Diego.

"I missed the class picnic," she said. "I wanted to say good-bye to Papa, but Mama said that we were getting late, and that, besides, he would probably be mad if we woke him up."

I thought of my sister, Sarita, in her apartment in San Francisco, writing newspaper articles three hours behind the East Coast light. Her girlfriend's voice always sounded so clear, so steady, when I called them, as if Sarita's nervous anticipation of the latest parental diatribe could only be balanced by Geeta's unwavering resolution. My parents always sounded relieved when they called and heard only my voice on the other end of the line, as if they constantly expected someone else to pick up the phone.

Isabel would smile when I recounted these family entanglements, as if she was indeed listening in on the domestic drama on a second line and could hear every measured word. She said she was tired of clearing up after Karma's parties, but she needed a break from California and had spent three weeks looking for a job after moving to New York. She missed her friends at the restaurant where she used to work in San Diego, but at least she could talk to me regularly. I kept thinking she must have understood what poured through the music I played, my latest salsa-bhangra mix blaring a cool, decadently air-conditioned beat.

I'd given up on the New York club scene, but one day one of the other store assistants, Hector, happened to hear my new musical hybrid and thought it would be perfect at the Café con Leche night, famed for its Nuyorican drag queen act. Then he introduced me to Sonia, who wanted me to spin at the Pink Cactus on Latin night, and I was soon coming home at three and four in the morning in the middle of the week, smoke and scat vocals clinging to my hair. I didn't have to get rent subsidies from my parents any longer and they were actually glad to hear that I was working—although I didn't tell them that I had been referred to in *The Village Voice* as the "new kid with the sexy Latin/Indian vibes who gets all the sisters grooving under the sheets." A couple of the sisters at the Pink Cactus made some gentle moves, and I had to play it carefully to keep my job, so I went to their after-hours parties and came home alone. Isabel knew I had stayed out late when I stumbled up the stairs to get some tea, and she always wanted to know if I had been listed in any newspapers again.

Since Karma had begun to retreat to his apartment in the afternoons to take air-conditioned naps, Isabel and I began meeting in her apartment and we had dinner together or went for walks in the park two or three times a week. I was enjoying the city at last—the heat was bearable if you kept the fans going all day—and I loved my night job. Lying in my room in the early hours of the morning, it occurred to me that I never did really think about the sounds of traffic outside my window because I was too tired. I still had this parched feeling, sometimes, but it wasn't just rain I wanted anymore. There was room in the elbow of the night to cradle another head, but I figured I was too exhausted and too busy.

When I think about it now, I shouldn't haven't been surprised at the way the summer ended. I had been so preoccupied with my own daydreams, and perhaps the dizziness of summer made me imagine phantoms, wavering mirages willed by my own thirst. I remember I hadn't had dinner with Isabel for a couple of weeks; Sarita had come into town with Geeta and they dragged me to the Pink Cactus every other night till I said it was interfering with my professional role and told them to find another club. I couldn't bear to see them, they fit together so perfectly and did everything in tandem, like a spoon and a fork.

One day after work I went up to Karma's apartment to ask Isabel to come with us to an outdoor concert. The door was open when I went in, so I should have realized that Karma was probably there, but I didn't hear any voices. The shades were still down, but there was a rustle in the bedroom and I saw the outline of a figure stretched out on the rumpled sheets. Isabel was standing in front of the mirror, zipping up her skirt. I could faintly see the white line of her bra across her back, her gray hair falling over her breasts. She saw me in the mirror and immediately raised her finger to her lips, turning softly and making a motion for me to wait outside. It didn't matter, because I was frozen, even though the air in the apartment felt warmer than usual. Isabel buttoned up her blouse methodically and tiptoed past the sleeping Karma, shutting the door behind her.

For a moment I saw her standing there with the blue mop, like I did the first day, and I realized now what I should have seen in the coil of her hair at her nape, what I should have sensed in the lightness of her fingers. She probably liked the pulse of Karma's music—the two-timing bastard—as much as I did. I felt a weird tug inside me again as I looked at her, but this time it was not sadness or wishfulness but something else altogether—the slow spreading clarity of remembering something you'd almost forgotten, finally sharpening the outlines of your waking dreams.

That night, I thought of taking a trip to California. I didn't care if it rained or not, and I wasn't afraid of El Niño's torrents, but I thought it would be nice to actually see Isabel's home rather than just fantasizing about it. I'd like to live somewhere for a while, not just move from one place to another, and get a real bed, maybe a queen size, who knows? I lay awake, hearing the rumble of the train as it rushed below the dusty, stained streets and then finally burst above ground on tracks shooting away from the city. There must be train tracks stretching across the entire length of the United States all the way to California, pikes struck into red earth by brown hands brought from Asia. Ships leaving San Francisco Bay for Hong Kong, turbans turned to the gray Pacific, watching the currents flowing, backward now, to the Bay of Bengal, back to the shouts on the docks in Calcutta. When the monsoons break, the rains will lash the piers where the men had waved good-bye to land and drench their fields at home. The men feel the hands of their wives, the fingers of their lovers, wiping the drops of sweat gently from their backs. Sometimes they caress in Punjabi, and then sometimes the strokes are in Spanish. It has been a long, hot, humid summer floating between shores.

Indran Amirthanayagam

Indran Amirthanayagam, a Sri Lankan Tamil, has published poems in *Grand Street*, *The Kenyon Review*, *The Massachusetts Review*, *Bomb*, *The Literary Review*, *Night*, *Hanging Loose* and other magazines. His meditations on plays have appeared in *The Chelsea-Clinton News* and *The Westsider*. He has an M.A. from Columbia University's Graduate School of Journalism and a B.A. from Haverford College. He teaches at Eugene Lang College, The New School, in Manhattan.

Let the Games Begin, Again
(November 4, 1995)

My friend: let the games begin, again.
No matter these silences between volleys
that we've got older in quiet pottering
with words and nostalgias apart, our books
written and unmade, Teofilio Stevenson boxed

four Olympics straight to gold, Duncan White
won the silver for Ceylon in London 1948
then left the scene, that undiscovered country
now a common item on the 24-hour news,
400,000 residents of Jaffna about

to leave the scene, what peace after
the bomb, I remember crows,
that awful cawing and my grandmother
falling down the last bomb dropped
the last time sarong-easy I shuffled

upon the tiles of my baby life, sugar
bread *seeni sambal* mutton curry
feast that disappeared without event
a planned transition from the rule
of kings, this walking up Broadway

to Penn Station, riding down
to Washington, American-out as diplomat,
reader of the culture again from *Time*
magazine, November 4, 1995, incomplete,
musing about Allen G's press relations,

Princess Diana's stepping out
of cars, arms pumped up, *People* mag
in all glory, the same old death and love

story, Clash calling from London's
Hammersmith Palais, New Yorkers in drag
gathering to resolve a few lingering

questions in lingerie from the days
of the Mineshaft and Anvil, in bovver boots
wondering who decided the 'shaft's dress code,
rugby shirt, tennis shoes . . . What other unsung
blessed rules skipped town with the sailors
and dead, the Disease and Dinkins?

Who will throw the party
for the peace of the brave?
Sander Lopez the kid who knuckled
you with sharpened rings at Walton High,
does he remember the standoffs

and staring down? Will he descend
upon your 25th reunion on the other side
of London, at the bottom of Fleet Street
and Borella Market, at Moishes Deli
in the East Village, where all experience
dissolves in a *rugallah* and coffee?

Who will greet the warriors
at the Staten Island Ferry back
in the city to remember the best
ride is across water, costs a quarter,
a half-dollar, a dollar? . . . plug in the correct

year of return, your post box
at Stuyvesant Station musty and webbed,
its spider exhausted, fly long dead,
are you spider or fly,
ant or lion, man? . . . no matter

Let the games begin, and let
them not end, let them not end
until we are together again,

until after the silences
have been accounted for,

until the proper history
of the disappearances
of certain species of human
from their ancestral lands
have been properly eulogized
and the blood money paid,

until we've puzzled
this destiny out that led
to the murder of Rabin
on this day of assessing
the culture, day of waiting
for the birth of my son.

Homage to Managua?
(May 23, 1985)

What are you doing down in Nicaragua?
have you drunk coffee yet at the Cafe Buena Vista,
have you met Cardenal?

A woman I know is so intrigued by your visit,
what about his lover, she said, doesn't she worry
about proximity to bombs, Contras,
Sandinistas, long lines of women after bread?

Would you live within an embargo,
she asked knowingly, as I sipped coffee

in my West Side room and thought
of the train that took a recent love
away, nothing more, not bread
or tea, fear of the yankee.

Your grandmother said you reminded her
of the boys that went to Spain.
Is there still Spain and a civil war?
Catalonia, Neruda, García Lorca.
Tell me, what are you doing down in Nicaragua?

I have not traveled in years,
I no longer know black or white,
naive yes, Botha is evil, true,
and the right wars, Jaffna,
Palestine, so I ask you again:
what are you doing down in Nicaragua?

To observe, you said,
to read and write
and keep your hands off, perhaps.

When you left
that early Sunday morning
shortly after dawn,
I imagined hair blown back
and dreams falling like flowers
off an unadorned tree,

waiting on Broadway for a taxi,
belongings sent off to London,
carrying a few clothes, notebooks, shoes,
a few too many socks,
but you could not think of everything,
a hat.

A wallet of single dollar bills
to live like a king
look and practise Spanish
(Rest your head in some dark, loping hair).

A good contrast to the Twin Towers, you said,
to see Nicaragua before you left the Americas,
to live in a revolutionary society.

(To walk in the blessing of morning
with the fisherman and cobbler,
preacher, drinker, market women,
I take the scene from "Under Milk Wood,"

but that's Dylan's wave
as he comes smiling to shore.)

Tell me, what are you doing down in Nicaragua
and what have you seen?

Bino A. Realuyo

"I am waiting for information from Canada when I can get my Immigrant visa. Aside from this, I am also waiting for the action of the INS regarding my citizenship application. I hope and pray that it will be approved, because if this citizenship application is the one that is approved, then it will take a very short time for you four to wait until I could petition for your joining me here in the U.S. . . ."

— Augusto Roa Realuyo, from his aerogramme to our family dated March 1, 1980

Biography

Bino A. Realuyo was born and raised in Manila, and as a teenager, moved to the United States with his family. He studied International Relations in the U.S. and South America. His poetry and fiction have appeared in literary journals and anthologies including *The Kenyon Review*, *Mânoa*, *New Letters*, *The Literary Review* and *Likhaan: Anthology of Poetry and Fiction 1996 and 1997* (Philippines). His first novel, *The Umbrella Country*, was published in 1999 in the Ballantine Reader's Circle Collection by Ballantine Books. He has also finished a poetry collection, *In Spite of Open Eyes*. He is the recipient of the 1998 Lucille Medwick Memorial Award from the Poetry Society of America. He is a cofounder of the Asian American Writers' Workshop.

Autobiography of an Aerogramme

February 9, 1979

Dearest Virgie, Berry, Albert & Alvin,

I arrived here in New York City safe & sound and was met at Kennedy International Airport by Mely and Dodoy. The whole trip was almost without a hitch from Manila to Tokyo, thence to Chicago (O'Hare International Airport) which was the port of entry, wherein our papers and luggage were carefully checked by U.S. immigration authorities before proceeding to our destination, New York. Chicago was still under 5 inches of snow and I was able to contact Agot Monasterio, Monona's husband, who went to see me at O'Hare Airport and I was able to deliver the letter of Clara for Tita Unding. Monona in turn was able to contact Mely by phone, so they were already very very sure of my arrival in New York which was right on time, as per schedule - 5:57 PM Saturday, Feb. 3.

The time of arrival in New York was a blessing, cause the whole city was already in its bright, blinking lights and I could see from above, the city, so beautiful, with its different patterns of multi-colored, blinking artificial lights in all its splendor. I hope you could all imagine in your own way, what I had seen and what greeted me on my arrival in this premiere city in America and in the whole world. I wish that in the not so distant future you will be able to see also this beautiful sight that greets all airborne visitors at nighttime.

At this writing, I had already disposed of all the letters and gifts sent thru me. I am still in the process of adjusting to the timetable here, as you very well know that when it's daytime in Manila, it's nighttime here in U.S. and since it's winter here, the temperature is always below zero, but it's a blessing that there is no snow here in New York. Only the very cold winds - so I don't bother yet to go out in the streets.

Marina was here yesterday and made arrangements that I be admitted at the hospital on Wednesday, Feb. 14, so I can have a full week of rest & adjustment. I don't know what I'll have to undergo at the hospital. I'll be communicating with all of you from time to time. Cesar called up from Oklahoma & said he'll try his best to come to New York, before he returns to Manila.

Well, this will be all for now, keep on communicating. All of you write in one airletter so as to economize. Inform me of when & what you'll need beforehand, say a couple of weeks before, so I can advise you, so I know of what is happening. Take care of yourselves.

Bye now. All my love & prayers to you all—

Love & Kisses,
Daddy

from "States of Being," *The Umbrella Country*

A year is not a very long time.

If you could count moons and stars and suddenly your ten years of waiting were over, I can also count mounds of red and black ants on the asphalt street and one day, a year will be over. One year. I want to go where you are, anywhere but here.

I'm afraid of this place, of what it's done, of what it's going to do to me.

So I squat here all the time, across our house, on the fence that never finished, holding the steel that sticks out of the concrete blocks, watching the window. I have seen you many times, the way I'm looking at you now. In my mind, you are always there, watching us play in the street, keeping Big Boy Jun away from Pipo and me, throwing peanut shells at the other marble-gambling boys for teasing us, cutting newspaper clippings about the States. The same things, again and again.

You may not know this, but you are always here.

I think about the States a lot more, wonder what is there. I know where you are but I'm not sure what it's really like. I think in circles—rain, flood, heat, sun, then back to rain again but where you are it's not like that. It's cold there, isn't it? Like sticking my hand in the Fridgidaire? And not too much sun. There is snow, isn't there? Before the snow, I think of the States as a coloring book house, wider than our street, sometimes green, sometimes white, sometimes you can lie on there and sometimes my feet could sink into the snow. Not like the houses here, with peeling paint that nobody thinks about repainting. These brown boxes all attached, one looking older than the other each day, like the faces of the people who lived in them. You don't live in one like that. Yours must be newly painted, the whole house, not just the doors. A Christmas Card house with rows of green trees outside sparkling with lights, snow half-melting on the twigs. I think about how you and Auntie Dolares walk together in the streets of Woodside, Nuyork. D'merica, sorry, that's the way you write it now. Sometimes you walk with my cousins too. You laugh. You forget all about the window. You forget all about the street that overlooked it. You forget about our bedroom, the noise, your *yantok,* how often it kissed Pipo's skin, the night you hit Mommy and broke the mirror on the wall, the only one we ever had. You forget about many things. I know. I can see you now. You laugh with Auntie Dolares, with her children. You practice your English with them. She tells you how you should learn to pronounce her name right, with an O not an A. Do-LO-res, she will tell you, just like what Ninang Rola said, but you are so used to saying her name your way, you don't hear her. I'm so used to saying her name that way too. You tell them about us. But you don't tell them what you did to us. Never once do you mention how you came home drunk from the embassy, thinking you failed your interview and beat up everybody and got rid of Ninang Rola and Maricon. You only speak of the paperboat times, the hours before the hitting. The ones after. You tell them how Pipo took after you, just like you. How you brought us up so well. They will see us soon.

Eat well, he always wrote.

Hunger, the taste of it I could never forget. It melted in my tongue when my stomach began to ask for something I could never get. Then I became conscious of little things, leftover of bread that the ants rushed to in a blink, or roaches. I gaped at children eating ice-cream, watched it melt on the cone, watched them lick their fingers, and when they finished eating, watched them go back to buy another one. I reached down my pocket and kept my hand there, wishing my coins would multiply. The corn vendor would roll by with his cart. Our neighbors ran to him, one peso for a corn, hot and steamy they burned their hands and their tongues as they licked the rounded surface before they bit into it and drooled. From our window, I watched all kinds of food being sold. In the morning, the taho man with his carts of soybean drink, in the afternoon till the evening, the parade of fishball carts, cotton candy, rice cakes, coconut that got chopped in front of you and many others as if they knew how hungry our street was, as if they didn't know that there were ones like me who only sat there and watched the whole time. So one day, I began to dry stale rice in the sun, mold them into balls to make crunchy rice cakes afterward. And fish, the taste of fish, dried and salted from the *tinapa* women—it became even more flavored because I'd want it to stay longer in my mouth, after dipping in vinegar.
Eat well, he said. But I wondered what he was eating now that made it easy for him to say that. When his letter arrived, I skimmed through it until I found the part where he listed what he ate that day, my new vocabulary of food, most of which I never heard of before: pizza bigger than your two hands, extra cheese, steak, medium rare, fish filet, a fish without bone he called it, without the head, how could that possibly be? He was saving money, he added, saving to rent a house for us.

A house full of food.

Because here, things were getting worse. Or maybe it had always been this bad, I just never noticed until now. I could tell by the way our neighbors looked. Everybody seemed to be complaining more, finding it more difficult to cope. Prices were going up too fast. Bread was shrinking in size.

That was when the States filled people's faces, blinked in everybody's eyes. And when they got tired of brownouts, the heat, the mosquitoes, the States appeared in every word they spoke:

So much food in California.

Ako? may sister *ako,* CPA *sa* Nuyork. She will send me a Balikbayan box, full of Fruitcake! Fruitcake, imagine, we don't have that here!

My son—*abogado* in Ha-why.

Look at my shoes. PX Goods. Stateside *'yan.*

Kumusta to your father, huh? Tell him not to forget us here, huh? Say hello for me, huh? But tell me, where's Woodside, D'merica?

When is he going to send me my Samsonite? He promised me you know? When is he going to send me Yardley and Ivory? Also, I want some Stateside Colgate, what do you call it there, Crest? They're not too expensive in the States I hear?

Every day, everywhere, a reminder of where he was.

VA Medical Center
May 27, 1979

Dearest Mommy, Berry, Albert & Alvin—

This afternoon, I just received your letter dated May 16th which was brought by Mely, together with some home cooked foods, underwear & pajamas. Since I just wrote you last Tuesday, May 22, informing you of my SECOND hospitalization at VA Med. Center in Manhattan, N.Y. and this time it is my THYROID, which the doctors here said that it is very much overworked resulting in my sudden loss of weight after gaining weight immediately after my discharge last March and palpitations of heart when tired, and trembling extremities. I am here now in the hospital and have undergone a couple of workups such as thyroid scan, blood tests for thyroid, thyroid therapy, etc. etc. My first day in the hospital I was brought to the medical intensive care unit (MICU) and given medicine and intravenous (IV). Two doctors were in attendance and when I asked one of doctors (Dr. K. Zachary) why I was brought to MICU, he said that when he examined me at the Ward (11 North), he said that I was already about to collapse. Well, I was a bit better next day Thursday May 24--so I was transferred to ward 11 North @ Bed # 39. I rested and Friday May 25 I was at Nuclear Medicine for Thyroid Scanning and Thyroid therapy. I was given a Nuclear cocktail to drink for my thyroid therapy to be given once a week, until when, I do not know. After I drank the cocktail, I was again surprised when I was transferred to a private room marked "isolation" and nobody could enter. And I could not go out for 48 hours. The nuclear doctor explained to me that after taking the cocktail, I was radioactive and nobody could come near me at least 6 feet . . . to avoid radiation . . . so I am alone in a room with toilet facilities like the one at Veterans Hospital in Q.C. that I occupied. From this room where I am now, I have a very beautiful view of East River, ships & boats coming & going, the U.N. Building, etc. At night, it is more beautiful with all the multicolored lights especially that of Washington Bridge . . . Oh, it is really a beauty . . . and I hope you all be here to see these beautiful sights . . . So you Berry, Albert and Alvin . . . study harder . . . and harder. For you Mommy take care of the children, very well, because I am sure we will be together in the near future. Among the addresses you sent me, I am not yet able to write Frankie, Dory. I was about to write them when I wrote you last May 22, but I was short of time . . . so I'll write them after I am discharged. I have here pictures with Nena at New Jersey which I will send you later, cause I cannot enclose anything in this aerogramme letter.

Well, so much for this now. I will be communicating with you from time to time, regarding this 2nd hospitalization . . . and write me often.

So long, Best wishes & regards to all. Keep everything going and take care.

Love, Prayers

Daddy

P.S. I haven't received any answer to my letter to Tesing. I hope she received it. My prayers for Mila.

March 5, 1998
VA Medical Center
(from a journal entry)

My vocabulary of war is a list of diseases; and my tongue has long refused to spill them out, afraid to taste the memory of illnesses that weren't mine. He named them last night, each word gravitated with fear—beri-beri, malaria, prostate cancer, amoebiasis, hyperthyroidism—to the medical interns who sat there muted by the anguish on this pale face framed by thick white hair. "How did it begin?" A young woman asked. I would have started by recounting what happened to him a week ago, on twenty-third street, where he almost fainted after a long walk. But he went back fifty years, in this hospital of all places, full of war-torn images of those who cough within these white walls every moment of what happened then.

Each word got caught in his throat. Each word a tear in his eye.

I had never seen my father cry.

So I am back here again, waiting for you. I am waiting again, for you. How many times do I have to do this in a lifetime of waiting for so many things. The walls are empty, nothing to distract me from the window. Except for two women having lunch to my right. They don't mind having me here. They are consumed by the buzz of the TV, greasy lips and fingers. Your stretcher will be rolled out of the elevators anytime now, back to the Cardiac Care Unit where you have been for the past week. I sat in my apartment this morning thinking about you, on the phone with Ma. She is supposed to be here. I wonder if she got lost again. She told me you cried again, afraid. You are now very old. You have been sick for so many years. I don't remember you being young. When I was born, you were almost fifty. Between us are years of estrangement and silence. Today is one of the rare moments I become your son, always when I wait for you to survive another terminal illness. Sitting here, I am restless. I become conscious of time, of the sound the elevator makes, of the people passing by the glass window, of the meaning of age.

Twenty years ago, there was a window too. In the VA hospital room in Manila, I reached over the window ledge to watch frogs leaping out of the small pond. I had never seen so many trees. There were older men on wheelchairs on the green. I didn't know how much time I had spent in that hospital. I didn't ask why you were becoming more emaciated each day. Hospital rooms carry a certain kind of smell. VA hospitals, in particular, add the smell of age and death. The war might have smelled the same way. During those months in the hospital as a child, I took pleasure in the attention from your relatives, the daily gift giving, the building up of boxes of crackers and candies in the corner of your bed, the constant mention of the States. I didn't know much about the war. I remember the wooden chest at the foot of the bed in our bedroom, full of war artifacts: rusty bayonets, helmets, bullet belts, cobwebs. When I opened that trunk, the smell of your darkest years escaped. The scent held no meaning for me. There were many things I didn't know then. I didn't think of what your ailing body meant to you, to me. After they took you to New York, I overheard our relatives say you were dying.

The war that never ended.

1942. Bataan Death March. Concentration Camps. Tarlac. World War II. Nobody would ever know what it was like. In my family, nobody dared ask. In many ways, our secrets become our weapons. Especially the ones we mention without us consciously knowing. We say them, at moments of fury, slipping at the tip of the tongue to be swallowed back and not completely revealed. His weapon was slow and winding. I was the child who listened yet was frightened by the facts that were left out. I heard about it from the people around me. I knew he was locked up in a camp. I knew he ate rats. I heard of the one ration of water in a tin can to drink, to wash his face, to bathe. The lack of sunlight. The constant wail of the dying. The emotion was strong, yet incomplete. I wasn't sure even then if it was something I had to know, I had to learn. Or perhaps I simply never paid attention as a child. It is hard when surrounded by deafening sounds of poverty. I had my own hunger to face. Hunger comes in so many different sounds. In this hospital in Manhattan, it's the sound of death creeping in: the dying old man without a leg on the next bed, or what happened to the other one on the vacant bed next door. History is in the body. Inside my father are many years of internalized fear. Out of the concentration camps he went, but he carried the dark cell with him. I wondered if he would be a better father without the taint of war. My mother said the reason he incessantly hid food and junk was because during the war, there was nothing. She is right, a trip to his bedroom in our house is to walk into a storage of unexplainable things: volumes of unread books, newspaper piles, boxes of foods, not to mention everything locked up in his secret closet. He never throws anything. He keeps them all like memory, tightly holding them as if the day he lets go, everything else will be taken away. He doesn't seem to remember that families, unlike time, don't simply walk away. Even if I don't understand him, I will stay here just because he is important to me. He is a man who doesn't say much, but on his face you can see years and years of thoughts. I must admit I never want to become like him, to carry the past with me, like some wound unwilling to heal. But every time I leave through the hospital's revolving door, I walk away with the same thoughts, the same scent of memory carried by a father whose wars have grown to include the very family for whom he was supposed to fight.

So you see, sitting here, waiting, I feel like writing you a letter. I want to tell you that as an adult, I can touch the contents of your wooden trunk. The helmet: I wear it on my head and slip it over my back: the bayonet; I place it between my arms, feel its tip with my fingers; the bullets: I slip them into my pockets and count them. In touch, I might learn history, one you never revealed. I want to follow the march. I want to see the mouths of the people whose dying voices I have been hearing all my life. I would like to visit the jail where they placed you. Sit there in darkness. Speak with the dying and the ones who survived.

Tell me what it was like, tell me what it was really like.

They tell me you are going to be okay.

On the twenty-third street crosstown bus, I'm moving away from the hospital's massive structure. The cold air creates mists on the window, blurring the street but slowly helping my thoughts to settle. You have been in this city for twenty years. When I read your letters we have kept over the years I remember our last years in Manila. The irony of it is that I owe much to your illnesses. If you didn't get fatally sick, you wouldn't have ended up in this country. If you didn't fear your impending death, you wouldn't have applied for American citizenship. Your survival became my American passport. We created a new home here, away from the country that had many times torn us apart. I thought it would be a chance to get to know you better, to create fatherhood, but I realized by then I had no need for a father. These VA hospitals have taken you away many times, and when you return, I often don't know what to do. There has been many years of absence: I have learned to become a man without you, to become a son with-out a father. But in the VA hospital, memories creep in. They come back in the faces of the sick soldiers who roam the hallways. The uneven slide of wheelchairs, the ghost of white uni-forms. I will walk away from the thought that I can't blame the war for your displacement. I won't blame the war for your illnesses as well. Blame is a weapon I am not willing to carry. In your most sickly moments, you petitioned for the rest of us to come here. You brought me to the city of my dreams. Your last opportunity to become a father occurred on your sickbed. I wonder now if your letters were meant to guide your children with words. Rereading them as an adult made me think of the warmth and security I felt when I first read them, those signs of hope, those beautiful passages about this wonderful New York City that we would all see some-day. They mean much now because slowly I begin to understand what your written pages mean to me. And what a beautiful city you brought me to, Daddy. Tonight, I decide to fold your aerogramme carefully in my thoughts. You have survived your operation. They opted for angio-plasty, bypass surgery being too dangerous at your age. You are healing. I am healing. Between us are years of wounds. Some inflicted by the war. Most by the haunt of memory. They will continue to follow me, as strong as the voices from the stories, the smell of the trunk. From you, I learn there are things too late to let go. From your letters, I have learned to write myself, to remember. Memory is the song of the wounded.

From *In Spite of Open Eyes*

1946:

8 Haikus

Your death has never been in a grave
in any country, anywhere.

\- Ryuichi Tamura

Flood of bullet shells.
In the rain, you hear the last
evening of the war.

*

A charcoal city.
Once the brown of reed mat roofs,
whistling walls of grass.

*

Barrack doors open.
You: bloated, muddy, almost blind.
Air pulls bodies out.

*

Scratches on walls.
Years of darkness written in
finger-scraped lines.

*

He looks like he's dead.
A woman places her ear
on your rib-thin chest.

*

Bayonet scars
map weeks of torture and sun.
"He is still breathing."

*

A city sees again,
much clearer than your eyes,
cataracts removed.

*

You multiply moons
in narrow white VA halls,
talking to yourself.

Mona Chen

Mona Chen was born in New York and grew up in New Jersey. She returned to New York to study art and has lived there since then. Her travels to China and Singapore, from where her father and mother immigrated over thirty years ago, have focused her interests in exploring the world and culture from which her parents came in an attempt to reconcile their world with her own.

Bharati Mukherjee

Biography

Bharati Mukherjee's newest book is titled *Leave it to me.* She was born in Calcutta and came to the United States in 1961 to study at the University of Iowa. She is the author of several fiction and non-fiction books, including *Jasmine* and *The Middleman and Other Stories*, which won the National Book Critics Circle Award in 1989. She teaches at the University of California at Berkeley.

Danny's Girls

I was thirteen when Danny Sahib moved into our building in Flushing. That was his street name, but my Aunt Lini still called him Dinesh, the name he'd landed with. He was about twenty, a Dogra boy from Simla with slicked-back hair and coppery skin. If he'd worked on his body language, he could have passed for Mexican, which might have been useful. Hispanics are taken more seriously, in certain lines of business, than Indians. But I don't want to give the wrong impression about Danny. He wasn't an enforcer, he was a charmer. No one was afraid of him; he was a merchant of opportunity. I got to know him because he was always into ghetto scams that needed junior high boys like me to pull them off.

He didn't have parents, at least none that he talked about, and he boasted he'd been on his own since he was six. I admired that, I wished I could escape my family, such as it was. My parents had been bounced from Uganda by Idi Amin, and then barred from England by some parliamentary trickery. Mother's sister—Aunt Lini—sponsored us in the States. I don't remember Africa at all, but my father could never forget that we'd once had servants and two Mercedes- Benzes. He sat around Lini's house moaning about the good old days and grumbling about how hard life in America was until finally the women organized a coup and chucked him out. My mother sold papers in the subway kiosks, twelve hours a day, seven days a week. Last I heard, my father was living with a Trinidad woman in Philadelphia, but we haven't seen him or talked about him for years. So in Danny's mind I was an orphan, like him.

He wasn't into the big-money stuff like drugs. He was a hustler, nothing more. He used to boast that he knew some guys, Nepalese and Pakistanis, who could supply him with anything—but we figured that was just talk. He started out with bets and scalping tickets for Lata Mangeshkar or Mithun Chakravorty concerts at Madison Square Garden. Later he fixed beauty contests and then discovered the marriage racket.

Danny took out ads in papers in India promising "guaranteed Permanent Resident status in the U.S." to grooms willing to proxy-marry American girls of Indian origin. He arranged quite a few. The brides and grooms didn't have to live with each other, or even meet or see each other. Sometimes the "brides" were smooth-skinned boys from the neighborhood. He used to audition his brides in our apartment and coach them—especially the boys—on keeping their faces low, their saris high, and their arms as glazed and smooth as caramel. The immigration inspectors never suspected a thing. I never understood why young men would pay a lot of money—I think the going rate was fifty thousand rupees—to come here. Maybe if I remembered the old country I might feel different. I've never even visited India.

Flushing was full of greedy women. I never met one who would turn down gold or a fling with the money market. The streets were lousy with gold merchants, more gold emporia than pizza parlors. Melt down the hoarded gold of Jackson Heights and you could plate the Queensboro Bridge. My first job for Danny Sahib was to approach the daughters in my building for bride volunteers and a fifty buck fee, and then with my sweet, innocent face, sign a hundred dollar contract with their mothers.

Then Danny Sahib saw he was thinking small. The real money wasn't in rupees and bringing poor saps over. It was in selling docile Indian girls to hard-up Americans for real bucks. An Old World wife who knew her place and would breed like crazy was worth at least twenty thousand dollars. To sweeten the deal and get some good-looking girls for his catalogues, Danny promised to send part of the fee back to India. No one in India could even imagine *getting* money for the curse of having a daughter. So he expanded his marriage business to include mail-order brides, and he offered my smart Aunt Lini a partnership. My job was to put up posters in the laundromats and pass out flyers on the subways.

Aunt Lini was a shrewd businesswoman, a widow who'd built my uncle's small-time investor service for cautious Gujarati gentlemen into a full-scale loan-sharking operation that financed half the Indian-owned taxi medallions in Queens. Her rates were simple: double the prime, no questions asked. Triple the prime if she smelled a risk, which she usually did. She ran it out of her kitchen with a phone next to the stove. She could turn a thousand dollars while frying up a *bhaji*.

Aunt Lini's role was to warehouse the merchandise, as she called the girls, that couldn't be delivered to its American destination (most of those American fiancés had faces a fly wouldn't buzz). Aunt Lini had spare rooms she could turn into an informal S.R.O. hotel. She called the rooms her "pet shop" and she thought of the girls as puppies in the window. In addition to the flat rate that Danny paid her, she billed the women separately for bringing gentleman guests, or shoppers, into the room. This encouraged a prompt turnover. The girls found it profitable to make an expeditious decision.

The summer I was fifteen, Aunt Lini had a paying guest, a Nepalese, a real looker. Her skin was as white as whole milk, not the color of tree bark I was accustomed to. Her lips were a peachy orange and she had high Nepalese cheekbones. She called herself "Rosie" in the mail-order catalogue and listed her age as sixteen. Danny wanted all his girls to be sixteen and most of them had names like Rosie and Dolly. I suppose when things didn't work out between her and her contract "fiancé" she saw no reason to go back to her real name. Or especially, back to some tubercular hut in Katmandu. Her parents certainly wouldn't take her back. They figured she was married and doing time in Toledo with a dude named Duane.

Rosie liked to have me around. In the middle of a sizzling afternoon she would send me to Mr. Chin's store for a pack of Kents, or to Ranjit's liquor store for gin. She was a good tipper, or maybe she couldn't admit to me that she couldn't add. The money came from Danny, part of her "dowry" that he didn't send back to Nepal. I knew she couldn't read or write, not even in her own language. That didn't bother me—guaranteed illiteracy is a big selling point in the mail-order bride racket—and there was nothing abject about her. I'd have to say she was a proud woman. The other girls Danny brought over were already broken in spirit; they'd marry just about any freak Danny brought around. Not Rosie—she'd throw some of them out, and threaten others with a cobra she kept in her suitcase if they even thought of touching her. After most of my errands, she'd ask me to sit on the bed and light me a cigarette and pour me a weak drink. I'd fan her for a while with a newspaper.

"What are you going to be when you finish school?" she'd ask me and blow rings, like kisses, that wobbled to my face and broke gently across it. I didn't know anyone who blew smoke rings. I thought they had gone out with black-and-white films. I became a staunch admirer of Nepal.

What I wanted to be in those days was someone important, which meant a freedom like Danny's but without the scams. Respectable freedom in the bigger world of America, that's what I wanted. Growing up in Queens gives a boy ambitions. But I didn't disclose them. I said to Rosie what my ma always said when other Indians dropped by. I said I would be going to Columbia University to the Engineering School. It was a story Ma believed because she'd told it so often, though I knew better. Only the Indian doctors' kids from New Jersey and Long Island went to Columbia. Out in Flushing we got a different message. Indian boys were placed on earth to become accountants and engineers. Even old *Idi Amin* was placed on earth to force Indians to come to America to become accountants and engineers. I went through high school scared, wondering what there was in my future if I hated numbers. I wondered if Pace and Adelphi had engineering. I didn't want to turn out like my Aunt Lini, a ghetto moneylender, and I didn't want to suffer like my mother, and I hated my father with a passion. No wonder Danny's world seemed so exciting. My mother was knocking herself out at a kiosk in Port Authority, earning the minimum wage from a guy who convinced her he was doing her a big favor, all for my mythical Columbia tuition. Lini told me that in America grades didn't count; it was all in the test scores. She bought me the SAT workbooks and told me to memorize the answers.

"Smashing," Rosie would say, and other times, "Jolly good," showing that even in the Himalayan foothills the sun hadn't yet set on the British Empire.

Some afternoons Rosie would be doubled over in bed with leg pains. I know now she'd had rickets as a kid and spent her childhood swaying under hundred pound sacks of rice piled on her head. By thirty she'd be hobbling around like an old football player with blown knees. But at sixteen or whatever, she still had great, hard, though slightly bent legs, and she'd hike her velour dressing gown so I could tightly crisscross her legs and part of her thighs with pink satin hair ribbons. It was a home remedy, she said, it stopped circulation. I couldn't picture her in that home, Nepal. She was like a queen ("The Queen of Queens," I used to joke) to me that year. Even India, where both my parents were born, was a mystery.

Curing Rosie's leg pains led to some strong emotions, and soon I wanted to beat on the gentlemen callers who came, carrying cheap boxes of candy and looking her over like a slave girl on the auction block. She'd tell me about it, nonchalantly, making it funny. She'd catalogue each of their faults, imitate their voices. They'd try to get a peek under the covers or even under the clothing, and Danny would be there to cool things down. I wasn't allowed to help, but by then I would have killed for her.

I was no stranger to the miseries of unrequited love. Rosie was the unavailable love in the room upstairs who talked to me unblushingly of sex and made the whole transactions seem base and grubby and funny. In my Saturday morning Gujarati class, on the other hand, there was a girl from Syosset who called herself "Pammy Patel" a genuine Hindu-American Princess of the sort I had never seen before, whose skin and voice and eyes were as soft as clouds. She wore expensive dresses and you could tell she'd spent hours making herself up just for the Gujarati classes in the Hindu Temple. Her father was a major surgeon, and he and Pammy's brothers would stand outside the class to protect her from any contact with boys like me. They would watch us filing out of the classroom, looking us up and down and smirking the way Danny's catalogue brides were looked at by their American buyers.

I found the whole situation achingly romantic. In the Hindi films I'd see every Sunday, the hero was always the common man with a noble heart, in love with an unattainable beauty. Then she'd be kidnapped and he'd have to save her. Caste and class would be overcome and marriage would follow. To that background, I added a certain American equality. I grew up hating rich people, especially rich Indian immigrants who didn't have the problems of Uganda and a useless father, but otherwise were no better than I. I never gave them the deference that Aunt Lini and my mother did.

With all that behind me, I had assumed that real love *had* to be cheerless. I had assumed I wouldn't find a girl worth marrying, not that girls like Pammy could make me happy. Rosie was the kind of girl who could make me happy, but even I knew she was not the kind of girl I could marry. It was confusing. Thoughts of Rosie made me want to slash the throats of rivals. Thoughts of Pammy made me want to wipe out her whole family.

One very hot afternoon Rosie, as usual, leaned her elbows on the windowsill and shouted to me to fetch a six-pack of tonic and a lemon. I'd been sitting on the stoop, getting new tips from Danny on scalping for an upcoming dance recital—a big one, Lincoln Center— but I leaped to attention and shook the change in my pockets to make sure I had enough for Mr. Chin. Rosie kept records of her debts, and she'd pay them off, she said, just as soon as Danny arranged a green card to make her legit. She intended to make it here without getting married. She exaggerated Danny's power. To her, he was some kind of local bigwig who could pull off anything. None of Danny's girls had tried breaking a contract before, and I wondered if she'd actually taken it up with him.

Danny pushed me back so hard I scraped my knee on the stoop. "You put up the posters," he said. After taping them up, I was to circulate on the subway and press the pictures on every lonely guy I saw. "I'll take care of Rosie. You report back tomorrow."

"After I get her tonic and a lemon," I said.

It was the only time I ever saw the grown-up orphan in Danny, the survivor. If he'd had a knife or a gun on him, he might have used it. "I give the orders," he said, "you follow." Until that moment, I'd always had the implicit sense that Danny and I were partners in some exciting enterprise, that together we were putting something over on India, on Flushing, and even on America.

Then he smiled, but it wasn't Danny's radiant, conspiratorial, arm-on-the-shoulder smile that used to warm my day. "You're making her fat," he said. "You're making her drunk. You probably want to diddle her yourself, don't you? Fifteen years old and never been out of your auntie's house and you want a real woman like Rosie. But she thinks you're her errand boy and you just love being her smiley little *chokra-boy*, don't you?" Then the smile froze on his lips, and if he'd ever looked Mexican, this was the time. Then he said something in Hindi that I barely understood, and he laughed as he watched me repeat it, slowly. Something about eunuchs not knowing their place. "Don't ever go up there again, *hijra*-boy."

I was starting to take care of Danny's errands quickly and sloppily as always, and then, at the top of the subway stairs, I stopped. I'd never really thought what a strange, pimpish thing I was doing, putting up pictures of Danny's girls, or standing at the top of the subway stairs and passing them out to any lonely-looking American I saw—what kind of joke was this? How dare he do this, I thought, how dare he make me a part of this? I couldn't move. I had two hundred sheets of yellow paper in my hands, descriptions of Rosie and half a dozen others like her, and instead of passing them out, I threw them over my head and let them settle on the street and sidewalk and filter down the paper-strewn, garbage-littered steps of the subway. How dare he call me *hijra*, eunuch?

I got back to Aunt Lini's within the hour. She was in her kitchen charring an eggplant. "I'm making a special *bharta* for you," she said, clapping a hand over the receiver. She was putting the screws on some poor Sikh, judging from the stream of coarse Punjabi I heard as I tore through the kitchen. She shouted after me, "Your ma'll be working late tonight." More guilt, more Columbia, more engineering.

I didn't thank Aunt Lini for being so thoughtful, and I didn't complain about Ma not being home for me. I was in towering rage with Rosie and with everyone who ever slobbered over her picture.

"Take your shoes off in the hall," Lini shouted. "You know the rules."

I was in the mood to break rules. For the first time I could remember, I wasn't afraid of Danny Sahib. I wanted to liberate Rosie, and myself. From the hall stand I grabbed the biggest, sturdiest, wood-handled umbrella—gentlemen callers were always leaving behind souvenirs—and in my greasy high-tops I clumped up the stairs two at a time and kicked open the door to Rosie's room.

Rosie lay in bed, smoking. She'd propped a new fan on her pillow, near her face. She sipped her gin and lime. *So*, I thought in my fit of mad jealousy, he's bought her a fan. And now suddenly she likes limes. Damn him, *damn* him. She won't want me and my newspapers, she won't want my lemons. I wouldn't have cared if Danny and half the bachelors in Queens were huddled around that bed. I was so pumped up with the enormity of love that I beat the mattress in the absence of rivals. Whack! Whack! Whack! went the stolen umbrella, and Rosie bent her legs delicately to get them out of the way. The fan teetered off the pillow and lay there beside her on the wilted, flopping bed, blowing hot air at the ceiling. She held her drink up tight against her nose and lips and stared at me around the glass.

"So, you want me, do you?" she said.

Slowly, she moved the flimsy little fan, then let it drop. I knelt on the floor with my head on the pillow that had pressed into her body, smelling flowers I would never see in Flushing and feeling the tug on my shoulder that meant I should come up to bed and for the first time I felt my life was going to be A-Okay.

Alison Park

After returning to New York - at the border where Canada meets it -
U.S. immigration questions my perfect English and my perfect
assimilAsian. *Route 332:* Who are you?

Biography

Alison Park was born in Chicago in 1982 and has been writing poetry since the age of ten.
Raised as a Korean American Roman Catholic, she has dealt with many frustrations as a
first-generation adolescent in the United States. Her writings reflect these frustrations. She
presently lives in Jackson Heights, Queens, with her parents, Soon-Young and Jung-Il. She
has a brother and a sister, Abraham and Agnes.

Maybe

Something
That would have been a dove.
The underside of wings
stained yellow and it landed
on orange claws.
The pigeon
maybe
is really a dove.
I should have been a man
in a man's world.
All the leaves are lying in the spectrum
between green and yellow.
Brown lies on the ground beside me.
I am singing my swan song
for the thousandth time.

The Players

Riding on noiseless trains after dark adds salt to life.
I clutch these grains and dissolve fear of something done.
Eyes wide and the weakers gather behind my gape as I realize that city lights are all
the color of tangerines glazed by the sun and that too many of them
at ten every square yard become plain and no sight
for my sore eyes.

Words should offer wisdom and they do not.
Noises gather in my basket as I step on every crack in the road.
And my skin is rough and parched from the cleansing
in the sanctuary of a fast-food restaurant's bathroom.
They are knocking on the door more frantically than the water and soap run together.
I shout, "Someone's in here!" But no one believes me and
they should not.

Memory

Skeleton leaves from skeleton branches drift downward. Pale.

The winter sky is purple and tastes of sad things.

Looking over the stretch of what they call *afterward*, I am convalescing after an ill-spent night in

the arms of Memory.

Across the street, multitudes gathered, dead leaves falling into their hair and

into their lashes.

Without reason they came in sympathy of my Valentine grief.

I soar and fly in the kisses.

Literature

Trees like ink.

That spills and explodes and goes dry.

I have been trying to express my everything as complete idea and thought

expressing ideas in clauses.

Not quite there yet, so green I am like ink from green pens.

What a surprise.

Leaves from my Iri cemetery trees fall and crumble into the snow

as I try to take a photograph with literature and show what my breath looks like

exhaled in the morning at the end of December.

To count the number of times one of us exhales and inhales since they are born to the day they

die would be a feat noteworthy and magnificent.

Until someone realizes that all those times are not created equal

and one breath will mean more than the next.

One breath more saving than another's.

Lena Sze

How funny you are today New York
like Ginger Rogers in Swingtime
and St. Bridget's steeple leaning a little to the left
here I have just jumped out of bed full of V-days
(I got tired of D-days) and blue you there still
accepts me foolish and free/all I want is a room up there
and you in it . . ."

                       - "Steps," Frank O'Hara

Biography

Lena Sze grew up in Chinatown in Manhattan. She is currently a sophomore at Swarthmore College. Her poetry has appeared in *Small Craft Writings*, *Asian Journal* and *Asiam.* She has won the National High School Poetry Contest sponsored by the Asian American Writers' Workshop and Bertelsmann's Literary Contest.

Observations From my Window

There are patches
of water in the street,
clumps of changed texture.

The bells of the old church
(a block and a half behind)
where ceremony and mourning
come together in draped black clothes—
no, they are not ringing tonight.

Down below,
people are wistful.
Silent.

The scene is full—
there is no emptiness in the city.
The sun gives its last breath of light.
Evening sounds are bearable.

and the remains of water fall
                    to the waiting drain:
tonight,
it is the rush of old rain
(and old water)
into grated
underground systems.

night

like eyes out of a brilliant sleep
after time away
the city skyline

juts out
the gray progression of avenues
in the october sunshine
light trickling through
empty streets and alleyways
that are always dark

nightfog breathes in and out
shooting its smoky wisps
into the side streets
the city hums from within
(cold air on skin)

playing with her hair
teasing the heartstrings
of a girl in love with the cold

reflections of light and warmth
from windows
are surrogate stars
rain grates and manhole covers
the sky
sacred night air

a memory of how she breathed:
the air in her mouth
and it settling in her like night.
when it becomes crackling and cold
in the dark
under the streetlamp's light
every movement is clear
and poised,
perfect as glass

as the air smoothes its back
against buildings and people
crystallized and moved to language

darkness will be worn by her
for walking,
for the night journey
through unborn city air.

tender night

the tenderness of city nights!
somehow gentle on the soul
with a velvet sky
so close as i walk

the tender night
makes the soft sky
seem so much closer
the glint of light
and a lonely street are enough
to make me live

the tender night
gives me glimpses of beauty
i can dream about for months—
sometimes i feel like
i can witness the world.

Betty Kao

How will he know now that the words I've written on my hand have smeared off?

Biography

Betty Kao, a second-generation Chinese born in Oregon, has lived in New York City since the age of six. She is currently studying art and environmental studies in the Pioneer Valley. Her awards include the Claudia Seaman Poetry Prize for 1997.

Don't Come Home

Brother says to sister:
"I don't care what you say."
Sister says to brother:
"I already knew, I just had to make sure."
The world turns black and gray.
You're not that powerful anyway,
                        anymore.
The sky expands,
the birds disappear.
It's night and the sky is stretched like taffy,
contorts like water waves,
sparkles like northern lights, doused with glitter.
Treetops bend together like
a flame following a baby's finger.
I want to scream,
but am too exhausted by everyone,
                      everything.
The only thing scarier than a deep blue sky
is a milky white one
sucked from a straw,
the indifference of us all is momentarily cast aside
as our eyes follow the heavens.

Whether the ground is wet from the rain
or the runaway's tears,
I don't know.

Hail hits hard.

My Mother's Journey

I see her face, contorted and perplexed.
She's five years old,
trudging toward an endless unlightened road,
clutching to her mother.
On their path they will confront rocky hills,
and corrupt soldiers carrying sacks filled with stolen heirlooms.
The darkness, the coldness take no excuses.
They must go forward.
The only directional guide is the sad movement of the herd,
each with their own pitiful stories of:
proud names, families and estates left behind.
She holds her mother's hand in a vise,
knowing that if she is lost, she will never be seen again.
The journey will not end there.
Ten years later she will leave her new home in Burma,
only to arrive in Taiwan alone, with no relatives to meet her.
She carries the equivalent of twelve dollars.
She will study hard to become a nurse,
persevering even with her shattered past.
One day a call comes, her brother has sad news of her father's death.
She struggles on,
forcing her own destiny
that so much has attempted to rip apart.
Here now,
my mother sits at home.
It's snowing bitterly outside,
and I don't want to go to school.
But as she brings me hot soup,
I remember all she has done,
and why I will go.

out of
the
square

That's not my times square.
Mine was a times square filled with pornography stores, old skeezy men jerking off in subways, gray and dreary faces attached to the sidewalk, right-wing Christian evangelists waving their propaganda through the smoggy air, and high-pitched Spanglish streaming from cheap junk-filled, immigrant-owned mom & pop stores with no memorable names.

Now times square has been taken aside, and washed away are the pornography stores. Now covered with rainbow paints, replaced with imitation old-fashioned breweries and promises of the new; slogans of the magical kingdom to come.

times square is no place to grow up.
times square is for grown-ups,   grown away.

And I should . . . shall be happy,
except for the soot and key-scratched lines permanently etched in my memory. The faces, the lingerings are all still there. The homeless feeding pigeons on a park bench stained with urine in the triangle of a busy street, looking around, staring, faces glued to the ground contrasting with the scattered rainbow crack-vial caps and their residue, lain bodies detached.

Sofiya Colette Cabalquinto

Had I the choice, I think I would have picked San Francisco.

Biography

Sofiya Colette Cabalquinto was born and raised in downtown Manhattan. Currently a sophomore at Swarthmore College, she is "taking a break" from the city in a small Pennsylvania suburb. Cabalquinto is a recipient of poetry awards, including third prize in the 1997 CCNY High School Poetry Contest, the Mark T. Rifkin Poetry Scholarship and the McGraw-Hill Scholarship for Poetry. Her work has appeared in such publications as *Poetry in Performance*, *Philippine Graphic*, *The Apprentice Writer* and *The Asian Pacific American Journal*. She is the daughter of the poet Luis Cabalquinto.

Omar, Are You Sleeping?

The morning I turned seven
my mother woke me up earlier than usual
and led me, crusty-eyed, to the living room,
where in a cardboard box lay a new Siamese.

And since that day I haven't
ever slept alone; beside me he lies all curled up,
head tucked against his belly
like any other cat would

except that his eyes are always half open,
the whites gleaming like pearl buttons through the slits.
And for that my father calls him Liberace,
after the piano great who had one too many face-lifts.

The Way This Water Does

Will I ever find a body
that touches the way this water does?

A tongue that moves into ears and navel,
warms all the way down and pauses between toes;

fingers that tickle and fingers that comfort,
a hand that is cool and clean;

palms that don't hesitate on the rough back and chest,
but glide along over, as if over roses.

If I should find the body
that touches the way this water does,

I'd stay with him until I'm left—
a contented, wet raisin.

Mindy and the Escargot

On our first date I took Mindy to Mon Maison:

"What would you like?"
"Oh, whatever you're having."

The plate arrives.

"Is that what it looks like?"
"It's delicious."
"It's snails!"
"Sure is, baby."

She shrieked as I grabbed one,
Kissed it,
Sucked it out of its shell—
Into my mouth.

Overdue

Tomorrow, my parents return me to their homeland
as they would ship their old blue jeans home
in a *balikbayan* box.

My aunt and uncle await my arrival,
prepare a mattress for "the American,"
set up a mosquito net around the bed.

I'm nervous about finding a toilet there;
last time, I fought back flies and critters
trying to do it in the outhouse.

My cousins, I know,
will think five feet, two inches
an impressive accomplishment.

But I will disappoint them
when I open my mouth.
They'll find my Tagalog a foreign tongue.

I hope I still get their names right;
my last visit was nine years ago.
Right now I can remember only

that they put me on a car tire
and floated me on the Pacific,
the only kin who couldn't swim like a tuna.

I gripped the rubber tightly,
though they were all around me
every time the sea coughed up.

We were brown bodies bonded to the sea,
common in that sunny land of
rope hammocks and roasted pigs.

We belonged there like mango trees,
like those butterflies rainbowing nearby
when we buried my grandmother.

In 1991, **Bino A. Realuyo** and a group of aspiring young writers founded the Asian American Writers' Workshop. He works full-time in the field of literacy and technology and teaches survival English to garment workers on weekends. He is widely published in literary journals and anthologies including *The Kenyon Review*, *Manoa*, *New Letters*, *The Literary Review* and *The Asian Pacific American Journal*. He is a recipient of the Lucille Medwick Memorial Award from the Poetry Society of America. His first novel, *The Umbrella Country*, was released by Ballantine Books in March 1999.

Rahna Reiko Rizzuto was born and raised in Hawaii. She is the author and editor of numerous articles and publications, including four young-adult mysteries under a pseudonym. Her work has appeared in *The Asian Pacific American Journal* and the *Salon* magazine anthology *Mothers Who Think*. Her first novel, *Why She Left Us*, will be published in September 1999 by HarperFlamingo.

Kendal Henry is an artist and public art curator who lives and works in New York City. He attended the School of Visual Arts in New York where he studied fine arts and photography. He has lectured on the subject of public art at School of Visual Arts, Long Island University and Yale University. He has been involved with the Asian American Writers' Workshop since its inception. Kendal is the manager of art programs at the Metropolitan Transportation Authority Arts for Transit Program.

From The Asian American Writers' Workshop

- *Tokens: Asian American Theatre On and Off Stage*
  edited by Alvin Eng

- *The NuyorAsian Anthology: Asian American Writings About New York City*
  edited by Bino A. Realuyo

- *Watermark: Vietnamese American Poetry & Prose*
  edited by Barbara Tran, Monique T.D. Truong and Luu Khoi

- *Black Lightning: Poetry in Progress*
  by Eileen Tabios

- *Contours of the Heart: South Asians Map North America*
  Winner of the 1997 American Book Award
  edited by Sunaina Maira and Rajini Srikanth

- *Flippin': Filipinos on America*
  edited by Luis Francia and Eric Gamalinda

- *Quiet Fire: A Historical Anthology of Asian American Poetry, 1892-1970*
  edited by Juliana Chang

For more information about the activities and programs of The Asian American Writers' Workshop, please contact us at

- 37 St. Mark's Place, Suite B, New York NY 10003-7801 |
- *tel* 212.228.6718 | • *fax* 212.228.7718 |
- email aaww@panix.com | • web www.panix.com/~aaww

To purchase any of these books, please contact Temple University Press,

1601 N. Broad Street, USB 305, Philadelphia, PA 19122.

Call toll-free 1.800.447.1656 | Fax 215-204-1128 or visit us on the web at www.temple.edu/tempress